# WARRIORS OF GOD

◆

◆

# WARRIORS OF GOD

## RICHARD THE LIONHEART AND SALADIN IN THE THIRD CRUSADE

# JAMES RESTON, JR.

DOUBLEDAY

NEW YORK    LONDON    TORONTO
SYDNEY    AUCKLAND

⚓

PUBLISHED BY DOUBLEDAY
a division of Random House, Inc.
1540 Broadway, New York, New York 10036

DOUBLEDAY and the portrayal of an anchor with a dolphin are
trademarks of Doubleday, a division of Random House, Inc.

Library of Congress Cataloging-in-Publication Data

Reston, James, 1941–
Warriors of God: Richard the Lionheart and Saladin in the Third
Crusade / James Reston, Jr.— 1st ed.
p. cm.
Includes bibliographical references and index.
ISBN 0-385-49561-7
1. Richard I, King of England, 1157–1199. 2. Saladin, Sultan of Egypt
and Syria, 1137–1193. 3. Jerusalem—History—Latin Kingdom,
1099–1244. 4. Crusades—Third, 1189–1192. I. Title.
D163.4 R47 2001
942.03'2'092—dc21
00-050890

BOOK DESIGN BY DEBORAH KERNER/
DANCING BEARS DESIGN
MAPS DESIGNED BY JACKIE AHER

ISBN 0-385-49561-7
Copyright © 2001 by James Reston, Jr.
All Rights Reserved
Printed in the United States of America
May 2001
First Edition
5  7  9  10  8  6  4

FOR DEVIN
*With love and pride*

# Contents

✠

✠

## The Principal Characters

### Crusader Kingdom of Jerusalem

| | |
|---|---|
| Guy of Lusignan | *King of Jerusalem* |
| Sibylla | *Queen of Jerusalem* |
| Conrad of Montferrat | *Lord of Tyre* |
| Raymond III of Tripoli | *Lord of Tiberias* |
| Reginald of Châtillon | *Lord of el Kerak* |
| Gerard de Ridefort | *Grand Master of the Temple* |
| Roger des Moulins | *Grand Master of the Hospital* |
| Balian of Ibelin | *Baron of the Old Guard* |
| Heraclius | *Patriarch of Jerusalem* |
| Godfrey of Bouillon | *hero of First Crusade* |

### Muslims of Egypt and Syria

| | |
|---|---|
| Saladin | *Sultan of Egypt, Arabia, Syria, and Mesopotamia* |
| El Melek el-Adel | *Saladin's brother* |
| El Melek el-Afdal | *Saladin's first son, Lord of Damascus* |
| El Melek el-Aziz | *Saladin's second son, Sultan of Egypt* |
| El Melek ez-Zaher | *Saladin's third son, Lord of Aleppo* |
| Nur ad-Din | *Saladin's predecessor as Sultan of Syria* |
| Rashid al-Din Sinan | *leader of the Assassins* |
| Mashtūb | *Grand Emir* |
| Karākūsh | *governor of Acre during siege* |

## CRUSADERS FROM EUROPE

| | |
|---|---|
| Richard I | *Plantagenet King of England and Duke of Aquitaine* |
| Philip II Augustus | *Capetian King of France* |
| Eleanor of Aquitaine | *Richard's mother, ex-Queen of France and England* |
| Louis VII of France | *Philip Augustus's father, Eleanor's first husband* |
| Henry | *Count of Champagne, Richard's nephew* |
| Frederick Barbarossa | *Holy Roman Emperor* |
| Leopold | *Duke of Austria* |

## OTHERS

| | |
|---|---|
| Henry II | *Richard's father and previous King of England* |
| John, Earl of Mortaigne | *Richard's brother and successor* |
| Berengaria | *Richard's Queen* |
| Alais | *Philip's sister, Henry's mistress, Richard's betrothed, Eleanor's prisoner* |
| Joanna | *Richard's sister, Queen of Sicily* |
| Tancred | *King of Sicily* |
| Isaac Comnenus | *Emperor of Cyprus* |
| Henry VI | *Holy Roman Emperor, Frederick Barbarossa's successor* |
| Celestine III | *Pope* |

# Foreword

✠

The crusader "movement," as it is sometimes called, stretched over a period of two hundred years, unleashing a frenzy of hate and violence unprecedented before the advent of the technological age and the scourge of Hitler. The madness was initiated in the name of religion by a Pope of the Christian Church, Urban II, in 1095 as a measure to redirect the energies of warring European barons from their bloody, local disputes into a "noble" quest to reclaim the Holy Land from the "infidel." Once unleashed, the passion could not be controlled. The violence began with the massacre of Jews, proceeded to the wholesale slaughter of Muslims in their native land, sapped the wealth of Europe, and ended with an almost unimaginable death toll on all sides. Bernard of Clairvaux, the great propagandist of the Second Crusade, would lament that he left only one man in Europe to comfort every seven widows.

There were five major crusades (and a handful of minor eruptions bred of the same instinct). Only the First Crusade was "successful," in the sense that it managed to capture Jerusalem and in the process make the streets of the Old City run ankle deep with Muslim and Jewish blood. All the others were failures. Three of the five got close to the object of the enterprise, the Holy City. Only because of the disunity of the Arab world did the First Crusade succeed in capturing Jerusalem. Precisely because of the unification of Egypt and Syria into a united Arab empire, the Third Crusade failed to capture it. In the Fifth Crusade, Frederick II of Germany negotiated his way into the Holy City, only to leave Palestine weeks later, pelted with garbage by his own people.

The Third Crusade, spanning the years 1187–92, is the most interesting of them all. It was the largest military endeavor of the Middle Ages and brought the fury of the entire crusading movement to its zenith. Perhaps most important, it brought two of the most remarkable and fascinating figures of the last millennium into conflict: Saladin, the Sultan of Egypt, Syria, Arabia, and Mesopotamia; and Richard I, King of England, known as the Lionheart.

That conflict of giants in a grand holy tournament still resounds in the modern history and modern politics of the present-day Middle East. Indeed, its resonance is even broader: with conflicts between Christians and Muslims wherever they may exist in the world, from Bosnia to Kosovo to Chechnya to Lebanon to Malaysia to Indonesia.

Until this day Saladin remains a preeminent hero of the Islamic world. It was he who united the Arabs, who defeated the Crusaders in epic battles, who recaptured Jerusalem, and who threw the European invaders out of Arab lands. In the seemingly endless struggle of modern-day Arabs to reassert the essentially Arab nature of Palestine, Saladin lives, vibrantly, as a symbol of hope and as the stuff of myth. In Damascus or Cairo, Amman or East Jerusalem, one can easily fall into lengthy conversations about Saladin, for these ancient memories are central to the Arab sensibility and to their ideology of liberation. On the bars of the small, dimly lit cell in the Old City of Jerusalem where Saladin lived humbly after his grand conquests is the inscription, "Allah, Muhammad, Saladin." God, prophet, liberator. Such is Saladin's relation to the Muslim God.

The Arab world, it seems, is forever waiting for another Saladin. At Friday prayer, from Aleppo to Cairo to Baghdad, it is not unusual to hear the plea for one like him to come and liberate Jerusalem. His total victory over the Crusaders at the Battle of Hattin is held up today as the everlasting symbol of Arab triumph over Western interference. In Damascus, near the entrance to the central Souq al-Hamadiya, a heroic equestrian statue of Saladin graces the main plaza of the city. When protests take place, as they did recently over the renewed negotiations between Israel and Syria about disputed lands, the gathering place is Saladin's heroic statue. In the office of the late president of Syria, Hafez Assad, an epic painting of the Battle of Hattin covered an entire wall, and Assad was fond of taking Western visitors over to it, as if to say that just as another Saladin will someday come again, so someday there will also be a second Battle of Hattin. Assad's death and funeral in June of 2000, when tens of thousands of Arabs filled the streets of Damascus, provided a pale reflection of what Saladin's funeral must have been like in March of 1193.

But it is not only for his military prowess that Saladin is venerated. He is also remembered for his humility, his compassion, his mysticism, his piety, and his restraint.

The legacy of Richard I of England is no less vibrant but somewhat different in nature. He is one of the most romantic figures of all of English history. In lore that has been embellished over the centuries and read to schoolboys at bedtime, Richard has become the very epitome of chivalry, the knight fighting bravely for his kingdom, his church, and his lady with ax, shield, and horse.

In my youth I was engrossed in the plays of Shakespeare and the novels of Sir Walter Scott that dwelt on this material. In the hills of northern Virginia where I grew up, I loved to ride behind the hay wagons and manure spreaders drawn by great sumpter horses, and to imagine these massive animals pulling the battle wagons of King Arthur and King Richard. In those same hills as I grew older, my favorite spot to watch the sun set over the Blue Ridge was a hill called Ivanhoe. I thrilled to the mail-clad warriors and their lovely liege ladies of the Hollywood movies: Elizabeth Taylor, Joan Fontaine, and Robert Taylor in *Ivanhoe*, Errol Flynn, Claude Rains, Basil Rathbone, and Olivia de Havilland in *Robin Hood*, James Mason, Rex Harrison, George Sanders, and Laurence Harvey in *King Richard and the Crusades*, Katharine Hepburn, Anthony Hopkins, and Peter O'Toole in *The Lion in Winter*.

There is something so wonderfully elemental about these romances. That in actual history, Richard Coeur de Lion did not quite measure up to the standards of his own legend does not dull his allure. He was a brilliant military mind and a fearsome general who understood the strategy and tactics of large forces far ahead of his time, just as in single combat he was unrivaled in bravery and recklessness. His enterprise, no matter what its final outcome, was incredible. And his return from the Holy Land and capture in Austria has the Homeric flavor of Odysseus. Richard is remembered for his bravado and cunning—and his extravagance. He is not remembered for his compassion, his tact, or his restraint.

In the story of the Third Crusade there is also a stellar supporting cast: a host of sterling knights on both sides who, like the white knight James d'Avesnes or the towering Arab knight el-Tawil, fought bravely and selflessly for their faith in the high tradition of medieval chivalry. The story has a brace of outrageous villains: Reginald of Châtillon, lord of el Kerak, who touched off the whole mess; Leopold, the duke of Austria, who broke the Truce of God and imprisoned Richard on his way home; Henry VI, the Holy Roman Emperor, who demanded the King's ransom and thereby nearly bankrupted England; Rashid al-Din Sinan, the head of the Assassins, who struck fear in the hearts of all, including Saladin; and Earl John, Richard's brother, later the king who inspired the legend of Robin Hood and signed the Magna Carta, and who tried to steal his brother's kingdom in his absence. The saga has Eleanor of Aquitaine, Richard's mother and Queen to both French and English kings, an original feminist, in whose glittering court at Poitiers, devoted to the supremacy of women, Richard was raised. Philip Augustus was the wily King of France and Richard's companion in love and war, who bridled at the dominance of his old lover in their joint military exploits and eventually betrayed Richard with the passion of the spurned. And Alais was the ultimate pawn of European royalty: mistress of Richard's father, Henry II, half sister of Philip Augustus, betrothed to Richard and then cast off by him, finally prisoner of Eleanor.

For this epic confrontation the Holy Land is the setting. To travel in one's imagination with Richard and Saladin over this sacred ground is very different from traveling it with Jesus or Muhammad. The tale begins in the wilderness of Moab, where Moses was held hostage for forty years, moves to the Battle of Hattin fought on the mountain where many believe the Sermon on the Mount was delivered, and then on to Jerusalem, which Saladin captures and defends and from whose Dome of the Rock the Prophet Muhammad ascended into heaven on his nocturnal journey to Allah.

It is not hard to imagine the exhilaration of the crusading foot soldier when he first stepped on the same mottled ground where Jesus himself had walked in Caesarea or Jaffa or Emmaus, and how deeply that must have affected his motivation to fight, and, ironically, to kill. Equally, it is not hard to imagine the extra effort required of the Muslim soldier to defend his land and its native faith. Jerusalem, sacred to Islam, Judaism, and Christianity, is the touchstone for all. Just as today where the bells tolling for nones mix with the cry of *muezzin* to prayer and the chant of the orthodox Jew, where the mosque of Omar is joined with brick and mortar to the Church of the Holy Sepulcher, and not far from the Western Wall, the Holy City lives in the dreams and the imagination of all the participants. The vibrancy of those feelings about Jerusalem, to capture it or to defend it for the faith, heightens the ferocity of the conflict. These same passions are no less vibrant today.

In my conversations with Arab scholars in Syria, Jordan, and East Jerusalem, I became aware early in this project how differently the crusading period is seen from the Arab side. There, the twelfth and thirteenth centuries are seen not as the history of five crusades but as a continuous struggle over more than a century to resist foreign invasion and to reclaim their land from foreign occupation. From the Arab perspective there are three periods, not five: the collapse of the divided Islamic world with the initial invasion of the First Crusade; the struggles to mobilize the power of many Arabian tribes, caliphates, and sects into a united response to the European invasion; and finally, the victory and culmination that was Saladin.

The symbolism of the Third Crusade hovers over the modern history and modern politics of the Middle East. On December 11, 1917, when General Edmund Allenby walked through Jaffa Gate to accept the surrender of the Turks after four hundred years of rule, the press made much about the consummation of Europe's last crusade. In July 1920, when the French general Henri Gouraud took charge of Damascus, he strode to Saladin's tomb next to the Grand Mosque and exclaimed, to the everlasting disgust of modern Arabs, "Saladin, we have returned. My presence here consecrates the victory of the Cross over the Crescent."

Across the centuries the Crusader fortress of Beaufort in southern Lebanon has been a strategic battle prize for many hostile armies in the Middle East and has changed hands many times. In 1982 it was besieged once again, this time by General Ariel Sharon, just as Saladin did nine centuries ago, and in May of 2000 the Israelis evacuated the fortress, just as Reynauld of Sidon had done in 1187, as Palestinians jubilantly took charge of the bastion once again. In today's Israel, Highway 1—known as Bab al Vad, the Gate to the Valley, between the plain of Ramla and Jerusalem—travels the route through the Judean Hills that Richard used in his thrust on Jerusalem in 1192. Now that same route is littered with the hulks of armor-plated convoy vehicles that were disabled in the Israeli War of Liberation in 1948.

"The difference is," said my friend David Passow, a veteran of the early Zionist struggles and now a professor of history at Hebrew University, "we made it, and he didn't."

In Arabic literature today the Jews are seen as the modern crusaders, essentially European peoples who have invaded and occupied the Arab homeland. Just as a handful of crusaders controlled the Arab masses with their network of daunting fortresses and tight urban communities, so today, say

Arab intellectuals, Israel controls the Arab majority with its American-backed military might and its fortified, barbed-wire-encircled hilltop settlements. It is an article of faith on the Arab side that through the slow and mysterious but inevitable forces of history, the Israelis, like the Crusaders, will eventually be forced out of Palestine. Arab ideology embraces the long view of history: It took eighty years for Saladin and his predecessors Nur ad Din and Zengy to displace the Crusaders. The state of Israel is scarcely more than fifty years old.

Now as in the twelfth century the problem for the Arabs is their disorganization and division. If it will take another Saladin to collect again the power of a thousand Arab tribes, a number of Arab leaders have been eager to assume the role. In the 1950s Gamal Abdel Nasser invoked Saladin continually in his efforts to forge the United Arab Republic and to force the British and French out of the Sinai and the Suez Canal. During the Gulf War, despite the guffaws of his fellow Arabs who supported the NATO coalition rather than him, Saddam Hussein reached for Saladin's mantle, making much of the fact that he and Saladin were born in the same town in Kurdistan, Takreet. After the collapse of the Middle East talks in the summer of 2000, the whole Gaza Strip welcomed the uncompromising Palestinian leader Yasir Arafat home from Camp David with a blaze of banners proclaiming him to be the "Palestinian Saladin." Once again, wrote the Israeli writer Amos Oz in the *New York Times*, "the specter of Saladin" hovered over the Middle East. And finally, when violence erupted across Israel and the West Bank in October 2000, after Ariel Sharon visited the Temple Mount, bands of Palestinian youth calling themselves the "Saladin Brigades" rampaged through the narrow alleys of East Jerusalem.

The Third Crusade was Holy War at its most virulent. Inevitably there was much about it that was unholy, indeed, sacrilegious: the pogroms of Jews, the lust for booty, the effusions of greed, the fighting and killing for their own sake—all in the name of piety. Here Holy War was in its infancy but practiced at the height of its ferocity. In the first instance it was a Christian Holy War that was met in response and in reaction by the Muslim concept of jihad. Jihad is, by definition, a defensive concept, conditioned upon the provocation of an unbelieving aggressor. In the Koran the believer is called upon "to fight in the way of God with those who fight with you . . . but aggress not: God loves not the aggressors" (2:190). From this holy and defensive fighting, great heavenly rewards will flow.

And so it is an irony of history that today, the word "jihad" strikes fear in the hearts of many Westerners and Western governments who associate it with terrorism and Islamic fanaticism. But there is nothing in Islamic history that rivals the terror of the Crusades or the Christian fanaticism of the twelfth century.

In the spring of 2000 the Crusades were back in the news. On the Sunday before his historic pilgrimage to the Holy Land, Pope John Paul II issued a sweeping apology for all the sins committed by the Roman Church in the name of religion over the past two thousand years. Called "Memory and Reconciliation," and following the 1992 apology for the treatment of Galileo, the proclamation was yet another act of digesting the dark episodes of church history at the millennium as part of a process the Holy See has called "historical purification." In the litany of atrocities against Jews, Muslims, women, and ethnic groups, the Crusades were specifically mentioned.

For the Muslim population in the Middle East, the papal pronouncement was cause for celebration. In the matter of religious apologies, the Crusades, at last, had received equal billing with the Holocaust. How the Pontiff might elaborate on his apology when he reached Israel was much anticipated. As it turned out, John Paul did not elaborate at all, and the Grand Mufti of Jerusalem was not pleased.

"There have been many massacres in the world," the chief Islamic cleric said. "Why is this Holocaust in particular more important? When it comes to our cause, nobody pays attention, whether it is the Crusader massacres against Muslims or the massacres against Palestinians committed by Israelis. And we don't keep using and using these massacres to remind the world what we are owed."

Only a few weeks after the Pope's visit, I was back in Jerusalem. It was Easter Week, holy to Christians for the resurrection of Christ, the Holy Day of Prayer for Muslims, Passover for the Jews. Amid the throng at the Holy Sepulcher, I came not as a pilgrim but as a writer. I wanted to see again the sword of Godfrey of Bouillon, which is stuck away, not quite in disgrace, not quite in glory, in the sacristy of Christianity's holiest church.

Mark Twain had also been interested in this dubious relic during his visit as an "innocent abroad" in 1867, and he was still living the romance. "I tried old Godfrey's sword on a Muslim and clove him in twain like a dough knot," he wrote. "The spirit of Grimes was upon me, and if I had had a graveyard I would have destroyed all the infidels in Jerusalem. I wiped the blood off the old sword and handed it back to the priest—I did not want fresh gore to obliterate those sacred spots that crimsoned its brightness one day seven hundred years ago."

By the confessional booth a stocky, gray-haired Franciscan monk sat alone in his brown habit, looking a tad forlorn, as he waited for a penitent. When I approached him, I learned that he was Brother Matthew from Pittsburgh, and he was glad for some small talk. Cheerfully, he agreed to show me the sword. During Easter Week in Jerusalem, I asked him, how should one best partake of the mystical quality of the city at this profound time? What service should I attend? What happened with the parade of cross? Where was the best pageantry? What church best celebrated the resurrection?

He looked at me indulgently. "Young man," he said, putting his pitying hand on my arm, "this is not Paris. We do not have great cathedrals here. What's important in Jerusalem is what's in your heart."

And then he pushed away a rack full of clerical vestments to show me the ancient sword.

JAMES RESTON, JR.
DECEMBER 2000

# PART I
# The
# Insult

*Fill my goblet, O cupbearer*
*I am overwhelmed with passion.*
*The day I see you is a day of joy;*
*You are as perfect as the full moon;*
*You are more graceful than the willow branch.*
*The garden is fragrant with your scent.*

*For the love of God, O you whom I love*
*Pour us out a drink, O pour into this goblet*
*For the love of God, O you who can cure me,*
*We accept all your words.*
*Rose, basil or lily,*
*You outshine all the flowers.*

MUSLIM DEFENDER SONG

# CHAPTER ONE

# A Sultan Is Born

ARLY IN THE TWELFTH CENTURY, IN THE CITY OF Tovin in northern Armenia close to Georgia, there lived an eminent family of Kurds, the master of whose house was surnamed Najm ad-Din, which meant "excellent prince and star of religion." Najm ad-Din had a boon comrade named Bihruz, a man of intelligence and charm, qualities matched only by his bent for trouble. Bihruz had the misfortune to be discovered in a compromising position with the wife of the local emir, who promptly had Bihruz seized and castrated and banished from his fief.

After this humiliation Najm ad-Din decided to accompany his disgraced friend to Baghdad, the seat of the Abbasid caliphate, where the Caliph, Al Muqtafi li-amri'llah ("he who follows the orders of God"), reigned supreme over the Muslim world of the eastern Mediterranean. In Baghdad the Sultan of Iraq noticed their talents. Since eunuchs were then favored as teachers and administrators, Bihruz became the tutor of the Sultan's sons and a companion to the Sultan himself in the games of chess and draughts. He rose quickly in power and influence and soon became responsible for building some of the great buildings of the land. In his rise to power Bihruz brought his friend, Najm ad-Din, along with him. Among the rewards the Sultan bestowed on Bihruz for his service was the castle at Takreet, on the Tigris River, and Bihruz in turn bestowed the command of it on his friend, Najm ad-Din.

At the castle in Takreet, Najm ad-Din was joined by his younger and more ambitious brother, named Shirkuh, and together these Kurds from the north seemed marked for greatness. For the Arab world had arrived at a critical juncture in its history. Forty years earlier, in the year 1098, Europeans had descended on Palestine, conquering Jerusalem in what the Franks called a crusade and establishing a powerful state called the Kingdom of Jerusalem, which stretched from Antioch in the north to Elath on the Red Sea. Along the coastline and in the mountains the foreigners built huge fortresses to protect their kingdom, and thus the Muslim world was fractured and invaded, beaten, and occupied.

In the year 532 (A.D. 1137 in the Christian calendar) a son named Yusuf was born to Najm ad-Din. In Arab lands this was an ambiguous name, which was associated with all the vicissitudes of the life of Joseph the Prophet, the low life as well as the high, the greed and falseness as well as the piety and truth. The circumstances of Yusuf's birth seemed ominous as well. For on the very night that Yusuf was born, the child's uncle, Shirkuh, had a dispute with the Isfahsalar, commander at the castle gate, after the officer had insulted a woman and she had come to Shirkuh in tears. In a rage Shirkuh snatched the halberd of the commander and killed him with his own weapon. When their powerful patron, the eunuch Bihruz, heard of this in Baghdad, he was appalled and banished the brothers from Takreet in disgrace. That so terrible an event accompanied the birth of Yusuf was considered a bad sign, but later it would be said, "Good may come of adversity when you least expect it. And such was the case with Yusuf." From Takreet the brothers went to Mosul in northern Mesopotamia.

In Mosul, in the face of the European occupation of Palestine, a strong Arab leader named Zengy had taken power and was making strides in uniting the far-flung domains of Islam, where Mesopotamia was traditionally divided from Syria, where Antioch fought with Aleppo, Tripoli with Homs, Jerusalem with Damascus, where the Sunni branch of Islam fought with the Shi'ite branch. In his quest to overcome the divisions of the Muslim world, Zengy called these Kurdish brothers to his service. Najm ad-Din became the commander of Zengy's fortress in Baalbek in the Bekáa Valley, while Shirkuh became a powerful commander in the vizier's armies.

In November 1144, Zengy's forces captured Edessa in northern Mesopotamia, and thus the first of the fledgling Crusader provinces fell. The fall of Edessa was a shock to Europe. Largely through the eloquence of the Cistercian monk Bernard of Clairvaux, a campaign for a new Crusade began, and among the first to heed this call was the King of France, Louis VII, and his Queen, Eleanor of Aquitaine. In 1146, before the new Crusaders arrived in the Holy Land, Zengy died, and he was replaced by an even more powerful figure, Nur ad-Din. Two years later the Crusader forces were crushed outside the walls of Damascus, turning the Second Crusade into a total disaster and emboldening the forces of Islam further in their quest for the reconquest of Palestine.

The boy, Yusuf, grew up in Baalbek and Damascus. Though he was slight of build, his intelligence, his mannerliness, his generosity, his piety, and his modesty were noticed in the palaces of Damascus. Like a few others of his age, he was drawn to wine and women in his adolescence, but the seriousness of the historical situation eventually impressed him, and he renounced these temptations. Later it would be said that from the education of his sovereign, Nur ad-Din, Yusuf—later called Salah ad-Din or Saladin—learned to walk in the path of righteousness, to act virtuously, and to be zealous in waging war against infidels. In the court of Damascus the principle of striving in Allah's cause was emphasized, and the youth took to heart this invocation in the Koran: "Those who strive in Our Cause, we will surely guide in Our way, for verily Allah is with those who do right."

In 1163 Nur ad-Din saw clearly the next step in the unification of the Arab world against the European occupation. In Egypt the Fatimite caliphate (which practiced the Shi'ite rather than the Sunni way of Islam) was in disarray, and this presented the lord of Syria with a target of opportunity. Nur ad-Din ordered Shirkuh, Saladin's charismatic uncle, to undertake a succession of invasions to the south and ordered the young Saladin, now twenty-six years old, to accompany his uncle. Reluctantly, Saladin complied.

As Shirkuh and Saladin headed south, Nur ad-Din himself laid siege to the greatest of all the Crusader castles, Krak des Chevaliers, in central Syria, but the fortress was impregnable and the Muslim forces were turned back. The time was not yet ripe for a frontal assault on the Crusader kingdom.

In 1164, with Saladin in command of the vanguard of the army, Shirkuh conquered Cairo. But within weeks he was forced to withdraw when Crusader forces came to the aid of the Egyptian caliphate. Three years later a second invasion failed, again due to the support of the Crusaders, for above all else the Crusader kingdom could not abide a united Egypt and Syria. So desperate was this crisis considered in the Crusader kingdom that any baron refusing to heed the summons forfeited 10 percent of his income. Two further invasions faltered, until on January 8, 1169, in the fifth attempt, Shirkuh entered Cairo in triumph. Gloriously, he proclaimed himself to be the new King of Egypt—and then, abruptly, died two months later. Poison was suspected.

Pondering this reverse in Damascus, Nur ad-Din settled on Saladin as his uncle's successor. The young soldier was chosen not because of his strengths but because of the perceived weaknesses of his youth and inexperience. In truth, Nur ad-Din did not want a powerful competitor in Cairo, and he was certain that he could control his malleable and polite ward. In this he would be disappointed.

At first Saladin was the compliant subordinate. Mercilessly, he followed Nur ad-Din's orders to expunge the Shi'ite way of Islam in Egypt and replace it with the Sunni way. He requested of his lord that his father, Najm ad-Din, be allowed to come to Cairo. "My happiness will thus be complete," he wrote to his lord in Damascus, "and my adventure will be similar to that of Yusuf [Joseph] the faithful." Nur ad-Din granted the request. When Najm ad-Din arrived in the spring of 1170, his son greeted him with honors, even offering to resign and turn the command of Egypt over to his father. But his father replied, "O my son, God would not have chosen you to fill this post if you were not deserving of it. It is not right to change the object of Fortune's favors." Two years later, while riding near the Gate of Victory, the Bab an-Nasr, Najm ad-Din was thrown from his horse and died.

Between 1169 and 1174, while successive Crusader attacks sought unsuccessfully to undermine the grip of Damascus on Egypt, Nur ad-Din and Saladin developed an increasingly tense relationship after Saladin balked at certain directives from Damascus. Finally, in early 1174, Nur ad-Din had

had enough of this impudence and mustered an army to invade Saladin's Egypt. But on May 15 of that year, as these preparations were under way, Nur ad-Din died. Absurdly, his power was handed to his eleven-year-old son.

A year later Saladin led an army out of Egypt and took control of Syria. He was proclaimed the Sultan of Syria and Egypt, and his vast empire now held the Crusader kingdom in its grip like a lobster claw.

Only because of the divisions among petty potentates, because of the feud between the Islamic sects of the Sunnis and the Shi'ites and between competing caliphates in Egypt and Syria and Turkey had the First Crusade succeeded. But gradually, with a slow inevitability that was almost providential, the Arab world consolidated its power in the face of the European occupation. The Arab recapture of Edessa had been the critical first step, and the failure of the Second Crusade gave the Islamic world confidence that it could drive the Christians into the sea. A succession of three strong Arab leaders advanced the union of the Arabs: the able Zengy who had recaptured Edessa and ruled until his death in 1147, the powerful Nur ad-Din who united all of Muslim Syria and Mesopotamia under Sunnism and subdued Egypt in 1169, and now Saladin.

When in 1175, at the age of thirty-eight, Saladin took power in both Damascus and Cairo, the centuries-old divisions evaporated. The Fatamid caliphate of Egypt was finished, and with its demise the Sunnism of the north supplanted Shi'ism along the Nile. In the spring of 1175, Saladin was declared King of Syria and was recognized as the Emperor of Syria and Egypt by the titular leader in the Middle East, the Caliph in Baghdad.

"When God gave me the land of Egypt, I was sure that he meant Palestine for me as well," Saladin proclaimed.

The dream of a united front against the Christians was a reality at last. That Arab dream was the Christian nightmare. For ninety years, through skillful alliances and offensive, destabilizing raids and strategic castles, the Latin Kingdom had kept its enemies off balance. The survival of the Latin Kingdom would now depend on its internal discipline and its military skill.

Before his final offensive began, the Sultan had one remaining task to accomplish within his own empire. He needed to subdue the last of the independent fiefs. In 1183, in the Muslim month of Safar (June) and after the death of a child-emir, he captured Aleppo. Beyond the military importance of the city, this triumph was fraught with symbolic importance. Aleppo was known as the Gray Castle, and among the public there was a popular saying that presaged even greater triumphs ahead:

*Thy taking of the Gray Castle in the month of Safar announces the conquest of Jerusalem for the month of Rajab.*

In 1186 the Sultan took Mosul in Upper Mesopotamia. He was well poised to strike. The month of Rajab was in the offing.

CHAPTER TWO

# The Kingdom
# of Heaven

✠

The Latin Kingdom of Jerusalem had come into existence eighty-nine years earlier with the First Crusade. In 1098 Godfrey of Bouillon had stormed the walls of the Holy City and massacred the Muslim defenders by the thousands. The stone streets of Jerusalem ran with blood, through which the victorious Crusaders waded before falling to their knees in a mass of thanksgiving at the Holy Sepulcher.

Thirty years later the small kingdom was at the peak of its power. Christian knights pushed its boundaries outward as if the Muslim world were a feather pillow. The kingdom had thrived on the division of the enemy. The thousand tribes of Arabia had their minor emirs and viziers, who aligned themselves with the caliphates of either Cairo or Baghdad, fought over petty disputes, and prayed as part of either the Sunni or the Shi'ite sects of Islam.

By 1131 the Crusader kingdom comprised the greater part of Palestine and the coast of Syria. The European invaders, who over time became known generically as Franks, concentrated in the important coastal cities of Latakia, Tortosa, Tripoli, Beirut, Tyre, Acre, Haifa, Caesarea, Jaffa, and Ascalon, as well as the inland cities of Edessa, Antioch, Tiberias, and, most important, Jerusalem itself. The rural areas were left largely to the native population, who outnumbered their overlords five to one. In their bucolic pastures the natives cultivated their crops in peace and were content to give half the harvest to their absentee landlords from abroad. These indigenous peoples were allowed to govern themselves.

In its entirety the population of the precious kingdom was about 250,000. Its leading cities of Jerusalem and Acre had about 25,000 residents (although in the aftermath of the massacre of Jerusalem, only a few streets were occupied and the new Crusader lords were forced to recruit inhabitants from other regions as the crusading army went home). The north of the kingdom was divided into nominally independent provinces: the principality of Antioch, and the counties of Edessa and Tripoli, whose lords were vassals of the King of Jerusalem to their south. With a few exceptions the grand personages of the Crusader kingdom had been the lesser personages of Europe, younger sons of minor households who had no real future on the Continent and had come to the Orient in search of wealth and position and adventure.

Against the seemingly inexhaustible manpower of the Muslim world the Christians had built their formidable network of great castles. This defensive system of strongholds stretched along the coast, and the castles were within sight of one another, so that signal fires could be seen from one to another. By a system of smoke and fire, the great fortress of el Kerak in the Transjordan, for example, could communicate with Jerusalem at night, over a distance of seventy miles. On mountaintops hovering over strategic valleys, these fortresses dotted the landscape at regular intervals.

The military monks, the Templars and the Hospitalers, were the backbone of Christian power. These zealots were former nobles who had given up their jewels and castles and ladies in Europe to take a solemn and chaste vow to defend the Holy Land. For a monk in a Christian order to bear arms spoke to the profound transformation that the concept of Holy War had wrought in the church. St. Martin had expressed the original orthodoxy in the fourth century: "I am a soldier of Christ. I must not fight." To shed blood in combat was sinful, and on no account could a holy man have anything to do with temporal conflicts. The church strictly forbade not only fighting but the bearing of arms.

A few decades later St. Augustine had challenged St. Martin's view. In certain instances war could be moral and even just. Just war must be defensive in nature when Christian soldiers took up arms to defend Christian lands against the enemies of Christ, and this concept fit very well with the defense of the Holy Land. Beyond that, war could also be holy, wrote St. Augustine, when God sanctioned it, and soldiers were servants of God. To preserve the purity of the church, to extend the faith—these refrains rationalized the new Christian combat. Charlemagne had put this new attitude into practice in the ninth century when he sought to conquer Muslim Spain and to create a vast Holy Roman Empire in Europe.

The new militants searched the Bible and the litany of saints for further sanction. In 2 Timothy 2:3–4 they found their certification: "Thou therefore endure hardness as a good soldier of Jesus Christ. No man that warreth entangleth himself with the affairs of this life; that he may please him who hath chosen him to be a soldier." St. Michael replaced St. Martin, for St. Michael slew the satanic dragon in the Book of Revelation. St. George, the patron saint of England, also slew the satanic dragon, and he had been a real soldier of the King.

The mass of St. Michael became the war liturgy, said with utmost reverence before a great battle in the Middle Ages. By the eleventh century even the prohibition against priests bearing arms was waning. The church now required chivalrous and moral gladiators. While the propagandists for the new militancy did not expressly say it, they were adapting the concepts of the Icelandic sagas to Christian warfare: Valhalla became Paradise, and Woden became Christ. Christian soldiers were like the heroes of the Niebelungen, the Jomsvikings, and the House-Carles of Svein Forkbeard.

In this transition from Christian sufferance to Christian militancy, the individual soldier was often flung into ethical confusion. "Frequently he burned with anxiety," read the biography of one soldier of the First Crusade, "because the warfare engaged in as a knight of the cross seemed to be contrary to the Lord's command to turn the other cheek. These contradictions deprived him of courage. But after Pope Urban granted remission of sins to all Christians fighting the Muslims, then at last, as if previously asleep, his vigor was aroused."

Before the capture of the Holy Land in the First Crusade of 1099, the Order of the Hospital had been established in Jerusalem to care for the poor and the sick. A papal bull formally chartered the Order in 1113 and put it under the direct authority of the papacy, making it independent from local control. In 1136 the Pope officially sanctioned the order to undertake military operations, and the Hospitalers would engage in major military operations in Eleanor's Second Crusade of 1147.

Parallel to the Hospitalers, the Order of the Temple was established in 1119. In 1128 its papal rule was promulgated with a central purpose to protect pilgrims along the perilous pilgrimage routes of the Middle East. It drew its inspiration from St. Bernard of Clairvaux, who declared that "killing for Christ" was "malecide not homicide" and "to kill a pagan is to win glory, for it gives glory to Christ."

A new knighthood was born in the holy chrism of the new chivalry. The warrior-monks took vows of poverty, chastity, and obedience like other monks. When they strapped on their armor, they promised, in battles with infidels, to be the first to attack and the last to retreat. In 1128 the Templars were given a white habit, signifying innocence, to which during the Second Crusade nineteen years later a red cross was added. In battle they had a black-and-white battle flag called the Beauceant, signifying their kindness to friends and their ferocity to enemies.

In principle, both the Hospitalers and the Templars satisfied the standards of Just and Holy War. The soldiers of Christ reported directly to the Pope through their Grand Masters. They were above the greed of temporal conflict and above the ignoble violence of the secular soldier. The military orders were at the height of their power.

Now on their mountaintop castles and urban bastions, these military monks looked east, across the tawny mountains and the vast deserts to the Muslim lands. Battalions of archers, squads of squires, and brigades of local mercenaries called turcopoles—soldiers of mixed blood who had proved effective over the years in fighting the mounted archers of the Arabs—supported these pious knights. Relying on the tactic of the cavalry charge of these passionate, well-armed, and heavily armored elite knights of Christ, the Christian army had proven itself to be invincible in pitched battle. But pitched battles were rare, and the Crusaders had done their best over the years to avoid them. In their tactical retreats they relied on their impressive castles.

With successive generations European traditions gave way to the customs and pleasures of the Orient. The short, stormy winters and long, hot summers transformed fashion and diet and lifestyle. The Franks shed their woolens and donned the burnoose and turban, the kaffiyeh and upturned soft slippers of the East. In the absence of wood for furniture and architecture, they sat cross-legged on patterned carpets and feathered divans, decorated their stone villas with silk and damask, perfumed their ladies with cosmetics and their rooms with incense, veiled them and took them shopping in open-air bazaars, bathed in deep tubs and discovered the joy of soap, cultivated exotic flowers in their gardens, became conversant in Arabic, spiced their rice with saffron and their tea with sugar and lemon, finished off their meals with melons and dates, and entertained themselves with Arabic lutes and native dancing girls. Life was good in this exotic garden of delight.

"The Lord made the wilderness so fat that where dragons and serpents had their dwelling there arose green reeds and canes," said a resident of Acre.

In due course some Occidentals intermarried with Syrian, Armenian, and Byzantine women. These unions created a new class of European Syrians known as poulains, which translated as "kids." The second- and third-generation Europeans came to think of themselves as Galilean and Palestinian rather than French or Roman, as citizens of Tyre or Antioch rather than of Rheims or Toulouse. Though they might dress in native garb and frequent the noisy *souqs* in comfort and even exhibit a degree of tolerance, the Europeans never lost their sense of being outsiders in their "Outremer." They adapted but they did not accept. They were not settlers but occupiers. They appreciated their vulnerability and impermanence as if they were intent to avoid being the last generation to experience these sensuous pleasures.

By the late twelfth century, visitors from Europe to the East were shocked at the corruption and hubris, the softness and even effeminacy of their distant cousins. "Among the poulains hardly one in a thousand takes his marriage seriously," wrote the Bishop of Acre about his wicked flock and their city. "They do not regard fornication to be a deadly sin. From childhood they are pampered and wholly given to carnal pleasures, whereas they are not accustomed to hear God's word, which they lightly disregard. Almost every day and night people are openly or secretly murdered. At night men strangle their wives if they dislike them and wives, using the ancient art of poison and potion, kill their husbands to marry other men. In the city there are vendors of toxins and poisons, so that nobody can have confidence in anyone.

The city is full of brothels, and as the rent of the prostitutes is higher, not only laymen, but even clergymen, nay, even monks, rent their houses all over the city to public brothels."

As the descendants of the First Crusaders lost their European discipline and values, they nevertheless felt like perpetual strangers in a hostile land. Over the past ninety years, including the Second Crusade in the year 1147, they had lived in a state of ceaseless conflict with the Arabs and had developed a special contempt for the Syrians. "They are for the most part untrustworthy," wrote the same bishop. "Double-dealers, cunning foxes even as the Greeks, liars and turncoats, lovers of success, traitors, easily won over by bribes, men who say one thing and mean another, who think nothing of theft and robbery. For a small sum of money they become spies and tell the secrets of the Christians to the Arabs, among whom they are brought up, whose language they speak rather than any other, and whose crooked ways they imitate."

The Jews were assigned a different scorn, for they were sunk in their "perpetual shame." "The Lord keeps them for a time like a log from the forest to be burned in winter, and like an evil vineyard, that brings forth only wild grapes," the pious bishop wrote. "For they remind us of Christ's death."

By 1187 the cultivated Arab nurtured an equal aversion to the European invaders. The white intruders had contributed nothing to the culture of the Middle East, no institutions of higher learning, no art or music, only grief and bloodshed. "The Franks (may Allah render them helpless!) possess none of the virtues of men, except courage," wrote a prominent prince from northern Syria. "They esteem no one but their knights upon whose counsel they rely." Still the prince distinguished between the families of the first Crusaders and the parvenus like Reginald of Châtillon, the terrible lord of el Kerak. "Those Franks who have come and settled among us and cultivate the society of Muslims are much superior to the others who have lately joined them. The newcomers are invariably more inhuman than the older settlers."

Among the newcomers was the King of Jerusalem himself. Guy of Lusignan hailed from a minor noble house in Aquitaine about which hovered the wonderful legend of descent from a serpent woman called Mélusine. Only a few years before, Guy had arrived in the East from France under curious circumstances. He had been banished from his native Poitou when he murdered the Earl of Salisbury as the pious earl was returning from a pilgrimage to Santiago de Compostela. In an irony of the Third Crusade, Guy's order of banishment was signed by the Prince of Aquitaine, Richard of Poitou, later to become Richard I of England, known as the Lionheart.

Seeking to turn disgrace into chivalry, Guy had conveniently taken the cross and headed for the Holy Land. He had achieved his status in Palestine, like Châtillon, by virtue of swagger and a well-placed bride. He was a better lover than a fighter.

Bold and ambitious and devilishly handsome, Guy had wooed the recently widowed sister of the King of Jerusalem, named Sibylla. Against the wishes of her family and against the advice of the church council, she had insisted on marrying this social inferior. An irregular ceremony was hastily performed during Eastertide, a time when marriages were generally forbidden, and abruptly this sly fugitive found himself in line to be King. William of Tyre, the great historian of the Latin Kingdom, remarked, patronizingly, that the lineage of this dashing upstart was "noble enough" to meet the bare essentials of royalty, but no one was pleased at the notion except Sibylla. With his marriage came a fief: Guy of Lusignan, descended from a serpent, banished from Poitou, fugitive and hustler, was now the lord of Jaffa and Ascalon.

From the moment of his marriage in 1180, Guy of Lusignan was flooded with good luck. The King of Jerusalem then was Baldwin IV, a wise and intelligent leader who had the misfortune to contract leprosy, which disfigured and blinded and eventually killed him and which, of course, prevented him from producing an heir. As Guy of Lusignan arrived on the scene, the King's condition was worsening with every passing year. His heir was his nephew, who was a sickly toddler. Between the King's illness and his heir's minority, Guy was appointed regent of the realm in 1184, and this put him in charge of the details of rule. The appointment further legitimized Guy and elevated his stature. But the resentment against this interloper among the indigenous barons was fierce, and it paralyzed the army. After he proved fainthearted in a confrontation with the Muslims at the springs of Tubania, Guy was dismissed from his regency. This did not affect his place in line for the throne, however, even though there were calls for Sibylla to divorce her husband and marry a more capable man. In the wars of succession, his rival in leadership and love was the patrician Count Raymond himself.

The leper King died in 1185, and his tiny nephew died the following year. Although Guy was resented and disliked by the barons and although the throne technically belonged to Raymond, Guy maneuvered his way skillfully to his ultimate goal. Once again a speedy ceremony was conducted in which the pretender donned the robes at the royal palace, and was hustled along to the Church of the Holy Sepulcher for the investiture by the Patriarch of Jerusalem. At Christianity's holiest shrine the Patriarch crowned Sibylla queen. And then he said to her, as if he could not bear to hear her answer, "My lady, you are most excellent. It is convenient that you have with you those who can help you govern your kingdom, whoever that may be. Take this crown and give it to whatever man can best aid you in governing your kingdom."

In this way the Patriarch divested himself of any responsibility for her frivolous choice. Naturally, she placed a crown on her beloved Guy's head. The new royals were then spirited down to the Temple Mount for a feast among carefully chosen guests. With this unseemly haste Guy became King in mid-September 1186.

"He will not last a year," an important baron grumbled. But the Poitevins in Guy's circle exulted. It was now the Poitevins against the poulains, the name given the indigenous knights. The Poitevins in Guy's camp taunted their opponents with a chant:

> Maugré li Polein,
> Avrons nous roi Poitevin.

This arrogant and contemptuous sneer, "Despite the poulains, we shall have a Poitevin king," created a resentment that would be long remembered. The new King of the Kingdom of Jerusalem never recovered the respect of his liege lords.

CHAPTER THREE

# The Flint and the Spark

✠

I N BIBLICAL TIMES THE FORTRESS OF KERAK had been the ancient capital of the Kingdom of the Moabites. It was not far distant from the town called Rabboth, which, apart from its three springs that served the bastion, was best known as the place where King David had wickedly seized the beautiful wife of Uriah the Hittite, taken her to bed, and impregnated her before he had the wretched Uriah slain at the city's gate.

He who controlled Kerak controlled all the trade, the pilgrimages, and the armies that passed through its bottleneck. The bastion was virtually a fortified city built on six stories, with an upper and a lower court. It was refreshed by thirteen cisterns, garrisoned by twelve hundred soldiers, appointed with multiple galleries, stables, storehouses, barracks, underground tunnels, a wine press, a kitchen with double sinks, and even a *souq*. Within its massive walls were stored provisions to sustain the bastion for a year. Constructed nearly a half century before on old Roman foundations and built quickly in just six years with local labor and slaves, its style was Byzantine. Its huge donjon in the south was surrounded by a high defensive wall punctuated at regular intervals by towers. Kerak was the finest example of military architecture of the twelfth century. Its location at the head of a cavern known as Wadi al Kerak, which sloped downward toward the Dead Sea in the west, allowed it to command all traffic from the Dead Sea. And it towered above the King's Highway as the road narrowed into a ravine.

Beyond its strategic location, deep escarpments protected the castle itself on three sides, except to its east, which was fortified with high walls and a dry moat, over which a drawbridge could be lowered as the only entrance to the fortress. Called the "Crow's Castle" partly because it hovered so closely and menacingly directly over the highway, the stronghold was considered nearly impregnable.

Saladin had found this out twice before. In 1173 he had mustered all his power against the citadel only to withdraw a few days later. He had tried again in 1184. "This fortress is a source of great annoyance to the Muslims," Saladin's court historian, Beha al-Din, had complained, "for it so effactually commanded the road to Egypt that caravans could not travel without a strong military escort. The Sultan resolved to put an end to this state of things and open the road to Egypt."

Again the assault had been a failure and did nothing more than contribute to the reputation of Saladin, for he had purposely interrupted his bombardment of the place while a wedding was under way within the castle walls. In frustration Saladin had withdrawn to Damascus, burning the city of Nablus along the way, and had not returned to Palestine since. The Sultan understood full well that the fortress of Kerak was strategically placed at the elbow of his newly formed empire joining Egypt and Syria. Unless the fortress could be subdued, the coordination between the two halves of his empire would always be difficult in any campaign that meant to squeeze the Crusader kingdom in a vise and drive the infidel invaders into the sea.

Thus the ruler of Kerak was arguably the most important lord in the entire Crusader kingdom.

In 1187 that ruler was Reginald of Châtillon. He was the most hated man in all the Muslim world. Like so many other second sons and landless lords, adventurers, and fortune hunters who populated the ranks of the European occupiers, Châtillon had come to the East in 1147 with the Second Crusade, more in search of wealth and power than for spiritual revenge. A minor noble from a northern French family with huge ambitions, he began his quest by seducing the recently widowed Princess of Antioch. That so eminent a royal lady, however flighty and pleasure-seeking she might be, should choose to marry down was a source of contention in Antioch, and both the King of Jerusalem and the Patriarch of Antioch opposed her union with so ordinary a knight.

Now the lord of the wealthiest city of the East, Châtillon made short order of this opposition. When the Patriarch refused to fund a punitive expedition to the Byzantine island of Cyprus, he was seized and conducted to the citadel, where he was stripped, honey spread over his entire body, and left for the flies in the blazing sun. When he came down from the tower, the Patriarch collapsed and opened his church's coffers. This atrocity so horrified and intimidated the King of Jerusalem that he sent a conciliatory envoy to assuage the renegade. In the raid on Cyprus Châtillon deepened his reputation for wild and ruthless action when his soldiers raped the women, mutilated the opposition, and pillaged their way across the island. At last, in 1160, this wild man was captured in a Muslim ambush as he was engaged in cattle rustling and was imprisoned in Aleppo.

He spent fourteen years in captivity. In 1176 Châtillon was ransomed for the huge sum of 120,000 gold dinars, but after his years deep in the dank dungeon of the Aleppo citadel he emerged in the grip of an even more passionate hatred of Muslims, and he was greedier and more bloodthirsty than ever. In the intervening time his lady of Antioch had died, and so Châtillon found in Stephanie, the Lady Eschive of the Transjordan, another widow of opportunity. With her came the strategic bastions of Kerak and Montreal and the control of the southern finger of the Christian kingdom, all the way to Aqaba and the Red Sea.

This black knight-errant set out to create an independent fief in the desert of Gilead. His reign at Kerak was infamous for its wanton cruelty, and it was

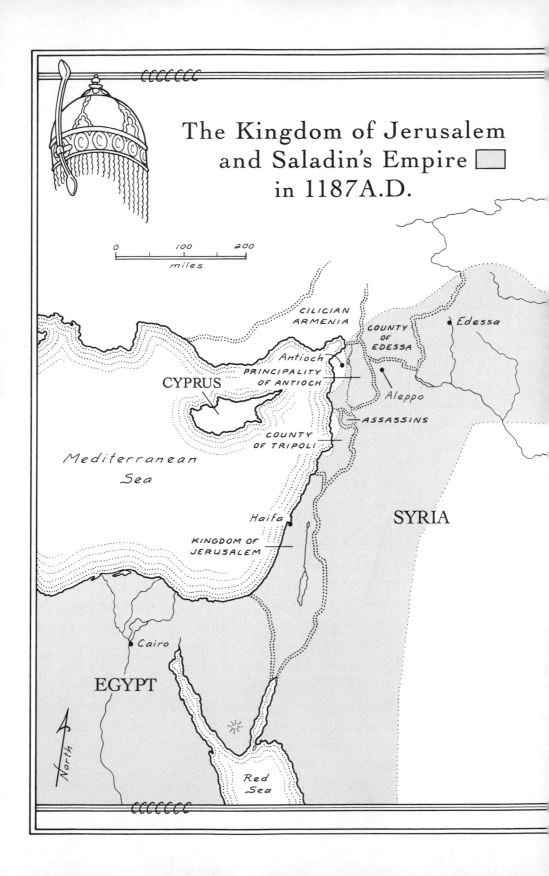

# The Kingdom of Jerusalem and Saladin's Empire in 1187A.D. □

0    100    200
miles

CILICIAN
ARMENIA

COUNTY
OF
EDESSA

Edessa

Antioch

PRINCIPALITY
OF ANTIOCH

CYPRUS

Aleppo

ASSASSINS

COUNTY
OF TRIPOLI

Mediterranean
Sea

SYRIA

Haifa

KINGDOM OF
JERUSALEM

Cairo

EGYPT

North

Red
Sea

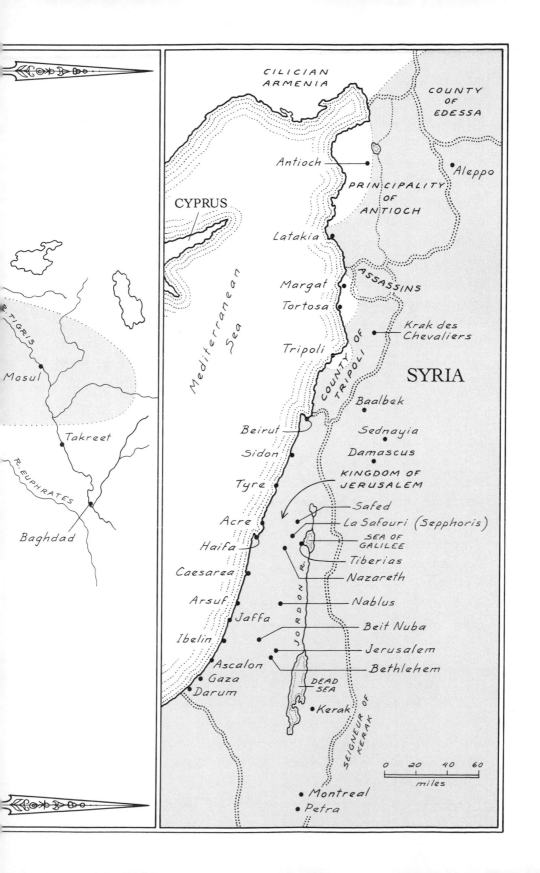

CILICIAN
ARMENIA

COUNTY
OF
EDESSA

Antioch

Aleppo

CYPRUS

PRINCIPALITY
OF
ANTIOCH

Latakia

ASSASSINS

Margat

Tortosa

Krak des
Chevaliers

COUNTY OF TRIPOLI

Tripoli

SYRIA

Baalbek

Mediterranean Sea

Beirut

Sednayia

Sidon

Damascus

Tyre

KINGDOM OF
JERUSALEM

Safed

Acre

La Safouri (Sepphoris)

SEA OF
GALILEE

Haifa

Tiberias

Nazareth

Caesarea

Arsuf

Nablus

Jaffa

Beit Nuba

JORDAN R.

Ibelin

Jerusalem

Ascalon

Bethlehem

Gaza

Darum

DEAD
SEA

Kerak

SEIGNEUR OF KERAK

0    20    40    60
miles

Montreal

Petra

R. TIGRIS

Mosul

Takreet

R. EUPHRATES

Baghdad

said that he encased the heads of his victims in a wooden box, so that when they were thrown off the high castle walls they would be conscious as they hit the rocks below. On his seal was the emblem of a griffin, the monster that was half eagle, half lion, with an inscription that touted the virtues of *"civitas."*

To the weak kings of Jerusalem this wild wind of the desert was uncontrollable. He was, however, active in the power struggles in Jerusalem and allied himself with the powerful militant monks called the Templars. He joined his fellow Europeans in battle against the Muslims when it suited him. In the great defeat of Saladin in 1177, for example, where the Muslim forces were cut to pieces in a swamp near Mont Gisard, he comported himself brilliantly. But his reckless independent actions gained him the most attention, and especially the ire of Saladin.

The most spectacular of these came in the winter of 1182–83. In his demented imagination Châtillon hatched a plan to attack the very heart of Islam—Medina and Mecca, the holiest of all cities—promising to defile and dishonor them before they were demolished. He would drag the Prophet Muhammad, "this accursed camel driver," from his tomb, he boasted, and he would raze to the ground the Ka'aba, the sacred black stone of Mecca, to which all Muslims turned to pray.

At Kerak, Châtillon built a fleet of ships, transported them to the Dead Sea for sea trials, dismantled them again, and had them transported 130 miles south to Elath, where, at the Crusaders' stronghold on the Isle de Graye at the northernmost point of the Red Sea, they were reassembled and launched. Crisscrossing the Red Sea, looting villages on the Arabian and Egyptian shores, these pirates sent a wave of terror through the Muslim world, but it was slow to react. Saladin's brother and his bedouins finally caught the pirates only a few miles from Medina. Inevitably, Châtillon escaped unharmed to the Moab while his buccaneers were strapped backward onto camels, taken to Cairo, and beheaded.

For this dastardly and contemptuous act Saladin vowed to catch Châtillon and personally decapitate him. The Prince of Kerak became something of an obsession for the Sultan, and he would spend the better part of the next two years trying to liquidate the threat. Meanwhile, the Caliph in Baghdad criticized the Sultan for failing to protect the pilgrimage route to Mecca, and this criticism hurt. In his defensive reply to the Caliph, Saladin tried to divert attention to rebellious stirrings in Mesopotamia.

"We are amazed that while we are defending the tomb of the Prophet (blessings be upon him), and are solely concerned with its protection, [the Prince of Mosul] is disputing the land which belongs to us and attempting to seize it unjustly."

But Saladin's raid against Kerak two years later was a failure. He retreated to Damascus and negotiated a truce with his Christian adversaries. "If the enemy incline toward peace, do thou also incline toward peace and trust in Allah," counseled the Koran. The Sultan waited for another opportunity—and another provocation.

He did not have to wait long.

## 2

# The CARAVAN

At the third beat of the emir's drum, in the winter of the year 583, known in the Christian world as A.D. 1187, the camels were saddled and loaded, and a large, heavy-laden caravan set out from Cairo, bound for Damascus along the traditional Transjordan route. It bore goods of extraordinary value: exquisite silks, metalwork with intricate floral designs, delicate pottery, spices, and heaps of gold and silver.

Because a truce had been forged several years before between Saladin and the Christian King of Jerusalem, it was considered reasonably safe to pass through the finger of desert that formed the southern portion of the Crusader land and then north along the hajj road. The master of the caravan was so confident in the truce, in fact, that his convoy was only lightly guarded, and it carried an important personage: Saladin's sister.

Across the Sinai south of the Dead Sea along the route that Moses took after he crossed the Red Sea, the camel train traveled at night to the light of torches carried by footmen. The procession came to al Raqim, mentioned in the Koran as the cave of the Seven Sleepers, before it at last arrived safely at the extraordinary ancient Nabataean city of Petra. It was here that Moses had twice struck a rock and water had gushed forth. Here the caravan would rest for several days.

At Petra the Egyptians encountered the first in the impressive chain of Crusader fortifications that stretched from the Red Sea to the north of Syria. Overlooking the main thoroughfare of Petra where the Arabian traders haggled in the roseate caves of the Nubian sandstone and where the breathtaking archways and temples and tombs of a lost civilization towered over them, the Crusaders maintained a small fort and listening post on a high place called al-Habees. Then a mile from Petra, in the valley the Arabs knew as Wadi Moussa, the Valley of Moses, a larger fortress called Wu'eira Castle was the command post for the region and was garrisoned by a strong force of Templar knights.

Still, the anxieties of the Egyptian travelers eased as they left Petra and passed Wu'eira Castle without incident and set out on the well-beaten hajj road. This section of the legendary pilgrim route between Damascus and Mecca had also been known since biblical times as the King's Highway. Moses had called it that when he pled in vain with the Edomites to let him pass through on his way to the Promised Land. "We will go by the king's highway," Moses had said. "We will not turn to the right hand nor to the left, until we have passed thy borders." The Edomites were unmoved. He was detained there for forty years.

Thirty miles to the north, above fertile fields abundant in corn, olives, and grapes, towered Shobak, which the Europeans called Montreal. This was an even more impressive high mountain fortress, which had been conquered by the first Crusader king, Baldwin I, as he consolidated the gains of the First Crusade and established the European realm in the Holy Land. The fort was added to the Christian domain in the year 1115.

This redoubt, too, was passed without interference. Eventually the convoy crossed the cavernous Wadi Hasa, the boundary between the biblical domains of Edom and Moab, and made its way languidly into the plain of Moab, the wilderness where Moses and his people had spent their forty years of waiting. To the west, far in the distant haze, was the Dead Sea, "that stinking lake" as the Arabs called it, the lake of Sodom and Gomorrah, where no living thing could survive and over which no bird could fly.

Finally the procession passed into the dangerous seigneury of Kerak. Four times the size of Montreal, the fortress of Kerak loomed ominously above the travelers. Within the shadow of the massive fortress of the dark knight, the rich camel train was attacked on the hajj road, its armed escort slaughtered, its rich hoard seized, and its travelers—including Saladin's sister—taken prisoner to the confines of the Crow's Castle. When the prisoners protested his action as a violation of the truce, Châtillon spat back, "Let your Muhammad come and deliver you!"

When word of the outrage reached Saladin, his fury settled into a smoldering resolve. Again he went to his Koran. "Against them make ready your strength to the utmost of your power including steeds of war to strike terror into the hearts of the enemies. Whatever ye shall spend in the Cause of Allah, shall be repaid unto you, and ye shall not be treated unjustly." The Crusaders had invaded his land and traduced the holy road to Mecca. Now this mad provocateur of Kerak had seized his sister and insulted his prophet.

He sent a message to Châtillon: "Where are the covenants? Return what you have taken!" Châtillon cast aside the message in contempt.

The Sultan renewed his promise that when God put this villain into his hands he would kill him with those same hands. To the newly crowned King of Jerusalem, the Sultan protested the outrage: The King was reminded of the truce that had been solemnly struck with his predecessor. He demanded a return of the caravan and all its wealth and the release of the prisoners. The Sultan found a receptive audience: Châtillon's action profoundly shocked the new king, and he insisted that the Prince of Kerak make restitution. But Châtillon refused to surrender his spoils.

"Just as he is the lord of his land, I am the lord of my land," he scoffed. "I have no truce with the Arabs." And thus, with this one action, the fragile Latin Kingdom of Jerusalem was divided and the powerful Sultan provoked.

Châtillon's treachery had elevated Saladin's prestige throughout his empire and made his cause righteous. It was written, "Should they intend to deceive thee—verily Allah sufficeth thee: He it is That hath strengthened thee with His aid and with the company of Believers."

A chain reaction began.

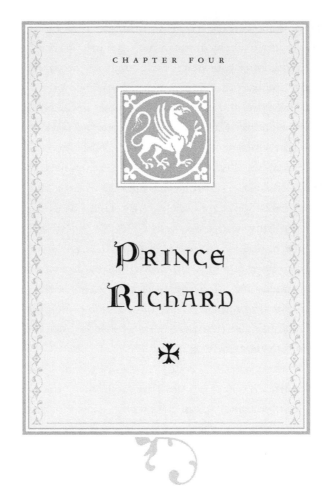

# CHAPTER FOUR

# Prince
# Richard

✠

The vast medieval duchy of Aquitaine in central France stretched from the Loire River in the north to the Pyrenees Mountains in the south. The land was rich in fertile fields, abundant water (including the Garonne River) from which it derived its name from the Latin word *aqua*, and abundant woodlands through which the dukes of Aquitaine had hunted since their line began in the year A.D. 660. Its history over the centuries was dramatic for the strong-willed, independent, and romantic bent of its people. "When they set themselves to tame the pride of their enemies," wrote a chronicler of the twelfth century, Ralph of Diceto, "they do it in earnest. And when the labors of battle are over and they settle down to peace, they give themselves wholly to pleasure."

The Duke of Aquitaine from 1087 to 1127, William IX, epitomized this bold and artistic spirit. He was a veteran of the First Crusade, which had established the Kingdom of Jerusalem, but when the battle was over, he became the first troubadour, beginning a two-hundred-year tradition in southern France of poets and minstrels who wandered through the landscape and sang of love and loss and amorous conquest in their native tongue, langue d'oc. In the years after William returned from the Holy Land, somewhat crestfallen at his less-than-heroic battlefield exploits but passionate about the Moorish songs he had heard in the Orient, he turned Aquitaine into the center of European culture. Of William it was said naughtily, "He knew well how to sing and make verses and for a long time he roamed all through the land to deceive the ladies."

If the duke could captivate the ladies and transport the literati, he had more difficulty in commanding the obedience of his vassals. Across his broad domain the viscounts of Limoges and the Vulgrins of Angoulême, the lords of Lusignan and Taillebourg, the counts of la Marche and Toulouse seemed always to be in dispute and often in open rebellion against their overlord in Poitiers. On a grander scale, however, if his vassals were contentious with the duke, the duke himself was most often in opposition to the King of France, to whom he owed homage for his entire duchy.

In 1137, however, a valiant attempt to reconcile the French throne with its rich, southern duchy was made with that most available of tools, a royal marriage. In that year the son of Louis the Fat, a sixteen-year-old, bloodless prince designated as Louis VII, was betrothed to the daughter of William IX of Aquitaine. The fifteen-year-old bride came to be known as Eleanor of Aquitaine. That she was strikingly beautiful, with a mouth, it was said, as soft as an apple blossom, is beyond question, but what distinguished her more was her brilliance, her learnedness, and her pluck. These qualities, in time, would prove to be too much for pale Louis to handle. But for a brief fifteen years the King of France held sway over Aquitaine as the Count of Poitiers, and the Duchess of Aquitaine was the intimidating Queen of France.

During those fifteen years Queen Eleanor produced two daughters. But child rearing was far from her only interest. At Easter of 1146, after the fall of Edessa in the Holy Land, the King and Queen of France went to Vézelay, where side by side on the wooden platform erected in a field they knelt before the great St. Bernard of Clairvaux, the mystical, charismatic Bernard who had become the great cheerleader of the Second Crusade and the official Vatican propagandist who promised the forgiveness of sins and eventually paradise in return for holy service on the battlefield. Bernard spoke of the "new chivalry" that service in Holy War would entail. Blessed were they who were called in the year of Jubilee. "Rejoice, brave warrior, if you live and conquer in the Lord, but rejoice still more and give thanks if you die and go to join the Lord. This life can be fruitful and victory is glorious. Yet a holy death for righteousness is worth more. Blessed are they who die in the Lord. But how much more so are those who die for Him."

When Louis Capet and Eleanor of Aquitaine rose from taking the cross, the cry went up, "To Jerusalem." Tiny crosses were distributed to the masses like tokens until they were quickly exhausted. The knights of the new chivalry had come together with the rest of Europe, "inflamed with the ardor of charity." Yet Louis and Eleanor had not gone to glory in Jerusalem but to embarrassment in Turkey and humiliation in Damascus. For years after that disaster the picture of Eleanor to the common foot soldier was haunting. It was to see her straddling a horse in full battle gear in the company of other amazon Crusaders, followed by a vast retinue of chambermaids and a huge train of excess baggage.

A deeper scandal lingered after the Second Crusade. It was said that at Antioch the self-assured Eleanor, then twenty-five years old, had first flirted with and then bedded her uncle, Raymond of Antioch, and for this the cuckolded Louis had put her under guard for the remainder of the Crusade. In the mind of the common man, therefore, Eleanor became the scapegoat for the failure of the Second Crusade. Within a few years the marriage of Louis and Eleanor was dissolved after Eleanor was blamed for failing to produce a son (though Louis's pious and effeminate ways may have had something to do with it). It was a costly divorce for France: With the departure of Eleanor the Duchy of Aquitaine was once again separated from the Kingdom of France.

In 1152 she married Henry II, and so her dowry of Aquitaine shifted to England. Henry II, wily, full-blooded, and tempestuous, whose pedigree could be traced to Noah and whose ambitions were huge, was much more suited to Eleanor's lusty and high-spirited ways. By him the sons flowed one after another. The first, William, died in infancy; the second, Henry, would turn on his father in rebellion at an early age; but her third, Richard, born in 1157, would become Eleanor's favorite. These affections were prophesied by no less a figure than Merlin the magician, who proclaimed that "the eagle of the broken covenant shall rejoice in her third nesting." It was an ambiguous prophecy, for no matter how much Eleanor loved Richard, she was an eagle who spread her injured wings over two realms. She had been divorced from France, and in due course she would be imprisoned in England.

Richard was to spend his youth mainly in Aquitaine with his mother, for the Queen of England was most comfortable in the bawdy culture of southern France, and she rarely ventured across the channel. From his childhood she had imbued Richard with her special code of courtly love: Woman was a goddess whom man must approach with respect and reverence and caution. The woman was the descendant not of subservient Eve but of the triumphant Virgin Mary, and it was to her that so many of the great Gothic cathedrals of the twelfth century had been dedicated. Woman's emotional and spiritual superiority was a gift to the benighted male—inferior, adolescent, violent dolt that he was—and it was left to these ethereal deities to bless a member of the inferior sex with her affection or to withhold it. A woman's power over a man was absolute.

In the court of Poitiers the ladies debated love the way the Greeks had debated politics, with the Socratic method: What is love? (It is inborn suffering.) Where does love get its name? (From the word for "hook.") What man is worthy of love? (Only a man of character.) What is the nature of jealousy? (It is the nurse of love. He who is not jealous cannot love. Real jealousy always increases the feeling of love.) What about lust? (Do not fall into the toils of a lustful woman. You cannot win her love no matter how hard you try—unless you know you are so potent at Venus's trade that you can satisfy her, and that would be harder for you to do than to dry up the oceans.) Ironically, the sensuality that marked these debates was derived, in part, from the influence of Muslim Spain.

In these entertainments Queen Eleanor was an enthusiastic participant. One day the question for discussion was this: A worthless young man and an older knight of fine character seek the love of the same woman. Whom should she choose? "Although the young man show that by receiving love, he might rise to be a worthy man," Eleanor opined, "a woman does not do wisely if she chooses to love the unworthy man, when a good and eminent one seeks her love. It might just happen that the character of the unworthy man would not improve with her love. The seeds we sow do not always produce a crop."

This brilliant court inspired a new romantic literature. In its salons some of the earliest lyric verse of the West was created, and its poetry, satires, and songs were called "the gay science." Under its influence Thomas the Britain imagined the love of Tristram and Isolde; Chrétien de Troyes conceived the romance of Lancelot and Guinevere, as well as the story of the Holy Grail. From their dialogues emerged rules of love, with the first and greatest of the commandments: Being obedient in all things to the commands of ladies, thou shalt ever strive to ally thyself to the service of Love. And the second like unto it: In practicing the solaces of love thou shalt not exceed the desires of thy lover.

Their troubadours spoke of romance in all its forms as it had never been debated before. The most common theme was courtly love, in which the vassal paid court to his liege lady or mistress, and when she satisfied his attentions, it was an honor. The apex of the minstrel's art was the chanson, a love song that could run to five stanzas and run the gamut of emotion from love lost to conquest gained to single combat fought in order to protect the name and reputation of the fair sex. The first two Crusades, with their pomp and parade, with their heroes like Godfrey of Bouillon and fantastic stories of bravery and loss, had advanced and heightened the troubadour's art and brought to its songs the Oriental instruments of the krummhorn, the shawm, and the naker. The romance of the Crusade had begun, in Eleanor's court, to replace the old romances of King Arthur. Eleanor's first royal husband, Louis VII of France, had taken his *légions de poètes* on his calamitous Crusade to Damascus, and her grandfather, the brave and irreverent William IX, was the father of the whole movement.

The speech could be raunchy. One court poet and musician, Marcabru, entertained the court with verses about unfaithful women who had victimized him and left him loveless. He railed at "those flaming whores," in mock offense, to the raucous laughter of the ladies themselves. He created a character called "Lady Good and Excited" and castigated "those cunts who are nymphos in bed." To much of this off-color discourse young Richard had listened intently, but to some of it he turned a deaf ear. For example, he ignored one enjoinder from the great codifier of love in the Poitiers court, André the Chaplain: "Love cannot exist except between persons of opposite sexes. Between two men love can find no place, for we see that two persons of the same sex are not at all fitted for giving each other the exchanges of love or for practicing the acts natural to it. Whatever nature forbids, love is ashamed to accept."

If emotionally Eleanor preferred France to England, so Henry's Continental holdings preoccupied the English King during the years of Richard's upbringing. The various rebellions by petty barons against their English king were unrelenting, as was the contention with the French King (and Eleanor's former husband), Louis VII. The irony is that after twelve years of strife, Henry II finally subdued these rebellions by 1169 and finally made peace with the King of France, only to have his sons, one after another, take up arms against him as they approached manhood.

Young Richard was no exception. The grievances of the sons were lodged in their anger over being conferred with titles that carried no power and in their divided loyalties between France and England. Richard's older brother, Henry, had been declared heir to the English throne, but for the English King's European lands he owed homage to the King of France. While this involved honor more than power, it put the sons of Henry continuously in the French court in Paris, where intrigue was rife and conspiracy the rule of the day. Richard, in turn, was made the Duke of Aquitaine, but he was a duke in name only. By the time he turned sixteen years old, he wanted more.

The defiance of his sons came at a particularly bad time for King Henry, since in England he was also contending with the defiance of his bishops, particularly his Archbishop of Canterbury, Thomas à Becket. Becket had placed the church's independence above his allegiance to his King, and this disloyalty sent Henry into a rage. Hearing the King's tantrum against this "idle, wretched, low-born priest," four nobles made their way to Canterbury and murdered Becket on his altar. Three years after his murder, Thomas was canonized, and a year later Henry II had publicly humbled himself before the martyr's grave. As part of Henry's penance for his complicity in Becket's murder, the Pope had required Henry to send to the Holy Land twice yearly enough wealth to support two hundred knights of the Temple and the Hospital in the field. That financial support would become critical to the defense of the Holy Land.

By 1173, the year of Becket's canonization, the sons were in open rebellion against their father, and their mother, Eleanor, always one to lead with her heart, sided with her sons against her husband. In the summer of that year young Henry, Richard, and their younger brother, Geoffrey, made a solemn pact in Paris "not to forsake the king of France," according to the chronicler Ralph of Diceto, "nor to make peace with their father, save through Louis VII and the French barons." Louis, in turn, swore "that he would help the young king and his brothers to the utmost of his power to maintain their war against their father and gain the kingdom of England for young Henry." During this family imbroglio King Henry, at least, was able to take care of Eleanor. His scouts caught her in the disguise of a man, trying to make her way from Aquitaine to Paris, and she was thrown in prison for the next sixteen years.

As Duke of Aquitaine, Richard's bequest came from his mother, and so his mother's imprisonment deepened the young prince's ire against his father. By early 1174 he was recruiting rebellious barons to his cause and even besieging minor castles loyal to Henry. Inevitably this filial disobedience got on Henry II's nerves, and he traveled to Poitiers to punish his son's insolence. At first Richard fled his father's presence, but soon enough the contrite son threw himself at Henry's feet and begged for forgiveness—which Henry promptly gave. Early in 1175 at Le Mans, Richard, along with his brother Geoffrey, participated in a formal ceremony of homage to his father. For the troubles he had caused, Richard was stripped of his title as Duke of Aquitaine and became beholden to the dictates of his father.

For the next five years those dictates were much to Richard's liking, for Henry vested him with the power and the authority to subdue the rebellious barons of Aquitaine and Gascony and to confiscate the lands of any barons who resisted him. It was during this period that Richard came into his own as a military leader. He was engaged almost continuously in battle, first attacking the castles of northern Aquitaine: Agen, Angoulême, Châteauneuf, Moulineuf, and Limoges, which had fortified themselves against Henry's rule. The young warrior then moved south into Gascony, humbling the rebels in Dax, Bayonne, Deols, and Châteauroux. With each new victory his reputation for ferocity grew. But it was not until 1179, when he turned his mind to malcontents in the Saintogne in the prosperous lower valley of the Charente River, that his reputation grew to continental proportions.

Shortly before Christmas 1178, he laid siege to the castle of Pons, the lair of a nasty rebel named Geoffrey of Rancon, who was leading the conspiracy against ducal authority. But Pons put up a stout defense, and four months later it was still in rebel hands. Richard was learning a lesson that he would later apply in the Holy Land about the exhausting nature of an extended siege.

After Easter, in 1179, he abandoned the siege of Pons to attack an even more formidable bastion, the fortress of Taillebourg. His comrades shook their heads at this folly, for Taillebourg was a remarkable fortress, perched high on a rocky outcropping above the Charente River, surrounded on three sides by steep cliffs. On its fourth side the township was fortified by a triple trench and a triple wall. For decades it had been ignored by Richard's predecessors, for it was considered impregnable. Thus, when Richard first turned up, its defenders were unconcerned. Instead of attacking the fortress, Richard began to lay waste the surrounding countryside. According to the chronicler, "he carried off the wealth of the farms, he cut down the vines, he fired the villages, and having pulled down everything else laid it waste; then at the approaches of the fortress he pitched his tents close to the walls, to the great alarm of the townsmen who had expected nothing of the kind."

Despairing at the scorched earth that Richard was producing all around them, the defenders made the mistake of launching a counterattack. But Richard outsmarted and outflanked the sally and gained access to the town by following the coattails of the defenders through the gates. Two days later he subdued the castle itself.

The word of this stunning and unlikely victory spread rapidly, first through the Charente Valley and eventually to King Henry in England. One after another the conspiratorial barons fell into line, and some of them went off to the Holy Land as punishment and penance. After destroying the walls of the rebel castles along the Charente, Richard journeyed to England, where Henry received him "with the greatest honor."

CHAPTER FIVE

JIhAD

✠

I N MARCh 1187, AFTeR The hOLY MONTh OF Ramadān, Saladin issued the call to Holy War. "When the forbidden months are past," it is written in the Koran, "then fight and slay the infidels wherever ye find them and seize them, beleaguer them, and lie in wait for them in every stratagem of war." From Aleppo and parts of Mesopotamia and over water from Egypt, Muslim troops poured in. They massed near Damascus and moved south. To impress the black knight in his Crow's Castle, the Sultan sent a detachment to Kerak to stage a show of power in front of the awesome fortress. Another caravan of Syrian pilgrims approached Kerak on their way home from their hajj to Mecca, and again it contained relatives of Saladin. But this time a heavy guard surrounded the procession, and Châtillon could only watch from his high perch.

Though the Sultan longed to get his hands on the villain, his next military opportunity lay elsewhere than the impregnable fortress of Kerak. In Tiberias, on the western shore of the Sea of Galilee, a more compliant and honorable Christian count ruled. Raymond of Tripoli represented the old guard in the Latin Kingdom. Born in the East, he could trace his lineage through various Levantine royals back to Raymond of St. Giles, one of the leaders of the First Crusade, and even further back to the royal blood of the Capetians in France.

Raymond was a noble figure, a wiry man of medium height with a great hawk nose and a dark complexion. Wise and magnanimous and well tested in battle, he was a great promoter of the Hospitalers, with whom he had shared many a struggle in the past years. Both Syrians and Christians alike had long recognized him as the most able man in the kingdom, and it was generally accepted early in the 1180s that he, rather than Guy of Lusignan, would be the next King of Jerusalem. Like Châtillon, he, too, had been a prisoner of the Muslims for some years. But instead of Châtillon's bitterness, he had acquired an admiration for Oriental beliefs. Raymond was fluent in Arabic and was a keen reader of Arabic texts. He believed in coexistence with his Arabic neighbors and proved it by welcoming Arabs into his court at Tiberias.

By marrying the widow of the Count of Tiberias, Raymond had taken over the most exposed and vulnerable fief in the Crusaders' land. His domain was the gateway to the Latin Kingdom. Tiberias was not more than sixty miles across the Golan Heights from Damascus, a three-day march at most. It would be the first prize for any Syrian incursion into the kingdom. His fief was hilly and included the sacred sites of Mount Tabor (where the Christian God had spoken out of the cloud and the disciples were "sore afraid") and Nazareth itself (where Jesus had been raised). Over the years Raymond had fought and had made peace with Saladin. He preferred peace.

Only three years before, in 1184, as Regent of the kingdom, he had made a good peace. During that year the whole of the Levant had experienced a terrible drought, and this thirst had prompted a peace initiative. Raymond knew that he could not protect his tiny, exposed country against a Muslim offensive in such a weakened position. Though it may have been counter to his best interest, Saladin had acceded to Raymond's plea for an end to the hostilities, and a four-year truce was concluded between them. In a surfeit of generosity to the enemy, Saladin provided water and food to the beleaguered county of Tiberias.

Naturally this consort with the enemy put Raymond in an awkward position with Jerusalem. The hawks of the kingdom, led by Châtillon and the Master of the Temples, Gerard de Ridefort, saw Raymond as a traitor and charged that he had become a Muslim and gone over to the enemy. There was wild talk about marching on Tiberias to bring Count Raymond to heel. The old guard, however, counseled caution. "There is a great force of knights inside Tiberias, both Christians and Arabs, and you have few people to besiege them," a great knight of the old guard, Balian of Ibelin, counseled King Guy. "You should know that if you go there not a man will escape, for as soon as you start the siege Saladin will come to its aid with a great army." Hatred is no good for anyone, he added, and he offered himself as an envoy to patch up the differences between Tiberias and Jerusalem.

Châtillon's rash attack on the caravan altered the situation. The truce was broken, and the breach provoked Saladin into mobilizing his jihad. And yet Raymond, the man literally in the middle, was still regarded as a friend and an exception—and a friend in interesting distress at that. If Raymond's Christian brothers actually attacked his bastion at Tiberias, Saladin was ready to come to the defense. The Latin Kingdom was on the verge of civil war, and nothing could be better from Saladin's viewpoint. Let the invaders fight and argue among themselves. The Sultan was in an advantageous position no matter what happened.

Saladin decided to roil the waters. With the sweetness of a lamb he presented Raymond with a terrible proposition. He requested permission for free passage past Tiberias so that a large Muslim force might stage a punitive raid deep in Christian territory as retaliation for Châtillon's raid on the caravan. This request put Raymond in an impossible position. To refuse Saladin was to provoke his wrath against Tiberias; to accept was to commit treason against his Christian brothers. And so, politician and conciliator that he was, Raymond sought a weak compromise. Saladin's troops could pass Tiberias without interference, he suggested, so long as they entered his domain at sunrise and left at sunset. They were not to raid any of his own towns or villages. To mollify his allies, he sent word to the Masters of the Temple and the Hospital and to the Archbishop of Tyre that Saladin's expedition was coming. Residents were to make themselves scarce, lock themselves in their homes, and let the enemy force pass harmlessly, without provocation.

Predictably, the response of the firebrands in the Christian kingdom was the reverse. The Master of the Templars, Gerard de Ridefort, sent out the alarm, for Raymond's insidious deal contravened the tenets of chivalry and the very Rule of the Order of the Temple. They could not permit this violation of Christian Holy Land. By their most sacred oath Templars were to be the first to attack and the last to retreat. Skulk away and hide while the infidels defiled sacred land, unchallenged? Never! They could be cautious in their operations, but they must not be deterred by superior strength. The order took its inspiration from Leviticus 26:7–8: "And ye shall chase your enemies, and they shall fall before you by the sword. And five of you shall chase an hundred, and an hundred of you shall put ten thousand to flight: and your enemies shall fall before you by the sword."

On the early morning of May 1, the feast day for St. Philip and St. James in the Christian calendar, the Muslim force crossed the Jordan in the deep crevice at Jacob's Ford and moved into Lower Galilee. The Islamic soldiers were prepared for battle, for this was a reconnaissance in force, an openly provocative expedition designed to lure the enemy into battle. It was also designed to test the commitment of their erstwhile ally, Count Raymond, and to force him onto the horns of a dilemma. They had no delusions that, when pushed, Raymond would side with the devil, and of the devil's promises the Koran writes, "The Devil makes promises only to deceive."

"He uses us," Saladin wrote, "to set to rights his own affairs and to terrify his fellow Franks."

Overnight the Templars mustered eighty knights from the Templar castles at Caco and La Fève. Ten Hospitalers joined the expedition, among whom was the Master of the Hospital himself, Roger des Moulins, who was on his way to Tiberias as a conciliatory envoy from the King in Jerusalem. A company of forty knights from the royal garrison at Nazareth joined this band before dawn, and they set out into the hills near Mount Tabor to search for the infidels. Sometime after midday this stalwart band came upon the force of seven thousand Muslim soldiers in a swale near a freshet called the Springs of Cresson, only two miles from Nazareth. The Muslims had completed their reconnaissance harmlessly, without injuring any castle or town, and were on their way home.

Looking down on the Muslim horde, the knights fell into a disagreement. Roger des Moulins and the marshal of the Templars, Brother James of Mailly, argued against a rash attack when they were so outnumbered. But Gerard de Ridefort, the Master of the Temple, scoffed at them as cowards. Roger recoiled in horror, protesting that he was not afraid of "these raging dogs who

flourish today but tomorrow will be cast into a lake of fire and brimstone"—
but he was still against this attack. Ignoring his rival, Gerard invoked the
Templar oath and their rule. He sneered at the naysayers' argument about
being outnumbered. Was it not written in Joshua 23:10, "One man of you
shall chase a thousand: for the Lord your God, He it is that fighteth for you,
as He hath promised you."

"Remember your fathers the Maccabees," Gerard shouted. "Their duty
was to fight for the Church, the Law and for the inheritance of the Crucified
One. You have already been carrying that out for a long time." He reminded
them that their forefathers "overcame the enemy not by force of numbers but
by faith and justice and observing God's mandates."

With that he wheeled his horse around and charged down the hill with his
rabid Templars behind. The doubters had no choice but to join. Hated and
feared though the Templars and Hospitalers were among the Muslim soldiers,
the foolish charge of this small brigade must have been a joyous sight. As they
were trained to do, the Muslims parted and let the knights ride into their
midst before they closed in around them and began to slice the Christians.
The slaughter was horrible. Sixty Templars, including Roger des Moulins,
were killed and then beheaded. By some miracle the perpetrator of this madness, the Master of the Temple, Gerard de Ridefort, escaped death with only
four of his brothers. Badly wounded, de Ridefort galloped back to Nazareth,
where he collapsed. At sunset the solemn procession of Muslim soldiers
passed by Tiberias as they had promised, on their way back across the Jordan
River, serene in having met their promise not to harm any castle or town, except that the heads of the slain Templars were skewered on their pikes.

The repercussions from this disaster at Cresson were great. The grisly
spectacle that unfolded before his ramparts at sunset revolted Raymond.
When he learned the details, his first emotion was fury at de Ridefort for his
arrogance and intemperance. De Ridefort and his Templars, in turn, were
equally furious at Raymond for his treason. But for the count's corrupt and
treasonous deal with the infidel, the disaster would never have happened! For
the precarious Latin Kingdom the catastrophe was more profound: It could
ill afford to lose more than a hundred knights, for there were only about
twelve hundred full-fledged, certified, battle-ready knights in all of the
Holy Land.

In Nazareth, King Guy's envoy, Balian of Ibelin, had missed being a part
of the ill-fated expedition of Templars only because he had remembered that

this was the feast day of the Apostles St. Philip and St. James the Less. Balian's morning prayers had delayed his arrival at the Templar castle at La Fève. Now he took in the horrifying details and passed them on to the Archbishop of Tyre, Josias, who had hastened to the scene after hearing the news.

The following day, with an escort sent by Raymond, the delegation set out for Tiberias. Count Raymond greeted them warmly as he braced for their indignation. By an Arab account his own soldiers vented their fury at their lord.

"You must surely have converted to Islam," one shouted. "Otherwise you could never tolerate what has just happened. You would not have allowed the infidel soldiers to cross your territory, to massacre Templars and Hospitalers, to carry off prisoners, without doing anything to stop it!" By this same account Archbishop Josias threatened to excommunicate Raymond for his treachery, before Balian stepped in, ever the chivalrous gentleman and the cool head, to calm the tempers.

Count Raymond was filled with remorse. What could he do to make amends? Roger des Moulins had been among his closest, truest friends, didn't they understand? Perhaps he should have foreseen what would happen, but he had not and had not meant for harm to come to any good Christian. He begged their forgiveness. Above all he wished to make amends and to rejoin the Christian brotherhood. What would they have him do?

Their demands were modest. He must return with them to Jerusalem, the ambassadors answered, to beg the forgiveness of his King and to swear again his allegiance. He must evict Saladin's agents from his city and put his military resources at the disposal of the kingdom. The Holy Land was in grave peril. The very survival of the Christian domain was at stake. For it to survive would require a supreme effort and sacrifice. Raymond readily agreed to these terms. The delegation soon set off for Jerusalem.

The bad day at Cresson reverberated far and wide. The battlefield was scarcely cold before the valor of James of Mailly, the marshal of the Temple who had argued so passionately against the attack at Cresson and whose courage had been questioned by de Ridefort, was turned into the stuff of legend. It was said that at the end, hemmed in by thousands of the enemy, he faced the multitude alone and that the Muslim soldiers, so admiring of his courage, had pled with him to surrender.

"He, however, turned a deaf ear to their exhortations, for he was not afraid to die for Christ," it was written. "But even though he was overwhelmed with the load of javelins, stones, and lances, rather than allow himself to be vanquished, he was finally with difficulty slain. His soul fled triumphant, bearing the palm of martyrdom to the heavenly kingdom. His death was rendered glorious, since by his single sword so large a circle of dead bodies had been heaped around him. It was sweet for a man to die thus, himself in the center, surrounded by the unbelievers whom his brave arm had slaughtered."

The story was soon adorned with the detail that James of Mailly had fought that day in white armor on a white horse. Perhaps, it was soon suggested, he was St. George himself.

Still, the recriminations persisted. Among the barons and the military monks, bitterness lingered. The odor of sedition hovered around Raymond. In time, word of Cresson reached Rome, for de Ridefort, as Master of the Temple, reported not to temporal men in Jerusalem but to the Holy Father himself. The Pope, Urban III, turned the news into an appeal to the English clergy to aid the Templars in their defense of the Holy Land.

"The Master of the Temple states that in this battle he has suffered serious losses of horses and arms, quite apart from the loss of men, and that the evil race of pagans is inflamed to attack more strongly than usual in accordance with the purposes of its iniquity. So we, to whom it especially falls to be solicitous for the safety of that land and desiring that they should be more concerned with its defense, call on you as brothers and command and order you to persuade and enjoin the princes, barons, and other faithful men by frequent exhortations and admonitions, so that, for the remission of their sins, for God and for their salvation, they may, by their strong hand, succor Christianity there: in their compassion they should not delay in aiding the brothers of the Temple with horses and arms whereby they may be better able to defend that land."

And so it was, as in most wars, that the call to Crusade began with an appeal for equipment and materiel. At this stage the loss of more than a hundred battle horses was a serious blow for the Latin Kingdom. Could the call for men as well as horses be far behind?

Much worse news was soon to come to Rome.

CHAPTER SIX

# Their Lions Were Hedgehogs

hen he heard the news of the glorious victory at Cresson, Saladin was at his camp at the Tell 'Ashterah, a watering hole east of the Sea of Galilee that could serve as a base for operations against either Kerak or Galilee. From his eldest son, now sixteen years old, el Melek el-Afdal, he received a poetic letter full of mixed metaphors. Of this first battlefield the son had ever witnessed, el-Afdal compared his victory to the conquest of "virgin girls, splendid in their beauty but difficult to attain, who are led in marriage only by those who can look after them and pay their dowry." Now his son had attained his first virgin "after a short courtship." He conveyed the good news to the "master of the prey" that his cub had stood in his father's place and triumphed with his sword.

By crushing this band of foolhardy cavaliers, Saladin perceived his wider opportunity in all its splendor. It was time to abandon his personal vendetta against the evil Châtillon, holed up snugly in his impregnable Crow's Castle, and to turn his mind to the strategic opening that now presented itself. With his main force he moved north to join the seven thousand troops returning from Cresson. Bedouins, Kurds, troops from Egypt and from Aleppo and Mosul flooded in, and the Muslim force swelled to more than twenty-five thousand.

The Sultan gathered his emirs together in a council of war. What should they do now? How should they seize the moment? Some argued to continue the strategy of harassment, since widely scattered raids had always worked well to spread out the thin resources of the enemy. To attack the Christian army en masse was to put the enemy on his most favorable footing. Referring to the continued strife between minor potentates in the Muslim empire, one emir said, "The people in the East are cursing us, saying that we no longer fight the infidels but have begun to fight Muslims instead. We must do something to justify ourselves and silence our critics."

At last, Saladin spoke. He appreciated that Islam had arrived at a critical moment of its history, and he was adamant. "We must confront all the enemy's forces with all the forces of Islam. For events do not turn out according to man's will. We do not know how long a life is left to us. So it is foolish to disperse this concentration of troops without striking a tremendous blow in the Holy War." In the weeks that followed, he reorganized his eclectic army into a central column and two wings, a vanguard and a rear guard.

Meanwhile, with his minders Balian of Ibelin and the Archbishop of Tyre, the contrite Count Raymond traveled to Nablus for his public apology and reconciliation with the King of Jerusalem. There the two weak factions of the kingdom came together warily. The well-established but compromised Count Raymond of Tripoli fell on his knees before the unpopular, disrespected, parvenu King, Guy of Lusignan. They made a great show of reconciliation and friendship and traipsed off to Jerusalem, where they appeared together in a grand procession. Together, with banners waving and refrains chanted, they vowed to defend the Christian realm. Afterward, the rejuvenated Raymond returned to Tiberias with the order to mobilize his forces and meet the King's men at the Springs of La Safouri.

But there was something forbidding in the air, a note off key or a confidence misplaced. No colorful spectacle of flag-waving, no windy expression of solidarity, no further benediction from bishops and patriarchs could mask the political and military weakness of the kingdom. When eyewitnesses later wrote this history, they pointed to apocalyptic signs in the heavens and in their dreams that portended an end-time dead ahead. "The approach of future destruction was foretold by diverse events: famine, earthquakes, and frequent eclipses, both of the sun and of the moon." In fact, in 1186 and 1187 there were six solar eclipses and two lunar eclipses. On March 26, 1187, as Saladin's troops were massing in the Golan Heights, three-quarters of the moon over London was in shadow. This same period had seen a dramatic cluster of planets in conjunction, once involving all of the five classical planets. The astrologers were worried. Three weeks after the disaster at Cresson, Jupiter and Saturn were in conjunction, in a way reminiscent of the same conjunction that was interpreted as the star the Magi saw. "And that strong wind which astronomers prophesied would spring out of the conjunction of planets was another indication. It was a mighty wind indeed, for it shook the four corners of the earth and foreshadowed that the whole of the globe was about to be stirred up to troubles and wars."

When the Christian soldiers massed at the citadel called La Safouri, the King's chamberlain had a terrible dream. He saw an eagle flying over the Christian army and holding in its talons seven arrows and a crossbow and screaming, "Woe to thee, O Jerusalem." In horror, the chamberlain leafed through his Bible and settled on Psalm 7: The Lord "has bent his bow, and made it ready. He hath also prepared for him the instruments of death." Did the seven arrows not stand for the seven deadly sins and the seven punishments that impended for the Christian army? Was Saladin himself to be the instrument of the wrath for the vengeful Christian God, disgusted with the sinfulness of his flock?

As Saladin's army massed east of the Sea of Galilee, the Crusader kingdom was in deep trouble.

On paper the Christian army was up to this latest challenge. For decades the forces of Christianity and Islam had clashed, with one side or another prevailing in bloody combat but with no fundamental shift in their position of parity. The adversaries knew their enemies' strengths and weaknesses and knew their tactics and strategy. Parts of the original Crusader kingdom formed in the aftermath of the First Crusade of 1098 had been shaved away, but the essential kingdom was still intact after eight decades of continuous warfare. The struggle boiled down to discipline versus manpower. But this reality came with the logical consequence that Saladin had more margin for error than did the Christians.

Saladin had had his victories in individual battles, but he'd had his share of defeats as well, most especially ten years earlier, when he had made the mistake of splitting his army in two and suffering a terrible disaster at the hands of the Templars in the swamps near Mont Gisard. Against his seemingly inexhaustible manpower the Christians had built their formidable network of great castles.

Now King Guy's heralds trumpeted the alarm throughout the kingdom. The infidel army was massing on the border. The defense was being assembled. Promising that every Christian soldier would be well paid, the King opened the coffers of a special English reserve, the treasure that King Henry II of England had sent for the defense of the Holy Land in penance for the murder of Thomas à Becket. But the promise of decent wages was not the only recruiting tool.

Guy now took the ultimate step. He ordered the Patriarch of Jerusalem to send the True Cross from the Holy Sepulcher. In the previous eighty years Christianity's most valuable relic had been brought into combat twenty times. Only four years earlier, in 1183, it had been taken on a raid deep into Syria, and its presence was credited with the ability of the Christian forces to hold Saladin in check. Now it was placed in the care of the bishops of Lydda and Acre and positioned at the center of the Christian host, as the final hedge against defeat. The Christian soldiers were now the bearers and keepers of their Lord's Cross.

Their numbers were formidable. Even with the attrition at Cresson, twelve hundred knights, virtually the entire noble population of the kingdom, gathered at the citadel of La Safouri. They were supported by twenty thousand foot soldiers. This was the largest army ever assembled in the Latin Kingdom.

La Safouri was only a short distance from Nazareth, and it was the traditional mobilization point for so large a host. A Crusader citadel stood on a hill that had once been a sophisticated city in Roman times, where the Romans had built an intricate system of underground aqueducts and cisterns. Once the place of baths and fountains, it possessed the largest reservoir in the Latin Kingdom. Below the citadel the fertile Rimmon Valley brimmed with provisions. In these fields Jesus had walked with his disciples, "plucked the ears of corn and did eat" (Matthew 12:1 and Luke 6:1). The parents of the Holy Mother Mary, Joachim and Anne, hailed from La Safouri itself. So long as the army remained in this fortified place of abundant food and gushing water, it was safe.

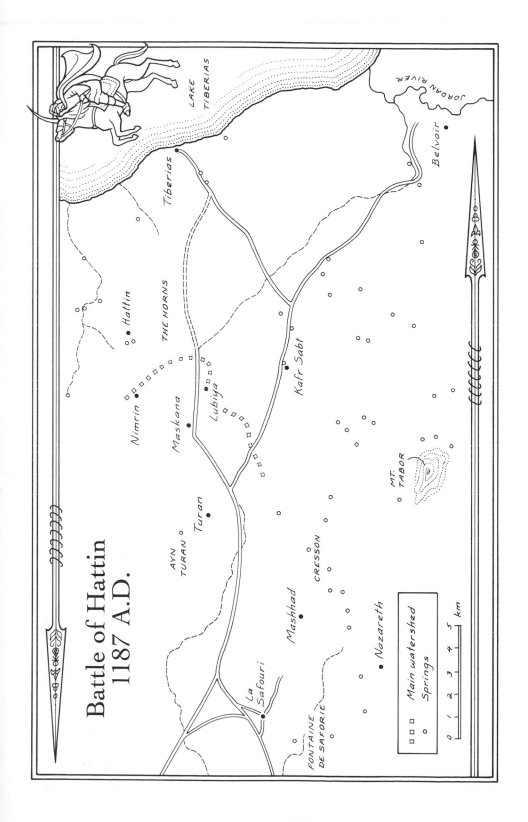

Battle of Hattin
1187 A.D.

LAKE
TIBERIAS

JORDAN RIVER

Belvoir

Tiberias

THE HORNS

Hattin

Nimrin

Maskana

Lubiya

Kafr Sabt

MT. TABOR

AYN TURAN

Turan

CRESSON

Mashhad

Nazareth

La Safouri

FONTAINE DE SAFORIE

☐☐☐  Main watershed
o        Springs

0  1  2  3  4  5  km

In these anxious days the rumors about the enemy's strength were wild, fueled by the reports that the Caliph's preachers had fanned out through Asia Minor and were stirring up the passions of Muslim youth. In truth, the size of Saladin's army was not much larger than that of the Christian army, perhaps thirty thousand in all, but its composition was different. Syrian and Mesopotamian and Egyptian contingents comprised the main body of Saladin's force, with Kurdish elements highly admired as the best soldiers and often providing the leadership.

The Muslim army had about twelve thousand mounted soldiers and an equal number to support them. These light cavalrymen were skilled horsemen, expert as mounted archers, deadly with their lances made of reed. With armor only of light wadded cotton called the *kazāghand*, they rode swift, small, maneuverable Yemeni steeds, noteworthy for their slender limbs, small fetlocks, thin manes, and easy, springy motion. These cavalrymen were divided into small squadrons and were highly trained in the tactic of charge and retreat. The Muslim army was well organized, well led, and disciplined, and it had a distinct advantage over the Crusader force: All of its soldiers spoke the same Arabic language. While its actual size was equivalent to the Christian force, legend aggrandized it, especially after it was victorious. The Pope was told of an 80,000-man force; by another account the Sultan was mustering 180,000 troops. (After the battle an estimate of the infidel army would soar to 800,000.)

Count Raymond had secured his vulnerable bastion at Tiberias, evicted the Muslims, and left his brave wife, Eschiva, in the citadel within the town's walls with instructions to flee on shipboard into the Sea of Galilee if Saladin should overwhelm the garrison. Then, together with his forces, the count joined the King.

2

# ALLAhU AKBAR

On July 1, to the exultant shout of "Victory over God's Enemy!" the Muslim army crossed the Jordan, south of the lake, under the watchful eye of the Hospitalers in their fortress of Belvoir, high in the Galilean hills above. The size of his host, as Saladin would later write, was such that a vast plain was too narrow to accommodate it, and "the dust cloud of their march darkened the eye of the sun."

At first the Muslims bypassed Tiberias and marched due west to Kafr Sabt, five miles east of Cresson. With satisfaction, Saladin surveyed the plain of Lubiya, north of his base, and proclaimed that it was here he hoped to lure the Christians into the final battle. To provoke the Christians, the Muslim troops set the brown, sun-baked fields ablaze. When this had no effect, they defiled the cone of Mount Tabor, the place where Jesus had been transfigured before his disciples and where they had heard the voice of the Lord from the bright cloud.

But however appalled the Christians may have been at this sacrilegious provocation, they did not budge. The ground was unfavorable.

On the following day, with some frustration and with full knowledge of the risk, Saladin split his army. He took a small but elite force to Tiberias, including his personal guard, which he fondly called the "burning coals" of Islam. These soldiers made quick work of the outer walls, undermining a tower and storming through the breach. The town was quickly overrun, with many inhabitants killed. Its wealth was plundered, its gold and silver piled in great heaps, its horses and cattle seized, its oil and cotton burned. With satisfaction Saladin turned to his Koran: "Fair in the eyes of men is the love of things they covet: women and sons; heaped-up hoards of gold and silver; branded horses and cattle and well-tilled land."

In the smoke Countess Eschiva cowered behind the ramparts of her citadel with her personal guard. Her escape to the Sea of Galilee was cut off. Hastily she fashioned a plea to her husband to rescue her: "The enemy has surrounded the city. They have pierced the walls and are just now entering against us. Send help at once or we shall be taken and made captive." Perhaps she could hold out behind the citadel's deep moat, but not much longer. The messenger galloped out of the burning town, unimpeded as he raced through the Muslim lines.

When the alarm reached King Guy, he called his barons together in a council of war. Eagerly, Châtillon and the fierce Master of the Temple, Gerard de Ridefort, called for the army to ride to the rescue of the lady in distress at once. The dictates of chivalry demanded an immediate response. "I require and summon you to go to the aid of Tiberias!" the knight of Ridefort insisted, as if he spoke from some higher law. If the King did nothing, now in the early days of his reign, he would play the fool in Saladin's eyes, and the villain would take advantage of his weakness.

At last the King turned to the knight most affected, Count Raymond, whose own wife was in danger and whose own fief was in flames. To the surprise of the assembly, Raymond counseled restraint.

"You know that we are in the height of the summer, in the hottest part of the year," he said. Let the Christian forces wait the Muslims out. "The strength of the kingdom and the heat will assail them. When they depart we shall be ready and shall pounce on his rear guard. We shall inflict so great a loss on him that, if it please God, we and the kingdom of Jerusalem will remain in peace."

Châtillon and Gerard de Ridefort hissed their contempt at this advice. It was "mingled with the hair of the wolf," said Châtillon, insinuating that Raymond's view was a corrupt blend of treason and cowardice.

After the meeting broke up, the King went out to review his troops, whose number continued to swell at the lure of the Holy Cross. When he returned, he sent again for his leading knights.

In the King's pavilion Raymond repeated his caution. "Sire, you know that Tiberias is mine," he said. "Any damage done there falls on me and on no one else. For the lady of Tiberias, my wife, the last thing I would want is for any harm to come to her. I have sent provisions and advised her that should Saladin's forces be so great that they cannot resist, she should take to the sea until we can rescue her."

Not only should the army not attack, he advised, but it should retreat to the vicinity of its strongest fortress at Acre, in accordance with the established practice that had often saved the Christian forces in times past. "I know Saladin is too proud and presumptuous to leave the kingdom without attacking you in battle. If the battle near Acre turns out badly for us, may God forbid, we can withdraw to the fortress. But if God gives us victory and we force him back to his own land, we shall have so reduced and shattered him that he will never be able to recover."

"This is the hair of the wolf!" Châtillon hissed.

Raymond pretended not to hear. "If all this does not turn out as I say," he said, "you may have me beheaded."

Châtillon would have none of it. "You have tried hard to make us afraid of the Muslims," he said. "Clearly you take their side and your sympathies are with them, otherwise you would not speak in this way." This time the barons swung over to the side of the hawk.

"Let us go and rescue the ladies and maidens of Tiberias!" they shouted in unison. Raymond's stepsons, the children of Lady Eschiva by her first marriage, also sided with the hawks and tearfully urged the King to save their mother. The call of chivalry was strong.

Again, as was his bent, the King vacillated. The barons vacillated with him, siding now with the Master of the Temple, now with the Count of Tripoli and his Hospitalers. As these discussions slid over into July 3, the majority swung back to Raymond's side. The Christians did not have the forces to dislodge Saladin from Tiberias. Raymond suggested that Saladin's army would probably disperse if it captured Tiberias. The debate disintegrated into a muddle of honor versus prudence. In the evening prudence won out. The knights were satisfied to sit tight for a few days in their comfortable, well-watered base camp, to wait for more soldiers to pour in, and to await further developments.

After nightfall the Master of the Temple slipped into the King's pavilion alone. His personal hatred for Raymond was extreme, for Raymond had once gone back on a promise to support de Ridefort's marriage to a wealthy princess. "Sire, do not trust the advice of the count, for he is a traitor. You well know that he has no love for you and wants you to be put to shame. I advise you to move off immediately. Let us go and defeat Saladin."

This time the Templar took the argument one critical step further, into the realm of personal honor and cowardice. In an oblique reference he alluded to the King's own removal as regent of the kingdom three years earlier, after Guy had allowed Saladin's forces to tarry near the springs of Tubania without attacking them for eight full days, contravening the dictates of chivalry and the most fundamental of laws of the Latin Kingdom. He had been pilloried for his cowardice then, de Ridefort pointed out. Now he could not make the same mistake. Should he falter now, in this, his first campaign as King of Jerusalem, Guy could not count on the support of the Templars in the future.

These were powerful arguments. Once again it seemed as if the pliable King was swayed by whoever stood before him. With his own courage and manliness now questioned, he reversed himself and announced that the army would move in the morning. The barons rushed to him in protest.

"Sire, our advice was that we should all stay put and remain here at least for tonight. By whose counsel are you making the host set off?"

Guy waved aside this impertinence. "You have no right to ask me by whose counsel I am doing this," he fumed, puffing himself up in his thin, royal trappings. "I want you to get on your horses and leave here and head toward Tiberias."

Raymond rushed in with his last appeal. "Tiberias is my city, and my wife is there. None of you is so fiercely attached, save to Christianity, as I am to my city. But we should not move away from water and food to lead such a multitude of men to death from hunger, thirst, and scorching heat. Our soldiers cannot survive half a day without an abundance of water. Stay, therefore, at this safe and fruitful halfway point—"

In this atmosphere of manly posturing and feverish belligerence, his words were ignored. With due obedience the knights fell into line and prepared to move. "As good and true men, they obeyed the King and carried out his commands," a chronicler wrote later. "Perhaps if they had not obeyed that command he gave them, it would have been better for Christendom."

According to the legend that later grew from these events, the horses of the Christian host refused to drink water that night from the fountain of La Safouri.

# CHAPTER SEVEN

# Still Water

S the crow flies, Tiberias and the glistening water of the Galilean Sea lay fifteen miles to the east of the wells of La Safouri, along the dry valley route with the hills of Nazareth to the south and Mount Turan to the northeast. Along this parched road, across the plain of Lubiya and over a high ridge known as the Horns of Hattin, the only water was in the occasional freshet and in cisterns, just enough to sustain the few residents of the villages of Lubiya and Maskana. Apart from the problem of water there was the question of speed. In years past, successful Christian campaigns had been unable to accomplish more than six or seven miles in a day against stiff enemy resistance.

On July 3, a day on which the heat was nearly unbearable, the army moved out. It was organized into three divisions. As the senior knight and the commander who knew the ground best, Raymond of Tripoli commanded a vanguard of Hospitalers; the King, together with his royal battalion and with the True Cross, was in the center; and Balian of Ibelin, the baron of the most distinguished house in the Latin Kingdom, commanded the force of Templars at the rear. By noon the army had marched, unimpeded, six miles at a steady clip and reached the south slope of Mount Turan. In the village of Turan was a tiny spring, and according to Saladin's report later, "the hawks of his infantry and the eagles of his cavalry hovered around the water" greedily.

Now King Guy had arrived at a critical decision: Should he push on in the terrible heat of midday or remain at this spring-fed place for the night? There could be no mistaking the enemy's presence; he was all around the Christian army, in the hills to the north and south and on the high ground ahead. The next six miles would not be so easy. And yet it was early, the lady over the ridge was in a desperate state, and the King's hawks screeched at him for progress. Perhaps the heat and the confusion addled King Guy, but Saladin had his explanation from the Koran for the King's lapse of judgment at this pivotal juncture: The devil had seduced him into doing the opposite of what was wise, and he "set out toward Tiberias, deciding, through pride and arrogance, to take his revenge." The lake was now nine miles in front, and the spring of Turan receded in the dust of his rear guard.

As soon as the Christian divisions left the oasis, Saladin's swift cavalrymen swung around behind by the thousands, cutting off a retreat and depriving the enemy of water. Instead of turning to meet the enemy's flanking movement, the Christians pushed deeper and deeper into the trap. In the scorching heat, Raymond of Tripoli was the first to appreciate the danger.

"We must hurry and pass through this area," he messaged to the King desperately. "Otherwise we will be in danger of making camp at a waterless spot!"

"We will pass through at once," the King replied airily, oblivious to the peril of their situation, as if passing through were something like a stroll.

With the King's concurrence Raymond sought to thrust north toward the village of Hattin, where there was plentiful water. But his way was blocked, and he stalled in front of the high ridge. Toward nightfall he looked back to see in horror that instead of the center moving up to help, the tents of the royal battalion were being raised at the arid village of Maskana. Surrounded on all sides, the stalled forces were without water and without hope of reinforcement. In front, more than a mile ahead, the Horns of Hattin, the site of the Sermon on the Mount, loomed, covered with the stubble of the enemy. The irony of their situation could not have escaped Raymond of Tripoli. The followers of Jesus were now indeed poor in spirit, meek, and mourning. The mountain of the Beatitudes was transformed into the horns of the devil.

"Alas, Lord God, the battle is over!" Raymond despaired. "We have been betrayed unto death. The kingdom is finished!"

A night of hell began. The Muslim forces crept close to the Christian camp, so close, it was later said, that if a cat escaped from the Christian campfire, the Arabs would grab it. Saladin distributed extra arrows to his archers and instructed them to aim for the Crusader horses. Without his horse the knight would have no charge. Without his horse the armored warrior would be a forlorn figure in the heat of this barren plain. Then the Sultan set fires that spread rapidly through the dry grass and filled the valley with terrible smoke. His fire, Saladin said, would give off sparks, a reminder of what God had in store for them in the next world. "That night," a Christian chronicler wrote, "God gave us the bread of adversity to eat and the water of affliction to drink." His bitter reference was to the Book of Isaiah (30:20), which continued, "Yet shall not thy teachers be removed into a corner any more, but thine eyes shall see thy teachers."

With the first light, even through the heavy smoke the Christians could see and hear their teachers all too well. After a night without water the Christian soldiers were already weakening and dispirited. In this bleak state four knights defected from Raymond's fold and were taken to Saladin himself, who had moved up in the night with his main force and who now surveyed the scene from the mountain.

"Sire, what are you waiting for?" the knights said to the Sultan. "Attack! They are dead men."

But Saladin waited—for the blinding sun to rise higher into the east, so the Crusaders would be looking directly into it as they tried to reach the lake, and for the heat and the wind to come up. On the plain of Lubiya a huge swath of dry grass had been reserved for the morning. Near noon this was torched, and the wall of wildfire and smoke moved swiftly toward the Christian forces, which were now surrounded in the open ground between the low hill of Lavi, named for young lions, and the hill of Nimrin, named for the tiger, and the Horns of Hattin directly ahead.

In the ensuing terror the foot soldiers in the vanguard formed a wedge and pushed up to the northern horn. From this high point they looked down on the brilliant blue of the Sea of Galilee, so inviting and yet so unattainable, and on the apricot sea of the huge Muslim force that blocked their way to the water. In this action the infantry was separated from the cavalry behind. Seeing the shield for his cavalry drift up the mountain, the King ordered the foot soldiers back to protect the True Cross.

They refused. "We are not coming. Can't you see? We are dying of thirst. We will not fight!"

Meanwhile, in a familiar pattern, the Muslim cavalry fell on the rear formation of Templars. The Templars responded with a series of charges, but as the Muslim chronicler later reported, "their lions had become hedgehogs." This rear guard was pushed backward toward the center. For some unexplainable reason the King ordered that tents be erected as a barrier, as if canvas and tent poles could blunt arrows and lances. Increasingly the beleaguered Christian soldiers crowded around the True Cross, hoping for the miraculous appearance of St. James himself, who might burst from a cloud, and slay the Muslims by the tens of thousands the way he had supposedly done in the miracle of Clavijo three hundred years before in Spain. But there were no clouds, and there would be no miraculous deliverance. The formations began to disintegrate.

A substantial force of Muslim horsemen split Raymond's vanguard from the royal battalion. Seeing this, the King ordered Raymond to charge the enemy force in his front. It was late for chivalry; the time for knightly glory was past. As the knights galloped into the Muslim force, it parted, as it had done at the Springs of Cresson, and then closed fluidly around the Christian brigade. The slaughter began. Raymond called out in the mayhem, "Those who can get through may go, since the battle is lost. We have lost even our chance to flee."

Perhaps he was speaking for himself. Again as if the Arabs knew exactly what to do, they made way for Raymond and a few of his lieutenants to gallop down the steep, narrow crevice known as the Wadi Hamman through their lines and to escape unharmed to the safety of the Templar castle of Safad in the north. With the leaders gone, the Muslim soldiers set about their grim task of butchery. When later Saladin offered his explanation for allowing Raymond's escape, he spoke obliquely, inevitably invoking his Koran: Count Raymond, "may God curse him," had turned on his heels and fled because he had seen the power of Allah. "Lo, I have nothing to do with you; lo! I see what you do not see. Lo! I fear Allah; for Allah's punishment is strict." (Koran 8:48)

As for the rest of the work, the Sultan saw it poetically. The hooves of his horses created a sky of dust whose stars were lance points. The eyes of the Muslim spears sought out the diseased hearts and livers of the unbelievers who were tormented by the fires of thirst. Rivers of swords came to water, and the infidels drank the cup of fate.

The Christian chronicler saw it differently: "What can I say? It would be more fitting to weep and wail than to say anything. Alas! Should I describe with impure lips how the precious wood of the Lord, our Redeemer, was seized by the damnable hands of the damned? Woe to me that in the days of my miserable life I should be forced to see such things."

Between terce and nones on the feast day of St. Martin Calidus, the forces of Allah secured their total victory over the Christian host. In the last hour of battle the Christian forces dwindled until only King Guy's red tent was erected on the southern horn of Hattin. When the King's tent went down, the battle was over. The prior of the Holy Sepulcher had been killed, and the True Cross was seized. King Guy and Châtillon and the Grand Masters of the Templars and the Hospitalers were captured. The day was lost.

Saladin called it a day of grace in which "the wolf and the vulture kept company, while death and captivity followed in turns."


# 2

# Rose Water Sherbert

As the sun set over the Sea of Galilee, King Guy and Châtillon were brought to the Sultan's wooden pavilion near the shoreline. The Sultan was seated, cross-legged, upon a raised divan covered with tribal carpets, surrounded by the apricot banners of his army. Bedraggled and dusty and gasping from thirst, the prisoners were presented to him. Terror was evident on the King's face, but Châtillon manifested only contempt. Saladin gestured gracefully for the King to take his place next to the Sultan himself. Châtillon then took a pillow next to his King. With a nod of his head to a satrap, the Sultan was handed a golden bowl of sherbert flavored with rose water, and he passed it to the King, who gulped it wildly and then passed the bowl to Châtillon.

"You did not ask my permission to give him water," the Sultan said quietly, with an undertone of menace in his voice. "Therefore, I am not obliged to grant him mercy."

This was a point of honor. In Islamic custom a captor who offers his prisoner food and water must spare him. Now Saladin said to Châtillon, "Drink, for you will never drink again." After the capture of the rich Muslim caravan on the holy road of pilgrimage, the imprisonment of his sister, Châtillon's disrespect toward Islam, after his pirate's raid on the holy sites of the Red Sea and his threatening Mecca and Medina and his many breaches of solemn truces, Saladin had made another vow that contemplated not mercy but justice. Twice the Sultan had vowed to kill this villain with his own hands.

"How many times have you sworn an oath and then violated it?" he said coldly to Châtillon. "How many times have you signed agreements that you have never respected?"

Châtillon grunted with loathing. "Kings have always acted thus," he said grandly. "I did nothing more."

"If you held me in your prison as I now hold you in mine, Prince of Châtillon, what would you do to me?" Saladin asked.

"So help me God, I would cut off your head," Châtillon snapped.

"Pig, you are my prisoner and yet you answer me so arrogantly!"

With a wave of his hand the Sultan ordered the vile prisoners away and then mounted his charger to welcome the return of his soldiers—and to collect himself. When he came back from his rounds, he ordered the prisoners to be fetched once again.

While King Guy was kept in an antechamber, Châtillon was brought in alone.

"Behold, I will support Muhammad against you," the Sultan said. To the Prince of Kerak the Sultan made his final offer: Convert to Islam, acknowledge Muhammad as the Holy Prophet, praise Allah as the only God, renounce the errors of the Christian faith. When Châtillon refused, Saladin took his crescent sword and brought it down across the tyrant's shoulder, severing his arm from his body, and then the slaves moved in to cut off his head.

King Guy was then brought in, trembling at the dreadful sight, preparing himself for his own execution.

"This man was killed because of his perfidy," Saladin said. Guy of Lusignan fell to his knees, but Saladin bade him to rise.

"Real kings do not kill each other," he said, offering another cup of rose water sherbert to his captive. "He was no king, and he overstepped the limits."

For days the exultant cries of "*Allahu Akbar!*" and "*La ilaha il' Allah*" lingered over the terrible battlefield, still strewn with the bodies of the Christians. The prisoners were herded together, bound with rope, and marched off toward Damascus, where the common foot soldiers were sold as slaves for three dinars, though one was sold for a shoe to make a point. A different fate awaited the knights. The Templars and the Hospitalers were the heart of the Christian defense. They were unshakeable in their dedication and commitment. Their will could not be broken.

"I shall purify the land of these two impure cults," Saladin announced, and he awarded fifty dinars to every man who had captured one of the militant monks.

And so, in a singular blot on his record of generosity, Saladin executed them all. Scholars and holy men and ascetics were accorded the privilege of delivering the blow. "There were some who slashed and cut cleanly and were thanked for it," wrote a Muslim observer. "Some who refused and failed to act and were excused; some who made fools of themselves, and others took their places." Ironically, only the Master of the Temple, Gerard de Ridefort, the worst villain of the flock, was spared, for he might prove useful as a bargaining chip.

"Unbelief was killed to give life to Islam," one Arab scribe wrote of this mass execution. "Monotheism destroyed polytheism." By contrast, the Christian chronicles later related that upon the bodies of these militant martyrs on the execution ground a ray of celestial sunlight shone down from heaven.

Meanwhile, the True Cross was pinioned upside down on a spear and carried to Damascus. To the Muslims this apparent sacrilege evinced their contempt only for the story of the crucifixion, not for the Christian Savior. For Jesus Christ remained a revered prophet in Islam. He was a great man, not a God; human, not divine; a prophet, but not a deity. For there was only one God, Allah. The Prophet Muhammad, with divine guidance, had clarified the mistakes and misinterpretations of Christianity.

Islam rejected the tale of Christ's death as unworthy of a great religion.

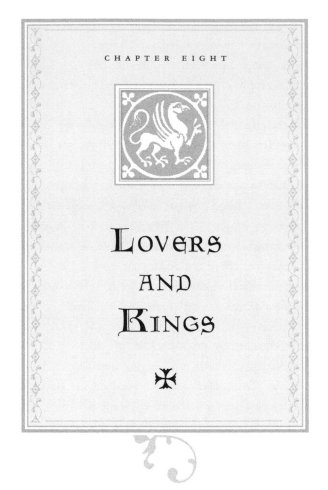

CHAPTER EIGHT

# Lovers
# and
# Kings

✠

hROUGh The DECADE OF The 1170s The pope
in Rome was the active and orthodox Alexander III, whose
dramatic papacy was to last twenty-two years and was to encompass various challenges by anti-Popes, several exiles from
the Eternal City, and the humiliation of King Henry II of England over the
murder of Thomas à Becket. Alexander had developed a reputation for being
sensitive to the needs of the poor and maligned. He had been particularly attentive to the plight of the Jews and counted among his closest advisers a
rabbi and scholar who held the honored position of steward in the Vatican
palace. On the lot of Jews, however, Alexander was a man of his time, as one
of his late decrees in 1179 showed:

"We do decree that those persons shall be excommunicated who shall attempt to prefer Jews to Christians, as it is right and proper that they should be beneath the Christians and be by them supported on grounds of humanity alone . . ."

It was not, however, the two hundred Jews of Rome so much as the millions of Muslims in the Holy Land who concerned the Pope the most, for he appreciated how fragile the Kingdom of Jerusalem was. Toward the end of his papacy—he was to die in 1181—Alexander III was greatly alarmed at the gains of Saladin in the Holy Land and frustrated at the apparent indifference of European monarchs toward the danger. "The Christian religion cannot sleep while such awful things threaten the Holy Land," he wrote. "May the zeal of God move you!" Particularly appalling to the Pontiff were those Christians who were profiting from the Muslim gains. As a consequence, he issued another decree in 1179, again using the threat of excommunication:

"To such a degree has shocking cupidity taken possession of the minds of some that whereas they glory in the name of Christians, they carry arms to the Arabs, and by supplying them with arms and necessities for the purpose of warring against Christians show themselves their equals and even their superiors in wickedness. Such persons we do order to be cut off from communion of the Church and for their iniquity to be subjected to excommunication."

The Pope's other main concern was the ferocity of the internecine conflicts in Central Europe. How pointless and narrow-minded were these unrelenting parochial struggles between important and petty knights in this so-called age of chivalry—and how distracting from the much greater threat in the Holy Land. The Crowns of England and France had to be reconciled if the Christian world was ever to have peace and to focus on the real threat to Christianity. But this reconciliation was not an easy task for the Pope who had punished the English King so harshly in the Becket affair. Alexander gave his blessing, nevertheless, to a truce between the two nations that was concluded in Gisors in 1180. But he had no illusions that this would be a permanent peace.

For England the increasingly crotchety and unpredictable Henry did the honors in Gisors, but there was a new king in France. He was young Philip Augustus, the son of Louis VII by his third wife, Adèle of Champagne. His birth in 1165 had seemed to be something of a miracle, since he was conceived when his father, the pious recluse Louis VII, was forty-five years old and had failed for decades with two previous wives, including the lusty Eleanor, to produce an heir.

To the Île-de-France the son became known as *Dieu-donné*, "God-given," for his birth ensured the continuation of the precarious Capetian dynasty in France, much to the disappointment of its rival, the Plantagenets of Henry and Richard. The citizens of Paris poured into the streets at the news, bearing candles and holding their ears against the loud ringing of the church bells. At Englishmen they brandished their fists, prophesying that the newest Capetian King would be a "hammer" to the British Plantagenets.

"Now we have a King given us by God, a mighty heir to the kingdom through God's bounty," said one woman in the street to an Englishman. "Through him shall fall on your King loss and disgrace, shame and heavy punishment, rich in confusion and distress."

The competition between the Capetians and the Plantagenets had been the central fact of the twelfth century. From his crib forward, Philip was imbued with the ambition to drive the Plantagenets from the Continent and to restore the glory of Charlemagne's empire to Central Europe. The news of Philip's birth dispirited the Plantagenets. Indeed, it occurred in a month when the English army was suffering reverses on the battlefield and two separate comets had appeared in the night sky over England. Royal astrologers generally interpreted these heavenly events to mean either the death of a king or the ruin of a nation.

Philip was a slovenly child. His princely garments were always askew and his hair so frequently tousled that he acquired the label *le valet malpeigné*. But in 1179 his father had an attack of paralysis and, fearing that he was about to die, decided to crown his son, Philip, as heir while he was still alive, even though Philip was then only fifteen years old. The boy would need to grow up in a hurry.

With great fanfare, on November 1, 1179, the coronation took place at Rheims, since the Archbishop of Rheims, Guillaume of Champagne, was Philip's uncle. For the festivities, *trouvères* were composed by the most famous troubadours of the day, including Blondel de Nesle, a boon companion of Prince Richard during their childhood in Aquitaine. "My joy summons me to sing in the sweet season," went Blondel's touching song, "and it accords with joy to love in a most refined way. When the occasion arises to give gifts generously; and to speak in a courtly fashion. He who follows these counsels will never fare badly." Another song anticipated "a springtime of peace opening the bosom of the earth." It's no wonder tears flow so freely at weddings and coronations.

For eleven months, until Louis VII's death in September 1180, France had two kings.

Philip Augustus was eight years younger than Prince Richard. Perhaps their physical attraction to one another was owed to their different natures. In any event, in their adolescence and early manhood Philip Augustus and Richard the Lionheart had been lovers. They were everywhere together. In the delightful verbal gymnastics of turning homosexuality into a lofty sentiment, Gerald, the Archdeacon of Wales, asserted that Richard "so honored Philip that by day they ate at one table, off one dish, and at night they slept in one bed. And the King of France loved him as his own soul."

Their intimacy flowered from the entanglements of the two dynasties. For some years Richard's father, Henry, had frequently held his conferences with his French counterparts, Louis and then Philip, under a famous elm tree in the northern French town of Gisors. At these conferences the young men had come together. Gisors was the chief town of the Vexin, that fertile contested part of Normandy that served as the buffer between the French and English monarchies and was claimed by both. In the early 1180s Henry II was old and raging against death, complaining sourly about bad beer and stale fish, followed by a circus cast of whores, actors, gamblers, and buffoons, spinning delusions about visiting the graves of the mythical King Arthur and Guinevere.

Because he had tired of these unending conflicts, Henry had come to an accommodation with the young King Philip and his advisers about the Vexin. The castle of Gisors and its surroundings were to be the dowry for Philip's beautiful half sister, Alais, who had been promised as Richard's wife in 1161, when Richard was four years old. As Richard's intended, Alais had been raised in Eleanor's court until Henry, never one to pass up a handsome trophy, snatched her away and took her to his own bed. This violation, of course, not only sullied Philip's blood and undercut his grand scheme, but it also undermined Alais's value as a bargaining chip. She was debauched and dishonored, damaged goods altogether. At this outrage Richard stood to the side unconcerned and probably amused, since he was not, in any case, interested in conjugal relations.

Thus the intrigue of the two courts became a set of interlocking triangles. There was raunchy old Henry; his imprisoned wife, Eleanor; and the beautiful courtesan, Alais; and the three raged at one another, as we know from the modern play *The Lion in Winter.* On the other hand there was Richard and

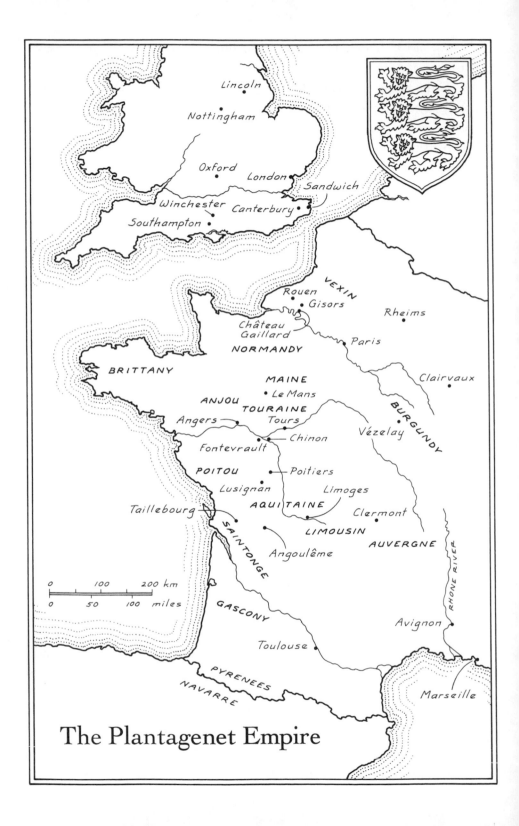

Lincoln
Nottingham
Oxford
London
Sandwich
Winchester   Canterbury
Southampton

VEXIN
Rouen
Gisors
Rheims
Château
Gaillard
Paris
NORMANDY
BRITTANY
Clairvaux
MAINE
Le Mans
ANJOU
TOURAINE
Angers
Tours
BURGUNDY
Chinon
Fontevrault
Vézelay
POITOU
Poitiers
Lusignan
Limoges
Taillebourg
AQUITAINE
Clermont
LIMOUSIN
AUVERGNE
SAINTONGE
Angoulême

0    100    200 km
0   50   100 miles

GASCONY
RHONE RIVER
Avignon
Toulouse
PYRENEES
NAVARRE
Marseille

# The Plantagenet Empire

Philip and Alais. That was a triangle of a different sort. Richard and Philip were the lovers, but Philip's ticket to the Vexin and a considerable payment from the English treasury was his deflowered sister, Alais. As he bedded down with Richard, Philip demanded that his lover take his sister, Alais, to wife.

That did not encompass the full complexity of the situation, however. Never mind the old King's carnal pleasures with Alais, the affair between Richard and Philip, and the young French King's dreams to restore the empire of Charlemagne to France. As if he counted on immortality, Henry was unwilling to cede any real royal authority to his sons. For years he had been scheming to disinherit Richard altogether. If Eleanor loved Richard the best, Henry despised his third son the most, probably because Richard was the most defiant, the most kingly, the most formidable, the most like Henry himself. Since the Duke of Aquitaine had received his fief not through his father but through his mother, Richard was the most serious threat. Instead of Richard, Henry lavished his affections on his youngest son, John, the most unworthy of his brood.

Between the years 1180 and 1187 the very thing that Pope Alexander III had so despised, the fratricidal wars between the royal houses, reached a level of total chaos. The great Plantagenet house was at war with itself, with its subjects, and with its rival in France, the House of Capet. From 1180 to 1183, Henry II demanded that Richard pay homage to his older brother, the younger Henry, as the next Angevin King. When Richard refused, his older brother invaded Aquitaine, with the blessing of their royal father, who bade young Henry "rise up and subdue Richard's pride." Richard's younger brother, Geoffrey, to whom Henry had ceded the least of the Plantagenet provinces, Brittany, enthusiastically joined in this campaign against Richard. But in Geoffrey the rebels had no great catch. To the chronicler Gerald of Wales he was "overflowing with words, soft as oil, possessed by his syrupy and persuasive eloquence, to corrupt two kingdoms with his tongue; of tireless endeavor, a hypocrite in everything, a deceiver and a dissembler." The lad had problems.

Mayhem ensued, with forces descending on Aquitaine from Brittany and Gascony, and barons within the duchy fortifying themselves against their own duke. In Henry the Younger these barons of Aquitaine saw an instrument to undercut Richard's rule in the duchy and gladly joined in the conspiracy against him.

Richard, however, rode out of the night with a small force and pounced upon one group of invaders a few miles south of Limoges, killing many and making prisoners of the rest. And then, as if he wished to deepen his reputation for ruthlessness as a warrior far across Europe, he had the prisoners taken to Aix, where, according to the chronicles, he caused some to be drowned in the Vienne, others to be executed with the sword, and the rest to be blinded. What had begun in Henry's mind as a disciplinary act against his third son was now out of control, and ironically, the aging King himself rode into Poitou to try to stop it.

Only when Richard's brother Henry took ill in June of 1183 and died did the madness cease. In one swoop Henry II's plans were dashed: His heir was gone, the insurgents of Aquitaine had lost their champion, and the villain himself—the independent, indomitable, ruthless Richard—now stood as Henry's eldest son and heir to the English throne.

At this unexpected turn of events the English King attempted a different tack. Since Richard was now heir to England, Normandy, and Anjou, something had to be done for Henry's youngest son, John, who was without any domain whatever. So the King demanded that Richard grant his beloved duchy of Aquitaine to John "and receive John's homage for it." This was an idea without legs, for Richard's life was Aquitaine. He had received it from his mother, not Henry, and if homage was due to anyone, it was to the King of France. Richard's reaction to this proposal was swift: He would never grant Poitou to anyone but himself. When Henry reduced his demand and pled with Richard to grant a portion of Aquitaine to John, the answer was the same. And so, characteristically, as he had done with Thomas à Becket and with young Henry's designs, the English King flew into a rage and gave John permission to invade Richard's land and fight him for it.

And so a new cycle began in which the father was alternately the provocateur, the mediator, the reconciler of his sons. The situation within the Plantagenet house was fast becoming a French farce—all the more so with the reentry of Philip, who was demanding that his former lover, Richard, marry his defiled half sister, Alais, who was then bedded with Richard's father, Henry. Henry's sons were one minute swearing their love and constancy at their father's feet and the next waging war against him. Sometimes they were in the English court and other times in the French court. And far away in the wings the imprisoned Eleanor stood by as a helpless witness.

With the Angevin princes in his Paris court, Philip was drawn (and no doubt amorously) to Richard's younger and oily and athletic brother, Geoffrey. King Philip made him the suzerain of France, largely to annoy old Henry. But Geoffrey was trampled to death in a jousting tournament on August 19, 1186, and was buried with great ceremony in the Cathedral of Notre Dame. So great was Philip's grief that he had to be restrained from jumping into Geoffrey's casket during the funeral.

The King soon got over his grief, however. By the spring of 1187 Philip had turned his affections back to Richard. When news of the scandal of these affections reached Henry, he was upset, wondering what the meaning of this "friendship" might be. The old King soon found out. Richard rode to Chinon, seized control of his castle on the Loire, and carried off all Henry's treasure, before he proceeded to Aquitaine and began to raise an army against his father.

But in the fall of that year, 1187, terrible and sudden news from far away rocked these royal adversaries and their petty rivalries at their foundations forever.

# CHAPTER NINE

# The Bride
# and
# The Camel

✠

Ａfter his great victory at Hattin on July 4, 1187, Saladin moved swiftly north, capturing Acre, Beirut, and Sidon without much of a fight. All were lightly defended and fell swiftly into the Muslim orbit. At Tyre, however, the Sultan was surprised. He expected the coastal garrison south of Beirut to fall as easily as the other Christian cities had. In his flight after the Battle of Hattin, Raymond of Tripoli had tarried briefly in Tyre but had quickly moved on, feeling that its defense was untenable. Indeed, Saladin had already negotiated an arrangement with a caretaker to surrender the city peaceably, in exchange for the safety of its citizens and the protection of their property. But when the Muslim legions came to Tyre, they found it well defended and well led. The appeasing knight had been displaced by a fierce, defiant latecomer. His name was Conrad of Montferrat.

The Marquis of Montferrat had arrived in the nick of time, only a few days before the Muslim army presented itself in front of the walls. A bold adventurer who like King Guy and Châtillon had a dubious past of murder and conspiracy, he had arrived on a Pisan ship, a fugitive himself from intrigues in Constantinople. His ship had appeared first off Acre, where he learned that the port had fallen to Saladin. And so the marquis had ordered the ship to turn north to Tyre, the last strategic foothold in the Latin Kingdom, where the broken remnants of the Crusader army were congregating.

The citizens of Tyre saw Montferrat as a godsend. Desperately they pled with him to take charge of their defense. This he agreed to do, so long as total homage was sworn to him as their sole leader. As the Muslim armies closed in on Tyre, the marquis buoyed the spirits of Christian soldiers and organized them into a stout defense force. When Saladin's troops appeared before the walls, the Sultan watched his apricot banners being ripped apart in a show of contempt.

Upon learning who was responsible for this sudden defiance, the Sultan realized that he held the marquis's father prisoner in Damascus. So William of Montferrat, a wily old veteran of Hattin, was brought forward and paraded in chains before the walls. Saladin sent an emissary to Conrad promising to free the marquis's father and bestow great wealth on him if the city were surrendered as promised. From the walls Conrad spat out his answer: "Tie him to a stake. What do I care?" he shouted. "I shall be the first to shoot him. For he is old and worthless." When William was brought closer to test this threat, he seemed not at all upset at his son's lack of filial loyalty.

"Conrad, guard well the city!" he shouted out to his son.

Conrad took a crossbow and shot at his father. Hearing of this, Saladin was impressed. "This man is an unbeliever and very cruel," he said. He knew that he would lose his advantage if he delayed for long in front of Tyre, mired in a protracted siege. His men were tired of fighting, but they were still eager for plunder. The Sultan could not get bogged down. To satisfy the greed of his own soldiers he moved swiftly to other targets where the pickings were easy. Moving south, he gathered Caesarea, Arsuf, and Jaffa into the fold before he stood outside of Ascalon.

Ascalon, one of the five cities of the Philistines, was the southernmost outpost of the Latin Kingdom. Shaped like a bow, its harbor was heavily fortified, fenced with high walls punctuated by a number of imposing towers.

Thirty miles south of Jaffa and only a day's march from Jerusalem, Ascalon's strategic importance lay in its relation to Egypt. Once in Muslim hands it could become a staging area for naval and land forces.

Well constructed though the town was, its defense was depleted, and Saladin felt he could have it easily. Wherever he could avoid a pitched battle, especially a siege, he was eager to do so. Time was of the essence, for the bride, Jerusalem, awaited him. Words from the Koran were his guide: "He for whom the door of righteousness is opened should take advantage of the opportunity, for he knows not when it may be shut against him."

To encourage the fortress's surrender, Saladin called for another important prisoner, Guy of Lusignan himself, and presented the erstwhile King of the Crusader kingdom with a deal. If Guy could encourage the town's elders to surrender the city to Saladin, he would be released. With that the King was escorted to the town's gate, to sing humbly for his own freedom.

"Gentlemen," King Guy said once he was with the skeptical councilmen, "Saladin has said that if I will surrender the city to him, he will let me go. It would not be right for such a fine city to be surrendered for just one man. So if you think you can hold Ascalon for Christendom, do not surrender it. But if you do not think you can hold it, I beg you to surrender it and deliver me from captivity."

He vowed more. Once free, the King promised to ask for help from the Europeans across the sea. At the King's propositions the burghers balked, for they trusted the disgraced King less than the Sultan. And so King Guy went back to the Arab camp empty-handed, meaning, of course, that he would remain Saladin's prisoner.

As these discussions proceeded, so did Saladin's sappers. With each passing hour the Muslim soldiers came closer to undermining the walls, and this seemed, at last, to concentrate the minds of the councilmen. Before they had no choice, they decided to capitulate. Saladin explained to his brother, el Melek el-Adel, his leniency toward the defenders.

"We granted them this," he said, "in the conviction that they were only being preserved from one fate for another. I wished out of pity to spare the wives and children of the Muslims in the town from the violence of the Christian army, as well as to protect the town itself from being ravaged by pillagers."

So the town whose capture thirty-four years earlier after a seven-month siege had marked such a high-water mark for the Latin Kingdom now slipped quietly back into Muslim hands. While the Sultan negotiated the surrender of Ascalon, his detachments harvested other lightly defended Christian outposts in the area: Gaza, Latrun, Ramla, and Darum. At the Templar castle of Gaza, Saladin used his second bargaining chip. He dispatched his prisoner, Gerard de Ridefort, the erstwhile Master of the Templars, to persuade his militant monks to surrender. De Ridefort proved to be more persuasive than King Guy, and as a result he gained his own freedom. He promptly led the pardoned Templars north to Tyre, and this would spell trouble for Saladin later.

Still, Saladin had achieved his immediate objective. The ring around Jerusalem was now complete.

The Sultan rested for some days in Ascalon, preparing himself spiritually for the final push on Jerusalem. After Mecca and Medina, Jerusalem was the third holiest city to the Muslims. According to Islamic scripture, the three cities (along with the city of Kufa in Iraq) were created from the same holy foam, even before the creation of the earth. Jerusalem was the ultimate prize, the goal of Saladin's life, the objective of his great predecessors, Zengy and Nur ad-Din, the burden of the last ninety years of Arab history, the final obligation of jihad. It was the dwelling place of Abraham and the abode of prophets, the spot where divine revelation descended. It was the place of the Rock, of the Gate of Mercy, of the Seat of Solomon and the Oratory of David, of the Fountain of Aloes. Its capture would complete the Arab reconquest of Palestine after nearly a hundred years of foreign occupation.

The sanctity of Jerusalem was at the very heart of Islam. Five hundred and eighty-three years earlier, so the canon tells, the Prophet Muhammad was flown from the Sacred Mosque of Mecca on the back of the beautiful winged horse called Buraq to the Farthest Mosque of Jerusalem. There all the prophets of the past, including Jesus, entertained him in a lavish feast. And then on the glorious night, the twenty-seventh day of the month called Rajab the Unique, from the Rock that originated in Paradise, the Prophet ascended the celestial ladder and was taken near the lote-tree, the symbol of heavenly bliss, into the Garden of Eternal Abode. Through the seven heavens Muhammad's vision never turned away, even at the Sublime Throne of Allah. The nocturnal journey of Muhammad from the Dome of the Rock is one of the great mythic stories of all religion.

Jerusalem, the bride, stood on the verge of liberation. Her reins hung loose, in the words of an Arab scribe, after eighty-nine years in the hands of the infidel. "Islam wooed Jerusalem," wrote a leading chronicler of the Arab cause. "We are ready to lay down lives for her as a bride-price, to bring her a blessing that would remove the tragedy of her state, to give her a joyful face to replace the expression of torment, to make heard, above the cry of grief from the Rock, the prompt echo of the summons which calls for help against the enemies, an echo to bring the exiled faith back to her own country and drive away from al Aqsa those whom God drove away with His curse."

In this moment of greatest anticipation Saladin struggled with his emotions. To his herald he "had tamed the indomitable colt of his desires and made fertile the meadow of his wealth." He struggled with his anger, with an understandable instinct for revenge and retribution against the blue-eyed invader.

On September 19 he broke camp and began his march. Entrusting his quest to the will of God, he hoped to find the door of opportunity open to him. The tramp of his soldiers raised such a cloud of dust that the sun was obscured and the day became dark and hazy. His soldiers shared his soaring expectation. As they marched, they raised their exultant cries to Allah. Their apricot banners fluttered in the wind, with their inscriptions, "There is no God but Allah, and His Prophet is Muhammad." Soon, they said to one another, the Muslim *muezzin* calling the faithful to prayer over the Holy City would replace the ugly sound of the Christian clappers. In the midst of this joyous cavalcade Saladin, the prosperity of the world and of the faith, the King who brings victory to the faith, rode triumphantly in his wooden pavilion.

The next day his soldiers stood before the Tower of David and the western walls of the holy city.

The weight of this historic moment could not have escaped Saladin. He knew the shame and the disgrace of the first Crusaders. Eighty-eight years earlier their leader Tancred had organized his forces on this very place and gazed upon the same Tower of David and an equally well-defended Muslim city. The ardor of their faith possessed those Crusaders just as much. Before they assaulted the walls, they, too, went through their spiritual exercises. They fasted, confessed, took communion, gave alms to the poor, listened to sermons, and walked barefoot as humble penitents. They, too, longed for the liberation of their Holy City, where their Savior had lived and died.

But the Christian soldiers were also in the grip of hatred. This was the flaw of their faith. They quivered with bloodlust. To them the supreme moment for revenge had arrived.

Their siege had lasted five weeks, from June 7 to July 15, 1099. Before the southern ramparts one of their leaders, Raymond of St. Giles, had filled the moat, had thrown wooden ladders against the walls, and was battering the ramparts relentlessly, even though the ground dropped off precipitously into the Valley of Jehoshaphat. While the soldiers attacked, the engineers built two siege towers, a huge battering ram, armored roofs, and more ladders. Four weeks into the siege Tancred gave up his assault on the Tower of David and moved east along the walls to the northern gate known then as St. Stephen's Gate (Damascus Gate) to join with the forces of their Crusaders' commander in chief, Godfrey of Bouillon. Godfrey was their supreme hero, the "slave of Christ," the paragon of knighthood, the advocate of the Holy Sepulcher, and later the first de facto Christian King of Jerusalem.

On July 15, 1099, the Dies Veneris, the Friday on which to the medieval believer Christ had redeemed the whole world on the Cross, Tancred finally breached the wall. His soldiers poured through the gap into the Jewish Quarter of the city known as Juiverie while Godfrey's soldiers were let through the gate of Jehoshaphat on the east. Almost simultaneously the forces of Raymond of St. Giles streamed over the southern wall. They converged on the Temple Mount, where an immense number of Muslims had taken refuge and were prepared to make their last stand.

There the orgy of slaughter began. For two whole days these Christian soldiers massacred every living creature that was not of their own kind. At the Temple Mount alone it was said that ten thousand were killed. According to Fulcher of Chartres, some of these had their bodies ripped open, because it was rumored that Muslims were swallowing gold bezants in desperation. For the whole city the estimate of the slain was forty thousand Muslims—men, women, and children. The Church of the Holy Sepulcher, the holiest church in Christendom, the site of Calvary, was a pool of blood. They found the Jews of Jerusalem huddled in their synagogue, ready for martyrdom. And they burned the prayer place down, dancing around the burning pyre and singing the *Te Deum.*

After the killing the looting followed. The mosque of Omar, dedicated to the second successor of the Prophet and contiguous to the Holy Sepulcher, was sacked. The tomb of Abraham was destroyed. The Crusaders went about

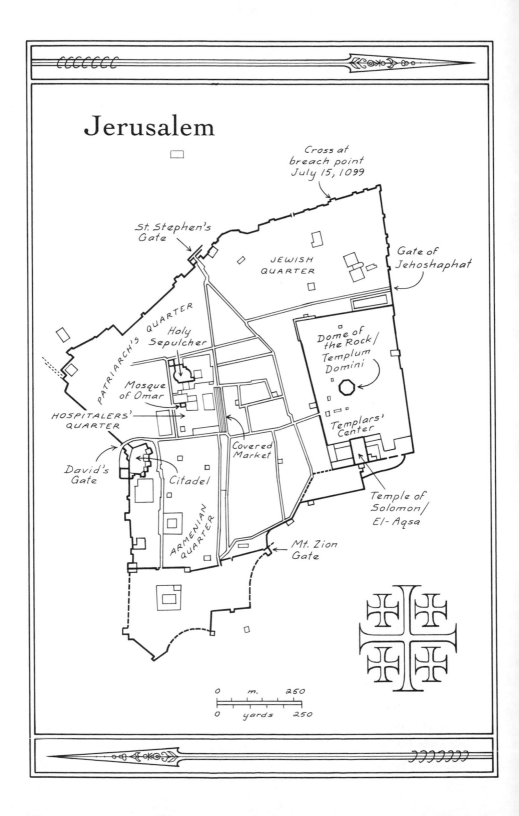

# Jerusalem

Cross at
breach point
July 15, 1099

St. Stephen's
Gate

JEWISH
QUARTER

Gate of
Jehoshaphat

PATRIARCH'S QUARTER

Holy
Sepulcher

Dome of
the Rock /
Templum
Domini

Mosque
of Omar

HOSPITALERS'
QUARTER

Templars'
Center

Covered
Market

David's
Gate

Citadel

ARMENIAN
QUARTER

Temple of
Solomon /
El-Aqsa

Mt. Zion
Gate

0        m.        250

0     yards     250

their work joyfully, confident in its righteousness, proud of doing God's work as in their humble mortality they saw it.

"In the Temple and the porch of Solomon, men rode in blood up to their knees and bridle reins," wrote one expansive participant, Raymond of Aguilers. "Indeed, it was a just and splendid judgment of God that this place should be filled with the blood of unbelievers since it had suffered so long from their blasphemies."

When it was over, Godfrey of Bouillon and the others removed their armor, washed the blood and gore off their cross-embossed surcoats and themselves, piously put on the robes of the penitent, and went to the Church of the Holy Sepulcher to offer prayers, sobbing with joy. They had done glorious work, they were convinced, in the highest tradition of chivalry as the knights of Christ. The Patriarch of Jerusalem led a holy procession to the Temple Mount, where a new canticle to the Lord was sung "in a resounding voice of exultation." From there the caravan proceeded to the quickly fashioned Crusader cemetery near the Golden Gate and then to the place where the wall had been breached. At this fresh monument a ceremony of thanksgiving was conducted, and the Patriarch delivered his benediction.

"If we consider the battles of Gentiles and think of great military enterprises in which kingdoms have been invaded, we will think of no army and absolutely no exploit comparable to ours," wrote a leading historian of the First Crusade, Guibert of Nogent. For the grotesque treatment of women, he had no apology. "The Franks did no other harm to the women whom they found in the enemy camp, save that they ran their lances through their bellies."

"O day so ardently desired," wrote Fulcher effusively, "desired because in the inner longing of the heart it had always been hoped by all believers in the Catholic faith that the place in which the Creator of all creatures, God, made man, in His manifold pity for mankind, had by His birth, death, and resurrection, conferred the gift of redemption, would be restored to its pristine dignity. They desired that this place, so long contaminated by the superstition of the pagan inhabitants, should be cleansed from their contagion."

What to one religion is glory becomes disgrace and shame to another. This was a memory no Muslim could forget. If the city itself still stank six months later from the carnage, the memory still stank ninety years—and nine hundred years—later. It was burned in Saladin's mind and psyche, central to his education and his determination, abhorrent in the extreme. At so inglorious a conquest as that of the First Crusade, Saladin had to harness the colt of his desires, the desire for rage, revenge, retribution, recompense, justice.

Now it was his turn.

For five days he reconnoitered the city. On the sixth, September 26, he began his assault. The Christian force was estimated at somewhere around ten thousand and they were noisy. Blaring their trumpets, they shrieked their chants from the walls: "True and Holy Cross!" "Save the city of Jerusalem!" "Protect the Holy Sepulcher!" They bolstered one another with the thought that each of them was brave and worthy enough to equal a hundred Muslim soldiers. They engaged in their rituals, passing around the "goblet of death" to prove their commitment. Of the initial attack one Christian reported that one could not show a finger above the ramparts without being hit, so thick was the shower of Arabian arrows.

But this aerial assault accomplished little. Within a few days Saladin changed his tactics. From the walls the defenders watched as the Muslim tents were struck on the Mount of Olives and Mount Joy and in the Valley of Jehoshaphat. For a fleeting moment it looked as if Saladin were actually withdrawing. "The King of Syria has fled," the jubilant cry went up in the city. "He cannot destroy the city as he planned." But the Sultan was only shifting his forces to higher ground, from the Tower of David to the northern wall around St. Stephen's Gate. His main force now stood exactly in the same place as had the force of Tancred and Godfrey of Bouillon eighty-eight years before.

Against the northern walls he brought forward his siege engines. First a huge petrary was rolled forward. A boulder was loaded into its spoon at the end of its colossal lever, the ropes were twisted tight to the breaking point, the arm was winched back and then released, hurling the stony projectile in an arc against the wall. On the following morning eleven such petraries stood in front of the walls. The Muslims also brought their arbalests into play, the oversized crossbows that shot javelins instead of arrows. "The bolts served as toothpicks to the teeth of the battlements," an Arab chronicler wrote later. The artillery barrage was constant. Meanwhile, the engineers worked to undermine the walls, digging holes underneath and then setting the supporting timbers aflame.

After two days of battering, the walls began to give. The Muslim sappers broke down part of the tower at St. Stephen's Gate. At the very spot of the

Crusaders' breach years earlier, a new breach appeared. The rocks tumbled into the moat, along with the cross that memorialized the Christian breach eight decades earlier. The defenders seemed to lose their courage and fled.

With the Patriarch of Jerusalem, Eraclius, as his spiritual adviser, the command of the Christian defense had fallen to the captain of the old guard, Balian of Ibelin. A tall man of noble bearing, this blueblood had for years reigned his fief well from his castle in Nablus as his father had done before him. It was Balian who several years earlier had carried the child King, Baldwin V, in his own arms to the Holy Sepulcher to be crowned after his father, the leper King Baldwin IV, had died. It was Balian who, as an ally of that other pillar of the establishment, Raymond of Tripoli, had counseled King Guy wisely and had commanded the Templars of the rear guard bravely at Hattin. Along with a few military monks he had miraculously escaped the awful carnage on the Lubiyan plain and made his way to Tyre. From a wealth of experience with the Arabs, Balian was accustomed to dealing with Saladin. And so it was not surprising that from Tyre he had petitioned Saladin personally for permission to go to Jerusalem to rescue his wife. The Sultan agreed to this, providing the knight not bear arms and spend only one night in the Holy City. But once he was there, the Christian population pleaded with him to take charge of the military defense.

Only in the age of chivalry would this request cause a crisis of conscience. Since Balian was a man of honor and since he had made a solemn promise to the Sultan, he appealed directly to Saladin to release him from his oath. This Saladin did, for he was not overly concerned about the defense of the city, no matter who led it. This noble and honorable knight probably did not need the moral counsel of Eraclius, for the Patriarch himself was something of a scandal. Though learned and clever, Eraclius lived openly with a mistress who was a draper's wife from Nablus and who was known in the Holy City as "Madame la Patriarchesse."

In Jerusalem there were only two true knights left, and the unpopular Templars had taken charge. But the citizens did not warm to the stern Templar rule and had beseeched Balian to take over. Reluctantly he acquiesced to this popular demand. Among his first acts was to send out foraging parties to stock the city with food. And then he knighted sixty surviving sons of eminent men to prepare for the defense.

But now at the first sign of the breach Balian knew that the situation was hopeless. If he needed proof that the fight was over and the battle lost, the

Patriarch of Jerusalem had offered five thousand gold bezants to fifty sergeants of the guard who would guard the breach. This was five hundred times the usual fee for a night's duty, and still the Patriarch could not find his fifty men. Already nearly twelve apricot banners were planted on the walls. The women of Jerusalem began to gather at the Holy Sepulcher, where they brought their children, filled basins with cold water, put their children in these basins, and cut their hair. This act of despair signaled an expectation of martyrdom.

Meanwhile, among the hotheads there were proposals for a last desperate charge at the infidel force, in the grand tradition of chivalry and knighthood. But the Patriarch advised against this blaze of glory. If the charge should fail, he said, and should the knights die, their women and children would be sold into the slavery of Islam and their souls would be prohibited from entering heaven. "The Arabs will not kill them but will make them renounce the faith of Jesus Christ, and they will all be lost to God," he said.

And so Balian was advised to sue for peace. He sent an emissary to Saladin, stating his readiness to talk. At first Saladin was uninterested.

"My wise men say that Jerusalem can only be cleansed with Christian blood," he said bitterly. Then he reminded the ambassadors of what had happened eighty-eight years before. "My counsel tells me to take revenge for those Muslims whom Godfrey slew in the streets and even in the Temple."

This harsh, menacing threat was softened slightly by Saladin's agreeing to consult once more with his learned men. A second embassy was sent and turned away, and finally a third came, led by Balian himself, to plead with Saladin to name his own conditions for the surrender. In return for the city he asked amnesty for the people of Jerusalem.

"Neither amnesty nor mercy for you!" Saladin growled. "Tomorrow will make us your masters. We shall kill and capture you and reduce the poor and the women to slavery."

At this terrifying threat Balian kept his wits and delivered his counterthreat. "If we must despair of your mercy, if we are sure there is no escape, we shall seek death like men," he replied steadily. "We shall hurl ourselves at you. We shall cast ourselves into the fire. Above all we shall not dishonor ourselves. No one will be wounded before he has first wounded ten men himself. We will burn the houses and pull down the Dome and leave to you the shame of reducing us to slavery. We shall tear up the Rock and leave you to enjoy the grief of losing it. We will kill every Muslim prisoner in our hands—and we have thousands. We shall destroy our possessions rather than hand them over."

He paused with effect. "What advantage do you gain from this ungenerous spirit?" he said softly. "You stand to lose everything."

With his promise to destroy the holy places of Jerusalem, including the Dome of the Rock, Balian got the Sultan's attention. When Saladin looked at the sad and determined face of his noble adversary, he knew that this was no man to make empty threats. And yet the Sultan would make no deal for a soft surrender, not here, with his ultimate prize in his grasp. It must be clear to all that he had taken the Holy City not by treaty but by force, not with compromise but with total victory. History demanded it. That had been his promise to his subjects and to his Prophet.

"I will tell you what I will do," he said to Balian finally. "I will have mercy on your people in a way that will save my oath. They will surrender to me as if taken by force. I will let them keep their wealth and their property. Those who are able to ransom themselves I shall set free in return for a set price. Those who lack the means to buy their freedom will remain as my slaves."

A period of haggling ensued, for now the only question was the price of freedom, not freedom itself. Proposal and counterproposal were exchanged; Balian and Eraclius were bargaining for the safe departure of the maximum number of poor Christians, about twenty thousand, since the wealthy could purchase their liberty on their own. It took some time and many messages back and forth before a price was agreed upon: ten gold bezants for each man, five for a woman, and one for a child.

Balian and the patriarch knew they could count on thirty thousand bezants from the Hospitalers' treasury from the money that Henry II had deposited in their coffers for the murder of Thomas à Becket. That would free seven thousand Christians. A collection for a freedom fund was taken in the streets, and this freed hundreds more.

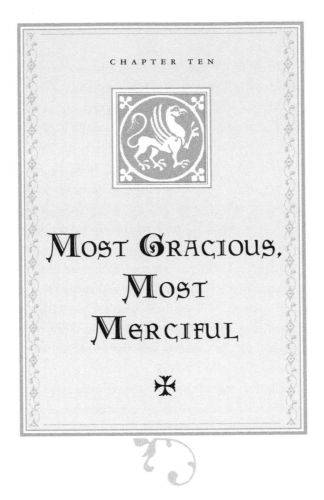

# CHAPTER TEN

# MOST GRACIOUS, MOST MERCIFUL

✠

ITh AN eYE TO hISTORY, SALADIN DELAYED his triumphal entry into Jerusalem for two days, so that he could reclaim the Holy City on Friday, the twenty-seventh day of Rajab in the year 583 (October 2, 1187). On this holy anniversary of the Prophet's ascension into the presence of Allah on his nocturnal journey, Jerusalem became Muslim once again. Within the city walls, Saladin proudly but humbly availed himself of a public audience to receive congratulations. Emirs and scholars, lawyers and poets, holy men and ascetics paid court to him. Orators declaimed his praises. They kissed the fringe of his carpet, presented him with gifts, read panegyrics to him. To one observer his throne seemed to glow with the umbra of the moon.

By contrast to the carnage of the Christian takeover in 1099, there was no mayhem. The only violence that marked this conquest was visited on structures. The doors of the Holy Sepulcher were slammed shut. Among Saladin's advisers were radicals who referred to the Holy Sepulcher as a dung heap, taking great delight in perverting the Arabic phrase for the Church of the Resurrection, *el-Kiāma,* into the word for shit, *el-Komāma.* They argued that the site should be destroyed, so that the shrine would cease to lure Christian pilgrims.

"When its buildings are destroyed and it is razed to the ground," said one, "and its fires spent and extinguished, and its traces rubbed out and removed, and its soil plowed up, and the church scattered far and wide, then the people will cease to visit it, and the longings of those destined to damnation will no longer turn to seeing it. Whereas if it is left standing the pilgrimage will go on without end."

To destroy or to preserve? The issue occasioned a hot debate. Other emirs responded that it was not the church of the Holy Sepulcher but the site of Calvary that drew Christians to Jerusalem. "They will not stop coming here even if the earth of Calvary is scattered to the sky," said one emir. Another, with a deep sense of history, pointed out that before the Christian conquest of Jerusalem, the Muslims of 1098 had debated this same issue and had decided, for sheerly political reasons, to leave the Holy Sepulcher intact. To destroy the holiest shrine of Christianity would only intensify the hatred of Christians for Muslims and fire their passion for retribution.

Saladin listened quietly to this debate. At length he made his decision. The Church of the Holy Sepulcher was not to be touched, he declared. To be a good Muslim was to venerate the holy sites of all religions. After his entry into Jerusalem, the Church of the Holy Sepulcher was closed for only three days, after which Christians were permitted to enter, for a small fee.

The victors found that the Dome of the Rock had been transformed into a Christian church. The Christians had covered the Rock itself with marble, so that the place where the Prophet's foot had trod could no longer be touched nor could its aura be felt. A grotesque tabernacle with marble columns had been built, together with graven images of animals, including the images of unclean pigs. In a cave beneath the entrance the Crusaders had made a confessional, which they regarded as the holiest place in their church. It was decorated with frescoes depicting the adulterous woman who was brought before Jesus and to whom Jesus replied, "Let him who is without sin cast the first stone."

Saladin ordered that all these Christian indecencies be demolished, so that the Rock again could be exposed to daylight. When it was finally exposed, pieces of the Rock were found to be missing. Chunks had been carved off and sold in Constantinople. In place of the Crusader confessional the Muslims restored their own sanctity to the cave, reclaiming the beloved Column of Abraham, on which they believed Abraham offered to sacrifice his son. Muslim warriors climbed to the top of the Dome of the Rock and pulled down the gilded metal cross that had been erected there. This was dragged through the streets in degradation and eventually made its way to Baghdad, a gift from Saladin to the Caliph of Baghdad, to whom Saladin still swore nominal fealty. The Caliph, in turn, embedded the symbol in the steps of the main mosque of his city, to be tramped upon by the faithful as they made their way to prayer.

Meanwhile, across the marble plaza of their Noble Sanctuary, the al Aqsa Mosque had been the headquarters of the Templars and stable to their horses. Now it was cleaned and purified with rose water, brought specially from Damascus by Saladin's sister, and made ready for the first preaching. Its *mihrab,* the niche marking the direction of prayer, was found to be a latrine. It, too, was scrubbed and purified and exposed again to the light, and Saladin had it lined with splendid marble in which his name was inscribed. The inscription read:

"In the name of Allah the Compassionate, the Merciful! Hath ordered the repair of this holy *mihrab,* and the restoration of the Aqsa Mosque which was founded in piety. The servant of Allah and His regent, the victorious King, Salah ad-Din, after that Allah had conquered the City by his hand during the month of the year 583. And he asketh of Allah to inspire him with thankfulness for this favor, and to make him a partaker of the remission of sins, through His mercy and forgiveness."

Images of human faces or animals, especially pigs, were erased from the temple. The famous Aleppo pulpit, the beautiful wooden *mimbar* of the master craftsman Hamed ben Thafir, which was made in the year 1168 and had the name of Saladin's predecessor, Nur ad-Din, carved into it, was brought from Damascus and draped with sumptuous cloth. The Koran replaced the Testaments in a sacred lectern. Carpets were laid on the floor. Along with the fragrance of rose water, incense perfumed the mosque. The cry of the *muezzin* calling the faithful to prayer wafted over the rooftops, replacing the familiar sound of the clapper that the Christians had used for their nones and vespers for so many years. Once again the strains of the first *sura* rang within the Dome, proclaimed by the most eloquent, clear-voiced, and pious of readers: "In the name of Allah, Most Gracious, Most Merciful; Praise be to Allah, the Cherisher and Sustainer of the Worlds. . . . Show us the straight way. . . ."

In the week after the Muslims occupied Jerusalem, dignitaries from across Saladin's empire, from Egypt and Syria and even Mesopotamia, streamed into Jerusalem. The Sultan's decision about who would deliver the *khotba,* or the first preaching, was eagerly awaited, for at this joyful moment the Sultan could confer no higher honor. All the eminent holy men in Jerusalem aspired to this privilege, frantically composing their draft sermons for Saladin's review, hoping to be chosen. Instead of an eminent elder, Saladin chose instead a vigorous, thirty-two-year-old seer who was the *kadi* of Aleppo. He was Muhi ad-Din, whose name meant "the reviver of religion." He was the future *kadi* of Damascus and a craftsman of pithy poetic masterpieces. It was his prophetic poem that had prophesied the fall of Jerusalem after the capture of Aleppo, the Gray Castle. As a result he had forever endeared himself to Saladin: "Thy taking of the Gray Castle in the month of Safar announces the conquest of Jerusalem for the month of Rajab."

After he ascended the Aleppo pulpit in a sumptuous black robe, the gift of honor from the Caliph in Baghdad, Muhi ad-Din did not disappoint the great congregation. For the next hour, in a swaying, eloquent, antiphonal declamation, he mixed exhortation and congratulation with scriptural sanction. The moral basis for this great victory was laid out. They were to rejoice at the good news, for God was pleased with their conduct. And the people of the green, the inhabitants of paradise, were rejoicing even more than the people of the earth.

"Beware," he warned, "lest Satan make you imagine that this victory was due to your sharp swords, your fleet steeds, and your fearlessness in battle. No, by Allah! victory cometh not from the Mighty, but the Wise!"

Muhi ad-Din explained the significance of Jerusalem to Islam and reminded his audience that, so sacred was the city, Muhammad had first directed the faithful to pray in the direction of Jerusalem instead of Mecca. The Holy City was like a strayed camel that had been abused by misguided polytheists for nearly a hundred years and was now back in the fold. "Rejoice at the purifying of this House in which God permitted his name to be mentioned." He drew the distinction between Islam and Christian trinitarianism, quoting the Koran about God as the only God, "who has no associate in his power, who begot no offspring, who never had any like unto him." He defined the correct Muslim attitude toward Jesus, the prophet, ennobled by God without raising him above the status of a mere mortal. And he did not shrink from the theme of vengeance:

"Labor to expel the evil which afflicts us and tear up the enemy by the root; purify the rest of the land from this filth which hath angered God and his Apostle; lop off the branches of infidelity and cut through its roots; for now the times cry aloud: Vengeance for Islam! God is mighty! God conquers and subdues! He humbleth the infidel!"

He ended with praise for Saladin: "thy trenchant sword, thy shining flambeau, the defender of thy faith, the champion and protector of thy holy land, the great helping prince who gave might to the declaration of true faith, who vanquished the adorers of the Cross, the welfare of the world and religion, the Sultan of Islam, the purifier of the Holy Temple, the commander of true believers."

It was a brilliant exhortation and benediction, a sermon that a witness described as eloquent and expressive, fluent and ornate, unsurpassed and marvelous, concise and diffuse.

Over the next forty days the sad evacuation of Jerusalem went forward. At each gate to the city an emir presided over the collection of the revenue. A black market quickly sprang into existence. Bribes were commonplace. Some Christians escaped over the walls on ropes, others inside baggage; still others disguised themselves as Muslim soldiers. In desperation, Christians sold whatever they had for a fraction of its value to raise their stiff ransom. The churches were stripped of their gold and damask and other valuables, and the clerics hoarded the rest, not to raise the ransom to liberate more of the poverty-stricken but to maintain the church's wealth. Among the worst offenders was the Patriarch Eraclius himself, who became the biggest looter of his own church. As the gold plating was being scraped from the wall on the Patriarch's orders, an aide to Saladin complained to the Sultan about the wanton greed of the priests.

"These are great riches. Their value is clearly over two hundred thousand dinars," he said in outrage, quoting a sum that was double what Saladin would bring into his coffers in the ransom of the entire population. "You permitted the Franks to take their personal property, but that was not extended to the churches and its [*sic*] property. Do not allow these rascals to keep this booty in their grasp!"

"If we block them, they will accuse us of breaking faith with the treaty," the Sultan replied calmly. "I prefer to make them obey the letter of the treaty, so that they are then unable to accuse the believers of breaking their word. Instead, they will tell others of the benefits we have bestowed upon them."

With all the deals and the bribes and the stinginess of the Christian Church, many thousands remained behind, abandoned and hopeless, to be sold off as slaves.

Saladin's heart was not, however, in this traffic in human beings. He seemed amenable to all sorts of last-minute special requests. The Patriarch appealed directly to the Sultan to liberate still others without ransom. This gained another five hundred of the poor. Orthodox Christians petitioned to remain in the city; Saladin agreed, exempting them from the ransom and requiring them to pay only a poll tax, allowing them to take over the Holy Sepulcher and to purchase the property of the Christians who had been driven out. Five hundred Armenians were released simply because they were Armenian. Another thousand were let go on the ground that they were merely guests in the city and came from Edessa. Queen Sibylla and all her court were allowed to leave, as was the widow of the wicked Reginald of Châtillon, for no apparent reason. Saladin took pity on the widows of dead soldiers and the wives of imprisoned soldiers. Not only did he free them, but he lavished them with gifts. Even Saladin's own brother, el Melek el-Adel, was so touched at the plight of the refugees that he bargained for more.

"Sire, I have helped you conquer the land and the city of Jerusalem," he said. "I ask you to give me one thousand slaves from among the poor people of Jerusalem." This Saladin did with the full knowledge that his brother would release them.

Balian tried to buy time for further softhearted expressions of mercy, for he suspected that in his heart Saladin wanted to free them all. But the acts of charity ceased when a fool was caught trying to slip his gold savings out in a wine gourd. A sergeant at one of the gates had stopped him, not suspecting the concealment of money but saying in high dudgeon that "it is because of wine that God has cleaned the city of the Christians."

Finally the figure of the poor to be left behind as slaves was whittled down to eight thousand. In exchange for these many thousands Balian and the Patriarch offered themselves as hostages. There Saladin drew the line.

"I cannot hold two men for eight thousand," he said. The haggling had come to an end.

Among this captive population, women were prized. To the Arab scribe Imad ad-Din, the wailing of the women was amusing, for he regarded all European women as licentious whores, glowing with ardor for carnal intercourse. The mere thought of them sent him into rapturous flights of medieval pornography. European women were "proud and scornful, foul-fleshed and sinful, ardent and inflamed, tinted and painted, desirable and appetizing, exquisite and graceful, seductive and languid, desired and desiring, pink-faced and unblushing, black-eyed and bullying, with shapely buttocks and nasal voices, broken-down little fools. . . . They dedicated as a holy offering what they kept between their thighs."

To see these strumpets wailing and weeping and clutching at their robes, as they contemplated their impending servitude to Arab men, aroused the Arab writer with sexual anticipation. "How many well-guarded women were profaned, how many queens were ruled, and nubile girls forced to yield themselves, and women who had been kept hidden stripped of their modesty, and serious women made ridiculous, and women kept in private now set in public, and free women occupied, and precious ones used for hard work, and pretty things put to the test, and virgins dishonored, and proud women deflowered, and lovely women's red lips kissed, and dark women prostrated, and untamed ones tamed, and happy ones made to weep! How many noblemen took them as concubines, how many ardent men blazed for one of them, and celibates were satisfied by them, and thirsty men sated by them, and turbulent men able to give vent to their passion. How many lovely women were the exclusive property of one man, how many great ladies were sold at low prices, and close ones set at a distance, and lofty ones abased, and savage ones captured, and those accustomed to thrones dragged down!" How many indeed. It was as if only against the women of Christianity did the Muslim men visit their revenge.

Because there were so many of them, the doleful train of refugees was divided into three contingents. The Templars and the Hospitalers were given charge of the first two groups, under the careful watch of Muslim guards. Balian and the Patriarch, with his wagonloads of church lucre, brought up the rear. Saladin assigned fifty mounted guards to protect each group on its journey. The refugees were escorted as far as the border of the county of Tripoli, in the direction of Tyre. As soon as the Muslim guards turned back toward Jerusalem, thieves fell on the procession and robbed the refugees of their last possessions.

As word of the fall of Jerusalem spread to Europe, a song of lament was composed:

> Rachel weeps again,
> whose want of sons
> discredits the womb.
> [a reference to Genesis 30:1–2]

> The temple having fallen
> the city which was formerly full of people
> now stands forsaken.
> [a reference to Lamentations 1:1]

By the exemplary behavior of his soldiers as they took charge of Jerusalem in 1187, Saladin did himself great credit as a wise leader, especially by contrast to the havoc of the first Crusaders in their conquest of the city in 1099. By his protection of the Holy Sepulcher and the other Christian holy sites, his tolerance of other faiths would be long remembered. His actions seemed to define what it meant to be a good Muslim. By his amnesties and various charities toward his enemies he secured forever his reputation for gentility and wisdom.

# CHAPTER ELEVEN

# The House
# of David

The GREAT CONFLICT OF 1187 SEEMED TO BE simply a clash between only two faiths. It was between the concept of a single Almighty God, Allah, versus the concept of God in Three Persons, Blessed Trinity; between the reverence for Calvary versus the reverence for the Rock, where the prophet Muhammad had trodden on his nocturnal journey to heaven; between the Holy Sepulcher and the al Aqsa Mosque.

What about the Jews? Was not Jerusalem equally holy to them?

It was the holiest of the holy. It was the Temple Mount, the site of the biblical First and Second Temples, whose remnant was the Western Wall. It was the place where Abraham was prepared to sacrifice his son, Isaac. It was Zion, the very center of their circle of faith, the place where Shekinah, God's presence, was palpable, the site of the Temple, which was destroyed for the second time by the Roman Emperor Titus in the year A.D. 70. Because of its magnetic lure, the rabbis of the city claimed the rite of fixing the calendar and the dates of festivities for the Diaspora. It was the place for the Jew to die and to be restored. Of its power a Jewish poet of the twelfth century wrote:

> *In the limits of the West, deemed as one who had died*
> *Until in Zion, the Lord's city, I revived.*
> *Zion! Though many cities of their charm make bold*
> *Yet like of her loveliness no human eye will behold.*
> *I know not if the heights before her bowed*
> *Or whether she it is who climbs to heaven's cloud.*

To the Jews of Palestine the white knights of Europe came as the ravens of the apocalypse. The news of the pogroms in the Rhineland and in the Danube Valley that preceded the First Crusade had spread quickly through the Near East. When the Westerners arrived, the sense of foreboding was tremendous and the preparation for martyrdom intense. Some holy men tried to persuade themselves that the appearance of these Christians presaged the coming of the Messiah. So many Christians there made the Holy Land into a "threshing floor," and soon God would command, as in Micah 4:13, "Arise and thresh, O daughter of Zion: for I will make thine horn iron, and I will make thy hoofs brass: and thou shalt beat in pieces many people. . . ."

The arrival of these brutal, hate-filled zealots sent the Computators of the End Time scurrying back to their calculations. A thousand years had passed since Titus's destruction of the Temple. Were these cross-bearing, hymn-chanting, vengeance-seeking legions the realization of that terrible, thousand-year vision? Had the day arrived when, in the words of Isaiah, the Lord shall hiss for the fly that is in the uttermost part of the rivers of Egypt, and for the bee that is in the land of Assyria?

"I saw the troops of the Ashkenazim, moving in their masses," one Jew remarked, "and I do not know where they will turn."

When the wall was breached in 1099, the Christian soldiers had swept first through the Jewish quarter of the Holy City and made Jews their first victims. About two hundred Jews lived in a section of their own near the Tower of David, and now they had been incinerated in their synagogue, with laughter, dance, and mocking hymns. For the next eighty years Jewish communities would revive precariously in places like Galilee and Acre, but not in Jerusalem. By edict of the Christian masters, no Jew could live within the city walls, although several hundred worked as cloth dyers just outside the walls. Overall, their numbers were never large. In the mid-twelfth century about four hundred Jews, mainly ship owners and glassmakers, lived in Tyre, and about the same number in Acre. In places like Hebron, Ramla, Bethlehem, and Beit Jibrin their numbers could be counted on a single hand. All in all, the Jewish population of the Latin Kingdom was fewer than two thousand. They were poor and isolated—and by the European occupiers they were reviled.

"They have become weak and unwarlike even as women," wrote the Bishop of Acre about the Jews, "and it is said that they have a flux of blood every month. God has smitten them in the hinder parts and put them to a perpetual shame. The Arabs among whom they dwell hate and despise them more than the Christians. They work with their own hands at the vilest and roughest trades. Yet they are not murdered by the Arabs any more than they are by the Christians, for the Lord keeps them for a time like a log from the forest to be burned in winter. They remind us of Christ's death. . . ."

Elsewhere in the Near East, especially in Babylonia, Jews were prominent in numbers and in wealth and in stature. They were often found as the goldsmiths and dyers of silk, the tanners and bankers, and they were the merchants who dominated the trade between Asia, Africa, and Europe. More than three thousand lived in Damascus and two thousand in Palmyra. Baghdad was the home of the Head of the Diaspora, the Prince of the Captivity who claimed to be descended from King David and who paraded through the city in silk as his minions commanded the crowds to part and make way for "Our Lord, the Son of David." Much farther to the east in Samarkand there were fifty thousand Jews. In Alexandria, Egypt, there were about three thousand, and in Cairo another two thousand who worshipped in two synagogues and had a president whose legitimacy was recognized by Muslim authority. Thus the connection to Palestine and Jerusalem for the Jews of the Orient was sentimental rather than actual.

In Saladin's empire if they were not exactly equals, Jews were certainly tolerated and widely appreciated. They fell into the broad category of nonbelievers, finding themselves lumped together with Christians and other non-Muslims. These *dhimmis*, "the protected ones" as they were called, were considered to be wards or clients of the state. The indignities they suffered were benign. They were not permitted to ride horses or mules, only donkeys. This rule extended to distinguished practitioners in medicine or government service. A number of Jewish doctors even treated Saladin himself. In general, he was well satisfied with the care of these learned men, except once when a Jewish doctor prescribed wine as a remedy for the colic from which the Sultan suffered. Since the consumption of liquor was forbidden under Muslim law, he ignored this medical advice.

It was natural, therefore, that among Saladin's early far-reaching pronouncements after his capture of Jerusalem was the call to Jews to return to their Holy City. He could remember with some sentiment that Jews had fought alongside Muslims in the defense of Jerusalem against the first Crusaders nine decades earlier. He wished to return the city to its status before the Western invasion, and that included restoring the city's diverse population before the Crusade invasion.

"Bid Jerusalem take heart in rebirth. All the seed of Ephraim who desire may return in mirth, who are left to Mosul and Egypt's dearth, and those dispersed to the uttermost ends of the earth. May all sides gather unto her and settle within her border."

This was how the Jewish poet Judah Al-Harizi remembered Saladin's proclamation, and it spread joy throughout the Diaspora. From all parts of the Near East and from the Magreb a motley group of Jewish immigrants streamed into Palestine and into their Holy City. A new Jewish quarter was established in the southern part of Jerusalem.

If Saladin's opening was noble, it was also practical. Apart from the conquering Muslim soldiers, Jerusalem had been rendered a ghost town. The Roman *cardo* was silent; the markets of the spices and of cloth were empty; even the street of the *mal cuisine*, that horrible-smelling place of raw and cooked and putrid meat, was starting to smell better for its emptiness. If any life was to be breathed back into the city, it needed a rapid infusion of new citizens. The Christian conquerors in 1099 had faced exactly the same problem. After the massacre of the Muslim and Jewish citizens, the city had been so depopulated that its inhabitants had been reduced to the few dwellers of a single street. The Christian masters had gone to considerable trouble to import Christians living in harsh conditions in Arabia. Similarly, after the

Muslim recapture of Edessa in 1144 Saladin's predecessor, Zengy, had moved some three hundred Jewish families into that city to replace the Christians who had fled.

The great Muslim Sultan now became a hero to the Jews. To them God had stirred up the spirit of Saladin. He had besieged Jerusalem, and "the Lord gave it unto his hand."

Saladin remained in Jerusalem for a month, presiding over the details of his occupation. Forsaking the grand spaces of the city's palaces, he took up residence in a small mosque called Al-Khanagah, dedicated to his God, "the most compassionate, the most merciful," not far from the Holy Sepulcher and the Via Dolorosa. Instead of spacious meeting rooms and banquet halls, his imperial office consisted of two dimly lit rooms where there was scarcely enough space for six men to sit in a circle. It was as if by this show of humility he was intent to avoid distraction and the corruption that his great military victories might induce.

He set about with determination to reinforce the walls and refurbish the moats, while he initiated vigorous efforts to restore the Muslim character to the city. As fast as the money was collected from the departing Christians, he dispensed it to his soldiers and emirs, to jurists and holy men and members of the mystical Muslim cult known as the dervishes. On the Sultan's orders the Patriarch's palace on the northwestern corner of the Holy Sepulcher was turned over to the dervishes for a hospice and prayer hall. The dervishes, in turn, named their new facility after the Sultan, the *khanqat Salahiyya*. In the eastern section of the city not far from the Gate of Jehoshaphat, through which Jesus had first entered the city on a donkey, Saladin appropriated one of the most elaborate Crusader churches, the convent of St. Anne's, and ordered it to be converted into a *madrasa*, or school for advanced study in Islamic law and theology. This, too, would be named for him, the *El-Madrasa es Salahiyya*. And as the Templar headquarters in the Temple Mount had been purified and reconverted to its original use, so the great Hospital of St. John in the Muristan section south of the Holy Sepulcher was transformed into a place of scholarly and religious contemplation.

For Saladin there was no time for rest. His advisers hounded him. His treasurers were distraught over the squandering of the Christian tax, and his military advisers called upon him to press the attack on the remaining coastal strongholds before the army melted away for the winter. The Christians will not draw back their hands from their possessions until those hands are cut off, one adviser wrote. Saladin's own chroniclers questioned his generosity.

"Every time he seizes a Christian stronghold such as Acre, Ascalon, or Jerusalem, Saladin allows the enemy soldiers and knights to seek refuge in Tyre, a city that has thus become virtually impregnable," wrote the scribe Ibn al Athir. "Ought we not to say that it is Saladin himself who organizes the defense of Tyre against his own army?"

On October 30 the legions of Islam finally left their Noble Sanctuary.

CHAPTER TWELVE

# ḥEATHENS IN THINE INHERITANCE

✠

IN NOVEMBER OF 1187 THE ARCHBISHOP OF TYRE Josias hastily boarded a ship in his eastern Mediterranean town and set out on a westerly course for Sicily. As befitted his sad mission, his galley's sails were dyed black. He could not be sure that when he was ready to return, the see of Tyre would still be in Christian hands. For Tyre was the last, vulnerable enclave of the Latin Kingdom of Jerusalem that had been established nine decades before in the First Crusade. For the present, Tyre had survived the furious assault of the infidels only because of a stout Templar defense. But no one could be sure how long it could hold out.

Besides his own recollections Josias carried with him the salacious and incendiary propaganda about the catastrophe, including a cartoon of Jesus being struck by an Arab, with blood running down the Savior's face and the inscription "This is the Messiah, struck by Muhammad, the Prophet of the Muslims, who has wounded and killed Him." He also carried a letter from the Master of the Temple, Gerard de Ridefort, who lived only through the grace of the Sultan. The Master's plaintive missive conveyed to the Christian world of Europe news at which the sun and the moon were "astounded."

"With how many and how great calamities, our sins so requiring it, the anger of God has lately permitted us to be whipped. We are unable, O sad fate! either in writing or in the language of tears to express. . . ." He provided details of Muslims swarming like ants. And then he issued his appeal: "Deign with all possible speed to bring succor to ourselves and to Christianity, all but ruined in the East, that so through the aid of God and the exalted merits of your brotherhood, supported by your assistance, we may be enabled to save the remainder of those cities. Farewell."

The idea was growing in the Christian world that the collapse of the Latin Kingdom had been due not so much to the power of Saladin as to the decadence of the Christians themselves. Was it not true that always before, even when Christian forces were outnumbered, they had prevailed in battle—especially so when the True Cross had been brought into the fray? Now their own God had permitted them to be scourged and defeated. Their own sins had caused the disaster and even required it. Saladin had become their Lord's terrible instrument of wrath. The Christian God had used the infidel to teach his own believers a lesson. Even as this notion took hold, the lore provided a rebuke to the wrathful instrument himself. It was imagined that after the Battle of Hattin a court jester appeared before Saladin.

"God has judged the Christians worthy of reproof and correction for their crimes," said the jester, "and he has chosen thee, O prince, as his agent in this matter. But sometimes a worldly father in anger seizes a dirty stick out of the mire, and when he has chastised his erring sons, he throws it back among the filth where he found it."

Pity the poor jester. There was, of course, no such a thing as a jester in Saladin's court, but even if there were, it is hard to imagine the great Sultan standing for such an impertinence. Still, the story found an eager and receptive audience in Europe.

In early December, Archbishop Josias reached the shores of Sicily, bringing with him the news that astounded the heavens. The Norman King, William II, received word of the calamity with such shock that he retreated for four days in sackcloth. On the fifth day he emerged determined to write all the potentates of Europe urging upon them a new Crusade, and with the 79th Psalm on his lips: "O God, the heathen are come into thine inheritance; Thy holy temple have they defiled; they have laid Jerusalem on heaps."

In Rome the shock was even more profound. Pope Urban III had died only a few days before Archbishop Josias arrived, and the Vatican was in the throes of an election. The new Pope was Gregory VIII. Brokenhearted though he was, the new Pope took up the call to crusade with vigor. The Christian world must take some responsibility, he said, for the loss of Jerusalem and the True Cross, for Christians had ignored papal entreaties of the past, and Christian princes had preferred their petty wars to the cause of the Savior.

Gregory threw his heart and soul into the cause. "Every person of ordinary discretion is well able to appreciate both the greatness of the danger and the fierceness of the barbarians who thirst for Christian blood," he said. "The goal of those who profane the holy places is nothing short of sweeping away the name of God from the earth." Noble men with contrite heart and humble spirit who would undertake the labor of this journey could expect indulgence for their sins and life eternal.

With his tortured appeal the Pope set out for Pisa and Genoa, the two great sea powers of the Mediterranean, to reconcile them in their differences and turn them united to the cause of Crusade. But the frail, heartsick Pontiff died from his exertions only two months after his investiture. Clement III succeeded him. This new Pope picked up the great cause vigorously, urging the princes of Europe to set aside their antagonisms and heed the call of Christ. The Vatican focused on England, since it was the wealthiest and mightiest of the European nations, and urged the English bishops to rally the poor and the powerful alike, lest "the unspeakable progeny of Ishmael" succeed in this unholy robbery. Clement dispatched Josias to Gisors, where the Kings of England and France were scheduled to meet early in 1188, so that the Archbishop of Tyre could make a personal appeal.

When Richard, the Prince of Aquitaine and the future King of England, heard this appeal in early December 1187, he fell to his knees and took the cross. He was the first Christian prince of Europe to do so.

On January 21, 1188, Henry and Philip came together once again beneath the elm at Gisors. Richard remained in the South of France, but the Kings had heard already what dramatic effect the calamitous news from the East had had on the future King. Now, the Kings listened at Gisors to Archbishop Josias about the loss of the Holy Land. His anger and despair were great, and later those sentiments would be reduced to a sad and haunting lament entitled *"Sede Syon, in Pulvere"*:

"Sit, Jerusalem, in the dust; sprinkle ashes on your head, put on the sackcloth. In the place where stood the firm foundation of hope, charity lacks a banner and faith privilege. In the heart of Jerusalem jackals give suck to puppy-dogs today. They cast the stones of the sanctuary into the marketplace, and Egyptians destroy the labors of the Hebrews."

At the archbishop's plea Henry and Philip also fell to their knees and took the cross. It was agreed that the French would wear red crosses on their outer surcoats, while the English would wear white crosses and the Flemish would wear green. The two Kings agreed to set off for the Holy Land in a year's time. It was at this conference that the idea of the Saladin tax was conceived, and it would be applied in both France and England.

For this brief moment it seemed as if the papacy's political motive behind its promulgation of Holy War had worked. Once again a Crusade was useful in diverting the raw energies of the European nobles from their pointless, destructive conflicts with one another. A common enemy should unite them into a glorious, holy enterprise for Christ. To stop the small, petty feuds on the European Continent and to harness the warring energies of the knights in defense of the Holy Land seemed like a winning idea. Moreover, it allowed the nobles to continue their love of personal combat, but for a good and lofty cause.

Because he was old and tiring of these unending conflicts, Henry was in an accommodating mood. At last, he was ready to come to an accommodation with the young King Philip and his advisers about the Vexin. The castle of Gisors and its surroundings were to be the dowry for Philip's beautiful half sister, Alais, who had been promised as Richard's wife in 1161, when Richard was four years old. Again Philip renewed his demand that the marriage take place.

The transcendent spirit of holy vengeance did not last many days after the

January 21, 1188, conference at Gisors. Soon enough the parties reverted to their petty vengeances. Henry's taking of the cross had been a transparent ruse to rid himself of his younger tormentors, and he had no real intention of going to the Holy Land himself. He had more than done his part for the cause, he felt, by sending his grudge money to the Templars and Hospitalers twice each year for his regrettable role in the death of Thomas à Becket. The old King receded to England and into the arms of Alais. But he still longed to control the Vexin, which Philip held in escrow as the dowry for Alais's long-delayed betrothal to Richard. By July, Henry's frustration burst into open hostility and even into blasphemy.

"Why should I worship Christ?" he bellowed. "Why should I deign to honor Him who takes my earthly honor and allows me to be confounded by a mere boy?"

In August, royalty was again under the elm at Gisors, until matters disintegrated and swords were drawn. In a fit of rage Philip had the famous elm cut down. When Henry saw the stump, he declared war. But he did not have the heart or the health for war. Prodded toward a settlement by Rome, the Kings met again in November, when old Henry was shocked to see Richard's intimacy with Philip. Their affection confirmed the rumors for the old King that his warrior-son was a homosexual. Yet again Richard demanded that he be proclaimed heir to the English throne. Yet again Henry spat out his refusal.

"Now at last I believe what heretofore has seemed incredible," Henry hissed, but he was not as surprised as he sounded. After Richard swore homage to Philip for his lands in France, they rode off into the sunset.

Rome was appalled at this new outbreak of internecine warfare, and a papal envoy was dispatched north to turn everyone's attention back to the common enemy in the East. The Pope's ambassador threatened an interdict against France and excommunication for anyone who did not cease local hostilities and did not rally to the desperate cause of Christendom. But the envoy was treated roughly. Philip Augustus sneered that Rome wanted peace only because it "smelled" English gold. And Richard had a ferocious temper tantrum in which he nearly pulled his sword on the legate.

Six months later Richard joined Philip in a military assault against Henry. They surrounded the old King in his birthplace of Le Mans and burned down the town. For this deed Henry placed the full blame on his third son. "You have vilely taken away the city I loved best on earth, the city where I was born and bred, the city where my father is buried," he shouted from a distant hill as he halted his speedy retreat to view the flames. "I will pay you back as best I can. I will rob you of the thing you love the best."

Richard set out in full gallop after his father. To slow the pursuit, one of Henry's lieutenants, William Marshall, who had been Richard's jousting tutor as a youth, tarried behind and caught Richard unprepared in an ambush.

"By God's legs, Marshall," Richard shouted in fear as he recoiled from the great fighting master. "Do not kill me. I wear no armor."

"May the devil kill you then," Marshall shouted back, "for I will not." And with that he thrust his spear deep into the bowels of Richard's horse.

In a few more weeks his foes finally caught Henry, exhausted and near death and deserted by all but a few flunkies, at a Templar house at Ballan. His disloyal servants had made off with the last of his treasure, "for it is true," wrote his herald, "that just as flies seek honey, wolves the carcass, and ants corn, this crew followed not the man, but his spoils." As his body shook with the death throes, he assented to final humiliations. He proclaimed Richard his heir, freed Eleanor of Aquitaine from her tower in Winchester, and gave up Alais so that Richard could marry her when he returned from the Crusade. He lost strategic castles in the border land and was forced to disavow his claim to the Vexin.

Richard knelt by his father's deathbed and wept, for he was not proud of his hostile actions against his father, and they would haunt him for the rest of his life. Henry was unmoved. As a thunderclap shook the house, he turned his head to his son and spewed out his last venom: "God grant that I may not die until I have had a fitting revenge on you."

This was the last gasp of a dying man. He was carried off to Chinon, where he passed away a few days later. His body was then carried to Fontevrault for burial at the Church of the Nuns, and this resting place among the nuns seemed to be a fulfillment of the prophecy uttered by a Cistercian monk the year before: "The womb of his wife shall swell against him, and in torments he shall suffer torments, and among the veiled women he shall be as one wearing the veil." Richard appeared at the funeral and was overcome with grief and guilt. When the son approached the bier of his father, so it was reported by Gerald of Wales, the chronicler of these events, blood burst from the nostrils of the corpse. This was a sinister and terrifying miracle, which suggested that Richard had somehow killed his father.

## 2

# A LION CROWNED

At the death of his father, Richard traveled briefly to England for his coronation. The English people eagerly anticipated the arrival of their strapping young king-to-be. Poetry and song filled the air. One song spoke of Richard as "a man mature in heart, yet young in years." The people should make ready "to receive the flower of chivalry whose word has a truth that comes from the heart."

Determined that her son begin his reign properly, the liberated Eleanor prepared the way. Barnstorming from town to town and castle to castle across southern England and emptying the prisons of her husband's political prisoners, since "in her own person she had learned by experience that confinement is distasteful to mankind and that it is a most delightful refreshment to the spirits to be liberated therefrom," she cultivated a hero's welcome.

With its great pageantry the ceremony took place on September 3, 1189, at Westminster. The air was redolent of hope and a sense of renewal. The troubadour of the age, Bertran de Born, expressed the sense of time with impish delight. "I like it when I see power change hands, and when the old leave their houses to the young—and a man can shove so many children onto his family that at least one should amount to something. Then I like it, because the world is renewed better than by flowers and bird songs. And whoever can change his lady or his lord, old for young, really ought to."

At the coronation of this ideal young King, gold was everywhere: four golden candlesticks, three golden swords, gold spurs, the royal scepter of gold, the King's slippers embroidered in gold, a golden cross, and, of course, the crown of gold, festooned with precious jewels. His coronation seal, carried by his brother John, depicted three lions, surmounted by a crown, set against a background of heraldic red, and bearing the inscription *"Corona et scutum bellipotentis regis Ricardi."* At the altar the prince swore three separate oaths, including the promise to cast out the evildoers against the church. He was stripped to the waist, whereupon the Archbishop of Canterbury anointed him with sacred oil before he was dressed in royal vestments and the crown of jewels was placed on his head. At the sumptuous coronation banquet after the ceremony only broad-shouldered men reveled in the accession of this glo-rious young King. No ladies were invited.

Beyond the lingering strains of the *Te Deum* and the procession of bishops and abbots, barons and earls, apart from the silken hoods and robes, the in-cense and the holy water, an ugly incident marred the spectacle. The trouble began at the bachelor's banquet after the coronation, when Jewish elders came to offer gifts to the new monarch. At the door they were barred and at-tacked, stripped, whipped, and thrown into the street. In the throat of the mob was a scandalous, anti-Semitic chant entitled *"Purgator Criminum"*:

> He *who purges sins*
> *Came forth from the right hand of the Father*
> *To heal the wounds of mankind.*
> *Acknowledge the Lord, O wretched Judah!*
> *The Old Law has come to an end;*
> *The old order has passed away.*
> *Nor is the rite of offerings cleansing sins,*
> *Nor the letter of the Law.*
>
> *O heart of a foolish people, harder than iron.*
> *You stare back at the dregs and do not see the oil.*
> *In eating the husk you do not taste the kernel;*
> *From choice grain you produce only bran bread,*
> *Nor do you fill your granary;*
> *You value barley higher than the mystic grain.*

One member of the deputation, Benedict of York, got away with his life only by agreeing to be baptized a Christian in the Church of the Innocents. The mob moved to the Jewish quarter of London and began to burn down the houses of Jews. Only when the fire spread to Christian property did the authorities move in.

The following day the new King was without sympathy for the Jewish victims, but he hanged a few culprits who had torched the nearby Christian houses. Then, perhaps as a curiosity, he ordered the new convert into his presence.

"Who are you?" the King demanded.

"I am Benedict of York, one of your Jews, sire," the wretched man replied.

"Did you not tell me that he is a Christian?" the King bellowed at the Archbishop of Canterbury.

"Yes, my lord."

"What are we to do with him?" Richard asked.

"If he does not choose to be a Christian, let him be a man of the devil," the archbishop snapped.

In relating this story, a chronicler of Richard's heroics, Roger of Hoveden, a Yorkshireman himself and a justice itinerant for the forests, invoked Proverbs 26: "As a dog returneth to his vomit, so a fool returneth to his folly." Richard's rank anti-Semitism grew into overt sadism. To him a good joke was to extract the teeth of Jews in a lingering process.

In succeeding months, as Crusader frenzy swept the island, Richard did little to stop the accompanying anti-Semitism, other than to send a perfunctory letter to the shires. After he left the country, his admonitions were promptly ignored. More attacks on Jews followed in York and Norwich, to the point that one commentator remarked, "Many of those who were hastening to go to Jerusalem determined first to rise against the Jews." In the days before Easter of 1190, the Christians of York drove some five hundred Jews into the tower of York. With a ranting crowd outside calling for their necks, an elder rose and said, "Men of Israel, listen to my advice. It is better that we should kill one another than fall into the hands of the enemies of our law." Not long after, they committed mass suicide. Benedict was probably among them.

One war correspondent, a monk from Winchester called Richard of Devizes, celebrated the passion of the massacres as just revenge and regretted only that his own town had been slow to join the pogrom. "On the very day of the coronation, about that solemn hour in which the Son was immolated to the Father, a sacrifice of the Jews to their father, the devil, was commenced in the city of London. The holocaust could scarcely be accomplished in a day. Other cities of the kingdom emulated the faith of the Londoners, and with like devotion dispatched their bloodsuckers with blood to hell. Only Winchester mildly spared its vermin. The city was unwilling to cast up violently the indigestion which oppressed its body. It was careful for its bowels, until it should be possible for it, at a convenient time for cure, to cast out the whole cause of the disease once and for all."

With this scourge corrupting the nobility of his start, Richard went about raising his army. But not all was corruption. Later the romance would be told that before he left for the Continent, Richard staged a three-day tournament at Salisbury. This romance was an adaptation of the story of Lancelot and Guinevere, except in this case the knight in different disguises would fight not for the hand of the lovely lady but for the palm of the Holy Land. The purpose of the tournament was to discover who were the bravest warriors in England. From the best fighters Richard proposed to choose his right-hand men.

Since only he was able to test their grit and mettle, the King himself was said to have assumed three disguises for his jousts. In the first his armor was black. The crest on his black helmet was a raven with its beak open wide and a bell around its neck. The raven signified patience in the face of hard work and pain, and the bell stood for the Christian Church. In this heroic garb Richard as a knight-adventurous rode into the lists and was opposed by three knights, one of whom he killed with his fourteen-foot lance along with his horse; the other two he unhorsed.

The Black Knight then disappeared into the forest and returned as a red knight. This time his helmet sported a red hound with a tail flowing to the ground, signifying the heathen hounds who debased the Holy Land. As the Red Knight, Richard fared less well when he found himself pitted against one of the great fighters in the land. After losing his footing in his stirrups from a bold thrust, he retreated, a bit dazed, into the forest.

Now he returned as the White Knight on a great white horse. On his shoulder was pinned a red cross, and the crest on his helmet was a white dove, signifying the Holy Land itself. This time a terrific blow from a mace knocked him senseless, and the brave cavalier had to be carried to his palace. Inevitably, as this application of the Arthurian cycle goes, his last two opponents became his chief lieutenants and swore a secret oath of fealty to the King.

Ten months later he found himself at Vézelay, with his Crusader army in place, side by side once again with Philip Augustus, with whom, it seemed, his destiny and his emotions had been intertwined from the start.

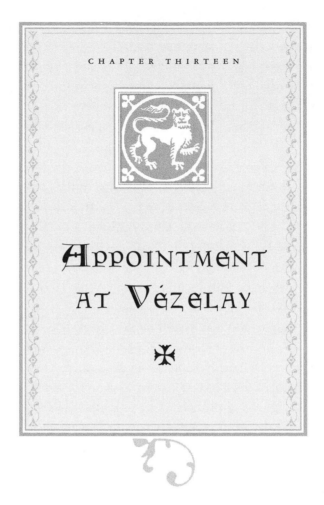

# CHAPTER THIRTEEN

# Appointment at Vézelay

✠

I N THOSE PLACID BURGUNDIAN FIELDS IN EARLY July 1190, King Richard cut the most magnificent figure. In his outward splendor he was the epitome of the noble and chivalrous knight. His frame was tall, lithe, and graceful, with the long legs and arms of an athletic warrior. On his head he wore an oblong helmet of Rhenish style, over his trunk was a hauberk of chain mail covered with a white surcoat bearing a red cross, and cinched around his waist was his heavy two-handed battle sword with its golden grip. In his left hand he held his battle shield, appointed with a single lion rampant toward the left against a brilliant red background.

There was about him a certain nervous trembling that stemmed from a rare form of malarial fever he had contracted in his youth, and it added to his fearsome aspect. Observers saw in these shakes an indication of the fierce workings of an overactive mind. It was somehow lionlike, "yea, more than a lion," said his chronicler Gerald of Wales, "while thus almost continually trembling, he remained intrepid in his determination to make the whole world tremble before him."

It was easy to imagine this awesome warrior cutting a man in two with a single slash of his blade, for, said another observer, "no arm was better adapted than his for drawing a sword, nor more powerful to strike with it." After fifteen years of fratricidal warfare across Brittany, Anjou, Maine, Poitou, Normandy, and Aquitaine—the last of which had been against his own formidable father—the stories of Richard's daring and strength were legion, as were the stories of his cruelty, his generosity, and his poetic sensibility. His troubadours claimed for him the valor of Hector, the magnanimity of Achilles, the stature of Alexander and Roland, the liberality of Titus, the eloquence of Nestor, and the prudence of Ulysses.

Above all he projected the air of command. He was the hero of Europe. Here was a real prince, the greatest warrior of the Continent, the very prince who had repulsed the efforts of his father, Henry II, to disinherit him and the efforts of his brothers to undermine his control of Aquitaine; who had prevailed over the past ten years in the constant skirmishes between the barons and dukes of Aquitaine; who was the favorite of his famous and ill-treated mother, the incomparable Eleanor of Aquitaine.

At the age of thirty-three, Richard's hair was still strawberry blond, his complexion ruddy. This might have been the only thing about him that seemed vaguely English. To this thoroughly Continental figure, French was the natural language of the chase, as well as the true tongue of love and war. England had merely been the easiest part of his realm to acquire and maintain, and he viewed its immense wealth as the cash cow for his Crusade. Without qualm he put high church offices, lordships, earldoms, sheriffdoms, castles, towns, and manors up for sale. From each city in England two saddle horses and one workhorse were requisitioned for his Holy War.

"I would sell London if I could find a buyer," the King remarked as he raised his Crusader army.

Upon the backs of the English, including their clergy, he had imposed a direct tax known as the Saladin tax. It was a three-year levy of one-tenth the subject's income. Each parish across the land collected the tithe, and those who did not pay were excommunicated. Those who joined the Crusade were exempt from the tax, and this, of course, was a powerful tool of recruitment. One knight was known to have sold his wife and all her possessions to raise his tax. Despite its noble intent, the tax, like all taxes, was not popular. Roger of Wendover called it "a violent extortion which veiled the vice of rapacity under the name of charity and alarmed the priesthood as well as the people."

With a vast array of colorful knightly pavilions in the foreground and Alps rising in the distance beneath the warm summer sky, the host was a glorious sight. The encampment gave the appearance of a temporary city. "There you see the martial youth of different nations equipped for war appearing able to subdue the whole length of the earth, and judge no place too hard or no enemy too fierce to conquer," wrote the chief chronicler of the Third Crusade. "They would never yield to wrong while they could aid and assist each other by the help of their valor."

In the sea of pennants and steel, the royal standards of two Kings were the most prominent. The red banner of Richard I, Plantagenet monarch of England and Aquitaine, was the standard of St. George: three elongated golden lions against a field of scarlet. This contrasted to the banner of Philip Augustus, Capetian King of France: a brace of golden fleur-de-lis against a brilliant field of azure blue. Their knights faced the Kings in the front rank. Mounted on their huge fighting horses, the best of which were French *turquemans*, many nobles wore proudly the tangible symbol of their solemn ceremony of taking the cross: the white smock with its prominent red cross sewn front and back. This surcoat covered a full body suit of chain mail—the hauberk, as it was known—whose links joined to form a single garment from head to foot that might stop the thrust of an Arabian arrow or at least blunt the point of an infidel's lance. Their conical and pot helmets sparkled in the sun, as did the points of their spears, to which were fastened the pennants of their noble houses. On one arm they carried kite-shaped shields whose points extended to their stirrups and protected their extremities. At their sides were their squires, who attended their persons, their weapons, and their steeds, and who stood ready to follow their masters into battle.

Behind the knights were the less-armored ranks of the foot soldiers and the engineers. Among these were a considerable number of holy men "who migrated from the cloister to the camp, and, exchanging the cowl for the cuirass, and the library for the study of arms, showed themselves truly Christ's soldiers." The crossbowmen in Richard's corps stood out, for the King had a fondness for the spring-fired crossbow called the arbalest. In deploying this powerful weapon, Richard was violating the will of Rome, for there had been papal decrees against its use, as if such a deadly device on the field of chivalry was immoral. But Richard fancied its range and penetrating fire and could be sure that his Oriental enemies had nothing remotely like these ballistic bolts and darts. His crossbowmen occupied a special place in the vanguard of his light infantry. In his battles across his realm in the previous decade he had relied upon them mightily in his battle tactics. The arbalest also came in a larger version called the ballista, a weapon that turned the concept of the mechanical bow into a small artillery piece. The story of the two enemy soldiers who had once been skewered with a single bolt from a ballista appealed to Richard's sense of humor, for it had become possible to pick the battlefield victims up with one hoist as if they were being carried directly to the kitchen for barbecuing.

The scene at Vézelay was enough to swell the heart and inspire the troubadour. Love, nobility, piety, and chivalry transported the army.

> You who love with true love
> Awake! Do not sleep!
> The lark brings us day
> And tells us in this hideaway
> That the day of peace has come;
> That God, by his kindness
> Will give to those who for love of him
> Take the cross and on account of what they do
> Suffer pain night and day
> So that he will see who truly loves him.

This was the host that God had stolen from Satan. "He took them clear and fair/'Twas for His sake they gathered there." In the abbey of Vézelay the bones of Mary Magdalene were enshrined, for the saint had come to southern France after Christ's death to spread the Gospel, so the lore went, and in the Maritime Alps she had died a hermit. The aura of the saint imparted a pious serenity to this solemn mobilization and sanctified it. By tradition, Vézelay was the starting point for a Crusade.

As their armies came together at Vézelay, the monarchies of England and France had become interwoven in tenuous, complicated ways, more complicated than most understood. In this new, Third Crusade their sons by different spouses were determined to avoid the mistakes of their parents in the Second Crusade. Richard and Philip Augustus were filled with passions larger than pilgrim's love. On the military side their challenge was more daunting. The entire Holy Land except the city of Tyre had been lost, not simply the important city of Edessa. Syria and Egypt were united and now had added Palestine to the Muslim empire. And in Saladin they faced the greatest Oriental general since Cyrus the Great.

Unmarried and in his prime, the French King had a delicate disposition. Richard knew him to be high-strung: quick to anger and quick to forgive. He was uncomfortable with risk, unenthusiastic about Richard's passions for hunting, tournaments, and poetry. While Richard composed his verses, Philip had failed to learn Latin and was therefore functionally illiterate. Next to Richard's magnificent Spanish horse, Philip preferred only the gentlest steeds. As the poet Bertran de Born expressed their differing visions, "Sir Richard hunts lions with rabbits, so not a one remains on the plain or in the woods. From now on, he counts on capturing the great eagles with kites and putting the goshawk to scorn with a harrier. . . . King Philip hunts sparrows and tiny birds with falcons, and his men don't dare tell him the truth, that, little by little, they are going downhill."

Though he was younger, Philip had been a king ten years longer. While he paled as a warrior and sporting man next to Richard, his ten years on the throne had necessarily involved considerable military exertions, especially with the troublesome Flemish. His reign also had shown him to be a cunning and determined diplomat as well as a brilliant administrator. If Richard looked his best on a horse, golden sword held high ready to strike, Philip looked his best in a brocaded royal chair, gnawing pensively on a green hazel wand and pondering his foreign relations. "The French King goes about so daintily that I am afraid he may spring on me," wrote Bertran de Born. The French King was often sickly and delusional. He was paranoid about his enemies and, compared to Richard's bawdiness, prudish in his speech and prissy about entertainments.

Richard took every opportunity to shock his intimate friend with the profane and frivolous songs and jokes of Aquitaine, delivered saucily in his southern drawl. That Philip was humorless and simpering made it all the more sport. Once, when Philip heard a knight swear in a gambling game, he had the coarse fellow dunked three times and then issued a proclamation against swearing for the entire land. Richard, by contrast, often went well beyond the oath "By St. George!" to swear upon Jesus' private parts and took great joy in insulting his clerics, knowing they could not respond.

Together they were something like the peacock and the crow in the medieval couplet in which the crow dresses up as a peacock, is stripped and found out, whereupon the peacock remarks, "He who climbs higher than he should falls from higher than he would like."

Beneath the magnificent spectacle of this colorful international army of Christ, spread out on the Burgundian fields like the flowers of spring, intrigue and conflict and suspicion swirled in the air. Even the chronicler of this heroic pilgrimage remarked upon the currents: "That immense army glowed with ardor and combined military discipline and goodwill. It could have been invincible to all the world. But it was riven with disputes and undermined by internal discord. Ties of fellowship were violated. A house divided against itself is made desolate."

In their personal dealings the Kings displayed the peevishness of ex-lovers. So long as Philip was the only King, his power counterbalanced Richard's charisma. Now their roles had been reversed. Along with Richard's dashing presence came his larger army, his more powerful fleet, his greater treasury, and his superior reputation as a warrior. He overshadowed Philip entirely, and Philip resented it. This resentment seemed to goad Richard even more to preen and strut before the French King, to show up his ally at every turn.

"Had their love lasted," lamented a chronicler, "they would have been honored for all time, and Christendom would have been exalted."

Instead they whined and chided and sniped at one another. Still, in their two days together at Vézelay they did manage to gloss over their personal differences enough to conclude a solemn treaty. They pledged a lasting peace, abjuring all conflict between England and France while they were in the service of the Lord. They promised to support one another in need and to act in good faith. Their respective realms were declared to be sacrosanct, so long as they were on their joint military pilgrimage. If one of them should be killed, the other was to take charge of the victim's army and redouble its efforts for Christ. He who broke this sacred pledge was subject to excommunication, and this punishment was stamped with the seal of their archbishops.

There remained the issue of Alais. For this, Richard uttered the obligatory words, "I would ask that you should put off the marriage until I come back. I swear to marry your sister within forty days of my return." For Philip that would have to do for the moment.

With these promises committed to paper, they reverently received the scrip and staff of the pilgrim from their holy men. On June 24, 1190, the feast day celebrating the Nativity of St. John the Baptist, their armies broke camp and set off. The plan was to separate after they crossed the Rhone at Lyons. Philip was to march to Genoa, where he had retained the services of the Genoese fleet for the eastern passage, and Richard was to march to Marseille to greet his English fleet. Then they would sail to Messina in Sicily and meet up for a final conclave before they sailed as one for the Holy Land. Through St. Leonard of Curbeny, Mulins, near St. Mary de Bois, the champions of Christ marched, more than a hundred thousand men in all. In Philip's cortège were many of the great men of France: Count Philip of Flanders, Count Henry of Champagne, and Count Stephen of Sancerre among them. Richard's troops joyously followed the scarlet standard with its royal lions of England.

Their ardor was apparent. Rome boasted that "it was no longer a question who should take the cross, but who had not yet taken it." To the deafening sound of the hooves, the rustle of a thousand banners, the flash of steel, the creaking of the wheels under heavy load was added their chant:

> *Lignum crucis, Signum ducis, Sequitur exercitus*
> *Quod non cessit, Sed praecessit, In vi sancti spiritus.**

The villagers turned out in force to cheer them and to weep. The poets sang their praise:

> *Oh, God of Majesty . . .*
> *These youths, where were they born and got?*
> *Gaze on their faces flushed and hot!*
> *Think on the sadness of their mothers,*
> *Their parents, sons, and brothers,*
> *Their friends and all who do belong*
> *To those that make this mighty throng!*

---

*Behind the wood of the Cross, the banner of the Chieftain
Follows the Army which has never given way
But marches in the strength of the Holy Spirit.

While the troubadours sang of valor, they also wept for young men marching off to war and cursed the "race of slanderers" for bringing this fate down upon them. "The new season, the month of May/the violet and the nightingale summon me to sing/and my gentle heart offers me such a sweet gift of love/that I dare not refuse" went a song of the fabled troubadour, Le Chatelain de Coucy, who himself was among them. "May God allow me to ascend to such high honor/that the one who has captured my heart and mind/ I might hold her just once, naked in my arms/before I go overseas."

At Lyons the Rhone River halted their advance. With the river swollen by summer rain, the Kings tarried to make an inspection before they passed over and camped in the meadows outside the town. When the main body of the army tramped over the wooden bridge, it sagged and gave way under the weight, and more than a hundred men fell into the torrent. This occasioned a three-day delay while Richard took charge and commandeered a flotilla of skiffs from up and down the river. Then the armies split as planned and went their separate ways, part bound for Marseille, part for Genoa. Along the way through Provence, Richard picked up a legion of converts, despite the common saying "Franks to battle, Provençaux to table."

CHAPTER FOURTEEN

# RED SAILS

✠

M EANWHILE, SHORTLY AFTER EASTER, IN THE year of the Christian Lord 1190, ten warships of the King of England gathered at the port of Dartmouth and began their pilgrim journey to the Holy Land. After passing a headland called Godestart (meaning "good start"), they charted a course across the Sea of Poitou for Lisbon, where they planned to rendezvous with the main body of the fleet. These other ships were coming from ports across England, Brittany, Normandy and Poitou—indeed, from across the whole expanse of the Plantagenet realm in the British Isles and the Continent. Once the main royal fleet gathered in Portugal, its plan was to pass majestically through the Straits of Africa and proceed to Marseille and its reunion with its dashing leader, known as the Lionheart, and his army.

Each of these original ten galleys carried three spare rudders, thirteen anchors, thirty oars, two sails, and three sets of ropes, a captain and a crew of fifteen. They were equipped to carry one hundred well-armed men. In design the warships were long and slender, sturdy enough to manage the high seas, but built to ride low in the water. They had two rows of oars and a pointed spur on the prow, painted with some distinguishing design. The purpose of the prow in battle was to pinion an enemy ship.

The admiral of this fleet was the estimable Robert de Sable. As befitted a holy undertaking, he was accompanied by his holy men, the Archbishop of Auxienne and the Bishop of Bayonne. De Sable was wealthy and of good family, a single man whose wife and son were dead and whose daughters were safely married off. His slate was cleared, therefore, to concentrate entirely on his mission. He was an experienced fighting man and a good administrator and, significantly, he was distantly related to the King himself. Not long after he guided the King's fleet to Palestine, Robert de Sable was to become the Grand Master of the Temple.

For this advance guard of the great Crusade the voyage across the Sea of Poitou proceeded calmly. But when the flotilla entered the Spanish Sea on the holy day of Ascension, a terrible storm struck and scattered the ships broadly across a wide expanse. The holy men fell to their knees and prayed for deliverance. And their prayers were answered. The ghost of Thomas à Becket appeared to them, it was said, not once but three times in three different places.

The ghost of the martyr spoke to the harried warriors: "Be not afraid, for I, Thomas, have been appointed by the Lord as guardian of this fleet of the King of England. If the men of this fleet will guard themselves against sin and repent of their former offenses, the Lord will grant them a prosperous voyage and will direct their footsteps in His paths."

With that the ghost disappeared, the wind died down, and the sea became calm.

Eventually nine of the ten ships limped into the port of Lisbon (the tenth having been blown south to the town of Silva, a village that only the year before had converted to Christianity and was under constant attack from the pagans of Islamic Spain; the local authority therefore seized the Crusader ship and broke it up for a barricade against the heathens). Thus saved by divine Providence, the crews of the remaining ships had much for which to be grateful, and their spirits rose further when a contingent of 63 more ships arrived in Lisbon from various ports of Europe. Not long after this a second battle group of 30 more ships appeared. That brought the royal fleet to 106 ships, including 6 cargo ships. These were the great three-masted galleys known as the camels of the sea, or busses, which had three tiers of oars and carried double gear of provisions and arms as well as more than forty horses.

Inevitably these mercenaries from all over Europe were keyed up and spoiling for a fight. They were certain of their divine protection, and their very overconfidence proved to be too much for their commanders to control. Brawls broke out between the Christian pilgrims and the Portuguese. Looters and scavengers in the Crusader army took advantage of these skirmishes by driving Jews and Muslims from their homes, plundering their property, burning their houses, and raping a number of women. This was scarcely the upright, pious behavior that the ghost of Becket had in mind when he calmed the storm. The gates of Lisbon were closed to the marauders, and more than seven hundred of the most unruly were thrown into prison.

Before the fleet had set sail, the illustrious King of England had made rules for insolent behavior among his soldiers. At his castle on the Loire known as Chinon, before he had departed for the mobilization point of his army at Vézelay, he had promulgated laws of military conduct. If a soldier should kill a man aboard ship, the offender was to be tied to his victim and thrown overboard. If the offense happened on land, the culprit was to be tied to his victim and buried alive. If a soldier should draw blood with his knife, he would lose his hand. If he only punched a fellow soldier without drawing blood, he was to be plunged three times into the sea. If a soldier cursed a comrade, he was to pay an ounce of silver for every instance of abusive language. If a Crusader was convicted of theft, his head was to be shaved "in the manner of a champion" before boiling pitch was poured over the top and pillow feathers scattered on the pitch.

The King's rules did not quite suit the mayhem of Lisbon, however, and these punishments went out the window. No one was tarred and feathered or plunged into the sea, for Robert de Sable knew he would need every able-bodied man for the fight against the Arabian horde. If his men must die, he preferred that their demise take place in war for the name of Jesus Christ. The offenses were overlooked, and the King of Portugal was very much relieved to watch the Crusader fleet disappear over the southern horizon.

With the great promontory of Calpe on the island of Jubaltaria on their left and the African Atlas mountain on their right, the ships glided through the Straits of Africa and past the southern coast of Spain. With infidel Spain behind them, the pilgrims knew that from that point forward in their Mediterranean passage, the lands on their left were Christian and the lands on their right were pagan. That made it even easier in their enterprise to divide the world into good and evil, white and black, Europeans and all others.

Upon this arrival in Marseille on August 22, the chronicles spoke only of the fleet's escape from "the dangerous sand banks and the perils of the terrible rocks, the stormy straits of Africa and all the dangers of the ocean" but did not mention the mayhem. The ennoblement of the endeavor had begun. The gangplanks were thrown down to receive their king, their lord who without rest after his coronation had left behind all the pleasures of his court and, as if chosen by the Lord God, had undertaken a journey so commendable and a work of "so great goodness, so arduous, and so necessary."

But the King was nowhere in sight. In fact, the ever-impatient Richard had arrived in Marseille three weeks earlier and, finding no fleet, had set off down the Italian coast in a commandeered ship for Messina, Sicily.

## 2

## ON TO SICILY

At Marseille on July 31, Richard was disappointed to find no fleet. His ships were still three weeks out to sea, just then passing through the Straits of Africa (though he had no way of knowing this). Since there was no telling how soon they would arrive, the English King quickly grew impatient, for he knew that in a perfect world and with perfect conditions he was only a fifteen-day sail from Palestine. He knew also that a German army, nearly equal in force to the combined British–French army, was stuck, tragically leaderless, somewhere to the north and west of Syria. Still, Richard loitered in the port city for a week, passing the time viewing the jawbone of St. Lazarus and conferring with the black monks in the Abbey of St. Victor. Eventually, he could bear the delay no longer and, hiring two large cargo ships and twenty galleys, he loaded his household troops on board and headed south.

He proceeded slowly, hoping his fleet would overtake him. At Genoa he put in to visit Philip, who was sick in bed. In his delirium Philip requested of Richard the use of five ships for his ongoing journey. As if he could not resist tweaking Philip, Richard offered three, a slight that annoyed Philip as Richard intended. The French King refused the offer. Farther down the coast, past the papal naval bastion of Civita Vecchia, Richard stopped at Ostia near the mouth of the Tiber. There he found another opportunity to annoy his allies. Two papal envoys greeted him warmly and issued an invitation to come to Rome for an audience with Clement III.

With theatrical hauteur Richard waved aside this summons. Ironically, the King despised the very man to whose call to crusade he had been the first to respond. The English monarch was no different from his predecessors in his tensions with Rome over the issue of church and state. Indeed, with a hint of the dispute that had led to the murder of Thomas à Becket nineteen years earlier, Richard began his reign by complaining to the Pope about the independent monks of Canterbury. Characteristically, Richard had dispatched a stiff letter to the Pope containing the threat of violence: "Unless the wisdom of the Apostolic See stand in the gap to crush the haughtiness of these monks," the new King had written, "we will more resolutely lay on them the hands of our royal severity. . . ." This bluster had gotten him nowhere, and other disagreements about various church appointments— including the appointment of his half brother, Geoffrey, to be Archbishop of York—continued the bad feelings.

Instead of hobnobbing with cardinals, the King took to the countryside to take in the sights. He hunted and frolicked along the Amalfi Coast, spent two weeks languishing in Naples and an additional week in Salerno. He was hungry for word of his fleet: Had they arrived safely in Marseille? Were his soldiers loaded on board and bound for Messina? Had there been any mishaps?

Tiring of the confinement of the ship, he rode through Calabria on horseback, ignorant of what was happening elsewhere, stopping by night at the local priories along the way, until he reached the ancient episcopal town of Mileto—and nearly lost his life. The disaster took place when Richard, accompanied by only one knight, was riding through a small, inconspicuous village. There he heard the cry of a hawk escape from a nearby peasant's hut. Since it was against the rules of chivalry for a lowly churl to keep a stately hunting hawk, the King in his boredom dismounted, entered the house, and seized the bird as if he were the local sheriff. For this foreign aggression he was immediately accosted by a mob of angry peasants who pelted him with sticks and stones. One brave soul actually drew a knife on the greatest warrior in Europe, an act that earned the wretch multiple blows from the flat of the King's sword, until the sword itself snapped and the King with his stub of a golden sword handle was forced to beat an indecorous retreat by throwing stones back at the angry peasants. He finally took refuge in the local priory of La Bagnara. Most of the chroniclers of the Third Crusade omit this undignified episode.

And what if Richard had died in this ignoble way? His mind must have gone to the terrible case of another crusading king, Frederick Barbarossa, Emperor of Germany. This venerable leader, seventy years old, was an audacious, chivalrous knight equal in every respect to Richard. Though his sandy hair and red beard had turned to gray, his eyes still sparkled with combative ardor. He was still broad of chest and tall in stature and cut a magnificent, manly figure for the ages. Like Richard, he had taken the cross immediately upon learning the catastrophic news from the Holy Land. With more dispatch and efficiency and single-mindedness and far less attention to royal squabbling, he had mobilized his crusading army from across the expanse of his Holy Roman Empire and marched off over the traditional overland route of Crusaders, through Hungary and Romania into Byzantium. By October 1189 he stood before Constantinople.

As befitted an honorable knight, Barbarossa felt obliged to write a letter to his great adversary, Saladin, warning the Muslim leader of the forthcoming invasion. "Now that you have profaned the Holy Land, over which we, by the authority of the Eternal King, bear rule, we will proceed with due rigor against such presumptuous and criminal audacity. . . . Restore the land which you have seized!" he demanded. "We give you a period of twelve months, after which you shall experience the fortune of war . . . You, God willing, shall learn the might of our victorious eagles and shall experience the anger of Germany: the youth of the Danube who know not how to flee, the towering Bavarian, the cunning Swabian, the fiery Burgundian, the nimble mountaineer of the Alps. . . . You shall be taught how our own right hand, which you suppose to be enfeebled by old age, can still wield the sword upon that day of reverence and gladness which has been a point for the triumph of Christ's cause."

Unlike the Crusaders before, the mighty German army had survived the sly intrigue of the Byzantines, the arrows of the Seljuk Turks, and terrible hardships of the Anatolian mountains. It had crossed the plateau of Asia Minor successfully, largely due to its discipline and strong leadership, and had arrived momentously in Armenia in the spring of 1190. Saladin was receiving continual reports about its progress from the Emperor in Constantinople, and he well appreciated the peril. At the prospect of so immense, well led, and disciplined an invading force, the Sultan sent out the call to jihad, Holy War, throughout his Muslim empire, to the lords of Sinjār, Jezīrat Ibn 'Omar, and Mosul, even as far away as the Caliph of Baghdad. Orders were issued for the wheat fields and storehouses ahead of the invaders to be burned. Fortresses on the border with Byzantium were abandoned, and the defenses at Sidon, Jaffa, and Caesarea were dismantled. Still, despite this panic, Saladin found time to reply to Barbarossa's provocative letter with some bravado of his own.

"If you count the Christians," he wrote, "my Arabs are many times more numerous. If the sea lies between us and the Christians, there is no sea to separate Arabs who cannot be numbered. Between us and those who will aid us, there is no impediment. With us are the Bedouins, the Turkomans, even our peasants, who will fight bravely against nations who should come to invade our country and would despoil them of their riches and exterminate them. We will meet you with the power of God. And when the Lord, by His power, shall have given us victory over you, nothing will remain for us to do but freely take your lands, by His power, and with His good pleasure."

On June 10, 1190, under the terrible heat of the dusty plain, the German Crusaders began to ford a small Cilician river called Calycadus, known as the Iron River, on their final push into Syria. Broiling in his iron suit of armor, the Emperor was barking orders in the shallow river amid a team of sumpter horses when suddenly the great beasts and then his own horse spooked, and the Emperor was thrown into the water. Even though the river was no more than hip deep, the weight of his armor pulled the Emperor down. In the shock of the cold water gushing through the crevices of his armor-plate across his overheated skin, he had a heart attack and drowned.

"The star of the Rhine casts Latium into ruins," ran a doleful lament about his death, "the star tumbles, and the star's fall holds the lands in darkness."

The consequence of the Emperor's death was terrible. His army was thrown into chaos and disintegrated almost immediately. Seeing their opportunity, the Turks attacked them from all sides, and the leaderless German soldiers melted into the countryside. Out of the nearly one hundred thousand men who had made their way through Byzantium, only about five thousand eventually limped into Acre weeks later.

It is well for the cause that on that unhappy day in July, Richard found refuge from the peasants' stones in a priory. His great Crusade was perilously fragile. Without a great leader it was doomed. As Saladin's chronicler remarked of the death of Frederick Barbarossa, "If Allah had not deigned to show His goodness to the Muslims by willing the death of the King of the Germans at the very moment he was about to prostrate Syria, men would say today, 'Syria and Egypt once belonged to Islam.' "

But Richard had happier news. The great English fleet was finally approaching Sicily. In hastening to join his men, the English King rejoiced. In his brief thirty-minute passage across the Straits of Messina, the symbolism of these waters could not have escaped him. There, ahead of him, was Faro Point and the Rock of Scylla, the twin terrors of ancient mariners, the rocks said to represent Greed and Arrogance. He could easily identify with Odysseus, scrambling to escape the whirlpools that Charybdis belched forth or the six-headed monster who sought to gobble up both him and his men. If the monsters did not devour Richard's Crusade, then there was the mirage known as Morgan Le Fay of the recent Arthurian legend. This apparition also lurked in these straits. She was the fairy enchantress who had learned her magic from Merlin and who could either heal the sorely laden or destroy in revenge for unrequited love.

Which, Richard might have asked as he passed over to Sicily, was to be his fate? If he was at all given to self-doubt, he might also have asked whether this grand goal of recovering the Holy Land was also a mirage.

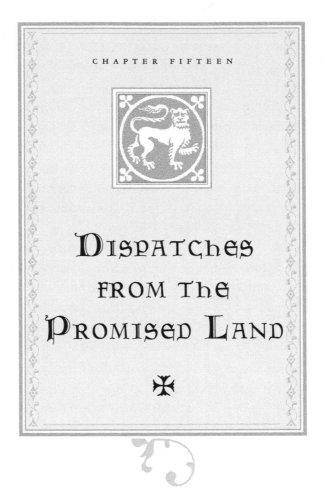

# Dispatches
# from the
# Promised Land

✠

I N the MONThs ThAT RIChARD WOULD TARRY IN
Sicily, he pondered the intelligence he was receiving about the
situation of the enemy and of his great adversary, Saladin.
In the nearly four years since Jerusalem had fallen to the Muslims, the Sultan had scarcely been idle. The Latin Kingdom of Jerusalem had
been swept out of existence. Its cities and its network of defensive fortresses
were no more. Its heart was reduced to a paltry few redoubts on the coast. All
ports south of Tripoli except for Tyre were in Muslim hands. Of the impressive network of colossal Crusader castles on the coast and inland, only Krak
des Chevaliers and Margat remained in Christian hands. And yet this was better than nothing. Richard had an objective, a strategic beachhead that still existed even after so many Christian reverses and from which he might launch

118
✦

his campaign to recapture the Holy Land. Tyre, this gift of a precarious enclave, was the product of a critical mistake that Saladin made immediately after his capture of Jerusalem. It would be the first of two critical mistakes.

In early November 1187, the Sultan had moved on Tyre for the second time. If he could capture this last vestige now, he would literally succeed in throwing the Christians into the sea. The rest was merely mopping up. Since Saladin's first assault earlier in that year, the able renegade, Conrad of Montferrat, had been able to strengthen Tyre's defenses considerably. Christian refugees continued to stream into the enclave from Jerusalem and other captured places. The city was veritably bursting at the seams with the beneficiaries of Saladin's tender and ill-advised charity.

Tyre was a magnificent, fortified city with a remarkable natural circumstance and with a high reputation for its glass and sugar, for its unique purple dye, for the amiable and welcoming disposition of its people, and for the fertility of the plains that surrounded it, of which Solomon in his Song had spoken as a "fountain of gardens and a well of living waters." In antiquity it had been the chief metropolis of the Phoenicians, the place where Jesus was denied entry on his walk along the coast, near where he walked on water, and where the Savior had said to the woman of Canaan whose daughter was possessed by the devil, "O woman, great is thy faith," before he healed her child. Like a hand stretching into the sea, the city was virtually an island, shaped like a quadrangle, surrounded on three sides by the rough water mined with hidden rocks, and connected to the mainland by a causeway about the length of a single bow shot. Twenty-five-foot-thick walls fenced this insular city, appointed with twelve strong towers. Facing its eastern land entrance along the narrow, man-made causeway named for its maker, Alexander the Great, were massive, lofty, contiguous towers. The ground upon which any assault might be launched was very narrow.

Only a combined ground and naval assault had any hope of capturing the place—unless an enemy was prepared to starve the city into submission with a prolonged siege of indeterminate length. That was not Saladin's style. Conrad of Montferrat could safely bet that in the absence of quick results, the Sultan and his army would grow impatient.

On the northern approach from the sea an entrance to a commodious inner harbor was the only break in the walls. Two towers flanked this entrance, and an enormous chain spanned it, to be lowered for friendly ships and raised when the enemy lay offshore, as five of Saladin's galleys now did.

This protected harbor was equipped to accommodate the largest warships of the day.

Saladin arrived outside the city walls in mid-November 1187 and commenced his siege. For his ground troops the going was tough, since Alexander's causeway was so narrow and exposed. Conrad promptly dispatched several galleys from his inner harbor to harass the Muslim soldiers and smash their engines from either side of the causeway, and many attackers were chewed up. To counter Conrad's ships Saladin ordered ten ships from the Egyptian fleet, which were then at anchor in Acre, to move to Tyre and set up a blockade. This created a standoff that lasted through Christmas.

Five of Saladin's warships were specifically tasked with the duty of the night blockade. Inexperienced and poorly trained sailors manned them, however, and Conrad must have sensed that he could make the greenhorns pay. On the night of December 30 the Marquis of Montferrat sprang a daring dawn raid. As the sun came up, the Egyptian sailors had been lulled into believing that their night duty was done, and they fell asleep happily, whereupon Conrad's seals woke them up with a start. Many Muslims leaped into the sea, and the Egyptian galleys were towed into the harbor. When Saladin was informed of the disaster, he ordered his remaining ships to make for Beirut in a hurry, for he was suddenly outgunned. But Conrad's ships gave chase, and in a panic the Muslims beached their ships and ran away. To complete the humiliation, Saladin was forced to destroy his beached vessels so that they would not fall into enemy hands.

With his naval capability decimated for the moment and the rainy season upon him, Saladin decided to cut his losses. The Muslim year of 583 (1187) had been such a glorious one. It would not do to sully the record with pointless exertions. Besides, his weary troops needed a rest for the next push forward. And so a few days into the new year he began to retreat.

Could this be the turning point? Watching from the walls as the enemy pulled back and proceeded to burn its massive siege engines that were mired in mud, the Christian defenders whooped their joy, for there was suddenly hope. So long as their city remained Christian, help from Europe was possible. During the rainy season the city would have months to strengthen itself and to widen its perimeter through the fertile countryside nearby. The Franks could have real faith that their spirited defense had discouraged the Muslim forces forever.

Tyre had survived. The Kingdom of Jerusalem, however small, still lived. And when news of it reached Europe, Conrad of Montferrat became an instant hero. The great troubadour of the time, Bertran de Born, sang his praise:

"I know now who has the greatest merit of all: Sir Conrad has the finest, no doubt, for he defends himself there at Tyre from Saladin and his wretched crew. God help him! For help comes slowly. He alone will gain the reward because he alone suffers the torment."

Within his own ranks Saladin was condemned for his self-inflicted wound. "No one can be blamed in this matter except Saladin, for it was he who sent the Frankish armies to Tyre," one Arabian commentator wrote disparagingly. Through the winter and early spring he pondered the lessons of the past year in Acre and Damascus and devised a strategy to complete the job. Its essence was to attack the weak and avoid the strong.

But it was as if he needed one further lesson to settle finally on this strategy. On May 30, 1188, his forces surrounded Krak des Chevaliers, the most impressive of all Crusader castles and known to the Muslims as the Castle of the Kurds. This colossus stood high above a valley. Its compact design of three massive semicircular towers, concentric rings of fortifications, and high thick walls were the crowning achievement of Crusader military engineering. Its imposing aspect quickly discouraged the Sultan, and he decided to move on. A lesson sank in.

From his experience at Tyre and Krak the new strategy for this northern campaign emerged. From now on, Saladin set out to capture the Crusader outposts that could be easily taken and bypass the fortresses of Krak des Chevaliers; the dark, brooding Margat overlooking the sea south of Latakia; and Safita, known as Castel Blanc, all of which were sure to put up an annoyingly stiff and prolonged defense. He knew he could isolate them from the action. To his troops he announced their next moves, where foraging from the countryside would be critical.

"We are going to enter the districts on the coast. Provisions are scarce there, and as the enemy will meet us on their own ground, they will surround us on every side. Therefore, you will have to provide yourselves with sufficient food for one month."

Good generalship though this may have been, it overestimated the immediate threat, for the Crusaders were in no position to surround anything. Their challenge was to avoid being swept into the sea. There was another rationale for this northern campaign. By mid-1188, Saladin knew that the news of Jerusalem's fall had reached Europe with devastating effect and that moves for a military response were under way. He had heard about a German crusade being organized and led by an impressive leader, the Holy Roman Emperor,

Frederick Barbarossa. From his sources in Constantinople, Saladin knew that the German army planned to move overland through Turkey and to enter Syria north of Antioch. His need, therefore, was to reduce the Crusader lands in northern Syria to a bare minimum so that it would be hard to provision the huge German army when it arrived. After leaving Krak des Chevaliers bottled up and harmless, he moved west to the sea and swept north in a great arc, capturing and burning Tartus, skirting Margat and negotiating the surrender of Jebela, then taking Latakia and all its enormous commercial wealth.

Before moving farther north to Antioch, he diverted his forces twenty miles inland to the remarkable castle at Sahyun, perhaps the most romantic of the Crusader castles. This amazing fortress sat high on a promontory above steep gorges, where two rivers converged below. Sahyun protected an important passageway from the Syrian desert east to the sea. Its walls skirted along the cliff's edge, creating a large lower courtyard that rose to an inner fortress and an impressive donjon. The only entrance to this magnificent base was across a drawbridge over a sheer crevasse that dropped fifty feet straight down and was protected by two huge, square towers. Like so many other Crusader castles, it lived comfortably, secure in the myth of its own impregnability.

Saladin commanded the assault personally. He gathered his main force on the high ground across the cut in the rock and pounded the towers unmercifully, but without effect. As perfect as Sahyun's situation was for defense, its garrison had been depleted, as had so many other Crusader outposts. Its strength lay in its imposing face across the crevasse, but its vulnerability lay in its long perimeter that traced the ridgeline of the spur high above the rivers. When the Sultan shifted his siege machines to the palisades on either side of the lower keep, its walls proved too extensive to defend. Saladin's mangonels reduced a section of the northern wall of the lower courtyard to rubble. With terrifying screams the Muslim troopers scaled the sheer ravines and poured into the place. After its capture Sahyun's name was changed to Qalaat Saladin.

Moving farther north, across the Orontes River, taking more legendary hilltop castles along the way, Saladin's army stood near the walls of Antioch in late September. Just south of the city he took the castle of Baghrās, an important bastion that commanded the entrance to the Beilan Pass and was a key defensive post along the Antioch-Alexandretta-Cilicia route. Once he captured it, Saladin gave orders for Baghrās to be dismantled, so that the German Crusaders could not use it when they arrived sometime in the future.

With this demonstration of power, Antioch itself sued for peace. As he had been with his charity toward the defeated of Jerusalem, Saladin was once again more lenient than wise. Judging that the European Crusade was still several years away from materializing, he allowed the residents of Antioch a space of seven months to surrender the city peaceably.

This most northerly of his objectives in hand, Saladin turned south to the Sea of Galilee. Two Hospitaler castles had long frustrated his direct access to the Holy Land from Damascus. Without much difficulty he took them both now: Belvoir, which commanded the heights south of the sea, and then Safed, which commanded the northern heights above the sparkling lake. At about the same time, another long-standing craw was removed from the neck of the kingdom: al Kerak—the Crow's Castle of the late, reviled Châtillon, the bane of the hajj road—fell to the forces of Saladin's brother after an eight-month siege. Saladin now held all of the land on both sides of the Jordan River.

Through this triumphant northern campaign the sense of its own righteousness transported the Muslim host. As the rope was being winched on one of his siege engines before the walls of Safed, his adviser turned to Saladin with satisfaction and invoked the words of the Holy Prophet: "There are two eyes that the fire of hell will never touch: the eye that has kept watch in the service of God and the eye that has wept in fear of Him." And with that the trigger was pulled and another huge boulder slammed into the walls. The Muslim army went forward into battle with the "sword verses" of the Koran in its throat: "When the sacred months are drawn away, slay the idolaters wherever you find them, and take them, and confine them, and lie in wait for them at every place of ambush."

Jihad was for the military host, yes, but it was also an individual concept for the true believer. Just as Saladin's army waged its jihad against the Christian invaders, so the Muslim soldier waged his own personal jihad: his jihad of the heart, where he struggled against his sinful inclinations; a jihad of the tongue, where he resisted the temptations of coarse speech; a jihad of the hand, which prohibited him from committing abominable acts; and finally the jihad of the sword for slaying idolaters and especially Trinitarians.

Richard did not underestimate the power of his enemy's passionate commitment on the battlefield.

In the summer of 1188, Saladin made his second critical mistake. For a year he had held the erstwhile King of Jerusalem, Guy of Lusignan, captive in Tortosa. But with his realm now a mere ghost of itself, with Ascalon in

Saladin's hands, the King seemed harmless. Saladin was prepared to release him on the condition that he renounce his kingdom, that he never again take up arms against the faithful, that he forever swear his allegiance to his liberator, and that he soon leave the Middle East. Moreover, the King's doting Queen, Sibylla, had made a personal appeal, and feminine requests always seemed to soften the Sultan's heart. In any case, Saladin could see some political value in presenting the more able Conrad of Montferrat with a rival and thus divide his enemy. And so in July 1189, in a move that was part sentiment, part principle, and part politics, Guy was freed.

The King broke his promise instantly. His promise had been made under duress, he told his clergymen, and they immediately absolved him of it. He repaired immediately to Tyre, where he had the temerity to demand the keys of the city from the marquis. Montferrat replied obliquely at first, "I am only the lieutenant of the Kings beyond the seas," he said sweetly, "and they have not authorized me to give the city up to you."

But the formalities were soon dropped, and Montferrat moved from the formal to the icy cold to the contemptuous. He heaped abuse on the fallen King for his battlefield incompetence. Indeed, said Conrad, Guy had forfeited his right to be King after the disaster of Hattin. As the last hero of the kingdom, Conrad himself now laid claim to the throne. With that, Guy was ushered unceremoniously out of the city. Saladin's bet that he would put the two rivals at one another's throats was paying off.

Contemptuous though they were of one another, Guy and Montferrat were able to reach some agreement about the remnants of the Crusader army. Partly because he wanted to relieve the strain on his overcrowded, chaotic city, which now teemed with restless, displaced soldiers, and partly because he had no special enthusiasm for combat far from the city he had saved, Conrad agreed to allow Guy to mobilize the survivors into a fighting force outside his city's walls.

Within a year the King had the core of his new force: seven hundred knights, mainly Templars, including the Master of the Templars himself, Gerard de Ridefort. Some nine thousand men joined this chivalrous elite. Moreover, the first elements of the Crusader force, which had begun to arrive in fits and spurts from Denmark and Holland, swelled the ranks. Once again the cry for Holy War was raised. The words of the prophet Isaiah were shouted to the winds: "I will bring thy seed from the north, and from the west I will gather thee together: I will say to the north, Give! and to the south, Do not forbid."

In August 1189 this new Christian army stood before the walls of Acre, eight leagues to the south of Tyre. With the forces at his disposal Saladin set out in pursuit, but again he was late. Already the city had been cut off, and his force was too small to overwhelm the revived and determined enemy. With his army spread from Aleppo in the north to al Kerak in the Moab, Saladin was incapable of snuffing out this new threat. The Christian soldiers dug in. On one side they besieged the city, and on the other side they hovered behind a huge trench that protected them from the charge of the Muslim cavalry. They were the attackers and the attacked all at once and could neither move forward nor retreat.

For more than a month, into October 1189, in thrusts and counterthrusts, the fighting was intense but inconclusive. On October 4, however, a violent and especially bloody clash took place in which hundreds were killed on both sides, in which the normally incompetent King Guy comported himself admirably, and in which Guy and his intense rival, Conrad of Montferrat, cooperated with one another efficiently. The outcome was a Muslim victory, but an inconclusive one in which both sides staged effective charges. At one point in the conflict Saladin's own camp was overrun, but he rallied his Mesopotamian horsemen and turned the tide in his favor.

In this battle the last of the Christian hotheads—Gerard de Ridefort, the Master of the Temple—was executed after he was captured in yet another brave but foolhardy charge. He was instantly canonized. It was said that his friends had beseeched him to relent and retreat, and he had gallantly replied, "I defy anyone to name the place where I have ever been when an enemy did slander the Temple and I did flee afraid." And so the firebrand became a martyr and saint.

"Happy is he upon whom the Lord conferred so great glory," one commentator wrote for his epitaph, "that he should gain the laurel which he had earned in so many wars and be admitted to the fellowship of martyrs."

But it was not a happy day for either side. In an effort to horrify and dishearten the Christians, the Muslims threw many of their victims into the river Belus near the town, so that the bloated, foul corpses would float downstream over the Christian lines. But this ghoulish maneuver backfired as disease spread on both sides of the trenches. Saladin himself fell ill with the colic from which he suffered frequently, and, worse, he fell into a melancholy. "Kill me with Mālik. Kill Mālik with me," he muttered a well-known verse miserably, by which he seemed to be saying that he was willing to die, if only his enemies died with him. His doctors viewed his illness with alarm, as did his emirs. Both urged the Sultan to withdraw for the good of himself and his exhausted army but also to allow the Christian force to retreat, if it would.

But the Crusader army did not withdraw. Instead it dug in deeper and settled in for the longest siege of the Third Crusade. When Saladin recovered from his illness in January of 1190, he renewed his call to the ends of the Muslim world, from Baghdad to Morocco, for fresh troops to break this infernal siege. "Islam asks aid from you as a drowning man cries for help," he wrote. The Europeans were like corn, which could be devoured only by soldiers like locusts. Moreover, he was receiving reports that the German Emperor, Frederick Barbarossa, was approaching Constantinople with a force estimated at 260,000 men, and this news put the Sultan into a state of high anxiety. He could not have known how quickly that force would disappear with the Emperor's death in July.

Saladin had his detractors now, and they were turning the Koran around against him. "When God wishes evil for a people no power can avert it, and no one else can protect them." Once again the parochial jealousies in the Muslim world were rife, and even within Saladin's own camp there was dissension. "Evildoers have multiplied and come into the open," wrote one Muslim chronicler. "They detect the scent of sedition—may God cut off the noses with which they smell it." This prevented Saladin from pressing his advantage against this gritty but small Christian force during the year when the massive Crusader armies were being mobilized in Europe.

And that is how the stalemate stood into 1191. As Richard the Lionheart of England and Philip Augustus of France arrived in Sicily for the trip to the Holy Land, they knew this: Tyre remained in Christian hands as a toehold. But its arrogant lord, the Marquis of Montferrat, could not be counted upon for his support. Frederick Barbarossa was dead, and his army had dissolved in Turkey. For nearly a year and a half Acre had been under siege, but the siege's commander was the weak King Guy, whose legitimacy was undermined by his poor judgment and incompetence.

CHAPTER SIXTEEN

# VISITATIONS IN SICILY

✠

IN THE LATTER YEARS OF THE TWELFTH CENTURY
Sicily was the crossroads of Mediterranean civilization. Here the
Arabs of the East, the Lombards of northern Italy, the Greeks
of Calabria and Byzantium, the Normans of Northern Europe lived
together in relative harmony within a nominally Norman state. With its
mixture of religions, languages, and customs, the island celebrated the di-
versity of the great inland sea. Its cosmopolitan scholars translated the science, mathematics, and philosophy of the East from Arabic into Latin and
passed the wisdom north. Similarly, the Arthurian romances and tracts on
chivalry were translated into Arabic and passed east. The proud Sicilians did

not take well to being treated as a lesser colony or as a mere staging area for other nations' ambitions.

To the natives of Sicily the arrival of the English fleet at Messina, was the most awe-inspiring sight anyone could ever imagine. As far as the eye could see on the horizon, the sea was filled with ships of war, packed with excited men-at-arms, streamers flapping from their spears, their bucklers and brigandines glistening in the sun, shouts of victory in their throats. The clanging of metal, the straining of ropes and beams, the sounds of trumpets and clarions filled the air. Such joy, such expectation. On the prow of Robert de Sable's command ship stood the magnificent Richard himself, resplendent in his royal robes and carrying the staff of his pilgrimage. This was a spectacle worthy of the grand quest, and above all else, Richard was a master of spectacle. He had taken heed of the dictum "As I see thee, thy worth I deem."

Only two days before, Philip Augustus had arrived quietly and unceremoniously, like a common merchant skulking into town on some low and unsavory errand. His fleet consisted of a single ship. He had circumvented the mob that waited on shore expectantly to welcome to their land so grand and noble a personage. His footmen whisked Philip away to a palace, and his greeters went home indignant, grumbling that no such king as this could ever be the savior of Christendom. Philip further alienated the local population when his French troops committed a few predictable transgressions on shore, as troops on liberty will sometimes do. The King turned a blind eye.

Once ashore, Richard had no intention of making the same mistake. Among his first acts was to erect a gallows and to hold a public hanging of a few random robbers and murderers. This display of authority distinguished him favorably from Philip and impressed the natives mightily. One of the starstruck was heard to remark, "The fame which preceded him fell far short of the truth when we saw him." Soon enough to the "Griffones" of Sicily Philip became known as The Lamb and Richard as The Lion.

At first the Kings and comrades greeted one another cordially, for they had much business to conduct and a few annoyances to discharge. Their first meeting did not bode well for the future, however. The very next day, as if he had endured a bad wedding night, Philip Augustus marched to his ship in a huff and set out for the Holy Land. His exit was more glorious than his return. During his first day out at sea he encountered rough weather—he was given to seasickness—and was soon back in Messina, in a better frame of mind to deal with Richard.

A more serious annoyance was the King of Sicily. He was Tancred, who had seized the throne two years prior, after the death of the legitimate king, William the Good (the good Christian king who had been the first to hear of the catastrophe in the Holy Land and had spread the alarm). William's widow was Joanna Plantagenet, Eleanor's youngest daughter and Richard's younger sister. When he appropriated the throne, Tancred had had the bad grace to imprison Joanna, and her incarceration did not sit well with Richard. Moreover, there was real money at stake here. Joanna's dowry, bequeathed to the English throne by William as a condition of marriage, consisted of a gilded chair that had been her throne as William's queen, a twelve-foot-long golden table, a large silk tent, twenty-four golden cups, twenty-four golden plates, and, not least, the use of one-hundred armed galleys for two years. When Richard complained about his sister's treatment, Tancred released Joanna with only her everyday furniture.

Along with the insults of the usurper King there was growing unrest among the natives over Richard's actions. In general, Sicilians were suspicious and resentful of Northern Europeans, and Richard's incursion into their land seemed to fit a pattern. He had moved quickly to seize strategic redoubts around Messina. Across the straits he took charge of the monastery at La Bagnara, fortified it, and placed his sister, Joanna, there, to keep her out of harm's way. Then he seized a monastery on an island in the River Far, threw out the monks, garrisoned it, and turned it into his arsenal. The Sicilians grew uneasy about these aggressive moves, which were viewed as merely a precursor to a full-scale occupation of their island.

The nasty situation began with insults, as Tancred's men made fun of the "long-tailed English," as if they had sprouted the devil's tail, and the English called the locals "low fellows of Arab extraction." Richard himself, in all the glory of his masculinity and homosexuality, called the Griffones "effeminate." The situation needed only a spark. It came in a dispute between an English soldier and a female vendor over the weight and price of a loaf of bread. For his grousing over the penny price, the soldier was attacked by street people, stomped underfoot, and left for dead. Soon enough, street rioting broke out, in which a score of unarmed English soldiers were murdered and thrown into privies. Richard himself tried to quell the turmoil. He rode through the streets and counseled calm, but the Sicilians taunted him unmercifully. Shortly thereafter the gates to Messina were closed.

This hostile act soon degenerated into general fighting. Privately Richard seemed to view the skirmish as a warm-up for the Holy Land, a good test for himself and a good way to test the mettle of his troops. Were they ready for Saladin? "The Lord sharpens them and grinds them and puts them to the whetstone like knives," the troubadour Bertran de Born had written, "but they're too thick at the tip and weak toward the cutting edge. Thanks to the grinder, they're more trusty than a prior; so they will all attain *vita eterna*." In high dudgeon the King went before his army, looking like, according to a reporter present, a "noble beast."

"O my soldiers! my kingdom's strength, who have endured with me a thousand perils, who have subdued so many tyrants and cities, do you see how a cowardly rabble insults us? Shall we vanquish Turks and Arabs? Shall we be a terror to the most invincible nations? Can we restore the kingdom to Israel if we turn our backs before these vile and effeminate Griffones? Methinks I see you restrain your efforts, perhaps to better contend with Saladin later.

"I, your lord and King, love you. I praise your honor. But I warn you again and again, if you leave this outrage unrevenged, your base flight will both precede and accompany you. Every enemy will think you runaways, and will redouble their energies against you. Old women and children will rise up against you. I will not command any one of you to stay with me, lest the fear of one shall shake another's confidence in the battle. For myself I will either die here or will revenge these wrongs. If I depart alive, Saladin will see me only a conqueror.

"Will you desert me, your King, and leave me alone to meet the conflict?"

His troops roared back their support. In a low growl the King professed his satisfaction. "You hearten me by your willingness to cast off disgrace," he said. He called for two thousand bold knights, "men who do not have their hearts in their boots," and two thousand archers. His engineers rolled out the battering ram, and the terrible battle flag with its grotesque dragon symbol was unfurled. Then the magnificent Richard strapped on his armor. When the brazen townsfolk saw the approach of this elite force, with King Richard in the lead, they ran as sheep before a wolf, so reported his herald. Not so fast. It was not quite so easy, for it took ten hours before the Plantagenet banners flew from Messina's walls. Still, the speed of the operation was memorialized in this couplet:

Plus tost eurent il pris Meschines
C'uns prestres n'ad dit ses matines.*

---

*Our King and his men have taken Messines
More quickly than a priest can say his matins.

The couplet might well have referred to the speed with which Tancred placed forty thousand ounces of gold before Richard as a settlement for the troubles.

Even though French soldiers had not participated in this police action, the fleur-de-lis was soon flying next to the English lions on Messina's walls, and Philip was demanding his share of the booty. He pointed to the agreement at Vézelay to divide equally the spoils of Crusade. Richard could not let this pass without a few choice words. "Who has more right to fly his flags?" he sneered. "The one who stands aside and lags, unwilling to share the battle, or he who sallies forth and dares?" It was just another spat among many. Richard relented, for they had more serious matters to discuss.

The property of the war dead, and gambling, and even the price of bread, for instance. At Vézelay, the Kings had settled the great affairs of kings and states, and at Chinon, Richard had laid down the law for military misconduct. But what about the property of war victims, or the malfeasance of his soldiers, or war profiteering? A few days after the capitulation of Messina, the Kings got down to these details. The incident between the soldier and the female bread vendor had a wider implication for policy. Trading needed to be regulated, especially the sale of bread and wine to the troops. So a principle was established that traders could not profit by more than 10 percent from their wares, or by one farthing per measure. No one was to buy dead meat for resale, nor could the meat of any living animal be sold unless it was slaughtered within the camp.

The regulations for gambling were more interesting. No soldier or sailor was permitted to play any dice game whatever for money (medieval craps, for instance). The penalty for this transgression was severe: The soldier was to be whipped naked throughout the army for three days and the sailor to be drenched in the sea each morning for three days. Not surprisingly, knights and clerics were the exception to this harsh prohibition. In their dice games they were not permitted to lose more than twenty shillings in a single day. A priest or noble caught losing more than twenty shillings must in addition pay one hundred shillings to the war chest for each time he had an unlucky day. Kings, however, could gamble as often and for as much as they pleased. For their high-stakes games there was no limit on the pot.

There remained a major point of contention between Richard and Philip. It was called Alais Capet, Princess of France, sibling to Philip, Richard's betrothed, Henry's sullied, and now Eleanor's prisoner in Rouen.

2

# A New Queen

had the mobilization of the Crusader force happened more swiftly and efficiently, the Christian army might have been in the Holy Land in late 1190. But it was now fall. Good winds and calm weather had given way to autumn storms, and Philip, with his dread of seasickness, was not eager for an uncertain, risky voyage. There would be no serious fighting in the mud of winter in any case. Moreover, the calamitous news from Turkey about the death of Frederick Barbarossa and the evaporation of his German army removed the urgency to coordinate the Christian invasion. The demise of the Teutonic army meant the Germans could no longer compete for glory or for spoils. The Kings decided to settle in for the winter in Sicily.

With Philip ensconced in the royal palace of Messina and the local population still hostile to English soldiers, Richard went happily about constructing a grand wooden palace for himself on a hill overlooking the town. He undertook the labor with great energy and called his masterwork Mategriffon, which meant "kill the Greeks," as a snub to Tancred and his local tormentors. Into the Christmas season the Kings made a show of comity. They visited one another's royal precincts for feasts and games, though the reality had not changed. King Philip suppressed his envy and resentment of Richard with, as one commentator put it, "the cunning of a fox." In due course the fox became ensnared in his own trap.

Into the new year of 1191, Richard found it politic to make his peace with the local tinhorn. And so on February 5, he and Tancred met in Catania to confer and to prostrate themselves before the shrine of St. Agatha, the martyr. In St. Agatha they could not have found a more complete victim of man's brutality toward women. For according to the Catholic book of saints, this third-century saint had been raped by a wicked magistrate who wished to steal her fortune, then tortured as hooks ripped her body and her breasts were cut off. "Cruel man, have you forgotten your mother and the breasts that nourished you?" she is supposed to have cried out before she was made to roll naked across burning coals.

The pilgrimage to St. Agatha seemed to put the Kings in a mellow frame of mind. The former adversaries suddenly wallowed in brotherly love, praying and feasting together and exchanging fabulous gifts. Tancred presented the English monarch with priceless objects of gold and silver, warhorses and rare silk, and, most important, four huge cargo ships and fifteen war galleys. In return, Richard placed before Tancred the most magnificent broadsword ever forged, which he professed, probably tongue in cheek, to be Excalibur itself, the magic sword of mythical and mighty King Arthur.

In this glow of comradeship Tancred blurted out a warning to Richard about King Philip, for the fox was crouching in his den and ready to spring. Tancred produced a letter from King Philip that called Richard a traitor and in which Philip promised to ally himself with Tancred, if Tancred would only pounce on the Englishman first.

"I am not a traitor, nor have I been, nor will I be!" Richard bellowed. "I cannot easily believe that the King of France sent you this about me."

Tancred swore by its authenticity and promised to produce witnesses. Naturally, when Philip was confronted with the letter, he pronounced it to be a forgery. But Richard had his pretext for doing what he had long wanted to do: he decided to end the sham of his betrothal to Alais Capet. To accomplish this desire of long standing, Richard summoned the Count of Flanders, who had recently arrived in Sicily with a significant troupe of Crusaders. The Flemish count was well known for his tact and eloquence, for he had a "tongue on which he set a high price." Richard placed the negotiation in his hands.

Philip's response was fierce: "If he does put her aside and marries another woman, I will be the enemy of him and his so long as I live." Upon hearing this latest threat, Richard quietly promised to produce many witnesses to prove how his own father had defiled the Capetian princess and even had a child by her. She was not fit to be the Queen of England. With their fates now so intertwined militarily, Philip could do little but whimper a meek parting shot and put out his hand to accept ten thousand pounds of silver for this unpardonable breach of promise. So many slights, so many resentments—the French King was forced to swallow one more.

While Richard's act lifted an emotional burden from his shoulders, it left open the larger question of succession to the English throne. If Richard did not marry and sire an heir, the crown might revert to his sniveling younger brother John, a nightmare from which all England and all Europe shrank with horror.

Far away in France the indomitable Eleanor of Aquitaine was taking

charge of this thorny succession problem. Now luxuriating in her new freedom, she stashed Alais in a tower in Rouen and began to canvass the royal
houses of Europe for a suitable replacement. She focused on Spain, where
Richard had gone to joust in Pamplona some years before as the Count of
Poitou. Beyond the Pyrenees he had shown some mild interest in the daughter of the King of Navarre, a comely and dreamy maiden named Berengaria.
That Eleanor was well aware of Richard's lack of interest in the opposite sex
was undeniable, but she brushed the matter aside. Where more important
things were at stake, sexual disorientation in a man could be overlooked like
so many of that gender's other faults.

Richard would just have to rise above his deviation for the sake of the
royal line. Duty called. After all, had he not consorted with women occasionally? Therefore, his sexuality was merely . . . ambivalent. To his court
troubadour, Bertran de Born, he was known as Lord Yes and No. Well, now
it would have to be Yes. Was it not true that he had even sired a boy with a
damsel from Cognac? (Richard had named his bastard Philip in a move that
could be interpreted two ways.) To Eleanor her favorite son simply had to
strap on his spurs and do the same for the glory and perpetuation of the Plantagenet dynasty.

While Richard marched his army to Marseille, Eleanor had quietly
tramped to Spain and taken charge of the placid Berengaria. The court historians bent the language to present this docile maiden in the best light. She was
"more learned than beautiful." (Did that mean she was plain?) She was a "prudent maid, a gentle lady, virtuous and fair, neither false nor double-tongued."
(Did that mean she was dull?) To Eleanor her greatest virtue was her compli-
ance, and the maid fell meekly in line behind the formidable Eleanor.

By the time the arrangements had been made, fall was sliding into winter, and a journey over the Alps was perilous. Not to Eleanor. With her lamb
bundled at her side, she forged through the snowbound passes toward her
lion and advanced her legend in her own time.

"Queen Eleanor, an incomparable woman," wrote a contemporary, ". . .
beautiful and chaste, powerful and modest, meek and eloquent, which is
rarely to be met within a woman; she is still indefatigable in every undertaking, and her power is the admiration of her age." It was as if Richard
sensed that his domineering, prepossessing mother was on her way to him.
He surely guessed that she was coming halfway across the Continent and over
its highest mountain range in winter to force upon him another woman.

A few weeks before Eleanor arrived with Berengaria, Richard gathered his archbishops and bishops around him at the chapel of Reginald de Moyac in Messina. There, proclaiming a visceral fear of the destruction of Sodom, he stripped himself naked and confessed the filthiness of his homosexuality. Throwing himself on the mercy of his Lord, he asked for forgiveness and strength to resist his unnatural impulses and desist from unlawful ways. He promised abstinence and repentance. In his attempts to deny his orientation, the biblical story of Balaam's ass bedeviled him. In that invocation the ass had turned away when an angel of the Lord stood in the road, sword raised high, and three times Balaam had struck the donkey for it. "Why have you struck your ass three times?" the angel would ask Balaam. "I stood in the way, because thy way is perverse before me."

His bishops declared his remorse to be genuine, set out the rules for penance, and proclaimed that the "thorns of lustfulness" had departed from his head. "O happy the man who falls so low and then will rise with greater strength still!" wrote his chronicler Roger of Hoveden. "O happy the man who after repentance does not relapse into a course of ruin!"

Richard may well have treated his public pronouncement of unnatural-ness as fortification against any nuptials his mother was coming to press on him. With a mixture of joy and trepidation he ushered her and her simper-ing maiden to their quarters in Mategriffon.

For the English and French soldiers who watched the grand entrance of Eleanor and her cortège, she was an ambiguous figure at best. Powerful, beautiful, indefatigable, sensuous, literary, an eagle soaring above mere mor-tals, mother of ten royal children she might indeed be. Nevertheless, in all her royal matrimonials she had failed to produce a male heir to the King of France and had been sacked for it. Rumors were rife about infidelities she may have had behind her King's back, from the King's own brother to Sal-adin (the unkindest cut of all)! She had produced five sons for the King of England, and he had been so grateful for it that he imprisoned her for six-teen years. Some regarded her as the Demon Mother who had once, in a bath, assumed the shape of a dragon. And Richard himself, perhaps in his despair over the "filthiness" of his deviant life, was to say of his ancestry that "they had all come from the devil and to the devil would return. With the root so entirely rotten, how can a fruitful or virtuous offspring arise from it?"

But these high affairs and low slurs did not concern the crusading army as much as Eleanor's tie to the catastrophe of 1147. To see this aged but still handsome queen mother stride regally from her galley with her military escort conjured up a nightmare of forty-four years earlier, with Eleanor straddling a horse in battle gear in the company of other amazon Crusaders, followed by a vast retinue of chambermaids and troubadours and a huge train of excess baggage. To see her now was to imagine the disaster at Mount Cadmos, where the Queen's baggage train had slowed and then split the Crusader army, leading to a terrible defeat at the hands of the Turks. It was to visualize a woman-dominated Crusade where a holy pilgrimage by day could be turned at night into a great pageant for poetry and music and dances and debates over love. Eleanor was the symbol of self-indulgence and defeat. It was because of her that the presence of women was discouraged on this Crusade.

"Many knew what I wish that none of us had known," wrote the monk of Winchester, Richard of Devizes, sorrowfully. "The same queen in the time of her former husband went to Jerusalem. Let none speak more thereof. I also know well. Be silent."

Eleanor stayed only a few days in Sicily. Her lamb was dutifully welcomed into Richard's den and placed in the care of his sister, Joanna, but the wedding bells did not seem to be ringing in anyone's mind, certainly not in Richard's. The season of Lent provided a handy excuse for delay. In his mother's hands Richard vested the power to manage certain political problems at home, before he put her back on her ship and pointed her toward Rome.

Then he turned his mind back to the Crusade.

Eager for spiritual preparation, Richard summoned the great mystic of Calabria, Joachim of Fiore, to his side for instruction and for his predictions. What lay ahead for the great war between the Christian and the infidel? Did the apocalypse of St. John have some bearing on their enterprise? It was said that this controversial Cistercian monk possessed the gift of prophecy and was most learned in his interpretations of the visions of St. John in the Book of Revelation.

As Richard and his bishops and archbishops listened intently for hours, the austere monk drew the picture, drawn from Revelation 12:1, of the Holy Virgin, clothed in the sunlight of justice, her feet firmly supported by the Holy Church, and upon her head a crown of twelve stars, signifying the twelve Apostles. Facing her was the seven-headed dragon, the devil himself. Seven is a finite number, the monk said, but his power for wickedness is infinite, for the devil's heads represent the wickedness that he can do. Still, the seven heads represent as well the seven principal persecutors of the Holy Faith, among whom were Herod and Muhammad. Five of the seven were dead, Joachim said, but two still lived. The last was the Antichrist, who, said the monk, was now fifteen years old and lived in Rome.

"If that is the case, the present Pope Clement must be the Antichrist," Richard announced gleefully. At the suggestion of the Pope as Antichrist, Richard's bishops howled their protest. In any case, Clement III was considerably older than fifteen years. Joachim pressed on: In due course the false prophet would become Pope and attempt to seduce the faithful, until this wicked one was revealed, and "Jesus Christ shall slay him with the breath of His mouth." At these ponderous imaginings Richard must have scratched his head.

The sixth principal tormentor of the church, said the mystic, was Saladin himself. Saladin was now the most terrible oppressor of the Church of God, and he must be defeated. For he had defiled the Holy City of Jerusalem and the Sepulcher of Our Lord and the land on which the feet of Our Savior had walked. Nevertheless, he would shortly lose his grip on these Christian possessions, to one who would bask forever in the glory of the faith.

"When will this happen?" Richard asked.

"When seven years have elapsed from the day of the capture of Jerusalem."

Richard made a quick calculation. Saladin had captured Jerusalem five years before. "Have we come too soon?" the King wondered.

"Your arrival is very necessary," the mystic replied, raising his hand to soothe the anxiety, "for the Lord will give you the victory over His enemies and will exalt your name beyond all the princes of the earth."

CHAPTER SEVENTEEN

# The Fruit of Aphrodite

✠

O N MARCH 30, 1191, KING PHILIP OF FRANCE left Sicily for the Holy Land in a pout. He left precipitously and unceremoniously, since he did not want to suffer the embarrassment of encountering Princess Berengaria, who was replacing his half sister Alais as Richard's betrothed. Regardless of his emotional state, Philip's voyage was smooth and unmarred by mishap, and he arrived at Acre three weeks later on April 20 in good spirits.

As in all phases of life, Richard's departure had more fanfare and his voyage more drama. With him would go the bulk of the Crusader fleet, which had swollen to an enormous size over the winter. The logistics of organizing the fleet for its Mediterranean passage were devilishly complicated. Having made his peace with the Sicilian king, Richard symbolically destroyed his provocative wooden castle, Mategriffon, before he said farewell in a frisky mood. On April 10 the immense flotilla moved out to sea, 219 ships in all, setting a course due east.

In three of his slowest yet sturdiest ships, called dromons or busses, he placed Berengaria and his sister, Joanna, along with a contingent of royal guards and a considerable part of his kingly treasure, and sent them ahead as the vanguard. These three regal busses became the point of an enormous triangle in the open sea. There were eight ranks, each of increasing numbers on through the seventh rank, which contained sixty ships spread out in a line. Richard brought up the rear with a few of his fastest galleys. From a distance the armada looked like a flight of birds, one chronicler remarked. In the gentle wind that blessed the first day at sea, the ships sailed in close enough order that ranks could communicate by trumpet and even with shouts. When night fell, the ships followed the light of enormous wax candles that were placed high in the lead ship and also in the King's ship at the rear.

But the gentle wind did not persist. On Good Friday the fleet was becalmed, and the next day, the Day of Preparation, a fierce wind arose. Before long the entire fleet was plunged into a furious storm. The sleek, geometrical lines of the armada were soon shattered, and communication was impossible. The captains could not hold their ships on course and had to ply all their skill simply to stay afloat. The soldiers hung on for their lives, and the priests in the fleet turned to Jeremiah, for this was surely the voice of the Lord "who causeth the vapors to ascend from the ends of the earth . . . and bringeth forth the wind out of his treasures."

When the sea finally settled down, the Crusader fleet was scattered far and wide, and it took some days for Richard to reassemble it. To one scribe his process seemed like that of a hen gathering her chicks. But some chicks were still missing—most important, the three dromons that had been in the lead, carrying the future Queen of England.

After ten days at sea the battered fleet dropped anchor at the foot of Mount Ida in Crete and consoled itself with the thought that this birthplace of Zeus was the traditional halfway point between Sicily and Palestine. A few days later the fleet set off again on a strong wind that persisted through the night. In the morning they found themselves off the rocky shore of Rhodes.

Amid the ruins of this ancient island, which once had been so great and now was a mere shadow of its former glory, Richard stayed ten days. While he waited for stray ships to limp in, he reprovisioned his fleet from the fertile fields nearby. From the rough passage the King was indisposed, but he was well enough to dispatch several of his best and fastest galleys on a search for his betrothed. In due course these scouts found her several hundred miles away in Cyprus. The fury of the storm had driven the three lead ships on a more southerly course. One of the three ships had been wrecked on the rocks of Aphrodite, not far from the port of Limmassol, but Berengaria's ship was unharmed and at anchor off the harbor. The princess was safe and suffering only from indignity.

The Byzantine ruler of Cyprus, named Isaac Comnenus, had treated the Crusader strays shabbily. Among those who drowned in the shipwreck was the King's vice chancellor, who always wore the King's seal around his neck. The Cypriot Emperor seized this royal pendant, along with all the money that could be recovered from the ship, imprisoned the survivors, refused to allow Berengaria to enter the harbor of Limmassol, and denied her soldiers access to the shore to obtain water.

The Emperor would come to regret his rudeness. Upon receiving the news of Berengaria, Richard flew into a rage. Who was this petty tyrant? he demanded to know. How dare he detain and rob pilgrims on the way to the Holy Land? Berengaria's welfare did not seem to be much on his mind; rather to Richard it was the principle of the thing.

His advisers conveyed to the King as much as they knew: that this Isaac Comnenus was the nephew of a Byzantine Emperor in Constantinople who as a youth had been captured in a war with the Armenians and imprisoned in chains for many years by Europeans. He had, therefore, a deep hatred for Latins and a phobia of chains. A usurper who had come to Cyprus six years before from Constantinople, he had succeeded in splitting the island away from the Byzantine Empire. Now he ruled Cyprus independently but was much reviled by his own people for his cruelty and his treachery. Many of his wealthy and productive subjects had fled the island, while those who remained were exploited and robbed of their wealth.

Of the calamity of Cyprus under Isaac, a monk named Neophytus had written, "Isaac not merely ill-treated the country and altogether plundered the substance of the rich, but even abused his own officers, inflicting penalties upon them daily, and oppressing them so that they all lived in despair."

Only by the dangerous intervention of a decent Cypriot (who was later

*Citadel of Jerusalem, overlooking Calvary, the Dome of the Rock,
and the Temple Mount, from* Picturesque Palestine *by C. W. Wilson*

*Statue of Saladin, Souq al-Hamadiya, Damascus*

(ANTOUN MEZZAWI)

*Statue of Richard the Lionheart, Parliament Building, London*

(JUDAH PASSOW)

*Rivers of Damascus, from*
Picturesque Palestine
*by C. W. Wilson*

*Ancient drawing of Saladin*

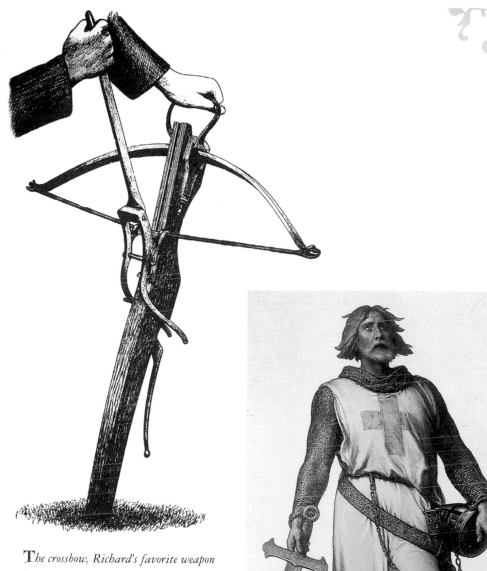

*The crossbow, Richard's favorite weapon*
(LIBRARY OF CONGRESS)

*Godfrey of Bouillon, the hero of the First Crusade*
(BELGIAN SENATE)

*Horns of Hattin, where the Kingdom of Jerusalem collapsed*

*Jerusalem from the Mount of Olives, from* Picturesque Palestine *by C. W. Wilson*

*S*aladin lays siege to
Jerusalem.

*C*aptured crusaders are
brought before Saladin.

*T*he Pope receives the bad news
of Jerusalem's fall.

*R*ichard embarks with his templars.

*Vézelay, the mobilization point for the Third Crusade*

(COMITÉ RÉGIONAL DU TOURISME DE BOURGOGNE)

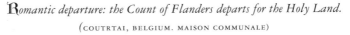

*Romantic departure: the Count of Flanders departs for the Holy Land.*

(COUTRTAI, BELGIUM. MAISON COMMUNALE)

beheaded for his troubles), had the survivors of the shipwreck escaped execution by the bitter Emperor. He had tried to trick the once and future queens into going ashore, but they had wisely demurred, awaiting deliverance by King Richard. It was said that Isaac was friendly with Saladin himself and that they had drunk one another's blood in a strange and barbaric ceremony of brotherhood. With this distressing portrait of a villain, Richard commandeered two of his swiftest galleys, fitted them with a company of crack troops, and hastened to the rescue.

He launched immediately into the broil of the Anatolian Gulf, where the currents of four seas clash and the *meltémi* winds are unpredictable. This treacherous expanse of water was a mariner's nightmare, and it was said that two awful curses were upon it. One came from the legend of the damsel who had refused a certain knight throughout her life. But on the night she died, the knight came to her and lay with her. The devil entered her body, and nine months later it gave up a child that was stillborn. The knight had the devil's child beheaded and kept the relic in a chest. Whenever his enemies attacked him, he had only to raise the head in front of them and they would be vanquished. But then the knight remarried, and his bride was curious to discover how her husband was able to defeat huge armies without a single soldier of his own. One day she searched his rooms and found the head in the chest. In terror, she raced to the water and flung the head into the sea. Thereafter mariners said that if the floating head was face upward, the sea roiled into a terrible storm, but if the head was face downward, it was calm and ships could pass without harm.

The other legend held that a black dragon of immense size haunted the gulf and that for one month out of every year it plunged its head into the sea and sucked up a huge amount of water. If sailors did not want to be sucked into the dragon's mouth, they must shout loudly and bang sticks together to frighten it away as they crossed the gulf.

Whether from the devil's head facing upward or the black dragon, the royal ships were tossed uncontrollably by the elements, spun around like tops, driven back by the current, and then driven forward by the winds. "Fearing the effects of its fury, we did all we could to guard against the dangers of the place, and pass over the waves that boiled and foamed all around us," wrote one pilgrim.

Eventually the ships made it through this dangerous patch and came upon a large ship on its return voyage from the Holy Land. From its sailors

Richard received the intelligence that Philip had arrived safely at Acre, was diligently building his siege machines, and was eagerly awaiting Richard's arrival. Richard pressed on in high spirits.

Outside the harbor of Limmassol he found Berengaria's ship at anchor in the open sea, tossing with the wind and waves, and the damsel in some considerable distress. Again the King's temperature rose. To this supposed Emperor he sent a message unusual for its restraint, given Richard's contempt for the lowborn bully. For the love of God and respect for the cross, the Emperor should release his captives and return their money and property, as well as the treasure seized from the shipwreck. Should he do this and thus perform a service to God, the Crusader fleet would move on directly to the Holy Land without further ado. To this message Richard received a curt rejection saying that the Emperor would neither release his captives nor give up their gold. Moreover, an emperor would have nothing to do with a mere king.

At this insult Richard strapped on his armor and gave the order for his entire army to do likewise. "Follow me," he said, hanging on to a yardarm, "Follow me, that we may avenge the injuries which this perfidious Emperor has done to God and to ourselves. He prates against the justice of God and keeps our pilgrims in chains." Looking out to the shore where the Emperor was prancing up and down on a horse and his soldiers behind their makeshift barricades were emitting a low, menacing growl, Richard said, "Fear them not, for they are without any real arms, and better prepared for flight than fight." Richard liked the look of the Emperor's horse.

The boats were launched, and the Crusaders hit the beach bravely. Their archers rained down arrows upon the hapless and knightless defenders, "like a shower upon the grass," said one observer. At first, with their bows and slingshots, the ill-trained Cypriots put up a stout defense, but the modern darts and bolts of the Europeans mowed them down unmercifully. The bulwark broke, and the defenders fled into a disorderly retreat, first into the city and then onto the plain beyond. On the beach Richard cadged a horse and tried to catch up to the Emperor so that he might challenge the villain to single combat. But the Emperor's magnificent steed was too fast, and Isaac slipped away.

Overnight the Crusaders brought their big horses ashore. But the beasts were sore from the constant pounding of the sea and flaccid from a month's confinement, and so they could not be pushed, certainly not pushed into battle. Very early on the following morning, therefore, the King and fifty knights trotted out gingerly five miles to the east near a castle called Kolossi, where Isaac had regrouped and was ready for a fight. Even in the glow of dawn, with the camp asleep, the local force looked daunting. One company clerk was bold enough to whisper to the King, "Sire, it appears to be a wise plan to decline a battle with so large and so powerful a multitude."

"Young man, you'd best confine yourself to your writing," the King snapped, "and leave the war to us. Take good care to keep out of the crowd."

The engagement at Kolossi was swift, violent, and short. The charge of the smaller force into the slumbering encampment dispatched the multitude. It was later reported that Richard either chased the Emperor in all his imperial nakedness through the warren of tents or was able to unhorse the villain. In whatever undignified state, the Emperor high-tailed it on his magnificent yellow Arabian stallion. While Isaac fled through the Troodos Mountains toward Nicosia, Richard came back to Limmassol with considerable booty, including gold cups and imperial tents and a gorgeous emperor's banner, which the King treated as a prized personal possession. But he wanted the Emperor himself—and his magnificent yellow stallion.

In the town he issued an edict to the local population in which he promised that any who came over to him would be treated fairly and decently, with their homes protected, whereas any who remained at arms would be treated harshly. The King underscored his deft piece of psychological warfare by garrisoning his soldiers outside of town in the nearby pastures, so as to cause no offense to the natives. The Cypriots streamed to the English side, and later a local Cypriot historian, Neophytus, would write bitterly that the English King, "the wretch," found Cyprus to be a "nursing mother." Had the Cypriots not been so compliant, the scribe wrote, Richard might have experienced on his island the fate that the German King, Frederick Barbarossa, had suffered in Turkey. But a nursing mother the island most certainly was.

Fresh from his thrashing of this local scoundrel, Richard must have been in fine spirits. Or he must have been particularly attentive to the geopolitics of his European realm. For on that day, a Sunday and the feast day for the martyr St. Pancras, and well after the season of Lent, he married Berengaria. In the land of Aphrodite and Adonis the ceremony had the veneer of romance and sensuality. Nicolas, Richard's personal chaplain, performed the marriage rite in a chapel of the Limmassol castle devoted to St. George, the dragon slayer. The ceremony had the full royal pomp it deserved. The royal watchers doted on this seemingly perfect and romantic couple:

*And there at Limmassol was crowned*
*The fairest bride that could be found*
*At any time and any place,*
*A virtuous queen with lovely face.*
*Now was the king most glorious*
*Because he was victorious*
*And because he had wed the wife*
*To whom he pledged his word and life.*

To the wet-eyed followers of the royal house the two made a romantic couple. "Later she was called Queen. Most dear," wrote a poet at the scene, "the King did love and revere her." Afterward, the Bishop of Evreux, attended by the Bishop of Bayonne and the Archbishop of Auxienne and Apamea, placed the crown on the bride's head and proclaimed this lady from the minor kingdom of Navarre to be the Queen of England.

Why would Richard do this thing that seemed so contrary to his character and proclivities? Why now? Why at all? Could he not have postponed the marriage until he reached the Holy Land? Or postponed it indefinitely on the pretext of his Crusade? Or could it possibly be that he meant now, through heroic effort, in the midst of his Crusade, to sire an heir to the Plantagenet throne?

A partial answer may lie in the unromantic area of geopolitics. He was clearly concerned about his far-flung Plantagenet kingdom receding ever farther from his grasp. In his marriage contract the King bestowed upon his new Queen all his lands in Gascony below the Garonne River. This troubled part of his domain in southwest France was torn by strife and populated with a number of obstreperous and independent nobles, who had no fondness for Richard nor allegiance to the House of Poitiers. But Gascony is contiguous to Navarre. Together Navarre and Gascony formed a bulwark against the province of Toulouse to the east, which traditionally had been openly hostile to the Duke of Aquitaine. If geopolitics did indeed compel the act, he had to do it here, in Cyprus, before he got to the Holy Land and into the presence of his vengeful, sensitive, cunning, and resentful former lover, King Philip of France. As for siring an heir, the proof of the pudding would be in the eating.

On the day of this propitious event the rest of Richard's fleet arrived in the harbor of Limmassol from Rhodes. This, much more than his sham marriage, may have accounted for Richard's especially high spirits.

km 0 ... 50
0 ... miles ... 30

Ⴞ Fortress
✕ Battle

Mediterranean Sea

Cape St. Andrea

St. Hilarion
Kyrenia
Kantara
KYRENIA MOUNTAINS
Buffavento
Nicosia
Famagusta
KARPAS PENINSULA
MESAORIA
✕ Tremathousa

TROODOS MOUNTAINS

Paphos

Kolossi
Limmassol

Cyprus

## 2

# SILVER CHAINS

The day before the marriage King Guy of Jerusalem arrived in Cyprus with three ships. He had come directly from the trenches of Acre, and he was accompanied by certain eminences of the Latin Kingdom and 160 knights. Even as the preparations were under way for the next day's wedding, Richard found time to row out to greet his ally and conduct him with full honors as an equal to his headquarters in the Limmassol castle.

Royal though his status may have been, Guy presented a sorry picture. His past four years had been hard. Saladin had kept him in captivity for a year after the Battle of Hattin and then had released him in July 1188 with the promise that Guy would never again take up arms against the Muslims. It took Guy about a year to put steel behind his broken promise. In July 1189 he mounted the siege of Acre, and it had dragged on nearly two years without success. Still unappreciated and widely blamed for the disaster at Hattin, he was now directly challenged for the leadership by the Marquis of Tyre, Conrad of Montferrat. To complicate his situation even further, Guy's wife, Sibylla, had died the previous fall in the epidemic that had spread through the Christian ranks, and therefore Guy's claim to the throne, which came directly through her, was considerably weaker. He was coming to complain to Richard that upon his arrival in the Holy Land, King Philip of France was siding with his rival, Conrad, and undermining his authority in the siege of Acre.

The threadbare King needed a bit of shoring up. And so Richard outfitted him splendidly. He presented Guy with two thousand marks of silver (a mark being two-thirds of a pound) and twenty precious cups, two of which were pure gold. In return King Guy swore allegiance to Richard as his leader. While this association had its short-term advantages, it solemnized yet another division within the Christian camp. Already there was the tension between the Hospitalers and the Templars, between the second- and third-generation Christians called the poulains and the parvenus, between King Guy and Count Raymond of Tripoli, between the English and the French, between Richard and Philip. Now it was Richard and Guy versus Philip and

Conrad. This was no way to begin an epic adventure to recapture the Holy Land. Saladin would be pleased.

On the day after the marriage the Emperor, Isaac, came skulking into Richard's presence, suing for peace. A meeting was arranged between the King and the Emperor on the open plain outside of Limmassol. Richard decided to make a real show out of the occasion. He draped himself in the finest of his royal livery. He threw his long legs over his immense Spanish stallion. His saddle sparkled with golden spangles, and the horse was caparisoned with a robe held in place by an ornament of two small interlinked lions of gold. Richard's spurs were pure gold. The King's loose vestment was rose-colored and decorated with silver crescents. Around his waist his woven belt held his great sword with its golden handle. On his head he wore a loose scarlet hat into which the shapes of various animals and birds had been woven. In his hand he carried the staff of his rule. He was magnificent.

Isaac fell down before this blinding apparition and swore his everlasting allegiance. Humbly he promised to contribute one hundred knights, four hundred horsemen, and five hundred foot soldiers to the Crusade and offered all the castles of Cyprus as strongholds for the Crusader soldiers. In settlement for his theft of the money from the wrecks of the two Crusader ships, he presented twenty thousand gold marks, and, as security, he offered up his only daughter and heir to Richard as a hostage. "My lords, you are my right hand," said Richard, turning to his council. "Does this peace do damage to your honor, which is here at stake? If it pleases you, it will be done, but not if it seems ill."

"We think it good, sire," they replied. "By such peace we are honored."

And so it was done. The truce was sealed with the kiss of peace, and the King rode back to Limmassol fully satisfied. He had the Emperor's captured pavilion returned to the villain as a gesture of friendship. It was erected ceremoniously on the very spot of their peace conference, under the careful watch of the King's guards, of course.

That night, however, in the spirit of another Cypriot treachery four hundred years later (Iago and Othello), a knight came to Isaac to sow the suspicion that Richard's assurances were a sham and that the English King really intended to seize the Emperor that night and clap him into chains. Chains? Isaac shuddered at the thought. From his years in a European prison, chains terrified him more than anything. The motive of this early-day Iago, who was in league with King Philip of France but was not acting on orders, was to delay Richard further with an intramural fight in Cyprus and thus give his lord, Philip, more time for singular glory in the Holy Land beyond Richard's shadow. Slipping past the King's napping watchmen, Isaac mounted his yellow stallion and fled to Famagusta. From there he conveyed his change of mind to Richard, declared his hostility, and swore to drive the foreign invader off his island.

Isaac's change of heart was probably exactly what Richard wanted. For it now gave the English King the pretext to subdue the entire island and to plunder its wealth. With its strategic location off the coast of Palestine and its fertile land, the island of Cyprus was the perfect supply base from which to launch his Crusade. If he could capture the island, it could provide him with a constant source of provisions for his entire campaign. Poor Cyprus. Aphrodite was ravaged yet again. Her island seemed forever destined to be someone's victim, someone's breadbasket, someone's strategic redoubt. In the end, from the people's perspective, Richard would turn out to be no better than Isaac. In the words of the monk Neophytus, Providence had driven out the dogs and had brought the wolves in their stead.

Richard's immediate problem—or opportunity—was to hunt down Isaac.

Splitting his fleet in half, he sent one battle group west around Paphos and the Akama Peninsula to Kyrenia, with orders to sweep up all the ships they could find, while he took the other half around Ayia Napa to Famagusta. Meanwhile he put King Guy in command of the army and had him march overland to Famagusta. Since the fall of Acre to Saladin four years earlier, Famagusta, on the eastern coast of Cyprus, had become the great port and emporium of the eastern Mediterranean. Much of Acre's population had resettled there. Its fortress and walled city faced the water, and a few centuries later the tower of that fortress was known as "Othello's Tower." Its harbor was the best on the island. Its narrow streets teemed with the trade of three continents. Isaac had good reason to flee into its vibrant chaos.

The sight of Richard's ships so soon in the harbor after his own arrival spooked Isaac once again, however. He fled Famagusta, into the great plain of the island, the Mesaoria, a vast shimmering ocean of grass dotted with olive trees and frequented by tigers and mirages. Behind this confusing expanse rose the spiny peaks of the northern Kyrenia range, upon whose heights Isaac's three colossal castles of Buffavento, Dieudamour, and Kantara were perched.

Before entering the Mesaoria, Richard tarried in Famagusta. Emissaries from Acre had come to visit and importune him there. King Philip had sent the worldly Bishop of Beauvais and his chief constable to inquire about Richard's costly delay in coming to the rescue of the Holy Land. Philip had built his siege engines and was ready, twiddling his thumbs. He would not begin his assault on Acre until Richard came. Where was his ally? The meeting was a tense one. The ambassadors verged on charging Richard with sloth and indiscipline. What did Cyprus have to do with their Crusade? The scattered King seemed to have lost his bearings. Why could Richard not keep his attention on the very reason for coming east? "Words were said that are not fit/Herein to be set down or writ," the poet reported. Richard did his best to contain his temper at these aspersions. But he would not be deterred from gaining his satisfaction. The scoundrel of Cyprus had to be subdued. Moreover, Richard wanted the Emperor's beautiful horse.

In Nicosia, meanwhile, Isaac was gathering all the soldiers he could still muster. His task was daunting, since so many had deserted to Richard. Even within his own guard he was being challenged. At dinner one night in Nicosia one of his nobles said to him, "My lord, we advise you to make peace with the King of England, lest the whole of your kingdom be destroyed." When the dissenter made this bold remark, Isaac happened to be holding a knife, about to attack a piece of meat. Instead of attacking his chop, the Emperor reached over and cut off the noble's nose.

With about seven hundred men Isaac eventually marched out of Nicosia into the plain and confronted Richard's forces at a place called Tremathousa. A brief pitched battle occurred there, but it was no contest. The skirmish was noteworthy for an attempt by Isaac to dispatch Richard with poisoned arrows. Isaac meant to hit and run, but he missed, and then he had to run very fast to the heights of Buffavento on his swift horse, because Richard was very angry indeed.

As he pondered his fate, Isaac's view from Buffavento was remarkable. His mountaintop castle was well named, since the ramparts of this bastion clung to cliffs of the second-highest peak of the northern range, and its walls were whipped by winds and often enshrouded in clouds. When the clouds parted, Isaac could look to the south over the Mesaoria to Nicosia, which was now in Richard's hands, and to the columns of the King's forces making their way toward him. To the north he looked out over the blue Mediterranean and down to the tiny harbor of Kyrenia, where he had his finest castle. Richard's galleys surrounded it now, and the great chain across its entrance was rendered worthless. Inside was his daughter. She soon saw that resistance to this overwhelming force was pointless, and she threw herself on her knees in front of King Guy. This display touched the King, perhaps because Isaac's daughter was quite beautiful. He packed her off to Limmassol, where she would become the lady-in-waiting to Queen Berengaria.

After the Kyrenia castle was in his hands, King Guy split his forces for the assault on the castles above him. When Isaac saw the forces converging on Buffavento, he abandoned it and moved to Dieudamour, his redoubt named for Cupid and often associated with the legend of Sleeping Beauty. Neither love nor legend could save him now, even if the fortress of Dieudamour was considered impenetrable. His troops lost themselves in their mead as they watched Richard's soldiers move up the mountain. The Emperor abandoned his besotted guards and moved east along the ridge to his last castle, Kantara, the fortress of a Hundred Chambers. But his situation was hopeless, his soldiers dispirited, and his foe determined. He was finally cornered at the tip of the Karpas Peninsula, the oxtail that pointed toward the Holy Land and was graced by the St. Andrea Monastery.

At Cape St. Andrea, the place where the Apostle himself first set foot in Cyprus, Isaac Comnenus was captured—and Richard greedily took charge of his captive's magnificent horse, which he renamed Fauvel, a corruption of the Latin word *"fulvus,"* for the steed's light yellow color. The Emperor fell to the ground before the English King and begged, above all else, not to be placed in iron chains. His fear of chains had become pathological. So Richard commanded that silver chains be made. When the Emperor was bound in them, he was put on a ship for the dark and dreary Hospitaler castle of Margat on the coast of Syria.

He was the last Byzantine Emperor of Cyprus.

With this annoying diversion now taken care of, the great Crusader King could turn his mind to the main business at hand. The Promised Land beckoned and beseeched his help. And Acre, the tormented city. It was the first destination and the first objective of this holy and glorious campaign. "If a ten-year war made Troy celebrated, if the triumph of the Christian made Antioch more illustrious, Acre will certainly obtain eternal fame," wrote the great chronicler of the Third Crusade, "as a city for which the whole world contended."

Acre. Gateway to Holy Land. The very name ached with excitement for the Christian host.

PART II

# The
# TOURNAMENT

If the King comes, I have faith in God
that I shall live
or shall be cut to pieces;
And if I live, it will be great good luck for me;
and if I die, a great deliverance.

BERTRAN DE BORN, TROUBADOUR

# CHAPTER EIGHTEEN

# The Holy Test

T LAST THE CHRISTIAN SOLDIERS BOARDED their warships in Cyprus to begin their true mission against the heathen, the mission to which they had committed their lives, their property, and their honor. They left with song in their throats as krummhorns resounded, trumpets rang out, and pipers added their shrill notes. "I have left evil behind me and have turned to a good life and want people to hear my song," went one rousing Crusader song called *"Parti de Mal."* "God has called to us in His need and no worthy man can fail Him. He humbled Himself and died on the cross for us; it is right that He should get His recompense; for by His death have we all been redeemed." But there was as much trepidation as joy. Few Crusaders seemed to return from this savage land, where the Arabs were treacherous and dangers were great. "I sing to comfort my heart," ran another song, about this epic Crusade in the "Outremer." "For I do not want to die or go mad despite my great torment. God! When they shout 'Outree,' help this pilgrim because I tremble."

Their first objective was to relieve the siege of Acre.

In the happier days of the Latin Kingdom, Acre had been the chief port of Palestine, the traditional point of disembarkation for the Christian pilgrims of Europe, the great marketplace of the eastern Mediterranean. The port was situated on a hook of land at the north end of the Bay of Acre across the water from Haifa, eight miles away, at the south end of the bay. Between the two cities the shoreline consisted of a wide swath of dunes and soft sand, the kind of sand prized by Persian goldsmiths for their work. From Acre's harbor the devout had traveled overland not only to Jerusalem but to Nazareth and Galilee and even to such distant places as the shrine of Our Lady of Sednayia. This holy place was only twenty-five miles from the lair of the infidel, Damascus, and so the journey was dangerous and had to be undertaken with a stout escort of Templars.

But the benefit could be great. The shrine's founding was said to have taken place in the year A.D. 547 when Justinian I, the Emperor of Byzantium, was warring with Persians of the region and had taken a respite from the fighting for a hunt. He gave chase to a gazelle, which in time began to tire, and the Emperor caught up with it near a rock by a small lake. As the warrior drew back his bowstring for the kill, the gazelle was transfigured into an icon of the Virgin Mary, and from this icon a white hand extended in protest.

"No, thou shalt not kill me, Justinian," a sonorous voice said, "but thou shalt build for me a church on this hill."

And this he did. It became a convent whose impressive domes and towers loomed high over the desert landscape. Inside there was an icon of the Virgin, painted by St. Luke himself, which was believed to have miraculous powers. The icon was said to have grown flesh from the neck to the belly, and from its breasts oozed a miraculous oil with an odor sweeter than balsam that could cure all sickness. And so in the years before the fall of Acre to Saladin in 1187, small bands of the sick and the lame set out from the port with their Templar guards, especially in mid-August and September to celebrate the

Assumption and the Nativity of the Virgin Mary, and braved the long and hot and perilous journey across the hills and into the Syrian desert in quest of a few drops of this amazing oil and holy cure.

To the medieval mind Acre was a spacious metropolis whose wealth was on par with Constantinople. Once the ancient southern city of the Phoenicians, it was a polyglot of religions and peoples at the confluence of three continents, where merchants from Venice and Marseille mixed with traders from North Africa and Yemen, where Jews and Armenians rubbed shoulders with Nestorians from Mosul and imams from Baghdad. And somewhere lurking in the shadows were Assassins from Masyaf and al Kahf. Its main street, the rue de la Boucherie, ran from the outer wall to the harbor and was a noisy, smelly, filthy, exciting fleshpot of teeming humanity.

Acre was a city with pious pretensions and profane proclivities. Its wealthy elite lived in splendor and comfort in spacious villas. Its archbishop railed at the corruption and the violence of this upper class. The city's murder rate was high and noteworthy for high-born wives poisoning their husbands. Its sex trade was centered in its many brothels, and its brothels included houses rented to harlots by monks. Its Muslim visitors complained about seeing Muslim women in chains, just as they salivated at European whores who "made themselves targets for men's darts, permitted territory for forbidden acts, offered themselves to the lances' blows, and humiliated themselves to their lovers." The Muslims hated the city's pigs and crosses and despaired over their mosques that had been made into churches and whose minarets had been made into bell towers. Only the *mihrāb* of the city's great Friday Mosque, now called the Church of St. John, had been left as a refuge for the believers in Islam.

If it could be heartless and brutal, Acre was also tender. Its "English street" was devoted solely to the care of poor pilgrims and included a hospice named for Thomas à Becket. The Hospitalers maintained the most impressive hospital and hostel in the entire Middle East. It was a virtual underground city of noble chambers with vaulted ceilings and beds for two thousand sick and wayward penitents. At the north gate and facing the plain where the northern wall met the sea, the Templars maintained a formidable garrison, and it was here that one arranged for an escort of militant monks across mountains and desert to Sednayia or down to Jerusalem.

The city was shaped like a triangular shield: two sides fronted the sea, while its eastern perimeter to the land side was protected by a double wall, various ditches and barbicans, and towers only a stone's throw apart. Like Tyre, it had an inner harbor where a heavy iron chain could be raised and lowered across its mouth. A forty-foot stone turret, known as the Tower of Flies, protected the entrance at the end of the breakwater. The tower's name was associated with Beelzebub, the Lord of the Flies, but that was the benign explanation. The rock on which it was built was also said to have been a place of human sacrifice in ancient times, where the victims' blood brought clouds of bluebottle flies. From the rooftops of the city it was not unusual to gaze out on a spectacle of eighty ships, moored in the harbor and anchored just outside. This forest of masts and flapping sails and yardarms brought to mind for the Muslim visitor that passage in the Koran about ships "lofty as mountains," great works created by man but made possible only by the grace of Allah.

When Saladin captured the city in 1187, he restored the city's Friday Mosque and the tomb of the prophet Salih to their former glory and then turned his mind to the city's defenses. The most vulnerable points were the damaged walls facing the plain of Acre. Most exposed of all was the salient at the northeast corner, where the walls came together at a protruding right angle upon which a high tower had been built. The Christians called this turret the "Accursed Tower"—*Turris Maledicta*—for it was said that Judas Iscariot's thirty pieces of silver had been minted here.

Upon the arrival of King Guy before Acre's walls in August 1189, the Christian forces had established their headquarters on a sandy, ninety-foot hill one mile due east of the city's gate. They named this position Le Toron, but the Muslims knew it as *Tell el Mosalliyin,* "the Hill of Those who Pray." From there the Christian battalions fanned out, setting up their siege engines along the northern perimeter and concentrating their firepower around the Accursed Tower. Across the neck of the peninsula on which Acre rested, they set about to dig an immense trench that might protect their siege lines from outside attack.

Saladin, in turn, had moved into the area slowly from the southeast, along the ancient road from Nazareth. At first he set up a forward position on a hill known as Aiyadida, but eventually he withdrew his base to a higher, more distant hill 250 feet in elevation, east of Mount Carmel, called Jebel el Kharruba or the "Hill of the Carob Trees." From there he could look down upon a vast battlefield, with the wide slit across the neck of the peninsula. Gradu-

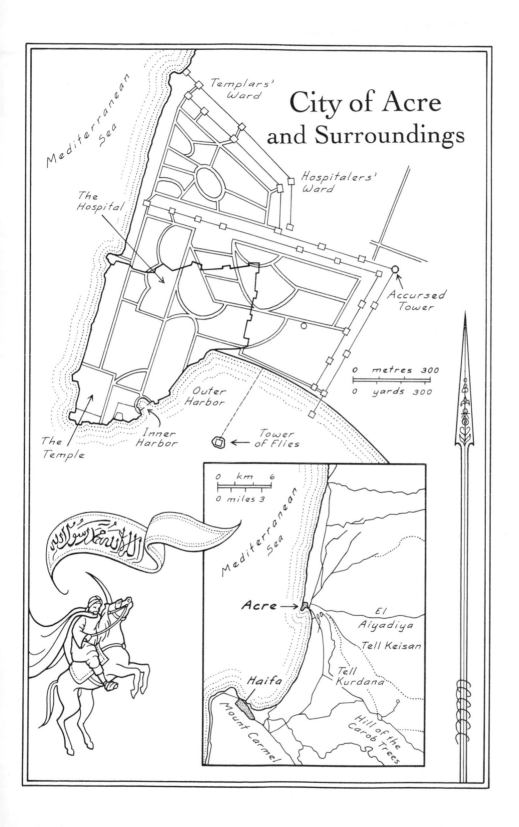

City of Acre
and Surroundings

Mediterranean Sea

Templars' Ward

Hospitalers' Ward

The Hospital

Accursed Tower

0 metres 300
0 yards 300

Outer Harbor

The Temple

Inner Harbor

Tower of Flies

0 km 6
0 miles 3

Mediterranean Sea

Acre

El Aiyadiya

Tell Keisan

Tell Kurdana

Haifa

Mount Carmel

Hill of the Carob Trees

ally he deployed his various divisions forward to positions near the smaller hillocks of el Aiyadida, Tell Keisan, and Tell Kurdana.

As the year 1191 began, there existed interlocking blockades. Acre was totally cut off and was slowly strangling. Together with an effective sea blockade, the Christian trench line stretched two miles across the neck of land that led to the city and prevented any access to it. But the Christians themselves were also besieged, blockaded by the wider encirclement of more than three miles that Saladin had set up in the surrounding hills.

Through the two winters the Crusader forces were encamped at Acre's walls, they also had difficulty getting enough supplies to sustain their effort. Many battle horses had to be slaughtered for food, and battle horses were not easily replaced. A dead horse had become more valuable than a live one. When one was slaughtered, the soldiers gathered like vultures. At this spectacle a chaplain could only shake his head and mutter the words of the evangelist: "Wheresoever the body is, thither will the eagles be gathered together" (Luke 17:37). Profiteering was rampant: A silver penny bought thirteen beans or a single egg, a hundred gold besants bought a single sack of corn, and ten soldi bought a horse's intestines. Whereas in peacetime a bushel of wheat cost a half bezant, now it sold for sixty bezants. At these prices soldiers reverted to eating grass.

To communicate with his besieged compatriots across the Christian trenches, Saladin had to rely on birds and swimmers. A Muslim soldier had trained a squad of carrier pigeons to carry dispatches back and forth and had built a commodious pigeon house of reeds for his messengers not far from Saladin's pavilion. The birds became revered heroes of the cause and were lauded later for their loyal service: "These birds kept secrets loyally," wrote one of the Arab chroniclers. "They ensured the flow of information, guarded the letters jealously, showed themselves as generous as the best of noblemen. They braved dangers, never made a mistake, and were prized as precious possessions."

Even more heroic were the swimmers who risked the perils of the ocean and the vigilance of the enemy to reach the desperate city and bring the defenders their pay. One legendary figure, much revered by Muslim soldiers, was named 'Aisa. He had become skilled at taking soldiers' pay through the ocean waters in a belt of oiled silk hitched to his waist, often diving beneath the Christian galleys. His method was always to release a pigeon to the Hill of the Carob Trees after he had arrived safely. When one day no pigeon arrived, his compatriots feared the worst. A few days later his body washed up on the rocks not far from the town. The money was found and delivered to its rightful owners. "Never before have we heard of a dead man delivering a message entrusted to his care," wrote the chronicler, much less of a soldier's being paid by a dead man.

If pigeons and swimmers and the occasional commando in a light skiff were the champions of the Muslim side, the messages that they bore from the city to the Sultan in their second winter were increasingly grim. The city was slowly starving and increasingly dispirited. Saladin himself began to despair over his chances to break the siege, largely because the Christian forces were being reinforced each day with fresh troops from Europe. The advance guard of Danes, Saxons, and Flemish had been followed by the arrival of Henry of Champagne, the grandchild of Eleanor of Aquitaine by one her of daughters from her marriage to the French King. This impressive young knight had the confidence of the French and English kings who were his uncles and whose precursor he was.

With his presence and his sanction as the kings' forerunner, Champagne imparted an overall central command to the Christian siege, which heretofore had consisted of brave but competing elements, which in turn led to brave but random assaults on the walls. As the specialists in maritime warfare, Pisans and Genoese were deployed north and south where the wall met the sea; between them came Hospitalers and Templars, the forces of King Guy and of Conrad of Montferrat, Flemish, Danes, Frisians, and Germans. At last the rabble had a supreme commander.

As the harbinger of good things to come, Champagne brought with him ten thousand soldiers, a number of important nobles and holy men—including the Archbishop of Canterbury (who would die several months later, in disgust, it was said, over the manner in which the Crusader army had given itself over to drink, women, and dice)—a fleet of ships to bolster the blockade and to provision the sieging army, and a number of siege engines. These mangonels were put into place and began their relentless pounding.

In the second year of the siege there were also random acts of great heroism on the Muslim side. Occasionally Muslim raiders would slip out at night and set ablaze one of the great engines, or, with a stroke of luck, a canister of Greek fire, the napalm of the twelfth century, which could burn through steel and could be snuffed out only with huge quantities of vinegar, would arc over the wall at the attackers and find its mark. Among the most celebrated of these brave acts was the wily plan to try to slip a cargo ship from Beirut, heavily laden with corn, sheep, cheese, onions, and other foodstuffs, past the tight Christian blockade.

For this daring mission a group of Muslim commandos put on European clothes and even shaved their beards, an extreme and selfless humiliation that was the ultimate act of devotion. The long and flowing beard was the signature of the virile Oriental man, and, in turn, the sight of ghostly European men with clean-shaven faces could inspire terror in the East. As if clean faces were not enough, the commandos also spread crosses around their ship and even allowed that most despicable of all animals, the pig, to run about freely and befoul the decks. A Christian galley came alongside the masquerading ship, and the captain shouted out, "You seem to be making for the city."

"You mean you haven't taken it yet?" the disguised Muslim shouted back.

"No, not yet."

"Very well, we will make for the army, but there is another ship close behind us, coming on with the same wind. You should warn them not to enter the harbor."

The Christian blockaders bought the bait and made for the ship behind, which was then coming onto the horizon, and the relief ship made a run for the harbor, to the great cheers of the starving inhabitants.

Not long after this episode, perhaps in anger at being so badly tricked, the Christian command decided to assault the Tower of Flies itself. This slender turret at the entrance to the harbor stood as a monument to the town's resistance; to ruin so visible a symbol would have a wonderful effect. This mission fell to Pisan sailors, who were the most ferocious and experienced fighters at sea. To accomplish their task the ingenious Italians constructed a huge wooden castle on the deck of one galley, covered its sides with hides soaked in water, and filled its top with bundles of sticks, which they intended to light when the galley came alongside and hurl through the windows of the tower. A second, shallow-hulled ship was mined with medieval napalm and other combustibles; the plan for this torpedo ship was to set it afire and launch it through the mouth of the harbor and into the Muslim fleet inside. On the deck of a third ship a roof was built to protect a company of assault troops huddled underneath from the missiles of the defenders above, until these marines could come alongside the breakwater and leap onto its rocks, whereupon they would lean huge ladders on the tower and scale its heights.

So bold and ingenious a plan, so disappointing a result. The fire ship was set ablaze as planned, but when it and the castle-bearing ship approached the Tower of Flies, the wind changed and the two ships began to drift away. As the attackers desperately tried to anchor their topheavy ship to the breakwater, the defenders of the tower rained down Greek fire, and eventually the ship, too, began to burn. Still, some of the Pisans got onto the breakwater. As they set their ladders against the tower, huge beams and still more Greek fire poured down on them, and eventually they had to withdraw. Meanwhile, the ship with the marines, seeing that disaster had befallen their comrades, fell into dispute and confusion. They were eventually taken without much of a fight. When this dramatic sea battle was over, the defenders raised a great din of joy with cymbals and the clanking of pipes. Inevitably they credited their God with the victory.

"These events were unmistakable signs of the will of God, and great wonders upholding God's religion," wrote the great Arab chronicler Beha al-Din. "It was a day of testimony."

For the Muslim side such triumphal moments were few. For each time that a skiff got through or a Christian mangonel was damaged or a Christian assault turned back, more Christian ships from across the sea seemed to arrive with fresh troops, fresh provisions, and more artillery. With the Christian siege becoming stronger by the day, Saladin felt compelled to pull back his divisions from their forward positions, leaving only a thousand soldiers on the Tell Keisan. With this pullback the circle around the Christian siege was enlarged. The Sultan obviously hoped that this breathing space would encourage the hotheads in the Christian camp to launch another of their foolhardy charges. It was hope against hope. For Saladin appreciated that more competent commanders were taking charge.

During the stalemate of the siege's second year there might be skirmishes and individual acts of valor on both sides, but generally the situation settled into a dull familiarity between the fighting elements. As the smoke of their campfires wafted over the besieged city or east over the tents of their own besiegers, Christian soldiers passed the time in telling and embellishing their heroic battle stories. As they have been passed down to us, many of these stories, like soldiers' tales in all times, were scatological: the Christian who is attacked by a Muslim on horseback when he is squatting to relieve himself and heroically fells his iniquitous adversary with a rock to the head; the Muslim soldier who makes a show of urinating on a cross high on the wall of Acre, only to receive an arrow through the heart; the brave Muslim admiral who stays behind to fight the Christians after his soldiers have retreated, only to be knocked off his horse while he holds a vessel of Greek fire, which breaks in the fall and spills over his genitalia, so that "what he had intended for our detriment became his own destruction."

Then there was the story of the Parthian and the Welshman who encounter one another in no-man's-land.

"I see that you are a good bowman," says the Turk boldly. "I am a Parthian by nation, brought up from childhood in the art of shooting, and my name is Grammahyr. I am a man of good reputation among my people for my deeds of renown, and well known for my victories. Of what country are you? And by what name may I be pleased to know you?"

The Welshman, true to his nation's character, answers sparely and roughly with the bare facts.

"Let us prove which is the best bowman, by each taking an arrow and aiming them against one another from our bows," says the talkative Turk. "You shall stand still first, and I will aim an arrow at you. Afterward you shall shoot in a like manner at me."

The Welshman, apparently one of the denser sorts, agrees to this proposition. So the Turk fits his arrow, spreads his legs, takes aim, fires, and misses. The well-satisfied Welshman then prepares to take his turn.

"No, I don't agree," the Turk objects. "You must stand another shot and then have two at me."

"You do not abide by your own condition," the Welshman cries as his dander rises. "If you will not stand, God will take revenge on you for your treachery." Whereupon he speedily launches an arrow through the heart of the Parthian, as the enemy, eyes averted, is selecting an arrow for his second shot.

"You stood not by your agreement, nor I by my word," the raw Welshman says over his slain opponent—and one can almost hear the cheers of delight at the end of the story around the fire.

The Muslim camp also had its stories, and many of them revolved around the generosity of their leader. In the early spring of 1191 a contingent of Franks had been captured at Beirut and had been brought before the Sultan. Among the prisoners was a very old man, and Saladin asked him why, given his age, he had come to Palestine. "I only came to this country to make a pilgrimage to the Church of the Resurrection," the old man replied. This answer touched Saladin, and he set the old man free, providing him with a

horse and an escort through the lines to his own people. His younger lieutenants objected and asked for Saladin's permission to execute the remaining
prisoners. The Sultan refused. When he was asked for his reasons, he replied
of the young hotheads, "They shall not become accustomed in their youth to
the shedding of blood and laughing at it."

Meanwhile, in his wooden pavilion high on the Hill of the Carob Trees, Saladin was concerned with more profound matters of strategy. The remnants of
Frederick Barbarossa's German army caused him great alarm. The Sultan had
been relieved when he learned that after the Emperor's drowning in Turkey, his
force had dwindled from 100,000 to merely 5,000. But those tough survivors
were already in Tripoli and moving south, under the capable command of the
Duke of Austria, to join the siege. Saladin's commanders urged him to attack
the German battalions as they made their way south over the the high and perilous seaside trail known as the Ladder of Tyre, but he refused.

His problem was far more serious than merely the German troops, however. From his spies in the enemy camp, from his sources in Constantinople,
and from the Catholic priests in Armenia, he knew also that the English and
French Kings were coming with vast armies. In order to shake the Sultan's
will, the Crusader nobles had long been boasting of the mighty English King
who was coming, a king so powerful that he had achieved mythic proportions in Europe. When this giant arrived, the tree of Hebron that had withered at Christ's death would sprout leaves again, the Christians boasted. If
Saladin could not break the siege around Acre by the local army, led by the
inept King Guy, how could he hope to contend with the vast invasion that
was nearly upon him, led by a giant?

The situation seemed increasingly desperate. The devout Sultan sought
solace in the Koran, especially the scenes in the Holy Test that described the
attack of the enemy of Islam on the holy city of Medina in what was known
as the Battle of the Trench. "Behold they came upon you from above you and
from below you and behold the eyes became dim and the hearts gaped up to
the throats, and ye imagined various vain thoughts about Allah! In that
situation were the believers tried: They were shaken as by a tremendous
shaking."

Then the hypocrites had taunted the faithful for believing in false hopes,
and Saladin had his own hypocrites and naysayers now in his own Battle of
the Trench. And yet Allah's grace had saved the Muslims in the holy story.
And it would save them again now. Saladin was sure of it.

He renewed his call to Holy War. To the emirs of his vast empire he pointed to the determination of their enemies. The Franks had spared no effort, had withheld no money, and now their mightiest kings were coming. Now was the time to cast off lethargy and for all believing men who had blood in their veins to answer this call.

"As long as the seas bring reinforcements to the enemy and the land does not drive them off, our country will continue to suffer at their hands, and our hearts will be troubled by the sickness caused by the harm they do us," ran his summons. "Where is the sense of honor of the Muslims, the pride of the believers, the zeal of the faithful?"

At last his appeal to the Muslim world registered. Reinforcements began to pour in from the far corners of the empire, the devout from Mesopotamia and even beyond the Tigris River as far as India, Egyptians from Babylon, and Africans all the way from Mauritania. It was appreciated that this was no ordinary jihad. This was shaping up as the final battle between the forces of Allah and the forces of the infidel.

2

GOD'S OWN SLING
AT THE ACCURSED TOWER

On April 20, 1191, King Philip Augustus of France arrived at Acre. The royal entourage consisted of six ships, packed with provisions and crowded with massive, large-jointed warhorses, which had been bred in Normandy and Flanders to carry warriors with the full panoply of plate and mail. On the sands of the bay there was great rejoicing at the King's appearance. In the absence of Richard, the French King acted positively Richard-like, as if he knew that his time as supreme commander would be brief. With banners flowing and horns blowing and with a magnificent white falcon of rare breed perched on his arm, he strutted grandly before the besieged city. So close to the walls did he pitch his tent that "the enemies of Christ often shot their quarrels and arrows right up to it." Upon his reconnaissance of the battlements and the siege engines already put in place by Henry of Champagne, the King declared rather tactlessly that "it is strange that with so many warriors here the town is still in enemy hands." Nevertheless, with his skills as an administrator and diplomat, he moved quickly in building on Henry of Champagne's efforts to coalesce the various allies into a coherent, integrated force.

Not long after his arrival his magnificent white falcon deserted him. Flying away from its royal master and ignoring repeated calls from the King and his falconer, the bird perched brazenly on the walls of Acre. This apparition thrilled the city's defenders, who immediately captured the snowy prize and treated this event as an omen of good things to come. The bird's defection did not amuse King Philip, especially since it meant that his first contact with his pagan enemy was his simpering plea to have his exotic bird back. The hefty reward of a thousand gold pieces was offered, but the Muslims did not dignify the offer with an answer.

Having surveyed the situation, King Philip decided to establish the French quarter directly opposite the angular salient known as Accursed Tower. This corner was at the same time the most heavily fortified and the most vulnerable point in the outer walls. He began at once to add his own siege engines to the forest of artillery already in place, but fortifying his various pieces with stone and iron to discourage any Muslim arsonist who might happen by.

Of his seven artillery pieces the most impressive was a huge stone catapult, which his soldiers dubbed the "Evil Neighbor." (Not to be outdone, the Muslims set up their own catapult inside the walls opposite the Evil Neighbor and called their piece the "Evil Kinsman.") And thus for a time the Evil Neighbor traded boulders with the Evil Kinsman. Another catapult, under the command of the Duke of Burgundy, was called "God's Own Sling." The French King erected a rampart and topped it with iron-reinforced breastworks. Behind this iron shield his crossbowmen and longbowmen began to rake the wall without letup. At certain points the outer moat was filled in, and sappers went to work undermining the walls beneath a contraption known as a "Cat." The Cat was a covered gallery with a prow in the shape of a plowshare and wheels, so that it slunk forward like a cat and stuck to the wall as if with claws.

At these points of attack the French King positioned his armored catapults, also called petraria or mangonels. He began to lob boulders against the walls and over them into the rue de la Boucherie and a plaza known as the "ox spring" that for centuries had been venerated by Christians, Muslims, and Jews alike as the place where the Lord brought an ox to Adam, and whatever Adam called every living creature, that was the name thereof.

As these preparations went forward, Philip Augustus turned his mind to political matters. He threw his weight behind Conrad of Montferrat as the rightful heir to the throne of Jerusalem. Under the circumstances, the throne of a nonexistent kingdom hardly seemed worth having, but both Conrad and King Guy wanted it desperately. Even in the abstract, the kingdom operated by the rules of the great houses of Europe, that is, by blood, even if by European standards the blood was dissolute. Guy had become King only through the royal blood of his wife, Sibylla, and now that she was dead, his claim was spurious, though he technically still held the crown.

The bloodline passed now through Queen Sibylla's younger sister, Isabella, but she was already taken. At a tender age she had married a cowardly homosexual named Humphrey of Toron, who was the stepson of Reginald of Châtillon. It had been their marriage ceremony a few years before at Châtillon's castle of Kerak that had been interrupted by the appearance of Saladin's soldiers. Now in a series of cunning moves, including making gifts and bribes to corrupt clerics, Conrad had succeeded in having Isabella's marriage to Humphrey annulled, and he married her himself. King Guy was so furious at this that he had challenged Conrad to single combat, but Conrad scoffed at the challenge. The Archbishop of Canterbury was so distraught at the behavior of the Christian leadership that he died, but that did not seem to matter much either. With Philip of France now solidly behind Conrad, King Guy's claim was further weakened, and this was the reason he sped to Cyprus to enlist King Richard in his personal cause.

By Philip's siding with Conrad, the intense competition within the ranks of the Crusade deepened: Richard against Philip, Conrad against Guy, the Pisans against the Genoese, the Templars versus the Hospitalers. It was a strange way to run a Crusade. Yet between Easter and Pentacost, despite these internal struggles, Philip made real progress in consolidating the attack. His constant bombardment began seriously to cripple the defense. Twice the wall was breached near Judas's Tower, only to be quickly shored up by the defenders.

Splendid organizer and diplomat though he was, Philip lacked the stuff of a supreme commander. He could set the table for Richard, but he did not have the determination or the patience to push the effort over the top without his English rival. Moreover, only a week before Richard arrived, another unsettling event distracted Philip and sapped his will to fight. On June 1, 1191, the noble Count of Flanders was killed in the siege. With its brilliant green crosses and its great commitment, the Flemish contingent had been stalwart in the Crusade from the first day that the news of Jerusalem's fall was received, and the Count of Flanders himself had been a pillar of strength. To his contemporaries he was "rich in material possessions and in honor, great in intelligence and in power, zealous in righteousness, courageous and skillful in arms." But he was also a proponent of the scorched-earth school of total war.

"Thus should war be begun, this is my advice," he was later quoted as having said. "First destroy the land and then one's foes."

Years before the Latin Kingdom was in jeopardy, the count had been a pilgrim in the Holy Land. When the Archbishop of Tyre had described the catastrophe at Gisors, he had been among the first to take the cross. After he'd raised a good deal of money, his force was formidable. The count had assumed the command of the Danish forces as well as his own. Among his fighters was one of the most gallant of all the knights on the Crusade, James d'Avesnes, a famous fighter whose crest was a field of diagonal gold and red stripes. If he was tough, the Alsatian count was also graceful. With great tact he had interceded in Sicily when the dispute between Richard and Philip over Alais threatened the alliance.

Now he was dead. This tragedy at the ramparts was a blow to the campaign. But in Philip's cunning mind it had profound political implications for his European domain. The Count of Flanders had died without an heir. That put up for grabs once again the coveted Artois and Vermandois, which the King of France had long coveted for his kingdom. Now, by rights, Flanders should be his, except that he was far away, here in the Orient, and he could not capitalize on the sad, interesting turn of events.

CHAPTER NINETEEN

# Waste Not the Hire

✠

IN Cyprus, Richard was growing impatient at
the good tidings of Philip's success at Acre. If the English King
did not hurry, his delicate rival might capture the prize and steal
the glory.

On June 5, 1191, he set out from Famagusta in his swiftest galley, which
he had christened *Trenchemere*, for the trough it cut in the waves. With the
rest of the fleet he left orders to follow as quickly as it could. On the following day the brooding hulk of Margat came into view through the haze,
high above the Syrian coast. Enemy territory completely surrounded the impressive Hospitaler fortress. As Richard sailed south, past Tortosa and

Tripoli, Sidon and Beirut, it was all enemy territory now until he reached Tyre. There his friends acted like enemies as well. Conrad closed the gates of the city to him and forced the King to camp, like some common outcast, on the beach.

On June 7, Richard was under sail again, when south of Beirut he came upon a huge buss with three masts, high decks, brimming with cargo, whose sides were streaked with red and yellow. Upon first contact the exotic ship identified herself as belonging to the King of France. Eagerly Richard moved closer, hopeful for the latest news. Then abruptly the strange ship changed her story and said she was really from Genoa, bound for Tyre. An Arab spy aboard Richard's ship recognized this colossus as similar to one he had recently seen in Beirut harbor, taking on a hundred camel-loads of weapons, boxes of Greek fire in bottles, and most terrifying of all, ampullas filled with two hundred deadly snakes. The truth was quickly apparent: This great camel of the sea was hovering outside Acre, waiting for the right moment to run the blockade. She was packed with 650 crack troops and a quantity of supplies that could sustain the starving city for months to come.

When the *Trenchemere* came alongside, arrows and darts and Greek fire rained down from the high decks of the enemy ship. This furious, unexpected assault repulsed the Crusaders, and they drew back. Richard heaped scorn on his cowardly men,

"Will you allow this ship to get away untouched and uninjured?" he shouted at them. "Shame. Shame. You have become cowards from so much sloth, too many victories over weak foes! The whole world knows you are in the service of the cross!" This spurred his men forward. Several dived beneath the enemy ship and bound its rudder with ropes to hamper its movements and slow its speed. Others renewed their assault, only to be beaten back.

What happened next is unclear. One report stated that Richard, realizing that his men could not take the ship, ordered his galleys to ram it with their iron prows. Another report stated that the Arab admiral, realizing that his cause was hopeless, scuttled the ship. In either case the result was the same. The leviathan began to sink, and suddenly the sea was strewn with men and supplies. Similarly, there were different accounts of Saladin's reaction when he heard that the great relief ship was lost. "Oh, God, I have now lost Acre," he was quoted as saying by one Christian source. "So bitter a loss. I am overwhelmed." But such whining was not in character. The Arab chronicle described his reaction differently. Serenely, he had retreated to his Koran and his finger had fallen on the line that read, "God wastes not the hire of those who do well."

On June 8, Richard finally arrived at Acre with his battle group of twenty-five galleys. From the sea his challenge was spread out before him: the crenellated walls of the tired city besieged and blockaded, the damaged but still-standing Tower of Flies and Accursed Tower, the colorful Christian lines outside the walls, punctuated with great siege machines, and smoke rising from the explosions of Greek fire around them. Muslim troops pressed right up to the Christian outer trenches, and the enemy's tents and apricot banners, including Saladin's own command post on the Hill of the Carob Trees, dotted the surrounding hills.

There was, of course, jubilation at Richard's arrival. That night huge bonfires were built on the beaches and near the Accursed Tower. The cheers of the throng rang through the hills, along with the blaring of trumpets and the clanging of cymbals. This clamor gave way in the night to choruses of Crusader songs: "*Lignum crucis, Signum ducis, Sequitur exercitus.* . . . The Banner of the chieftain marches in the strength of the Holy Spirit," and then to Virgil's chant: "*Una salus victis nullam sperare salutem.* . . . There is one help for the vanquished, to hope for no help." Then to devout ballads. And finally to the mournful wail of the Scottish pipe, the beating of tambourines for the dancing under a thousand torches, the strains of the harp. To the Muslims in the surrounding hills it seemed as if the whole valley was on fire. They had heard of this King of Kings and of his daring exploits. Now he had come, and they feared the worst. As he listened to the din and beheld the spectacle below him, Saladin was calm, for he counted on his God's favor and protection, and he was serene in the purity of his motives.

When Richard set foot on land, Philip greeted him cordially and escorted him to a royal tent that had been prepared. They spoke excitedly about how to subdue the broken city with dispatch. It was not long, however, before they fell into a squabble over money. As the harder-pressed of the two, Philip was given to bad decisions where land and gold were at stake. Now he foolishly demanded half the booty from Cyprus, in accordance with the agreement they had made at Vézelay. Very well, Richard replied, he in turn would require half of Flanders. These demands were absurd on both sides, for the Vézelay agreement applied only to lands jointly conquered in Palestine. Somehow they managed to get over these ploys, perhaps with a wink and a flirtatious glance, and move back to the serious business at hand.

Philip's proclivity for making bad decisions on money matters did not end here. When his dutiful subject and nephew, Henry of Champagne, came to him in need of new supplies, after his many months of conducting the siege alone, Philip offered him one hundred thousand Parisian gold pieces, but on the condition that his nephew cede his fief of Champagne to the French Crown. Shocked and disappointed at this ingratitude, Henry replied, "I have done what I should. Now I will do what necessity forces upon me. I wanted to fight for my King, but he has no use for me except for what is mine. I will go to him who will receive me and who is more ready to give than to take." Richard seized the opportunity happily, heaping upon Henry four thousand measures of wheat, four thousand pig carcasses, and four thousand pounds of silver.

Philip was cheap, and Richard saw his old companion's failing as a quick way to put Philip in his shadow. Hearing that Philip was offering soldiers in his command three gold bezants a week as pay, Richard's heralds spread the word that the English King would be paying his men four gold pieces a week. Once again Philip was stumped and trumped and overshadowed, and he withdrew for a few days in a huff. "When Richard came," wrote an English chronicler, "the king of the French was extinguished and made nameless, even as the moon loses its light at sunrise."

As Philip had appropriated the salient at the Accursed Tower as his area of attack, Richard set up his siege engines opposite the northern gate. The thirteenth-century Arab historian Abulfaraqio would later report that more than three hundred catapults and balistas were now deployed by the two Kings outside Acre's walls. Since the Genoese had sworn allegiance to Philip, Richard brought the Pisans under his command. On his third day in country he reconstructed his wooden citadel called Mategriffon, whose rafters he had brought from Sicily, and sheathed its walls with cords and skins soaked in vinegar as cover against Greek fire. From its height his archers began to spray the walls of the Accursed Tower with arrows. His miners began to undermine the walls. His men threw up their ladders. His mangonels were smaller than Philip's, but he had brought granite boulders from Sicily that were far more effective than the soft limestone of Palestine. These dense bombs were now trained on the north gate. Richard himself was a study in perpetual motion. "The King was running up and down the ranks, directing some, reproving some, and urging others. Thus he was everywhere present with every one of them, so that whatever they all did ought properly to be ascribed to him."

During these days of furious activity, as he prepared to crush the city of Acre and wreak vengeance on his enemy, Richard must have wondered what manner of man was this whom he faced. For soon after his arrival he received not bombs but gifts from Saladin. Baskets of pears, of Damascene plums and other fruits, along with other small gifts came to Richard and to Philip as a gesture of peace and willingness to talk. At this curious way of treating the enemy, Richard arranged to send an envoy to Saladin through the lines and to suggest that the two leaders meet face-to-face.

Saladin demurred. "It is not customary for Kings to meet," he replied, "unless they have previously laid the foundations of a treaty. For, after they have spoken together and given one another tokens of mutual confidence, it is not seemly for them to return to making war upon one another."

## 2

## A Mighty Shout

Toward the end of June there was an eclipse of the sun that plunged the battlefield into darkness for three hours and unsettled the Christian host. The fact that this unnatural phenomenon coincided with the nativity of St. John the Baptist made the apparition even more terrible. And indeed, a bad development followed immediately. A grotesque illness drove King Richard to his bed. Besides a high fever he was visited with a terrible soreness in his mouth and gums. After a few days his hair began to fall out, and his fingernails became loose. Shortly thereafter Philip Augustus came down with the same scourge. Their doctors diagnosed the problem as arnaldia or leonardia, commonly called trench mouth or scurvy, an ailment probably brought on by a deficiency of vitamin C in their diet.

While Richard was sick, diplomatic contacts between the two sides continued over the possibility of a meeting between Richard and Saladin. For a time it appeared that Saladin had relented and would agree to the meeting, to be conducted on the plain of Acre between contingents of the two armies. Rumors came to Saladin's camp that strong objections against such a meeting were being expressed in the Christian ranks. Then another message came from Richard: "Do not believe the reports that have been spread as to the cause of my delay. I am answerable to myself alone. I am the master of my own actions. But during the last few days sickness has prevented me from doing anything at all.

"It is the custom of Kings," he continued, "to send each other mutual presents and gifts. Now I have in my possession a gift worthy of the Sultan's acceptance, and I ask permission to send it to him."

"He may send the present provided he will accept a gift of equal value from us," Saladin's brother, el Melek el-Adel, replied.

"Our present might be falcons from beyond the sea," the Crusader ambassador then said. "But just now they are weak, and it would be a good thing if you could send us a few chickens which we could feed the falcons to revive them, and then we will send the falcons to you."

This was greeted with a guffaw. "The King wants the poultry for himself," surmised el-Adel.

The diplomatic exchanges seemed to deteriorate from there, until finally the Christian envoy said, "Have you anything further to say? Speak, so that we may know what it is."

"It was not we who made advances to you. You came to us. If you have anything to say, it is for you to speak and tell us your views. We are prepared to listen."

With that the conference was over, and the envoy was shown the door, after he was given a royal robe as a present. The Muslims concluded that the motive for engaging in these exchanges was merely to determine the enemy's state of mind.

Since Philip had been cut out of this diplomacy and since his trench mouth was somewhat less virulent than Richard's, the French King was ready to return to the battle lines on July 1. In his delirium Richard pleaded with Philip to wait a few more days for the final assault. Most of his English fleet and the bulk of his Norman army was stuck in Tyre, detained by adverse weather known as the Arsuf wind. In only a few more days he would be better, and his full force would be with him. Philip declined. Perhaps he thought this was the moment to snatch all the glory for himself. He deployed defensive guards along the trench and proceeded to assault the Accursed Tower with tremendous force.

The Crusaders had some sense of the desperate state of the city behind the walls, for they had an anonymous spy within who sent them regular reports that were always prefaced with the blessing "In the name of the Father and of the Son and of the Holy Ghost, Amen." But if the city was in desperate shape, it was not apparent in the way the defenders fought. Before the city was cut off, nine thousand soldiers defended it, but the attrition over time had been great, and still the bravery and vigilance of the defenders was impressive. The command of the city's defense had been entrusted to two important emirs, known to the Christians only by their shortened names of Karākūsh and Mashtūb. Karākūsh, the Turkish word for "eagle," had been in charge from the beginning of the siege two years before. He was a eunuch who had originally been Saladin's slave in Egypt. But his talents had been evident from the beginning, and the Sultan had invested him with great responsibility. In Egypt he had rendered loyal service as a builder, overseeing the construction of the citadel of Cairo, known as the "Castle of the Mountain," as well as of the walls of the city and the bridges that led to the Pyramids. He presented a grandiose air of self-importance, and he was sometimes caricatured, even by his own people, for his apparent stupidity. But he was an estimable and trusted emir.

Mashtūb was the most distinguished of all Saladin's emirs. He was a high-minded Kurd known for his generosity and his lofty spirit. His name meant "scarred," for he had a great scar across his face. For years his relationship to Saladin had been close, so close that when a son was born to his friend, the Sultan wrote to his emir, "We rejoiced by the star which hath risen from behind its veil; and we hope for joy from the fruit of the date tree still remaining in the bud." Mashtūb held the unique title of grand emir and had assumed overall command of Acre only the previous February.

The emirs now sent messages to the Sultan informing him that the city was in dire straits, the garrison exhausted, and the buildings in shambles, especially around Adam's ox spring, from the daily bombardment. The health conditions were desperate, not only from the lack of food and the presence of their own dead but from the carcasses of dead horses and cows that the Christians were lobbing over the walls with their catapults. Some soldiers were leaping to their deaths in despair, and others were defecting and even accepting baptism in the Christian faith. If Saladin did not break the siege, they would have to surrender soon.

Try to hold out for another week, Saladin replied. A flotilla of Egyptian ships was on its way from Cairo, and a contingent of reinforcements was coming overland from Baghdad. Frantically he was writing to the Caliph in Baghdad and the Emperor in Cairo, "They have mined the walls and the city is in danger. . . . Nothing remains now except that God should overtake it with grace. If help does not come now, when will it come? Whoever comes, but not when he is needed, has not come at all."

As Philip pressed his attack on the Accursed Tower, a smoke signal and a roll of drums went up from the city, the indication to the command post in the far distant hills that the enemy had commenced another attack and that it was time for Saladin's troops to move close onto the trench. Soon after, the Sultan's forces pressed right up to the ditch's edge, trying courageously to fill in certain sections, thus to pass over into the Christian ranks. Here and there individual soldiers succeeded in making it across the trench and tearing up Christian tents and creating havoc. But in general these Muslim commandos were repelled. They did, however, succeed in landing a bundle of brush wood, soaked in Greek fire, on one of Philip's cats, setting it aflame. This, in turn, blunted the French attack on the tower, and at day's end Philip gave up his solo assault. As was his lot in life, it seemed, he would have to wait on Richard once again.

July 2 broke hot and bright. It would be a day of furious activity. At last the English fleet appeared offshore, bringing with it a number of notable Norman and English field commanders. They had arrived just in time, for once again Muslim troops, commanded this time by Saladin's nephew, appeared at the outer trench and sought again to make a bridge across it. Philip's sappers finally made strides in undermining the Accursed Tower. Deep underground, just as the foundations were about to give way, their tunneling was met by countertunneling from Muslim sappers within, and there were terrible hand-to-hand fights in close and dark spaces. The countermine turned back the Christian sappers, even as the wall was collapsing with thunderous noise above them in a breach.

As the rampart was caving in over at the Accursed Tower, Richard could bear his indisposition no longer. Sore gums, depleted hair, and all, he had himself carried to the north gate in a litter made of his royal quilt. From the top of Mategriffon, in a reclining position, he reached for his crossbow and began to pick off Muslims scurrying along on the walls below. Especially gratifying for him was the shot that placed a bolt through the heart of a defender who had had the temerity to don the hauberk of a fallen French chevalier.

Meanwhile all Richard's battle elements were brought into play. His sappers worked beneath the gate's tower. His ram worked on one portion of the wall, while his mangonel bombarded another portion with its Sicilian bombs. With his difficulty at shouting orders, the King nevertheless had his heralds spread the word that he would pay any soldier a week's wages of four gold bezants for every stone he could personally remove from the walls. Even at this unspeakable danger and terrible odds, many sergeants and squires leaped at the chance, and many fell as a result. Eventually the tower gate began to tilt and soon fell into itself. Even then courageous Muslims rushed to protect the ruin. Neither the exhortations of the Bishop of Salisbury nor the inspiration of the Count of Leicester's banner nor the ferocious courage of the Pisan warriors could overcome the stouthearted defense.

By July 4, Mashtūb and Karākūsh had had enough and launched their first peace feeler. Under the white flag, the eagle and the scarface were escorted to the Templars' tent near the north gate and into the presence of Kings. There they laid down their proposal. They might be prepared to surrender the city, they said, and to pay considerable gold and silver, if their lives were spared, their property protected, and if their people might receive safe conduct. "We have taken cities from you," exclaimed the grand emir. "Even when we carried them by storm, we have been accustomed to grant terms to the vanquished. We have taken them to places in which they wished to take refuge, treating them with all kindness. Accordingly we will surrender the city to you if you will grant us similar terms."

"Those you took were our servants and slaves," Richard snapped. "You are likewise our slaves."

"We would rather kill ourselves than surrender the city," Mashtūb said stagily. "Not one of us will die before fifty of your greatest have fallen."

Richard was unimpressed. "The ransom for your bodies shall be your heads," he said coldly.

But Philip was tantalized. He was quite ready to seize this chance and end the conflict. He, too, had had enough: more than a year of slights at the hand of Richard and six weeks of this infernal siege. He was tired of being humiliated and overshadowed, tired of war, and fretful about neglecting unattended opportunities in Europe. He wanted a quick way out.

Richard flatly demurred. He was a warrior who loved war most of all. The glory of victory by force was the true object of war. There was no glory in the negotiated, conditional capitulation of the enemy. He had not come all the way from Europe with his soldiers, sustained the loss of many brave knights, risked his own kingdom at home, only to enter an empty city. With the towers of Acre in ruins and its walls crumbling, with his forces on the verge of pure victory, he meant to complete the job.

Still, he made a counteroffer. In exchange for their lives and the safety of their property, King Richard would accept the return of the entire Latin Kingdom as it was defined forty-four years before when Louis, the King of France, had been in Jerusalem. In addition, the True Cross, captured at the Battle of Hattin, must be returned.

The emirs were horrified. "Without the assent of our lord Saladin we could never comply with these exorbitant demands," they protested. "Give us a truce of three days so that we might confer with the Sultan."

Back in the city, as the bombardment continued without pause, they wrote a message to the Sultan and sent it by pigeon to the distant hill. "We are so utterly reduced and exhausted that we have no choice but to surrender the city. If you do not effect anything for our rescue, we shall offer to capitulate and make no condition but that we receive our lives."

But Saladin was not ready to give up. He still expected further reinforcements from the south and east. Persevere, he commanded his emirs. If he was unable to relieve them in a few days, he would sanction an honorable capitulation. Immediately he launched a furious assault on the trench. This time he led it himself. According to his chronicler, he rode from battalion to battalion, "as restless as a mother weeping for her lost child," crying out to his men, "On for Islam!"

But the Christians presented a solid front. His soldiers came back with incredible tales of bravery on the part of the Crusaders. One huge Crusader had held a parapet on the trench even though he was pierced by more than fifty arrows, and he was felled only when a Muslim flame-thrower hurled a bottle of napalm at him and burned him alive. Another story was told of a Crusader woman, wrapped in a green cape, who kept killing the attackers with shots from her longbow until she was finally killed. Her longbow was brought to Saladin, who was amazed.

After his day at the ramparts Saladin returned to his pavilion exhausted and melancholy and receding into ceaseless prayer. Again he sought solace in the Koranic line "God does not waste the hire of those who do well."

When he arose the following day and made ready to assault the trench once again, he met resistance from his own men. "You are placing all Islam in jeopardy. Such a plan cannot have a successful outcome." And so Saladin relented and stayed in camp.

On July 8 the enemy had penetrated the outer wall on the east and was working on the inner wall. In response, as if he already understood that Acre was lost, Saladin burned the village of Haifa, to the south across the bay from Acre, so that its port and ship-building facilities would be worthless to the enemy. His despair was deepened when a swimmer made it through the blockade with another letter from the grand emir: "We have sworn to die together. We will fight until we fall and will not yield the city while there is breath in our bodies. You must do all you can to occupy the enemy and prevent his attacking us. Since we are resolved, be sure that you do not humble yourselves before the enemy or show yourselves faint-hearted." With their pact of mass suicide, the defenders were already wrapping themselves in the green mantle of martyrdom.

As Haifa burned, Saladin came back with a counterproposal. He offered to return the True Cross and to effect a prisoner-for-prisoner exchange to redeem the defenders of Acre: three thousand Christian prisoners in exchange for the populace of Acre. But Richard refused again. Only *all* the Christian prisoners in Saladin's hands and *all* the cities in the Latin Kingdom would satisfy him. Saladin scoffed at Richard's preposterous greed and stubbornness. He was not dealing with a man sophisticated in subtle diplomacy, he concluded. "They play at being cunning, and God, too, plays at being cunning," Saladin quoted from his Koran. "But He is a better player."

At the breakdown of this "diplomacy" Philip launched yet another ferocious assault on the Accursed Tower, for there was now an eleven-yard breach near the parapet. But again he was turned back at the cost of forty men. It was after this frenzied, fruitless attack that each side was visited by a miraculous apparition. According to Roger of Hoveden, an important chronicler of the Third Crusade, a light shone down from heaven, and the Virgin Mary appeared before the Christian guards at Judas's Tower. "Be not terrified," she said benevolently, "for the Lord has sent me hither for your safety. As soon as the day shall have dawned, go and tell your Kings, in the name of Jesus Christ my Son and Lord, to cease leveling the walls of this city. Four days from now the Lord shall deliver it into their hands." At her disappearance the earth shook with an earthquake. It startled and frightened the Muslim side as well, but a soldier stepped forward with an explanation. He had seen a thousand cavalrymen appear suddenly, shaking the earth, and they were all dressed in the green of martyrdom. And thus the martyrs of yore were joining the Muslim host. Deliverance must be imminent.

Four days later, on July 12, 1191, Acre fell. To secure the surrender and to bargain for their lives, Mashtūb and Karākūsh took the initiative on their own, and when their deliberations were completed, they simply informed Saladin. Once again the emirs trekked out to the Templars' tent to meet the Kings. The surrender terms were stiff. Along with the city, five hundred Christian captives and two hundred thousand gold bezants would be handed over. Two thousand Muslims would remain captive, and, in addition, one hundred of the richest, most eminent personages in the town would become hostages. Mashtūb and Karākūsh would be among this number. Perhaps most important, the emirs promised to return the True Cross of Christ to the Christian side within a month. When the money was paid and the hostages were in prison, the remaining inhabitants of the town could leave, taking their possessions and their wives and children with them.

Within a day the evacuation began. Christian soldiers lined the road to the Toron hill to watch the refugees depart. They expected a bedraggled, threadbare, dejected lot. Instead the Muslims left the city with their heads high, their dignity intact, their pride on display. The Christians watched in amazement.

"If they were not unbelievers," one astonished observer remarked, "it would have to be said there were no more decent and brave people than these." The Arabs, wrote another, showed themselves to be renowned for their courage and valor and esteemed for their magnificence. "They bore no marks of care as they came forth," wrote the chronicler, "nor any signs of dejection at the loss of all they possessed. In the firmness of their countenances they seemed to be conquerors by their courageous bearing."

Grieving as if he were a father who had lost his child, Saladin was despondent. He could see the shouts of jubilation and watch the banners and standards of the Crusader factions go up on the walls and on the minarets of the mosque. He had wanted to disapprove the terms of this treaty, but a swimmer had brought him the terms, and by the time he got them, the surrender of Acre was a fait accompli. With the shouts of joy ringing in their ears, the Muslims retreated into their laments.

Their harp was turned to mourning, their mirth to heaviness. Saladin went to his Holy Book, finding comfort in the passage "We come forth from God, and to Him we must return." There was no further point in maintaining his forward positions. Soon enough Saladin broke camp and retreated to the south, as his counselors persuaded him to attend to the coastal cities and to Jerusalem itself.

Once the Muslims were out of Acre, the Kings entered in triumph, to music and dancing and a "mighty shout." In their throats were the words of Zacharias (Luke 1:68): "Blessed be the Lord God of Israel; for He hath visited and redeemed His people." Philip took charge of the Templars' palace, with its three impressive towers overlooking the sea, while Richard installed himself and his Queen, Berengaria, in the royal citadel in the city's center. Philip's prize captive was Karākūsh, while Richard took the grand emir, Mashtūb. In due course the grand emir would be ransomed for thirty thousand bezants while, to the distress of his own sense of self-worth, Karākūsh brought only eight thousand. When they were settled in the city, the Kings proceeded to divide the spoils evenly between them.

The surrender arrangements at Acre had shocked Saladin. He disapproved profoundly, but his hard-pressed satraps had simply gone around him. When he learned of the terms, including his own obligations under the agreement, the red and azure-blue and green banners of the enemy already flew colorfully from the parapets of Acre, most especially from the minaret of the Friday Mosque, and his people were already being herded into a special quarter of the city. In the days afterward, sunk in his doldrums, Saladin held out a faint hope that the hot-blooded chevaliers in the Christian army would charge out for one more glory day, whereupon the Sultan could sweep down upon them and rectify this terrible disgrace. But no brigade of Christian fools presented itself.

Only ambassadors from the European Kings appeared, armed with demands to know, in graceful but firm phrases, how and when the Sultan would produce his captives, tender his gold, and convey the True Cross of Christ. Were the prisoners, the gold, and the Holy Rood with the Sultan, or did they need to be brought from Damascus? It would later be suggested in the Muslim chronicles that the Holy Cross had actually been shown to the Christian envoys on the Hill of the Carob Trees and that they had fallen down in the dust in great awe and reverence. But this seems unlikely.

Saladin's answers to the envoys' questions were vague. The ambassadors interpreted this vagueness as a suggestion that there were problems in satisfying the terms. The Sultan proposed an installment plan, the first of three installments to be produced within the month. Still, there was some confusion over the time period, with some Muslims understanding that they had three months to deliver on their promises.

Saladin attempted to confuse the picture further with several conciliatory gestures. Instead of the surrender provisions on the table, he offered a sweeping permanent peace in which all of southern Palestine would be returned for their Latin Kingdom, except for the fortresses of Kerak and Montreal on the hajj road, if they would only lend him two thousand knights and five thousand foot soldiers for one year to suppress the rebellion of dissident elements in Upper Mesopotamia. When Richard rejected this silly proposal, Saladin sent, along with lavish gifts, an inquiry about the Christian faith itself, as if he were seriously contemplating conversion. Richard did not fall for this gambit either and returned the lavish presents.

With the European envoys trundling back and forth to Saladin's camp, Richard prepared for the next phase of his operations. He dismantled his siege engines and packed them away in their traveling kits. The walls of Acre were repaired and the fosses cleared out of dirt, stone, and offal. As the day drew closer for Saladin to return the Cross, Richard wrote to England of his great successes. Expect him home, triumphant, by the following Lent, he wrote.

One month after the fall of Acre the envoys came to collect the goods. Saladin had some captives, but he was having trouble meeting the full complement of six hundred. Moreover, absent among the number he offered that day were certain eminent warriors who had been specifically named by the envoys. Saladin tried to gain time by asking for the Muslim prisoners to be released first before he paid his ransom.

These transparent ploys more than annoyed Richard. When Saladin satisfied his obligation in full, the Muslim captives would be handed over, said the English King. And the Sultan had better be quick about it. The agreement was disintegrating. Either Saladin could not come up with sufficient money and captives or he distrusted this famous warrior. Once Richard had his money, his prisoners, and his Rood, Saladin suspected that would be the end of the exchange—and perhaps the end of his captives.

With the air full of charge and countercharge the deadline slipped by until, several days later, Richard demanded, for the last time, immediate satisfaction of the terms. If his lucre, icon, and champions were not produced forthwith, he threatened to execute all 2,700 Muslim combatants in his possession. A few more days passed without resolution. While Saladin was stalling, perhaps he believed that Richard was bluffing. He was not.

On August 22, 1191, the Crusader King who had come so piously to restore the Promised Land to Christianity and to Jesus had the 2,700 Muslim soldiers tied together. They were marched out of the city on the road to Nazareth, where they were arrayed on a plain between the forward position of the Christian army on the Tell Aiyadida and the forward position of the Muslim army on Tell Keisan. And there, one by one, they were slaughtered.

"For this be the Creator blessed!" wrote the chief poet of the Crusade.

CHAPTER TWENTY

# ḷome Fires Smoldering

✠

EVERAL MONTHS BEFORE THESE PRODIGIOUS
events in Acre, the indomitable, the incomparable, the
irrepressible Eleanor of Aquitaine left her favorite son,
Richard, in Sicily and made her way north toward Rome.
Among the dignitaries in her retinue was the Archbishop of Rouen, whose
crusading vow had been annulled in Messina to free him for more important political work. By depositing Berengaria in the King's cortège with
firm instructions that she and Richard were to be married after the
Lental season, wherever they might find themselves—Eleanor could
scarcely have imagined Cyprus as the nuptial site—she must have felt

content that she had solved at least one fundamental problem of the future.

The perpetuation of the Plantagenet dynasty from Scotland to the Pyrenees was scarcely the only dilemma pressing on the Plantagenets, however. With the King preoccupied with his Crusade, far away in Palestine, it fell to Eleanor—or, more aptly, she seized the chance—to quell the home fires and hold the vast realm together until Richard returned. Eleanor would now become more than a queen. She became a kind of supermonarch.

Her immediate challenge was to hold in check the pretenders to Richard's throne, most especially her youngest and least favorite son, John. Two years before, when the new King was coronated, Richard had been extraordinarily generous toward his younger brother, even though he harbored an older brother's disdain for John's wimpy and erratic ways. He brought John back to England with him just so the prince could take part in the pomp of the coronation ceremony. At Westminster Abbey, John, holding one of the gold royal swords, led the King-in-waiting decorously to the altar. After the ceremony Richard confirmed John's fief as the county of Mortaigne in Normandy, the county of Nottingham, and the castle of Marlborough. In addition, the counties of Dorset, Somerset, Derby, and Lancaster became his, along with the earldom of Gloucester. Within a few weeks the new King put his brother in command of an expedition to suppress a rebellion in Wales. When this was successfully accomplished, Richard added the county of Devon to John's domain as a reward. Only a few years before, John had been ridiculed as Jean sans Terre, John Lackland. Now the whole of West England fell under John's rule.

For all his generosity, Richard had not proclaimed his younger brother as the successor to the throne, and this rankled, particularly since there was a good chance Richard would be killed in the Holy Land. Indeed, it tormented the suspicious and perpetually outshone John, who suspected that his luminous brother might impulsively name the son of their late brother, Geoffrey, as heir. As a further annoyance to John, Richard had placed the reins of the nation in the hands of a chancellor, one William Longchamp, naming the stout and diminutive Norman as chief justiciar and making him Bishop of Ely. Once he was Bishop of Ely, Longchamp persuaded the Pope to make him papal legate for all England, Wales, Scotland, and Ireland, so that, in the words of the chronicler Richard of Devizes, "thus triple titled, and triple headed, he might use both hands instead of the right one alone, and that the sword of Peter might aid the sword of the general."

Longchamp spoke no English (and never would acquire the tongue). His main qualification for the regency was his unswerving loyalty to Richard, whose chancellor in Aquitaine he had been. The chancellor was also shrewd and ruthless, just the stern qualities that an absentee monarch would need in a powerful surrogate to protect his interests at home. To ensure that John would not interfere with his chancellor's authority, Richard at first demanded that John leave England for three years. Although Eleanor persuaded the King to discard this demand, the stage was set for a battle between John and Longchamp in Richard's absence.

There was a third player in this backstage drama. He was another Geoffrey, the bastard son of Henry II by an anonymous Englishwoman. He was an overproud, tactless, intemperate, irascible character who carried his illegitimate birth on his sleeve and acted as if he were owed plenty for his embarrassing indignity. Emotional and unpredictable, he seemed to swing between stubbornness and fawning humility. Having been forced by her husband to bring up the unwanted boy in her court, Eleanor hated this offspring of Henry's lechery with the passion of a cuckolded stepmother. The bastard had served his father well, however. He had demonstrated a considerable talent for administration and had risen heroically to his father's defense during various rebellions. And so Eleanor and Richard knew they had to satisfy Geoffrey's rightful claims. Henry's own wishes seemed to offer an admirable solution. Upon his deathbed Henry II declared his wish that his love child be Bishop of York. This seemed to serve Eleanor and Richard's interests admirably. Being made a bishop, Geoffrey was removed from any claim to the throne. In York he was exiled far to the north. Then they gleefully downgraded the See of York in importance.

The solution was brilliant, except for the fact that it did not work. Various bishops challenged Geoffrey's appointment as invalid, for he seemed wholly unsuited for the miter. By temperament he was a fancier of two-handed swords, fine hawks, and swift greyhounds rather than the cope and crosier of the holy man. He was slandered as a murderer and the son of a whore. The Pope was asked variously to consecrate the appointment and then to nullify it. Geoffrey appealed to Richard, hoping to stay on his good side by promising to raise money for the Crusade, then falling on the King's bad side when he failed to fulfill his promise. Richard alternately despised his half brother and found him useful.

In Sicily, Eleanor had brought the bad news to Richard that both his brother John and William Longchamp were out of control. John was parading around the country as if he were King, seeking to subjugate the kingdom to himself and proclaiming that Richard would never come back from the Crusade alive. Longchamp, in his turn, aspired not to be king but to be dictator of England. He traveled through the countryside "with a sneer in his nostrils, a grin on his features, derision in his eyes, and superciliousness on his brow." So proclaimed his erstwhile friend the Bishop of Coventry. The chancellor moved with such an enormous parade of minions, dogs, hawks, and horses that the privilege of having His Majesty's emissary as your guest for the night would bankrupt you for years. The good Bishop of Ely appropriated lands for himself and his family at will. He forced the sons of English noblemen to humiliate themselves and their families by serving him on bended knee, and he settled in Oxford with his court of Normans and Flemings, whose chief amusement seemed to be the ridicule of the English people.

A wave of revulsion against Longchamp swept England. The Canon of Yorkshire wrote of Longchamp that "the laity felt him to be a King and more than a King, and the clergy a Pope and more than a Pope, and both of them as an intolerable tyrant." Because he was Norman, he acted as if he belonged to a superior race. Indeed, "he seemed to strive to put himself on a level with God." Gerald of Cambridge, one of the chief scribes of the Third Crusade, colored his prose in an even deeper hue of purple. Longchamp was, he wrote, a man low in birth and in stature, deformed in body and moral character, a cross between a dog and an ape, having "lame and bandy legs, enormous feet, a potbelly, big head, swarthy skin, black and deep-set eyes, a hairy face, and a sinister smile." Gerald did not like the Norman.

In the warm months of 1191, as Richard hammered the walls of Acre, the dispute between his brother John and William Longchamp had finally come to blows. Longchamp was besieging the castle of Lincoln, while John besieged the castles of Nottingham and Tickhill, and it was only the alarm of various bishops that prevented the situation from disintegrating into full-scale civil war. These bishops prevailed on the parties to relent and declare a truce. The agreement was more about the future than the present, since it presumed that "our lord the King" would probably depart this life in the pilgrimage. Even though for the present the status quo was safeguarded, the parties were dividing up the castles of the post-Richard realm between themselves already.

In Sicily, Eleanor and Richard perceived the urgency of confirming Geoffrey the Bastard as Archbishop of York, for he was still popular in England. To be the son and brother of an English king, as well as the son of a common woman, captured the imagination of the common people. This very popularity might serve as a counterweight to the excesses of John and Longchamp. Richard placed in Eleanor's hands certain sealed letters that were intended to bring the disputants into line. But letters drafted so far away might not be sufficient.

The troubles in England fell under the wide rubric of the most solemn document of the Crusade. This was the Truce of God. Its essence was the ultimate vow of any Christian King or prince during the time of a military pilgrimage in a just and holy war. The concept had its roots in the Second Crusade. Under it, potentates agreed never to take advantage of the absence of crusading monarchs. The Truce of God was always sealed with a kiss of peace. Eleanor and her then-husband, Louis of France, had sworn this pilgrim's vow before they departed for the Holy Land in 1147. Her next husband, Henry II of England, had reaffirmed it with Philip Augustus of France under the elm tree at Gisors in 1187; and Philip Augustus and Richard had planted the kiss of peace on one another in Vézelay as their armies gathered in 1190.

The instruments Eleanor carried to Rome and later announced in England and Normandy invoked this solemn document. The conflict between John and Longchamp made them out to be disturbers of this sacred truce, and Eleanor wanted the Pope's blessing to curtail the civil strife under its provisions. She arrived in the Eternal City on the very day that a familiar eighty-year-old cleric named Hyacinthus Bobo was consecrated as Pope Celestine III. Celestine III had been an archdeacon of the church during the terrible crisis over Thomas à Becket many years before, and thus he knew well both the dangers and the opportunities that existed in disputes between Kings and bishops. The new Pope was, of course, a great supporter of the Crusade, but he had no illusions about the motivations of its participants. "It was certainly not the fear of God nor any stirring of penitence that inspired them," he was to say later, "but pride and vainglory directed all their enterprise."

Still, the Pope was well disposed to Eleanor's petitions. The pallium was formally conferred on Geoffrey as Archbishop of York, and the Archbishop of Rouen was consecrated as a superlegate, which placed him in a superior status to William Longchamp in the chancellor's capacity as Bishop of Ely. Together with the authority conferred upon her by Richard in his sealed letters, the papal sanction upon Eleanor's designs strengthened her hand as superregent who acted on Richard's behalf. With these assurances she left Rome, sped past Aqua Pendente and over the Alps. By midsummer she was ensconced in the castle at Rouen casting a wary eye across the channel and a loving eye across her Continental lands.

If Richard was intent to curtail the excesses of his stout chancellor, he did not mean to undermine his authority. Indeed, on August 6, as he waited for Saladin to meet the terms of surrender at Acre, he wrote to Longchamp about his current situation. In an upbeat assessment, the King conveyed the news of his conquest of Cyprus and his capture of Acre and predicted that he would be home in England by the following Lent, in triumph and Christian humility, with Jerusalem and the Holy Sepulcher once again in their rightful hands.

In Eleanor's wake, Geoffrey, armed with his papal appointment to the See of York, made his way toward England. The agents of William Longchamp detained him in Normandy and forbade him to cross the channel, asserting that King Richard himself had left orders before he departed for the Holy Land that Geoffrey was not to return to his homeland for three years. Geoffrey's protestations concerning Richard's more recent orders fell on deaf ears. Geoffrey ignored the warning, crossed the channel to Dover, and was immediately arrested by Longchamp's police. The arrest was especially nasty, for the archbishop had ridden swiftly to the local monastery called St. Michael's Priory, where he was celebrating mass, when Longchamp's men laid siege to the place. After five days of hostilities they broke into the church and dragged the prelate in his episcopal vestments from the altar and through the streets of Dover amid the protests of the people to Dover castle. There he was thrown into prison.

This trespass handed Earl John the opportunity he had long sought. He ordered Geoffrey released, a demand to which Longchamp acceded, and then mobilized the clergy of England against the chancellor. With the specific injury of Geoffrey's arrest as the centerpiece of the complaint, a long list of grievances was drawn up against Longchamp. And the Bishop of Coventry added a sweeping accusation:

"He and his revelers had so exhausted the whole kingdom that they did not leave a man his belt, a woman her necklace, a nobleman his ring, or anything of value even to a Jew. He had likewise so utterly emptied the King's treasury that in all the coffers and bags therein nothing but the keys could be met with, after the lapse of these two years." As the campaign against him grew in strength, Longchamp took refuge in the Tower of London. There he loudly protested the charges against him.

"I declare that the Archbishop of York was seized without my knowledge or my consent," he fumed. "I am ready to give an account to the last farthing as to why and for what I have spent the King's money." And then in a lapse into honesty, he confessed, "I fear the King more than I do you."

The cries of the people drowned these hollow words. "Perish he who hastens on the ruin of all things!" they shouted, and then evoked St. Luke: "That he may not crush all, let him be crushed. If he has done this in a green tree, what will he do in a dry one?"

The judicial proceeding of barons and bishops that gathered to hear the charges against Longchamp was remarkable for its decorum, its orderliness, its attention to the nascent jurisprudence that had been so advanced in England by the late Henry II. Even John, the Earl Mortaigne, acted with consummate political skill and uncharacteristic restraint. He allowed the rule of law to prevail without interference. He had carefully gauged the mood of the judges and never stepped too far ahead of their sentiment, for he appreciated keenly that more was at stake for him in this proceeding than the mere discharge of Longchamp.

For the chancellor the outcome was foreordained. One of King Richard's letters from Sicily was unsealed and read before the court. If Longchamp acted against the will of Richard's royally appointed ministers, the letter ordained, he was to be deposed and replaced by the Archbishop of Rouen. This closed the case. Longchamp was excommunicated as well as discharged.

Now John turned the proceeding to his most fervent wish. Solemnly the court, together with the citizens of London, proclaimed that should King Richard the Lionheart die without issue, John, the Earl of Mortaigne, was the rightful heir to the throne.

Longchamp was not present for his sentencing. He had fled to Dover. For a short time he toyed with the pious thought of taking the cross and joining Richard's Crusade as a way out of his disgrace. Instead he decided to protest his "mistreatment" in Rome, for he still had a legion of supporters abroad.

But how to slip out of the country? Shedding his sacred robes and the acces-
sories of his temporal power, he disguised himself as a woman in a long, flowing green cape and large hood and then waddled down to the shoreline
to wait for a boat. Later the Bishop of Coventry made great sport of this
spectacle. "He pretended to be a woman, a sex which he always hated,
changed the priest's robe into the harlot's dress. Oh, shame! the man became a woman, the chancellor a chancelloress, the priest a harlot, the bishop
a buffoon."

A fisherman happened by as Longchamp sat wanly on a rock, and according to the Bishop of Coventry, "perhaps wishing to be made warm," he cud-
dled up and embraced the lady, only to have the hood fall back and reveal the
swarthy mug of the ex-chancellor. Jumping up in astonishment, the fisherman called for his friends. "Come all of you and see a wonder. I have found a
woman who is a man!" he cried. A crowd gathered quickly for the freak show.
The women wanted to know how much the "hermaphrodite" (a creature of
the sea with both male and female sexual organs) wanted for her/his gown.
But since Longchamp did not understand English, his silence only angered
the crowd further. Things turned ugly. "Come let us stone this monster,"
someone shouted out. Instead they dragged him by his green sleeves across
the beach and through the town and finally deposited him in Geoffrey the
Bastard's cell in Dover castle.

Eventually Longchamp made it to the Continent, where he was able to
make trouble for some months to come. Among his acts was to inform
Richard of John's designs on the throne and then to turn back to John and
pay the earl a handsome fee to reinstate him in his old job. In pleading his
case he directed his ire with special vigor at his false friend, the Bishop of
Coventry, who had so publicly and gleefully disclosed the scandal of his feminine disguise in Dover. Such a bishop, Longchamp wrote, should be strictly
avoided by everyone, "so that in future a sheep so diseased cannot blemish
and corrupt the flock of the Lord." That the learned men of this time knew
how to insult one another is beyond question. But no insults against his detractors could save Longchamp now, and he receded from the stage.

The upshot of the Longchamp affair was harmful to King Richard. His
younger brother, John, was now in a powerful position to disrupt his rule.
Indeed, the continuation of domestic unrest was in John's interest. Richard's
iron hand at home was stayed. The Truce of God was proving worthless. The
lure of England was strong, and if the absent King did not heed the call, he

risked being seen as a truant and stood to lose everything. As word of these troubles reached him piecemeal in Palestine, even as he basked in the triumph at Acre, he might well have questioned whether the cause was worth the risk.

Only a few weeks after the fall of Acre an even mightier blow befell him, one that multiplied his risk exponentially.

# 2

## Spoils

It is certainly true that only through the arrival of the overwhelming English and French forces had the city of Acre fallen. But after the city was taken, Richard and Philip proceeded to gather the spoils entirely to themselves with breathtaking high-handedness, as if they felt they and only they had been involved in the heroic enterprise. Blithely the two Kings ignored their lesser allies, oblivious to the fact that much of the loot belonged to their own people. They scoffed at the claims of local barons of the Kingdom of Jerusalem who had lost their property to Saladin four years before, who fought and starved and toiled to preserve a Christian toehold in the Holy Land. It was they who had persevered for two years against tremendous odds before the arrival of the well-provisioned European forces.

Now the Kings dismissed the role of Italian and Flemish, German and Austrian soldiers. The contempt of the English soldiers for the remnant of German army had the most dire consequences. After the news of Frederick Barbarossa's death, his half brother, Leopold V, the Duke of Austria, had rushed to the Holy Land to take command of the German survivors at Acre. In their jubilation over the capture of the city, Leopold's men had spontaneously raised the red-white-red-striped banner on an important building, only to have English soldiers rip it down and throw the shreds into a ditch, cackling with derisive laughter and mocking their German brothers. Thereafter guards were posted, and only English and French were permitted to enter Acre; others were restrained with a violence that was extraordinary. Thirteen non-English or French soldiers paid with a severed foot for the folly of trying to enter the city without sanction. Oblivious to other claims and seized with greed, the French and English accountants set up their scales and began the time-consuming process of counting and weighing the booty and dividing it equally between their respective camps. Outside this counting-house the others with worthy claims remained empty-handed.

Not surprisingly, this arrogance evoked considerable resentment. In response to the desecration of his banner and the mockery of the enormous sacrifice of the German soldiers, Duke Leopold packed up his army and left the Crusade in considerable umbrage and with an ominous vow of revenge, muttering about Richard and his wild Viking blood. Only when the local knights banded together and forced the Kings to hold an assembly was the matter of property claims addressed. At the gathering in the Templars' castle the barons made their case pointedly. Of their homes, one baron said, "The Arabs took them by force, and you have come to liberate the Kingdom of Jerusalem. It is not right or lawful that we should be disinherited. Your knights who have appropriated our houses say that they have conquered them from the Arabs. We beg you not to allow us to be dispossessed!"

Philip was the first to see the justice of these claims, for he seemed to be mellowing and losing his stomach for war in arid places. "For my person," he said, "I say that we are not come here to win land or to take anyone's property away from them. But we came here for the sake of God, to save our souls and to conquer the Kingdom of Jerusalem from the infidels. Since God has given us this city, it would not be right to take it away from those for whom it is their inheritance." The assembly agreed, and provisions were made for the indigenous knights to reclaim their houses—but not until the English knights were ready to move out.

The complaints lingered. "The Church and posterity may judge if it was suitable in accordance with the majesty of kings that they kept for themselves, without blushing, that which other people won over two winters and with their blood and suffering," wrote an Italian. "Instead of thinking only of themselves, they should have been thinking that the bones of many other peoples were whitening in these holy fields. This victory cannot be ascribed to two Kings, but to God." Adding to the solemnity of this claim was the fact that in the cemeteries around Acre, especially those of the Hospital of the Germans and the Hospital of St. Nicholas, many thousands of soldiers had been buried, victims not only of the sword but of plague and starvation.

And so this moment of triumph dissolved into recrimination. Had the victory at Acre united and inspired the remaining Christian host, it would have presented a juggernaut that would quickly sweep from Acre to

Jerusalem. But Richard's avarice and condescension strained the fragile alliance. In early July, Philip came down with a fresh case of dysentery, and he began to look for a way out. Having lost his hair to arnaldia the month before, he was now delirious and had lost control of his bowels, and that concentrated his mind.

In a malicious French account of this important juncture, an improbable story is told of Richard paying a call on Philip at his sickbed, as if to comfort his ailing ally but really to make him sicker, even to kill him from shock. After perfunctory inquiries by Richard about how his former lover was faring, and weak replies from Philip, Richard said, according to the French chronicler, "And how do you console yourself in the matter of your son, Louis?" This was a delicate subject, for Philip's hard-won son by Isabella of Haignaut had been born only four years earlier and was Philip's sole heir to the French throne.

"What has happened to my son that I should need consolation?" the feverish Philip muttered.

"Why, that is the reason I have come," Richard replied. "To comfort you . . . because he is dead!"

Scurrilous chronicler. This naughty fabrication was intended to cast Philip as Richard's victim once again and to provide for history some sympathy for Philip in the events that follow. Not to be outdone, an English chronicler produced his own fabrication. Philip, wrote Richard of Devizes, the monk from Winchester, had ordered his scribes to forge a diplomatic message from France beseeching the King to return on account of the desperate illness of his son. In both cases the accounts are written long after the Third Crusade was over.

There is evidence that the boy, Louis, was indeed ill in France, also from dysentery, at about the same time as Philip lay ill in Acre. But the Kings could not have known about anything going on several thousand miles away in Paris. To place a miraculous spin on the impossible tale, the French account described a solemn procession to St. Lazarre, where the dukes and dauphin prayed for Louis's recovery. When the ailing boy touched the holy relic in the church, the nail from the Cross of Calvary, he was instantly cured, so we are to believe, as was his father, far away in Palestine.

From whatever natural or supernatural force, Philip did begin to feel better, and in better-supported developments he found his pretext to leave. After the victory at Acre the thorny question of who was the rightful King of Jerusalem again arose. Perhaps realizing that his champion, Philip of France, was weak and not long for the Holy Land, Conrad of Montferrat came to King Richard. He fell on his knees before the English King, asked his forgiveness, and beseeched him to settle the matter. Inevitably, Richard and Philip quarreled bitterly over their respective candidates. Richard berated Philip for promising to cede his hostages and his future conquests to Conrad of Montferrat if the King should die or have to leave.

"It is not fitting for a man of your name to give away or promise things that have not yet been won," Richard rebuked Philip in this public forum. "If Christ is indeed the reason for your pilgrimage, when you at last take Jerusalem from the enemy's hand, you will turn the kingdom over to Guy, the lawful King of Jerusalem. Remember! You did not take Acre without help. One hand should not parcel out what belongs to two, by God's throat!" At least in this case Richard swore by God's public parts.

Eventually an agreement was reached. But the spectacle of Kings lambasting one another publicly made the price high. Richard's candidate, Guy of Lusignan, in recognition of his service in commencing the siege of Acre and bravely commanding the siege forces, would retain the crown. But his heirs, if there were any, would not inherit the throne. Instead, upon Guy's death, Philip's stronger candidate, Conrad of Montferrat, would become King, and his heirs would succeed him. Conrad was to retain his dominion over Tyre, Beirut, and Sidon; Guy's brother, Geoffrey, would take over Jaffa and Ascalon—if Jaffa and Ascalon could be retaken from Saladin. All the revenues of the kingdom, as it now existed, were to be divided equally between the two rivals. Even though Guy and Conrad fell on their knees and swore to abide by the terms of this agreement, the heat of the debate took a toll on the alliance.

On July 22, only ten days after the fall of Acre, King Richard received a delegation from Philip, including the Bishop of Beauvais and the Duke of Burgundy. The French delegation offered a fawning apology for the absence of their lord, professing him still to be under the weather, but Richard guessed immediately the reason for their coming in so formal a way and with their chagrined, downcast manner bespeaking their shame.

"Your lord wishes to go home, and you have come for my permission," Richard said frigidly, for he supposed that Philip was no longer sick at all but merely did not have the spine to appear in person.

The French envoys blathered and jabbered and sputtered excitedly. Their

King feared he would surely die if he remained in Palestine. He was anxious about his son and his crown; he was worried about the succession to the throne of Flanders, for which he had done such careful planning; these matters required his personal and immediate attention.

Richard listened stoically. Perhaps his mind flashed across the pull of his own domestic problems in England and Normandy and Anjou, the challenge of his brother John and the tyranny of Longchamp—across all that he himself risked by persevering in this noble but dangerous Crusade. Perhaps he also thought about the vows at Gisors and Vézelay, where they forswore worldly concerns, sewed on their surcoats the cross of Calvary, and embraced the possibility of martyrdom.

"For the King of France and his land it will be a disgrace and a dishonor if he leaves without bringing our effort to completion. I advise him not to do this," Richard said at last. But there was no room for negotiation here. He knew he could not dissuade Philip from his course. "If he sees his choice as being between dying here and going home, then he should do what he wants." His words all but said good riddance.

News of Philip's desertion spread rapidly through the armies, and it caused great consternation. The following day the French King was visited by a number of his knights, who burst into tears and pleaded with their lord not to dishonor the glory of the royals who had come before him nor to visit shame on the monarchs who would come after. There was nothing so shameful as to break the pilgrim's vow, they said as they struggled to contain their loathing for their King. Philip remained unmoved.

On July 29, 1191, a week after his shocking notice of betrayal, Philip again sought Richard's official blessing to leave. Having no choice, and perhaps glad to be shed of his fainthearted companion, Richard could only extract a promise. Under no circumstance was the French King to do harm to any of Richard's lands in Europe, so long as the English King remained in the Holy Land. Solemnly Philip proclaimed his vow and swore it on the medieval equivalent of a stack of Bibles (the Holy Disciples themselves). The French King pledged to keep this sacred oath until forty days after Richard's return from the Crusade.

In theory this was a renewal of the Truce of God. Soon enough it would be transformed, as had happened so many times before, into the breach of men. Before Philip left Palestine, he turned half of his treasure from Acre over to Conrad of Montferrat, and a few days later all of his valuable Muslim hostages, including Karākūsh. He placed the command of his army in the hands of the Duke of Burgundy, lavishing upon this vassal another chunk of his spoils.

Thus disgraced, reviled, and considerably poorer than he had been a few days before, with thinned hair and sore jowls, the King of France skulked out of the Holy Land with five ships, two of which he had "borrowed" from Richard. The air was thick with abuse for the oath breaker. "For shame, you forsake and abandon the land of the Lord," ran one howling rebuke. "Spiting all the saints, spiting God himself, he slinks back. Evil shall his reception be. A scoundrel he is, villainy will be his sermon." Richard himself would write home about the King "who basely abandoned the purpose of his pilgrimage, and broke his vow, against the will of God, to the eternal disgrace of himself and his realm." It was not long before their strife was likened to that between Abraham and Lot in the Book of Genesis. They were brethren who could not live together, and so Abraham had remained in the land of Canaan whereas Lot departed and tilted toward the wicked land of Sodom.

The first part of Philip's return voyage was uneventful as he passed through Antioch; past the river Salef, in which the Emperor Frederick Barbarossa had drowned; along the coast of the kingdom from which hailed the Three Kings who brought gold, frankincense, and myrrh to baby Jesus. But when he entered the terrible Anatolian Gulf, where Richard's ships had been scattered and Queen Berengaria's galley had been driven toward Cyprus, a fierce storm tossed his ship about, and his knights cowered around him, proclaiming that either the devil's head was facing upward or the huge black dragon had begun to suck them toward his terrible mouth. According to the French account, King Philip waved aside the fears of his companions about devils' heads and black dragons. "Let the Jew from Juvenal believe that, I will not," he said grandly. Suddenly he became brave and heroic. Puffing himself up with a noble, imperious air, the royal deserter asked calmly what time it might be. Midnight, came the answer. "In that case, fear not," said Philip Augustus grandly, "for at this very hour the monks in our land are awake and pray to God for us." Not long after, the tempest calmed, and the ships arrived safely at Brindisi.

The royal train passed through Rome on its return journey. There Philip complained loudly to the Pope about Richard's rude behavior and asserted with a bald face that Richard had forced him to leave the Crusade against his will. He begged to be released from his oath not to attack Richard's lands.

This shabby behavior merely confirmed Pope Celestine III in his low opinion of the base and corrupt motives of the champions of the Cross. Piously the Pope gave the King palm fronds and put a cross around his neck. But contempt was in his voice when he reminded the French King of the Truce of God and forbade him, under the pain of excommunication, to raise arms in anger against the last crusading King in Zion.

Philip fared better with the Holy Roman Emperor, who was related to the spurned duke of Austria and to the Emperor Comnenus in Cyprus. Philip regaled the Emperor with the stories of Richard's humiliation of his relatives, and he received an assurance that if Richard attempted to pass through the lands of the Holy Roman Emperor on his way home from the Holy Land, he would be seized.

In the quest to recover the Holy Land, Richard the Lionheart now stood utterly alone.

CHAPTER TWENTY-ONE

# The Plain of Sharon

✠

I N THE MONTH BEFORE THE ARMY LEFT ACRE, KING Richard busied himself in repairing the damage to the city's walls and raising their level to a formidable height. As a military engineer he was unparalleled. A constant study in motion, he could be seen striding nervously along the breastworks, barking orders and exhorting his men to greater effort. At the same time, his artillery—the great mangonels and catapults—were carefully packed for the sieges that surely lay ahead. As the days passed, the King became increasingly concerned about the corrupting influences of this fleshpot, where women were many and the temptations were great. Consequently he ordered his licentious pilgrims out of Acre and into tents pitched on the plain outside of town. No damsels except washerwomen were permitted in the encampment. Slowly and peevishly the soldiers left the city, with the French soldiers the slowest and most peevish of all.

To appease the discontent, it would be imagined centuries later by Sir Walter Scott that King Richard, after victory and after massacre, held a grand jousting tournament for the entertainment of his tired and victorious warriors. In the "lists of St. John of Acre" the brave Saxon knight Ivanhoe of yore did overthrow the evil Norman knight Brian de Bois-Guilbert. And when the language of England came to be called "Middle English," romantic poetry was composed about Richard's prowess at Acre, especially his use of a great ax, well made and twenty pounds in weight. When his galley, *Trenchemere,* had approached Acre, and Richard had seen that a great chain was across the mouth of the harbor, the poet imagined the scene as follows:

> *And kynge Rychard, that was so good,*
> *With hys axe in foreschyp stood.*
> *And whenne he come the cheyne too,*
> *With his ax he smot it in two*
> *That all the barouns, verrayment*
> *Sayde it was a noble dent.*

A noble dent indeed—even if it existed only in the poet's fancy.

Two days after the atrocious massacre of the Muslims and on the holy sabbath dedicated to the feast of the Apostle St. Bartholomew, the herald sounded the call to ranks. At dawn, bonfires were lit, as was the Crusader custom before a march, and the army arranged itself into three divisions. Each man was to carry ten days' rations, while the bulk of the supplies was loaded onto barges. Barges and smacks, laden with the food and weapons, would parallel the army as it made its way south along the ancient coastal road of the Romans. Empty galleys followed behind, available to board troops in an emergency. Richard took his place with the vanguard of Templars, Normans, and English. King Guy was in the middle with his indigenous forces and the honor guard that surrounded the Crusader standard.

The great battle flag of the Crusade was mounted on a high mast and rolled along in a cart of its own, drawn by four magnificent sumpter horses, each of which measured eighteen hands. The standard could be seen f' miles. More than a battle flag, it was invested with biblical significanc' was meant to be like the root of Jesse signifying the descent of Jesus fr'

royal line of David, the standard around which the faithful had rallied in biblical times. In the rear came the Hospitalers and the whining French, who
were still smirking about leaving behind the pleasures of Acre and still chagrined at the departure of their King.

The army crossed the River of Acre and made its way through the sandy
plain and the dunes toward Haifa. As it approached the tells and hills of the
Carmel range, the enemy began its harassment. Saladin was watching the
slow progress of the Crusader army from his command post high in the hills,
and when the moment was right, he dispatched his raiders. They poured
down the slopes in bands of twenty or thirty and attacked the points furiously. To the Crusaders these raiders were like an annoying fly. "If you drive
it away, it will go. But when you cease, it will return," wrote a Christian
chronicler. "As long as you pursue, it will fly, but it reappears the moment
you desist."

The fly took a considerable toll in the first days out, however. A number
of French stragglers were killed, as well as four hundred irreplaceable horses.
For a brief moment the last division lost contact with the middle division,
and had Saladin's son, el Melek el-Afdal, had more troops, he might well
have succeeded in cutting off the French. "If we had been in full force, we
should have taken them all prisoners," el-Afdal's dispatch to his father read,
but by the time the message arrived and Saladin sent more troops, the French
had stepped up their pace and reestablished contact with the forward units.
In the process the Muslims captured an important count of Hungary who
had allowed his frustration to get the better of him and had ventured far out
carelessly in pursuit of his tormentors.

The progress around the spur of Mount Carmel was slow, since, apart from
the harassment, the coordination between the land elements and the navy offshore was difficult. Still, Richard's patience belied his modern generalship.
He was manifestly in no hurry. He marched his men in the cool of the early
morning and rested them in the broiling afternoon. Since there were few
beasts of burden, nearly half the soldiers became porters beneath the searing
heat. The Crusader army inched past Haifa, the first of the old Crusader
strongholds that Saladin had dismantled four years earlier, and then around
Mount Carmel, toward a halting place called Casal of the Narrow Ways.

Meanwhile, in the hills, the Hungarian count was dragged before Saladin
just after the Sultan's midday prayers. With his noble bearing and elegant
fingers and square, rough-hewn head, the Magyar count cut a splendid fig-

ure, and Saladin's court was much impressed with him. From their captive they extracted valuable information about the last few days. When they had what they wanted, Saladin waved the count away and gave the order for him to be beheaded—but, as a courtesy in deference to his rank, his body was not to be mutilated.

This qualification was a concession, since Saladin was still furious over Richard's massacre of a few days before. In retaliation he had permitted his soldiers to satisfy their revenge by hacking their prisoners to pieces. Under the circumstances the Koran seemed to sanction this savage retaliation: "Life for life, eye for eye, nose for nose, ear for ear, tooth for tooth, and wounds equal for equal." It would be some time before Saladin could ever execute enough Christians to equal the number of his own victims. Sensing his end, the Hungarian excitedly asked for a translation of Saladin's order.

"But I will give you one of the important captives at Acre," the count exclaimed after hearing it.

"It must, by God's mercy, be an emir," Saladin said coldly.

"But I cannot get an emir released!" the count protested. Saladin shrugged. The matter was of no consequence to him. Still, his own emirs prevailed upon the Sultan to relent. He would think things over on his afternoon ride, and he mounted his horse to review his troops and reconnoiter the enemy forces arrayed below. He must have been impressed by what he saw. When he returned, he had the Hungarian summarily beheaded—and two other Christian prisoners as well, for good measure.

After Casal of the Narrow Ways, the Crusaders were entering unfamiliar territory. Before they came to the Holy Land, they had imagined a desolate place of sand and rock, of rounded hills with rounded boulders through which it was easy to picture Jesus walking in his sandals and ministering to the multitude. "O Holy Land, from the moment my sinful eye first looked upon you, I have been living in a noble way for the first time," ran a Crusader song. "What I have always wanted has come about, for I have reached the place where God walked in the flesh."

A different sort of landscape awaited them now, as they rounded Mount Carmel and came into the Plain of Sharon. Rather than desert and dunes, they found marshland covered with high, luxuriant vegetation. Their Bibles promised a countryside of fountains and clear streams, of fertile fields of sugarcane and pastures full of lily of the valley and rose of Sharon. Muslim soldiers would not be their only danger. Lions, leopards, oryx, ostriches, cheetahs, panthers, and hyenas were abundant in the Palestine of that day, providing both danger and sport to the barons of both sides.

"What other business does a man have than to hunt and fight?" asked one Syrian knight, who had fought as many lions in his life as Franks. And hunting falcons were prized, especially the falcon with thirteen feathers in its tail, for such a bird, if it were properly trained, could hunt herons and cranes and even gazelles.

In the streams and dunes and grassland of the Plain of Sharon and in the Carmel Hills lurked snakes and spiders and crocodiles as well as Muslims. Around the campfires the men shuddered at the story of the terrible poisonous snake that reproduced in so cruel a way: The male came to the female in season, put his head inside her mouth, and planted his seed, whereupon the female bit off the old boy's head and then happily produced their brood of one male and one female "worm." Veterans spoke of the "deaf adder" of these parts, which plugged up its "ears" with its tail and thus did not hear the soldiers' approach. The soldiers should also be careful in harvesting frankincense and myrrh for vespers or for sanctifying their dead, for the gum trees of Palestine, it was said, were infested with flying serpents whose evil skin was spotted with many colors and whose bite was deadly. On their way to Jerusalem they would have to cross the River of Crocodiles, a stream full of the hateful reptile who loved to devour all men but was said to be especially fond of Christian pilgrims. So vile a creature it was: It had no way to excrete its masticated food, they said around the fires, so after its meal it fell asleep along the riverbanks, and snakes crawled into its yawning mouth and down into its belly and acted as its "janitor." And so its hapless Christian victims would be twice eaten by serpents.

Scorpions and tarantulas were so abundant that the soldier was well advised to clang pots ferociously as he moved through the tall grass, so that the vermin would flee, even if the clanging brought the enemy closer. To keep the infidels and the reptiles and the spiders at bay at night, the Crusaders huddled around their fires and deputized one of their number to be their cheerleader. "*SANCTUM SEPULCRUM ADJUVA*. HELP! HELP! FOR THE HOLY SEPULCHER!" he would call out, and the soldiers would respond en masse, "*SANCTUM SEPULCRUM ADJUVA!*" Amid wailing and weeping, the chanting seemed to calm the soldiers' fear and anxiety, and so, over the hills and flat land, this eerie call-and-response wafted plaintively night after night.

Dunes and high grass buffered the coastal road to the east, creating a natural barrier between the marching soldiers and their enemy in the hills. Thus for some miles the Crusader army rolled south toward Caesarea in relative safety. Only their great standard was visible from the hills to the east, on its mast, high as a minaret. Still, the summer heat was terrible. It caused many to faint and even die in their claustrophobic, ninety-pound armor.

In the hills the Muslims shadowed the Christians, and Saladin himself kept up a frantic pace, consulting with his commanders, reviewing his troops, pondering strategy, his activities always punctuated by midday and evening prayer. Handfuls of Christian captives were brought before him, including a group of fourteen that included a woman in full battle gear. All were executed. The Sultan was not in a merciful mood.

He had moved his main force southeast through the valley of Jezreel, quartering them at Tell Keiman (Caymont) while his scouts kept watch from the hilltops. The sultan rode fitfully between his main army and his outlooks. In one day alone he rode thirty-five miles, racing past the mound of Megiddo, where the Battle of Armageddon was supposed to take place, hooking back through Scariathus (by some believed to be the home of Judas Iscariot, although Carioth south of Hebron was generally accepted as the birthplace), to Caesarea ahead of the Christian vanguard. Perhaps here—at the town he had destroyed four years before so that the coastal fortress could not be reused by the Crusaders—perhaps here the Sultan would make his stand.

Personal illness complicated his movements. Mysteriously, terrible blisters broke out on his lower body, and he could scarcely sit up from the dreadful pain they caused. Still, out of duty and a sense of emergency, he mounted his horse and carried on, bearing the pain of the boils without complaint.

"The pain leaves me when I am on horseback," he confided in his aide, "and only returns when I dismount."

Caesarea. The ancient Roman city, once famous for its palm trees and orange groves and buffalo milk, where Herod had built a harbor of marble, where Peter had baptized Cornelieus, where lived Philip the evangelist, who had four daughters, virgins all, who were prophets. Caesarea was now an empty ghost town.

Still, Saladin held off. Patience was one of his greatest virtues, and in it he was guided by the Koran. "To those who fight strenuously in the cause of God and are patient," it is written in the Koran, "verily, thy Lord will be forgiving and merciful." He was cautious about committing his full forces, for he still hoped for further reinforcements. To his emirs he grumbled about un-responsive nobles who lacked sufficient animosity for the enemies of Islam. For several days he was critically indecisive, as his heavy and light baggage was moved to and fro, as if to prepare for a major attack and then to decline. At best he wanted to slow down the march until he could catch the enemy in a disadvantageous position and commit fresh troops, which he expected any day. But neither the perfect battleground nor the reinforcements materi-alized. The Crusaders entered the ruins of Caesarea without incident and then moved on three miles south to the banks of the stream called the River of the Dead.

Upon their leaving the abandoned city, the skirmishing grew more fierce. As the pace of hostilities picked up, King Richard moved to the center to command the defense, leaving King Guy in command of the vanguard and the "sons of the Lady of Tiberias" in command of the rear. To the Muslim at-tackers the discipline of the Crusaders was an impressive sight. While the fleet horsemen poured down on the Crusader ranks, the Christians drew themselves up smartly into a precise order of battle, as if this was all in a day's work, with their well-mailed archers and slingers in front and their cavalry behind, waiting for the order to charge. "They shot at us with their great ar-balests," wrote an Arab chronicler, "wounding the Muslim horses and their riders. I saw some Frank foot soldiers with ten arrows sticking in them and still they advanced at their ordinary pace without leaving the ranks." To an-other chronicler the Christian soldiers looked like hedgehogs with so many arrows sticking out of them.

"The Muslims discharged arrows at them from all sides to annoy them, and force them to charge, but in this they were unsuccessful. The Franks ex-ercised wonderful self-control. They went on their way without any hurry. One cannot help admiring the patience displayed by these people who bore the most wearing fatigue."

This close-ordered march was a reflection of their commander.

Over the dunes and marshes the din of battle was terrific. Drums and trumpets competed with shouts of *"tahlīl"* and *"takbīr"* ("There is but one God! God is Great") and *"Sanctum Sepulcrum Adjuva"* ("Save the Holy Sepul-cher"), and from the Templars *"Ha! Beau-séant!,"* the name of their half-white, half-black banner, where the white was meant to symbolize their fairness toward Christians and the black to symbolize their fierceness toward infidels.

*Arab soldiers, twelfth century*

(LIBRARY OF CONGRESS)

*Tyre*

*Gate at Acre, from* Picturesque Palestine *by C. W. Wilson*

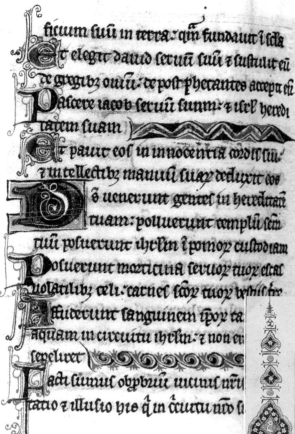

Medieval Psalter:
Words of the Seventy-ninth Psalm:
"O God, the heathen are come into
Thine inheritance; Thy holy temple
have they defiled; they have laid
Jerusalem on heaps.
(WALTERS ART MUSEUM)

Page from a rare medieval Koran:
Sura 47, Verse 19: Lā ilāha illā Allah.
The credo of Islam:
"There are no gods but Allah."
(LIBRARY OF CONGRESS)

 *Entrance to Holy Sepulcher, from* Picturesque Palestine *by C. W. Wilson*

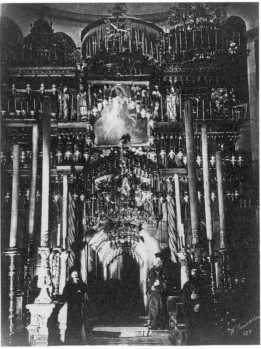

*Holy Sepulcher*

*Facade of El Aqsa Mosque,
from* Picturesque Palestine
*by C. W. Wilson*

*Dome of the Rock*

*Ancient Jaffa, from* Picturesque Palestine *by C. W. Wilson*

*Richard the Lionhearted departs Ascalon for the final push on Jerusalem.*

*Tomb of Saladin, Damascus*

*Muezzin chanting at Great Mosque, Damascus, from* Picturesque Palestine *by C. W. Wilson*

*Dürnstein*

*Tomb of Richard the Lionheart, Rouen Cathedral*

(GAINES POST, JR.)

HIC · COR · CONDITVM · EST · RICARDI
ANGLORVM · REGIS · QVI · COR · LEONIS · DICTVS
OBIIT · AN · M · C · XC · IX

While the squadrons clashed, there were individual contests, and in one of these a famous Islamic knight fell heroically. He was el-Tawil, a giant called the "long man," who carried so huge a lance that no two were larger or thicker or heavier in all of France. The Muslim champion had gained quite a reputation already among the Crusaders for the many times he had engaged in single combat in the medium ground between the forces. Among the Muslims he was known as "the audacious, the man-eating lion, the stabber, and the giver of blows," and a man with a "will of fire."

"To the screaming he is the best listener," wrote an Arab scribe. "He is the first to bless the sneezing clouds of war-dust. He is the first to mount a horse, and last to dismount it. When others turn backwards, he goes forward. He races to harm without delay; always calling for a duel, and running to execute it. He travels on the back of his arrows to the warrior of warriors, borne on the litter of his hatreds. How many a hand of infidelity he has curbed! How many a virgin of victory he has led in solemn procession! How many an idolatrous nose he has amputated!"

Now the lion waded once again into contested ground, challenging any Christian hero to meet him. But this time he seemed more reckless, as if he were seeking out martyrdom by his flagrant challenges, as if he aimed for a quick trip to paradise and happiness. Instead of a single champion, a pack of Christian wolves set upon him. By the Arab account "many noses of unbelievers" were struck off before the Arab giant succumbed. He did so, according to the Islamic rendering, only because his horse betrayed him by allowing itself to be cut down beneath the great warrior. Like a beached, overturned turtle, el-Tawil was helpless against the swarming Christian attackers, unable to move under the weight of his armor. "When his comrades reached him, they found that he had passed away to accompany the living in heaven—not the dead—on behalf of God and his religion."

There was great mourning at the champion's death. In their grief, Muslim warriors cut the tails from their horses. They buried their lion at a place called Mejahed Sheikhah, "the place where chiefs fought in Holy War." And later the Christian chronicler gave him his due: "He was a man of gallantry and of such strength and mastery that there was no man who could beat him, and none even dared compete with him."

It was also at the River of the Dead that King Richard received the first wound of the Crusade. He was in a melee when a spear struck him a glancing blow in the side. The wound seemed to excite him further, and he waded still deeper into the fray. As this skirmishing proceeded, the King's chief concern was the loss of horses rather than men. It appeared that the Muslim attackers were targeting his animals, knowing full well that the big-jointed European battle horses and the huge sumpter horses could not be replaced. One estimate put the loss at one thousand. At night soldiers haggled over the fallen horses for their meat, and this required Richard to issue the directive that a knight who lost a horse would be given a fresh one, provided that he donated the horse meat of the first to his hungry men.

"And thus, they ate horseflesh as if it was venison, and they reckoned it most savory, for hunger served in the place of seasoning."

For several more days this bloody attrition continued without altering the basic situation. The Crusader army moved relentlessly south across the plain of Sharon. In its disciplined order of march it moved at a snail's pace, marching only in the cooler morning, protecting itself skillfully against harassment as it went, and taking advantage of rivers to camp beside for several days of rest and regrouping. In fifteen days the army had covered only sixty-two miles. Yet it was now within striking distance of the old Crusader stronghold of Arsuf, a walled town on the seacoast with a small fortress appointed with towers.

This was the ancient Greek city called Apollonia, another in the chain of coastal fortresses of the former Crusader kingdom that, like Haifa and Caesarea, had been destroyed by Saladin after 1187. Its reoccupation would have grave implications. If Richard were not halted here, Jaffa (Tel Aviv) was only six miles farther south. "From Jaffa," Richard wrote, "we will promote the interests of Christianity and pursue the object of our vow." With Haifa, Caesarea, Arsuf, and Jaffa back under their control, the Crusader army would turn inland and move on Jerusalem itself, the city of the living God. It would be nearly impossible to stop.

The countryside around Arsuf had abundant woods and fertile fields. The woods of Arsuf stretched twelve miles north of the town and comprised one of the very few forest lands in all of Palestine. In the woods Saladin perceived a military opportunity, for he could hide his soldiers virtually until the point of attack. It was his best chance to halt Richard. He must do it now. He began to lay his plans. The Christian commanders suspected as much, and the rumor began to spread that an ambush awaited them. When they entered the woods, the "pagan cattle, the unbelieving black-faced brood" would try ~et the forest ablaze.

Then, surprisingly, there was a peace feeler. Saladin was jolted out of his preparations with word of an enemy contact with his advance guard. An interview with his brother, el Melek el-Adel, was requested. Seeing no harm in the request, for it seemed to be a test of his will, the Sultan authorized the meeting, and el-Adel rode to the front lines. Overnight he conferred with the Crusader envoys, cordially enough, and the following morning he conveyed the essence of the Christian proposal in a message to headquarters:

"The war between us has gone on for a long time, and a number of brave warriors have fallen on both sides," the Franks were reported to have said. "We only came out from Europe to help the Franks of the coastal regions. Make peace with them, and let the two armies return each to its own country."

The Sultan could not believe this to be a serious overture. "Try to protract the negotiations," he wrote back to his brother. "Keep them where they are until we receive the reinforcements we are expecting."

When Richard soon learned that el-Adel himself was present at the forward position, he requested a personal audience with the famous commander. The King rode out with a splendid cortège, waving banners and clanking steel and having at his side the son of Humphrey of Toron as his translator. Henfrid of Toron was a devastatingly handsome young soldier, a fact noted by a Muslim chronicler, although Henfrid's clean-shaven face was also noted. This was regarded as both a sign of effeminacy and something terrible that tended to frighten Muslim children.

Richard began by proclaiming his desire for peace.

Accepting this expression of goodwill with a bow, el-Adel said, "If you wish to obtain peace and desire me to act as your agent with the Sultan, you must tell me the conditions you have in mind." He leaned back, preparing himself for a long, protracted conversation, which was his mandate.

"The basis of the treaty must be this," Richard replied. "You must return all our territory to us and withdraw into your own country."

This was an insult, a display of hauteur that the Muslims had come to expect from the Europeans. El-Adel was appalled. "While the Unbelievers got up in their hearts heat and cant, the heat and cant of ignorance, Allah sent down His Tranquility to his Messenger and to the Believers and made them stick close to the command of self-restraint. . . ." was written in the Koran. But el-Adel could not exercise self-restraint. An argument broke out immediately. Not long after, the Muslim commander was back in his ranks, livid and bristling for a fight. So much for a protracted negotiation.

When he heard of Richard's affront, Saladin wheeled his divisions into place on the plain south of the woodlands. The Crusader army marched closer, from the Salt River, through flat sand and saltwater ponds to the River of the Cleft. The enemy was now only six miles from Arsuf. It was the evening of September 6, 1191. Two more unlucky Crusaders were brought before Saladin that night. Now, almost as a spiritual preparation and a witness for the clash that was coming the next day, the Sultan had them cruelly beheaded. To Richard's pavilion in turn, the scouts brought back the report of Muslim soldiers covering the whole of the earth ahead of them and outnumbering the Crusader army three to one.

The following day was the vigil for the birthday of the Virgin Mary.

CHAPTER TWENTY-TWO

# The
# Fourteenth
# Day of
# Sha'bān
# The Honored

✠

I N The Muslim Calendar The Fateful Day of
September 7, 1191, was the fourteenth day of Sha'bān the Honored, *May God Let Us Know His Favor*, the eighth month of the
year and the month before Ramadān the Sublime, the most holy of
all months and a time for fasting and spiritual renewal, not fighting. No

doubt Saladin, the defender of the faith, was as intensely aware of the march of time toward the holy month as he was of the march by the Christian invaders below him. So many times before, his army had melted away when its warriors heard a higher calling. Now was the moment for the big battle, the biggest of his life, the second Battle of Hattin. On this ground, more than fifty miles from the Holy City, Jerusalem had to be defended. He could put off the confrontation no longer. Now was the time for the final, triumphant, decisive victory of his jihad.

The Crusaders were camped near the mouth of the River of the Cleft. A large, impassable swamp called Birket el Ramadān protected their encampment from an inland attack, and so Saladin would have to wait to pounce until the Crusaders moved into open country. At dawn the Crusaders lit their fires, broke camp, and struck out at the sound of the clarion, with the sandstone fortress of Arsuf as their objective, five miles south. At first they marched across a sandy landscape, dotted with dunes, where the ground was too soft for the fast Muslim horses to ply their advantage. But within a mile of the River of the Cleft a line of low hills rose parallel to the coastal road. This higher, firmer ground stretched all the way to the orchards outside Arsuf.

For several days Richard had anticipated this great confrontation, and his soldiers were on high alert. For these critical miles ahead, the King had reorganized his order of march into five fighting divisions. The Templars were joined in the vanguard by a contingent of Turcopoles, native cavalrymen who were lightly armed, fast and mobile, and specifically trained to counter the Muslim raiders on their spry Yemeni horses. After the Templars came the soldiers of Aquitaine, Richard's own European subjects, Angevins and Poitevins along with the contingent of Bretons. They were commanded by King Guy, whose generalship was improving. Then came the Normans and the English, guarding the battle standard. And in the rear were the French, fortified by the fearsome Hospitalers, leavened by a number of local Syrian barons, commanded by Richard's cousin, the capable Henry of Champagne, and graced by the presence of the Flemish count, James d'Avesnes, who apart from Richard was the most gallant and chivalrous warrior of the entire European army. Richard and the Duke of Burgundy, the surrogate for King Philip of France, rode along the full length of the march, urging the soldiers to maintain compact ranks. So close were the men, wrote a chronicler, that an apple, if thrown, could not have fallen to the ground without hitting a man or horse.

Peering out from his battle station in the high ground, Saladin permitted the Crusaders to march down the road several miles before he unleashed his offensive. The turbaned Muslim horsemen poured out of the oaks of the forest. Estimates varied from two thousand to ten thousand mounted warriors, but the Crusaders noted their complexion as much as their numbers. The black bedouins, "blacker than soot, as if they had been cursed by God as a savage race," seemed to terrify the Christian ranks the most. These desert nomads led the charge. Behind them came a well-ordered and well-commanded force that was divided into precise regiments and companies and whose unit designations could be seen on their swallowtailed yellow banners, streaming from their lances. Beside the dust and the pennanted pikes and the horrid black faces, a fearsome clamor rose from the Muslim charge. The attackers shouted for Allah; the sound of trumpets mixed with the clattering of gongs and the shaking of tambourines. Their Sultan rode among his squadrons, exhorting them forward for the faith, having as his personal bodyguard only two pages who led a horse between them, in case the Sultan's own was cut from beneath him. His pages could do little about the arrows that whizzed by.

By contrast to the Battle of Hattin, the sea protected the rear of the Christian line this time, so that the Muslim riders could at least not get behind the flanks. Instead the attack forced the Christian ranks into an ever more compact formation, almost to the point of suffocation. And this was especially so when Saladin committed his main force to the fray.

The brunt of the attack fell on the rear. The Hospitalers and the French were forced and herded into a smaller and smaller space. The press of the attack became nearly unbearable. "Our people, so few in numbers, were hemmed in by the multitudes of the Arabs," wrote one eyewitness, "that they had no means of escape, even if they had wanted one. Neither did they seem to have sufficient bravery to withstand so many foes. They were shut in, like a flock of sheep in the jaws of wolves, with nothing but the sky above and the enemy all around."

The commanders sent word to Richard that they could not be squeezed further. They must break out in a charge, they said. But Richard would not allow it. He knew too well the disastrous consequences that could come from a precipitous charge. Despite the pressure, the line continued to inch southward toward Arsuf, and Richard could sense the frustration of the Muslims at not being able to rupture his line. Still, these hard-pressed warriors in the midst of the tightening vise felt more and more like "martyrs of Christ," and later their scribe would invoke Psalm 129 for their condition: "The plowers plowed upon my back: they made long their furrows." While their mail and armor and felt covering could withstand many arrows, a terrible toll was taken on their battle chargers. To the Crusaders it seemed as if "the fury of all Paganism had gathered together," while the flower of Christian youth was united into one body, "like kernels of corn on their ears."

Among the Hospitalers the anger and frustration began to boil over. "O excellent Saint George," the Master of the Hospitalers, Garnier de Naplouse, cried out in supplication to the patron saint of all Crusaders. Perhaps St. George would come again to the aid of Crusaders, as it was said he had done in the First Crusade at the Battle of Antioch in 1098. "Will you leave us to be put into confusion? The whole of Christendom is on the point of perishing because it fears to return a blow against this impious race." Pushing his way through the crunch, the master made his way to the center and found King Richard.

"We are violently pressed by the enemy, my Lord," he shouted over the din at his commander. "We're in danger of eternal infamy, as if we do not dare to return their blows. Each of us is losing our horses. Why should we bear this shame any further?"

"Patience, good Master," the King said. "It is you who must resist their attack. No one can be everywhere at once." The line must hold and push south to the safety of Arsuf's walls, and it was only through the discipline of his military monks that this would be possible. If there was to be a charge, it must happen all at once, all up and down the line, and there was a plan for that.

Garnier de Naplouse was not consoled, for this inaction flew in the face of his vows as a military monk and his allegiance to his native Syria. Still highly agitated and distraught, he returned to the rear flank to find it under even greater stress than before and with his knights on the verge of mutiny. "Why do we not charge them at full gallop?" they shouted at their master. "We shall forever deserve to be called cowards. Never has such a disgrace befallen so great an army in combat with unbelievers! Unless we defend ourselves, we shall be an everlasting scandal. So much the greater, the longer we delay." The master had no response, for he agreed with the sentiment.

The situation flew rapidly out of control. The left flank could be compressed and compressed only so long before it exploded. In advance, Richard's high command had decided upon a signal that would initiate a disciplined, coordinated charge of the whole line, should it be necessary in desperation. Two distinctive trumpet blasts from the front, center, and rear of the line, synchronized and shrill to be heard above the general din, would unleash the charge. In the best of conditions this wave of galloping knights would not only overwhelm and rout the Muslim force but would envelop and annihilate it. Instead the combustion was spontaneous.

From his vantage point above the fray, Saladin could see the explosion coming. "The enemy formed in one body," wrote his scribe, "and knowing that nothing but a supreme effort could save them, they resolved to charge." It did not quite happen that way. Instead the spark came from two knights, a marshal of the Hospital and a Flemish knight and boon companion of Richard. Without authorization they burst through the protecting line of infantry, shouting an invocation to St. George, and began to attack the attackers. Instantly, as if a stretched rubber band had snapped, the infantry line parted, and the rest of their Hospitalers charged. The commander, Henry of Champagne, had no choice but to follow, as did James d'Avesnes. The charge of the rear guard spread quickly to the center. and then to the vanguard of Templars. It was as if this brilliant, dynamic strategy had been planned. As with the rear, the infantry line parted in the center, and as if on cue, without the King's lifting his hand or a trumpet's sounding a single order, the cavalry charge became general.

The effect of this rolling wave was devastating. The Muslim ranks broke in terror and general confusion. The front line of the Muslim attackers, who were pressing close in and who had dismounted from their horses, was cut down totally. "Their bearded heads lay thick as swaths at harvest time." And the soldiers behind them fled in disarray. "I was in the center," wrote the Muslim eyewitness, "and when that body fled in the wildest disorder, it occurred to me that I might take refuge in the left wing which was the nearest to me. But when I came up with it, I found that it, too, was struck with panic, and had taken to its heels even quicker than the other. Then I turned to the right wing, but when I reached it, I found it in still greater confusion than the left." Finally he looked for the spot where Saladin's own personal guard should have formed a rallying point, but he found only seventeen men there, furiously and futilely beating on the drum. Over a two-mile swath, according to a Christian account, the Muslims could be seen fleeing in all directions. *"Pedibus timor addidit alas,"* Virgil's *Aeneid* was quoted gleefully by the Christian scribe. "Fear alone added wings to the feet."

To the front of the Hospitalers' line the carnage was awful. Across a wide expanse, bodies of Muslims were strewn in the sand, probably by the thousands, amid the carcasses of horses and camels. The frustration of being so hard-pressed and so hemmed in translated now into savage vengeance by the military monks. Amid the hacked and headless bodies was a horde of discarded weapons—scimitars and lances and crossbows, enough to fill twenty wagons. Later Richard would boast proudly that only a third of his men had routed Saladin's superior army.

When Richard himself saw the spontaneous charge, he galloped forward on his gigantic Cypriot bay stallion, called Fauvel, screaming out, *"Adjuva nos, Deus!"* and *"Sanctum Sepulcrum!"* He raced from the center to the head of the Hospitalers on the left and contributed substantially to the slaughter. In building his lore later, his scribe would write, "The fierce, extraordinary King cut down Arabs in every direction. None could escape the force of his arm. Wherever he turned, brandishing his sword, he carved a wide path for himself. With repeated strokes of his sword, he advanced, cutting them down like a reaper with his sickle."

Some distance away, Saladin stood like a reed, nearly helpless in the flood of fugitives who were running for the hills as fast as they could. Desperately, he had a few deserters dragged to him to berate and shame them and threaten terrible punishment, but he soon gave up the effort as hopeless. The drum beat constantly, plaintively, an empty call to rally and regroup, but its thump only added to the general clamor.

When it reached the edge of the Arsuf forest, about a mile from the infantry line, Richard halted the charge and forbade his knights to enter the woods. Too many times in the past, Crusaders had paid a heavy price for pursuing the enemy too far. In halting, Richard displayed again his restraint, his maturity as a military leader, his prowess in generalship far ahead of his time. It had been his very restraint in the early part of the day that had led later to the crushing rout, as if he knew instinctively that bottling up his Hospitalers would make them terrifying counterattackers.

As the Crusaders halted, so did some units of the Muslims. Taki-el-Din, Saladin's nephew and the former viceroy of Egypt, who, it was said, "felt the most hate for the Christian state," managed to rally some seven hundred troops beneath his unique banner, with its curious symbol, the trousers of Ayubbid nobility. Behind these britches they launched an effective counterattack. This impertinent resistance impelled Richard to launch a second charge and then a third, until the remaining brave souls among the Muslims were scattered far into the hills.

"The rout was complete," the Arab scribe wrote.

That night the Crusader army camped in safety within the ruined walls of Arsuf. They had accomplished the most complete victory of their Crusade. Compared to some seven thousand of their enemy, with some thirty emirs lost, the Christian toll was a tenth as much, about seven hundred. Still, in their grief over the fallen they found in Psalm 34 their solace: "Many are the afflictions of the righteous: but the Lord delivereth him out of them all." As for their victims, they also found in the Psalms (78) a justification for their enemy's destruction: "They kept not the covenant of God, and refused to walk in His law."

Around the Crusader campfires that night, to paraphrase Job 31, their harp was turned to mourning, their organ into the voice of them that weep. For among the fallen was a man of great distinction, slain in Taki-el-Din's charge beneath his royal trousers. He was the Flemish baron known as James d'Avesnes, a man who on both sides of the conflict enjoyed nearly equal fame. This noble figure had been among the first wave of Danes and Frisians to arrive in the Holy Land in 1189. It had been he who assumed command of the siege of Acre from the inept King Guy, who presided over the digging of the defensive trenches, and who held the command until the arrival of his superior, Henry of Champagne. If he was the very epitome of chivalry, so he had been its beneficiary. For during a skirmish outside the walls of Acre he had been thrown from his horse, and a sergeant had saved him by giving away his own horse, only to pay for the noble deed with his life. In his bravery and leadership the Flemish knight was much admired by the Arabs, so much so that it was said that Saladin once sent for him during the siege and tried to bribe him to join the Muslim side. As el-Tawil was to the Arabian side, James d'Avesnes was to the Christians.

The following morning a detail of Templars and Hospitalers, together with a squad of Turcopoles, ventured back out onto the terrible battlefield to search for the champion among the fallen. To identify him even among so many dead was not difficult, since his uniform included a distinctive shield of six diagonal stripes of gold and heraldic red. Eventually, amid the gore and discarded equipment, they found his disfigured body, minus an arm and a leg. Around it lay fifteen dead Muslims. (Later, as the hero went into legend, it would be said that even minus his appendages he fought on, and at the point of his death he screamed, "Richard, avenge my death!") The corpse of the hero was washed and wrapped and brought back to Richard in Arsuf, whereupon the King and King Guy carried the body to the church dedicated to Our Lady the Queen of Heaven, whose birthday it was that day. There a proper funeral was held.

"In counsel," wrote a Christian chronicler, "he was a Hector, in arms an Achilles, and in honor he surpassed Regulus."

## 2

## The Puzzle of Ascalon

In the hills Saladin was inconsolable, barely able to eat and barely able to converse with his closest aides. "Allah alone could conceive the intensity of the pain which broke his heart following the battle," wrote his scribe, who had tried unsuccessfully to move the Sultan out of his lethargy. The Sultan now stood twice defeated by this awesome, invincible English King. The spirit of the Muslim army was broken, and only with difficulty had Saladin been able to restore a semblance of order to his scattered ranks.

His emirs were in open rebellion. As they had after the fall of Acre, they had begun to question once again the competence of Saladin's leadership. After Acre some soldiers had even refused to follow orders to attack the enemy on its way to Haifa. What would they do after Arsuf? Some doubted that the Sultan would be able to persuade his allies in the hinterland to send replacements for his fallen.

It had been proved that he could not defeat the invaders when they were entrenched, as they had been at Acre. Nor could he apparently defeat them when they were on the move, in their disciplined ranks, holding back their terrible charge as their ultimate weapon. At all costs he must avoid another pitched battle and return to his proven method of harassment and skirmish and grudging retreat, joining forces with the heat of the desert and great expanse of the Arab hinterland and the salve of time to discourage the invaders.

The way to Jerusalem now seemed open to the invasion. Jaffa lay less than ten miles to the south. From there the old Roman road cut directly southeast past Ramla and Latrun to the Holy City, a mere twenty-five miles away. Saladin's only hope was to slow the enemy's march once it turned inland. Separated from its naval support, the Christian army would have to lengthen its supply line to the coast and be concerned about water. The Arab horde must contain and harry the enemy without confronting it directly.

As he emerged from his doldrums, Saladin realized that his army was intact. He held sway over the countryside and the ridges. He had taken a terrible toll on the horses of the enemy knights and the mules of their franklins. While he may have lost ten times as many men as the Crusaders at Arsuf, the Crusaders had lost many men at the siege of Acre, perhaps as many to pestilence as to war. Saladin had the ability to replace his casualties, and his enemy did not. Perhaps once the enemy forces turned inland, they would make a mistake. Perhaps he could provoke them into another foolhardy charge, as had happened several years before at the Springs of Cresson. Perhaps the Sultan could catch the Christian ranks without adequate water, surround them, and apply the lash of Hattin once again. To use King Richard's own description of Saladin, the Sultan would be "the lion in his den, secretly lying in ambush in the more elevated places for the purpose of slaying the friends of the Cross like sheep destined for slaughter." He needed to shore up his own southern supply line to Egypt through his southern base at Ascalon. And he must reinforce Jerusalem itself to ensure a long and painful siege for Richard.

Later, Christian accounts reported that after the Battle of Arsuf, Saladin had gathered his emirs around him and scolded them. "Are these the deeds of my brave troops upon whom I have heaped so many gifts?" he asked. "You were once so boastful, but now the Christians roam the whole country at will, for there is no one to oppose them. Where are my swords and spears to threaten them? Where is the victory you promised? Where are the disasters for the infidel foretold in our scriptures, written down of old? We are a disgrace to our noble ancestors who wrought such violence upon the might of Christian insolence!"

At this tirade shame and silence reigned until Saladin's third son, his favorite, the eighteen-year-old el Melek ez-Zaher, finally spoke up. Now the governor of Aleppo, the young warrior was quiet-spoken and studious, known for his lofty spirit and his sense of justice and as a lover of poetry. And so his speech carried weight. "Most sacred Sultan," the youth said earnestly, "these words are unfair, for we fought with all our strength against the Franks. With fearless hearts and zeal we attacked them, but they are armed with armor that no weapon can pierce, and so our blows fell harmless as if against flint. Moreover, among their number is a leader superior to any man we have ever seen. He charges on his immense horse before the rest and slays our men by the score. No one can resist or escape this man they call Melech Ric. Such a King seems born to command the whole world."

From these words, ironically, the sultan gained hope. Within twenty-four hours of his crushing defeat at Arsuf, Saladin was capable once again of menacing the Christian army.

After a day of rest, of burying their fallen champion and praying to the Virgin Mary, the Crusaders were on the move south again toward Jaffa. Saladin positioned his soldiers to block their way, spraying the Crusaders with arrows and hoping to provoke another charge, for which he would be better prepared. But there was no charge. The column moved relentlessly forward, and Saladin retreated in front of it. More Christian prisoners were brought before the Sultan, including more women in full battle gear. After their interrogations they were summarily beheaded.

From one of these interrogations the Muslim command learned that Richard had decided to tarry some days in Jaffa, where he planned to rebuild its walls and redig its defensive trenches, so that the bastion might serve as the new gateway to the Holy Land for future pilgrims.

But where would the enemy turn after Jaffa?

Jaffa was not the best naval seaport in lower Palestine. That was Ascalon, thirty miles farther to the south. In the past ninety years the important city had changed hands four times. The first Crusaders had captured it from the Muslims in the year 1100, but then the Muslims retook it, only to lose it again in 1154, until Saladin returned it to Muslim control in 1187. Now it was the fulcrum for Saladin's united Arab empire of Syria and Egypt, his forward naval base. To lose it to Richard would break the communication between the two halves of his empire.

Ascalon was a lovely and much-cherished city to the Muslims. It had been one of the five principal cities of the Philistines, the place where Samson had slain thirty men in anger and Herod had been born. Outside the town was the Valley of the Ant, where, according to the Koran, in a parable of the mighty and the small, Solomon spoke the speech of birds and feared that he would step accidentally on the lowly ants, prompting one of the ants to say, in Koran 27:18, presumably beyond Solomon's earshot, "O ye ants, get into your habitations, lest Solomon and his hosts crush you underfoot without knowing it."

The port had a four-hundred-year-old mosque called the Mosque of Omar and a fine, vibrant bazaar upon a marble plaza. It was renowned for its olive and sycamore trees, for its famous silkworms, and infamous for its ferocious sand flies. A double wall, fifty-three towers, and strong outer ramparts fortified its bow-shaped harbor. Its strategic location meant that the Arabs could mobilize a military force quickly from Egyptian resources that could threaten the Latin Kingdom at will. The city's very name meant in Arabic the "head of Syria."

If Ascalon was the forward post for an attack on the Crusader kingdom and the fulcrum of the united Arab empire, it was also the first line of defense against a Crusader invasion of Egypt and against any threat to the holiest places of Islam. At this point Saladin could not be sure that Richard would turn inland toward Jerusalem at all. Who was to say, regardless of his talk about a "Holy Crusade," that his ambitions were limited to Jerusalem? He might instead pursue the historic quest of his European forefathers to capture Egypt and to reign again as the Emperor of the Mediterranean, like Caesar Augustus or Alexander the Great.

From a military viewpoint this would make sense. If the English King moved south along the coast, he would be supported by his superior, unassailable navy. After his conquest of Egypt, Ascalon could be to the new ruler of the Near East as Alexandria had been to Caesar Augustus and Alexander the Great. And so the situations would be reversed. Instead of being the fulcrum of a united Arab empire, it would be the crux of a new and expanded Crusader kingdom, with Jerusalem its jewel.

Egypt, after all, carried the wealth of Saladin's empire. The burden and the glory of Arab history in the past ninety years had been the supreme effort to unite Egypt and Syria into one empire, under the Sunni way of Islam, just so that a European presence in the Middle East would be untenable. Saladin's own rise to power had come precisely in this quest for unity, against the efforts of Frankish kings to prevent it. Five times, from the years 1163 to 1169, a Crusader King had tried to invade and capture Egypt just to prevent this junction of Arab lands. During the wars against the Franks in Egypt, Saladin's own father had been thrown from his horse outside the Gate of Victory in Cairo. His own uncle, Shirkuh, had been the conqueror of Egypt and thus had delivered the land to the Emperor in Damascus. And when the Franks had finally been turned aside, Saladin himself had become the Emperor of Egypt.

Unity was not only the achievement of recent Arab history, but blessed by the Prophet in the Koran as an eternal value.

*Created though he was in the best of moulds*
*Man fell from Unity when his Will was warped,*
*And he chose the crooked path of Discord.*
*And sorrow and pain, selfishness and degradation.*
*Ignorance and hatred, despair and unbelief*
*Poisoned his life, and he saw shapes of evil*
*In the physical, moral and spiritual world,*
*And in himself.*

What was to stop this Melech Ric now, this daunting warrior whom Saladin's own son saw as destined to command the world, from going straight for the gold of Cairo? Who could forget the obscene raid of Reginald de Châtillon on the holy places of Medina and Mecca in the year 1182? Perhaps this giant of a king was a grandiose version of Châtillon whose quest was not merely the recapture of Jerusalem but the very destruction of Islam itself. And so the nightmares of Saladin were prodigious.

What, then, should be done about Ascalon?

To address this strategic dilemma, Saladin called his emirs together for a consultation at his latest retreat, at Ramla. Could Ascalon be defended? Or, put differently, were they capable of defending both Ascalon and Jerusalem simultaneously, fighting a two-siege war at once? Twenty thousand men were required to defend each city. From what reserves, from whose units, were these defenders to come?

The disaster of Acre was painfully fresh in all their minds, and at the thought of another protracted siege—with its hardships, its starvation, and, quite likely, its massacre at the cruel hand of Melech Ric in the end—the emirs blanched. "If you wish to defend Ascalon," said an abrasive Kurdish emir known as Al Samin the Fat, "go there yourself or arrange to send one of your sons. Let your filthy scoundrels do this. No one will go with them, since we do not relish the thought of a fate like that of Acre."

These insolent words verged on mutiny. Since the dissension showed how weak his position had suddenly become, Saladin chose to ignore the insubordination for now. But his own people as "filthy scoundrels"? The contempt dispirited the Sultan, and he withdrew alone into his pavilion for a day. How could one of his own proud Kurdish race say such a thing? Beyond the advice of the emirs he looked for enlightenment in prayer. "He sought counsel with God, and God made him see that it was necessary to destroy Ascalon since the Muslims were unable to protect it." After much agonizing, he decided that Ascalon would be dismantled and abandoned.

Four days after his defeat at Arsuf, Saladin took the fateful step of splitting his army. He left a token force with his eldest son, el Melek el-Afdal, near Jaffa to keep an eye on Richard's efforts at urban renewal, while the Sultan himself struck out with his brother, el-Adel, for Ascalon. With them were the heavy equipment and the bulk of the Muslim army. After a half day's march they arrived at Yubnah, a Samaritan town on a hilltop, known to the Christians as Ibelin, which to Saladin was better known for its fine mosque, as the burial place for companions of the Prophet, and as the garden for excellent Damascene figs. There he gave his soldiers a rest, and as the night came, his anxiety about his decision concerning Ascalon weighed on him. After a talk with his son el Melek el-Afdal, he turned to his chief adviser. "I would rather lose all my children than cast down a single stone from the walls," he said miserably, remembering that the capture of Ascalon had been his stepping-stone to Jerusalem four years before. "But God wills it. It is necessary for the Muslim cause. Therefore, I'm obliged to carry it through." It was as if by giving up Ascalon he was scuttling the united empire, abandoning the achievement of the past thirty years, squashing the most cherished Arab dream, maligning the sacred principle of unity.

A day later he was camped outside the city. The workmen gathered to hear an announcement of their grim mission. From house to house the Sultan's soldiers went recruiting additional hands for the destruction. The outcry was general. Women wailed at this terrible fate, sold what goods they could at fire-sale prices, and set off for Egypt or Syria in a sad procession with whatever they could carry on their backs. Ten hens went for a single dirham.

To destroy so ancient and beloved and well-built a city was a considerable undertaking. The walls were often nine or ten cubits thick (a cubit being the length from the elbow to the tip of the middle finger, or about eighteen inches). To one soldier the thickness was measured differently. The ramparts were as thick as his battle lance was long. The towers drew special attention. At each an emir was assigned to command a company of miners; the most special attention of all went to the particularly stout Hospitalers Tower, a massive citadel with a commanding view of the sea. On the first day of

Ramadān it was filled with logs, and it burned for two full days before its mortar and joints began to weaken and its stones were friable enough for the miners' picks to make a dent.

As the demolition went forward, the Sultan urged his soldiers and miners on to superhuman effort. They were already exhausted from fighting, and the native workers were understandably lethargic in obliterating their own homes and defenses. But Saladin feared that Richard would find out about the destruction and hasten to the attack. The Sultan's encampment was moved closer to the walls, so that his camel and ass drivers could be detailed to the effort.

Daily messages arrived from his son, el-Afdal, at Jaffa, and so there was good intelligence on Richard's activities. The Christians were camped outside the walls, and in Jaffa's pleasant gardens partook themselves of the exotic pomegranates and figs and grapes that were abundant. Their fleet had arrived from Acre with reinforcements and supplies—and with women. Later a Christian scribe would blame the ladies, as if this were a collective tale of Adam and Eve. "Women came to them from Acre, to stir up men's passions and multiply their misdeeds. The whole people became corrupted, the zeal of the pilgrimage waxed cold, and all their works of devotion were neglected." A number of Richard's soldiers returned to Acre with the ships and fell into even more indolent debauchery. Saladin's spies gleaned no word of such sloth. Skirmishes between the lines remained a daily event. As Ramadān set in, these clashes grew in intensity. Once again Saladin salivated at the thought of bushwhacking the Crusaders in some narrow pass.

Then abruptly word came from his son about another diplomatic contact. Henfrid the Beautiful, the son of Humphrey of Toron, had again requested a meeting. Could it be that the Crusaders were tiring of the fight? The Christian side proposed now that Saladin surrender all the coastal cities without further resistance. In return for what, was not clear. Since the Crusaders had already captured all the important coastal cities north of Jaffa and since Saladin was destroying Ascalon, all that remained to the south were the minor fortresses of Gaza and Darum. Several emirs argued that after the Muslims extracted the maximum concessions, the proposal should be accepted. Saladin, however, did not consider the feeler to be serious. Moreover, to cede the coastal cities to Richard so easily and formally played to Saladin's paranoia about a possible invasion of Egypt. But the initiative was useful in delaying further hostilities. The probing skirmishes of the enemy interested Saladin more. With Ascalon shrinking by the day, he marshaled his forces once again for a march to Ramla.

"We are delaying matters as long as we can," el Melek el-Adel wrote to his brother of his peace talks. "We will prolong the negotiations as long as possible to give you time to complete the destruction of the city."

# CHAPTER TWENTY-THREE

# Angst and Delirium amid the Pomegranate Trees

✠

I N EARLY OCTOBER 1191 A PATHETIC BAND OF DIS-
gruntled, bedraggled refugees from Ascalon were intercepted with
only a few possessions on their backs, and from their loose tongues
the Crusaders learned of the destruction of the southern outpost.
While the King did not doubt the veracity of the reports, he needed to know

the extent of the demolition before he could analyze its meaning. And so he outfitted a strong galley, put the brother of King Guy—Geoffrey of Lusignan, a competent commander—in charge, and dispatched it to the waters off Ascalon. Geoffrey of Lusignan was a fire commander, but if anything, he was even more vain than his brother. "Since they have made *him* a king," Geoffrey would say, "Surely they should make *me* a god!" When the ship returned with the shocking details of toppled towers and burning houses, Richard was ready to spring into action.

"The Arabs are afraid to meet us in the field," he told his council. "They are dismantling Ascalon, and I think we should endeavor to save it, as a protection for future pilgrims who pass that way."

But Henry of Champagne and the Duke of Burgundy and the other French commanders objected strenuously to this idea. Smaller as a town though it was, Jaffa was closer to Europe and fully adequate to the needs of future pilgrims. It could serve handsomely as the port of entry. The men had already expended considerable effort in clearing its moat and refurbishing its ramparts. By contrast, Ascalon was a diversion, an outpost, a vestigial appendage of the Crusader kingdom. It was too exposed and too far to the south to help any except pilgrims from Africa, and it was not likely that there would be many of them. Whether by the vehemence of their argument or their sheer numbers, the French argument proved convincing to the assembly, and Richard was outvoted. "Our differences may not only be useless but dangerous to the army," was all Richard could grumble at having lost the argument.

"Foolish counsel! Fatal stubbornness of indolent men!" an English chronicler later wrote of this decision. "By concerning themselves with their immediate comfort, intent as they were to avoid further labor and expense, the French did what they would later repent of: If they had then saved Ascalon, the whole land would soon have been clear of infidels."

Even the maverick marquis, Conrad of Montferrat, who was sitting out the Crusade in his northern redoubt at Tyre, sent an insolent message to Richard about his inaction in the Ascalon situation. According to an Arab source, Montferrat wrote, "Saladin destroys Ascalon, and you sit there on your ass and do nothing. After you understood that he had begun to demolish the city, you should have marched in great haste against him. That would have made him decamp from Ascalon, and you could have made yourself master of the place without lifting a weapon."

On October 4, 1191, Richard sat down in Jaffa to write to the Abbot of Clairvaux (the successor to St. Bernard of Clairvaux, the herald of the Second Crusade and the Pope's representative in the disputed district of the Loudunais, north of Poitiers). His letter contained a significant insight into his state of mind and about his aspirations for the future. His portrayal of his advantage over the enemy had the odor of exaggeration: Saladin was leveling Ascalon only because he had heard that Richard was "marching with hasty steps" toward it. The Sultan did not "dare" to engage the Christians, and he had "deserted and set at nought the whole land of Syria."

Richard's embroidery of the situation had an ulterior motive. Contrary to Saladin's fear of a wider conflict, the King, in this letter, seemed to be shrinking his ambitions rather than widening them. He evinced no interest in Egypt, no ambition to be the new Caesar Augustus of the Mediterranean. Instead he seemed intent to capture Jerusalem and get out of this infernal desert as fast as he could. His mind drifted toward his own departure for home. Of Saladin's supposedly desperate straits Richard wrote, "We consider this to be grounds for sanguine hopes that in a short time, by the bounty of God, the inheritance of the Lord will be entirely regained. As the inheritance of the Lord has already in some measure been regained, and as we have endured the heat and the burden of the day and have now exhausted all our money . . . not only our money but our strength of body as well . . . we do notify unto your brotherhood that we are not able to remain in the country of Syria beyond the arrival of Easter."

With this notice of departure in six months, the King entreated the papacy to begin mobilizing an army of occupation "to defend and protect the kingdom of the Lord, of which we, by the mercy of God, will by said time of Easter, more fully gain possession." Where the Pope might find such an army of occupation was his problem. Easter of 1192 was the deadline. The letter was more than notice; it was a warning: "to the end that we may not be reproached with slothfulness and negligence, in case we had in any way neglected to forewarn a man of such position and so holy a life on the urgent interests of Christianity. The most urgent need calls upon you with all earnestness to arouse the people of God to act." In short, he had done his part. It was for the Pope to pick up the pieces.

But the October 4 letter to the Abbot of Clairvaux was not the last word on Richard's state of mind. Only two weeks later, on October 11, he wrote a letter to the admirals that was totally contradictory. If his goals were smaller on October 4, they were far grander on October 11. "You should know that next summer, for the honor of God and for the confusion of the pride of the Muslims, we shall, if you are agreeable, hasten with all our forces into Egypt, to Cairo and Alexandria. . . ." And he proceeded to imagine all the bounty that was to be had in this expedition. Perhaps this was only a ploy to bring more Genoese vessels into the war, out of sheer greed. But still, Richard had not, just yet, given up the notion of becoming Caesar Augustus.

2

STALEMATE

The decision to hunker down in Jaffa led to a two-month hiatus, and it was as if, in this relaxation amid the fig and pomegranate trees, the fire went out of the Crusade. Ships passed back and forth between Acre and Jaffa, with cargos of foodstuffs and well-stuffed women.

*Back to the host the women came*
*And plied the trade of lust and shame.*

So wrote the chief poet of the Crusade. Many soldiers, in turn, hopped a ride with the returning galleys, only to lose themselves in the taverns and brothels of the larger fleshpot. Richard unwittingly contributed to the easing of discipline by summoning his Queen, Berengaria, and his sister, Johanna, the former Queen of Sicily, from their safe fortress at Margat. They came with their train and court, their music and the rustle of their fine clothes. If the King acted in so mellow a fashion, how were his soldiers to maintain their fighting trim?

After a few weeks Richard realized the drain on his forces and dispatched King Guy to Acre to round up the strays and bring them back for the next phase of the campaign. Despite his recent recovery as commander under Richard, Guy still enjoyed little respect among the rank and file. "For King Guy they made a sluggish return," wrote a chronicler wryly, and it became necessary for Richard himself to make the trip to Acre to scold and threaten and whip his soldiers back into line. While the King succeeded in bringing back the slackers, he somewhat undermined his purpose by bringing back also a company of manservants and a cache of valuables to make the royal stay in Jaffa more comfortable.

During this furlough in Jaffa a catastrophe nearly visited the Crusader side. On the eighth day of Ramadān, Richard, eager for some benign sport, went out for a day of hawking with only a small escort. Undoubtedly he hoped for game, but he was ready to pounce upon a few Turks as well if any turned up. Arguably there was a legitimate military purpose to the foray: Richard needed to scout the landscape that lay ahead of him as he moved on the old Roman road, southeast toward Ramla.

After some hours of hard riding, he was not far from Lydda—perhaps he had gone to visit the great church dedicated to St. George there—when he lay down in some woods and went to sleep. A strong patrol of Muslims happened onto this tranquil scene, and when they saw the sentry asleep, they thundered down on the careless party. The noise awakened Richard, and he barely made it onto Fauvel before they set upon him. The hunting party was badly outnumbered, and their capture was certain and imminent. Only the cunning of a Norman knight interceded. William des Préaux, one of the royal retinue, saw the full scope of the catastrophe at hand and began to scream out that he and no other was the daunting Melech Ric, and they had no right to take him captive, which of course the enemy immediately did.

In the confusion Richard was able to gallop away. He was, wrote a chronicler, "reserved by the divine hand for greater things." Poor William des Préaux had to languish in a Muslim prison until the end of the Crusade, when he was ransomed for a dear price. When news of this near-disaster spread through the troops, there was great consternation at the risk taken by their leader. A few knights reproached him for his rashness to his face, but Richard dismissed their alarm with a wave of the hand.

"No one can turn my nature out of doors, even with a pitchfork," he said wryly.

On another occasion a group of Templars found themselves in a hopeless situation, and Richard's aides pleaded with him not to attempt another heroic rescue.

"My lord, it would be crazy, with our small body, to resist this multitude," said one. "We are not able to save our men who are fighting. It's better to let them perish than to expose your royal person and all Christendom to certain danger, whilst we still can escape."

"What!" exclaimed Richard. "If I neglect to aid my men whom I sent forward with a promise to follow them, I shall never again deserve to be called a king."

Beneath this bravado Richard's misgivings about his entire enterprise were growing. Ahead of him on the old Roman road to Jerusalem lay the Plain of Ramla. Ramla was the ancient capital of Palestine, and though it did not exist in biblical times, it had, in the past four hundred years of its existence, once been as large as Jerusalem. It was noteworthy for its pleasant baths and spacious homes and for its large Jewish population, about three hundred in number, who had lived unmolested and in harmony with the town's Muslim population and with its Crusader overlords.

Now Saladin's army was entrenched in force there. On the Crusaders' reconnaissance missions it had been discovered that Saladin was dismantling every installation with any military value that lay between the armies. From a strategic viewpoint the Sultan's plan was to dismantle and retreat, while tactically he harried the Crusader soldiers at every turn.

As Richard's detachments moved out from Jaffa to scout or to forage, waves of enemy horsemen swooped down upon them. While these waves were gallantly repulsed, each engagement brought new casualties. Each fight seemed to add more luster to the legend of some noble and brave knight, while other, lesser but still precious knights fell on the field of battle around their champion. Given the constant harassment, the guard for the foraging parties had to be strengthened, and the distance from the main army had to be shortened.

In more than one such skirmish Richard himself had ridden to the rescue, with all the prodigious risks that involved, only to find that his horse was not swift enough to overtake the nettlesome and frisky Muslims. To pursue too far courted disaster. The King sent his engineers out to rebuild the Casal of the Plains and Casal Maen, two small outposts along the Ramla road. But once they were rebuilt, who would garrison them? And how long would the garrisons remain before loneliness or defeat or starvation displaced them? Even in his rear, in territory captured expensively with Christian blood, there were reports of organized Muslim thieves who were slipping into the Crusader camps, killing garrison soldiers, and carrying off supplies. How long would the Christians put up with that? Was this not a glimpse into the future? Meanwhile Richard learned that Saladin had destroyed the handsome cathedral of St. George at Lydda and had demolished the fortress at Ramla.

By the account of the Arab chronicler Beha al-Din, Richard signaled on the twenty-sixth day of Ramadān, or October 17, 1191, that he wished to talk. A meeting was requested with Saladin's brother, el Melek el-Adel. At Yazūr, a crossroads three miles from Jaffa and eight miles from Ramla, envoys of the two sides met with great fanfare, and a letter from Richard to Saladin was decorously handed over. The embassy then proceeded to Ramla and into the presence of the Sultan himself.

"The Muslims and Franks are bleeding to death, the country is utterly ruined, and goods and lives have been sacrificed on both sides," the Sultan read in Richard's letter. "The time has come to stop this."

With that remarkable pronouncement the letter defined Jerusalem, the Holy Cross, and the Latin Kingdom as the fundamental points of conflict between them. "Jerusalem is for us an object of worship that we could not give up even if there were only one of us left." Richard demanded that the entire domain of the old Kingdom of Jerusalem be restored as a hereditary right. In addition, as if he were indeed Caesar Augustus, he demanded Cairo as a tribute.

And lastly, the Cross: "To you the Cross is simply a piece of wood with no value. But for us it is of enormous importance. If the Sultan will deign to return it to us, we shall be able to make peace and to rest from this endless labor."

As with many diplomatic initiatives, this opening salvo was most important for its subtext, and Saladin read it and reread it carefully. On their face the demands were absurd coming from one who, despite his victories at Acre and Arsuf, found himself surrounded, with his army dispirited and his alliance disintegrating. But the opening words bespoke fatigue and suggested a longing for an honorable exit. Saladin would need to be cunning in handling the gambit. He knew that he, too, was war-weary. With any more serious reverses, his whole army might well evaporate.

"Your King demands what I cannot agree to without dishonoring the True Faith," he said to the Christian envoy. "Nevertheless, I will offer him the whole land of Jerusalem, from the river Jordan to the Western Sea, on the condition that neither Christians nor Muslims shall ever rebuild Ascalon." At this remark the Crusaders' ambassadors must have taken heart. But when Saladin sat down to write his reply to Richard, he made no such counteroffer.

"Jerusalem is ours as much as yours," Saladin replied. "Indeed, it is even more sacred to us than it is to you, for it is the place from which our Prophet accomplished his nocturnal journey and the place where our community will gather on the Day of Judgment. Do not imagine that we can renounce it or vacillate on this point. The land was also originally ours, whereas you have only just arrived and have taken it over only because of the weakness of the Muslims living there at the time. God will not allow you to rebuild a single stone as long as the war lasts. As for the Cross, its possession is a good card in our hand. That Jesus died on the Cross is a falsehood for us. The Cross cannot be surrendered except in exchange for something of outstanding value to all Islam."

It had become a game of tit for tat. In diplomatic parlance, they had enunciated their respective statements of principles and had a frank exchange. Their disagreement seemed intractable. And yet words are not everything. El-Adel himself became the messenger for Saladin's tart reply to Richard's letter, and when the Sultan's brother arrived in the Crusader camp, he was received warmly. Richard was indisposed and could not receive the emissary, for the King was being bled. (He was not sick but merely receiving preventive therapy, for bleeding was recommended at this time of year for all travelers to ward off sickness.) At the King's direction el-Adel was lavishly entertained that evening with an elaborate feast. The following day the Arab leader returned the favor by conveying the precious gifts of seven camels and a splendid tent to Richard. Between the King and the prince a familiarity and understanding was developing.

From this serious exchange, softened by gifts and courtesies and banquets, the situation lapsed briefly into farce. How the silly proposal evolved is unclear, but Richard's attitude toward women as pawns was well established, and el-Adel had been the beneficiary of Western hospitality enough times to gain an appreciation of Western ladies. However it emerged, el-Adel returned to his brother's pavilion in Ramla with an astonishing proposition from Al Anketār, as Richard was also known at the Muslim court.

Solemnly el-Adel presented the new proposal to his brother: he, el Melek el-Adel, known as the "Sword of Religion," would become betrothed to King Richard's sister, Joanna, the former Queen of Sicily. Once married, the couple would become the joint rulers of the new Kingdom of Jerusalem, with their royal seat in Jerusalem. Saladin was to hand over all his Palestinian lands to his brother, and Richard was to hand over all his territory to his sister. The two halves would then be amalgamated into the hybrid kingdom, although the Templars and Hospitalers would be allowed to keep their fortresses to ensure the safety and well-being of future pilgrims, and Christians would be free to visit the holy sites in Jerusalem without difficulty. The True Cross was to be returned, and once it was, Richard would leave the Holy Land.

Even before el-Adel formally presented this outrageous idea to the Sultan, word of the proposal spread rapidly through the Muslim camp, and its transparent appeal caused great rejoicing among the common soldiers. Could peace really be at hand? In deference to his estimable brother, Saladin decided to play out the scene though he must have had difficulty restraining himself from breaking into uproarious laughter. Until now he had not suspected King Richard of being a practical joker.

For starters the Koran forbade a marriage with an unbeliever. Spiritual harmony between husband and wife in the Garden of Bliss was a central tenet of Islam. A couple must see the truth of God in the same way. "Do not marry unbelieving women until they believe. A slave woman who believes is better than an unbelieving woman, even though she allure you," the holy text reads. "Unbelievers do but beckon you to the Fire." For the marriage to work, Joanna would have to convert to Islam.

If by some miracle there could be a joint Christian-Islamic marriage ceremony, one could hear the poet wax eloquent about el Melek el-Adel. Later a *kasida*, the testimonial poem of Arab lands, was written about him: "In every land his unsullied justice has formed a paradise watered by the heavenly stream of his liberality. So just is he that the wolf passes the night in the torments of hunger, although the brown gazelle is before his eyes. No believer in the true religion can be troubled by a doubt respecting the excellence of him. He is a sword of which the surface has been polished by glory, and of which the metal denotes the excellent temper. His generosity leads him to pardon the gravest offenses, and his noble pride turns him from obscene discourse. You need not listen when the history of other kings is read. Hear this! The flesh of the wild ass has the taste of every sort of game."

It was hard to imagine the royalty of Europe standing silent to swallow these touching sentiments about their mortal enemy.

Still, as was the custom for such matters of state, Saladin gathered his council of emirs together, and the proposal was read three times. To each reading the Sultan answered his solemn agreement, knowing full well, as the Muslim chronicle makes clear, that Richard would never sanction such a thing and had proposed it out of sheer mischief. Whatever else might be involved in this ludicrous proposition, the Muslims bought precious delay in the hostilities.

But the play had to go forward. Upon hearing of the proposal, Joanna fell down shrieking her objection and swore on all that was holy that she would never marry a Muslim. In situations like this Richard was not at his best. When the Muslim envoy came for his reply, the abashed King reported his sister's distress and said, "If el Melek el-Adel will but consent to become a Christian, we will celebrate the marriage." Seemingly oblivious to the un-likeliness of this, he nevertheless pressed forward as if they were closing in on an agreement. His formal message to the Sultan dealt with Jerusalem and the proposed division of lands.

"I wish for your friendship and affection," he wrote his enemy. "I told you that I would give these regions of Palestine to your brother, and I want you to divide the land. But we absolutely must have a foothold in Jerusalem. My aim is to ensure that you divide the lands so that the Muslims may not blame your brother and the Franks may not blame me."

If Joanna was unwilling, Richard had a backup. He offered his niece, Eleanor of Brittany. Perhaps she was not a queen, but she was a pliable vir-gin. In putting this maiden of his ward forward, he would not need papal as-sent, as he would with a former queen, and to secure the permission from Rome would require an annoying delay of at least three months. But when this message came to el-Adel, he balked. He had his heart set on a Christian queen, and only a Christian queen would do. The players were being difficult.

In the midst of this charade a bizarre subplot complicated the picture fur-ther. On the very day that Humphrey of Toron was meeting with Saladin on Richard's behalf, another local baron, the Prince of Sidon, arrived unexpect-edly in the Muslim camp. He was bearing tender messages from the Marquis of Tyre, Conrad of Montferrat. To the Muslims, the Prince of Sidon was a fa-miliar figure. For many years he had been the lord of Beaufort, the colossal fortress in southern Lebanon. He had escaped the Battle of Hattin only to be taken prisoner in other action and held captive in Damascus until recently. His castle at Beaufort had been besieged by Saladin's troops for over a year beginning in 1189 and had only been starved into submission. He had now allied himself with Conrad in hopes of recovering his coastal town, which the Muslims held.

Conrad, of course, had turned his back on Richard's entire enterprise after

Richard had sided with King Guy. He had left Acre in a huff before it fell, had associated himself with King Philip of France, and had received Philip's prisoners and half the French booty before King Philip had absconded for France. As if Conrad were Philip's surrogate, the tensions had continued as Richard marched south. When Richard sailed from Jaffa to Acre after the battle at Arsuf, his purpose, beyond collecting the drunken slackers, was to patch up his differences with Conrad and his French naysayers. In this he had entirely failed. Because of his proven ability and courage and animal energy, Conrad remained the most feared of the local barons to the Muslims.

So what was on his mind now?

After old Humphrey of Toron was ushered out, the Prince of Sidon was ushered in, and he put before Saladin a remarkable offer. Conrad of Montferrat had had enough of this arrogant English bully. He was now prepared to ally himself with Saladin to throw the bastard out of the Holy Land. The price of this unholy alliance was that Saladin must give up the cities of Sidon and Beirut. Moreover, Conrad was prepared to lay siege to the Crusaders in Acre. Should Acre fall to him, he should have the right to it as well. So it was not hard to guess at what Conrad imagined: a different sort of state altogether, made up of the northern cities of Beirut, Sidon, Tyre, and Acre; populated by the ancestors of the First Crusade rather than these interlopers "from beyond the seas"; and ruled by this renegade of the Piedmont.

Saladin was elated with this separate offer. The prospect of splitting the Crusaders between the natives and the invaders was too delicious. By accepting Conrad's offer (which Saladin was inclined to do immediately), he would set the pale-faced Europeans at one another's throat. If Conrad stormed Acre, Richard would have to halt his advance on Jerusalem and turn back to defend old turf.

A splendid tent was prepared for the Prince of Sidon in the Muslim camp, with plush carpets and soft cushions. He was feted at lavish feasts and taken on rides with Saladin's brother, el-Adel, to inspect the battle lines. Thus treated like a caliph or a pasha, the Prince of Sidon needed to be entertained for some days while the emirs considered the two competing offers on the table.

In this air of unreality the envoys shuttled back and forth between the various camps. At one point a special tent was set up between the lines, furnished magnificently, where el-Adel and Richard held their convivial meetings and bonded over lavish dinners and toasts. They parted, an Arab chronicler reported, with "mutual assurances of perfect goodwill and sincere affection." On October 16, Richard presented a magnificent war horse to el-Adel as a gift for the Sultan.

In a subsequent round with Richard's envoy, the issue of prisoners arose. "If there is peace, it will be a general peace," the Sultan quipped to Humphrey of Toron. "If there is no peace, the matter of prisoners will be moot." When the envoy left, Saladin turned to his chancellor and said, "When we have made peace with them, there will be nothing to prevent their attacking us treacherously. If I should die, the Muslims would no longer be able to muster an army like this, and the Franks would have an upper hand. We had better carry on the Holy War until we have expelled them from Palestine . . . or death overtakes us."

Still, the Sultan called his emirs together as a formality to ask their solemn judgment about the two proposals. If Richard's proposal were genuine, they responded, it was preferable, since long experience had taught them that an honest agreement with the local barons was impossible; they always betrayed their promises. More recent experience showed them that any measure to get rid of Al Anketār and his army was to their advantage.

And so Conrad's initiative languished. In a few days the Prince of Sidon ended his regal repast in the Muslim camp and departed. Meanwhile reality asserted itself on the matrimonial front. It did not look as if the Third Crusade would end in a blaze of brotherly love. Richard's final message evoked the horror in the Christian camp over the marriage proposal, not only from Joanna but from his bishops. If the holy text of Islam forbade marriage to an unbeliever, so the Christian Bible could be invoked in opposition. "Neither shalt thou make marriages with them; thy daughter thou shalt not give unto his son" was written in Deuteronomy. "For they will turn away thy daughter from following me, that she may serve other gods: so will the anger of the Lord be kindled against you, and destroy you suddenly."

The dissent was manifold. "The Christian people disapprove of my giving my sister in marriage without consulting the Pope, the head and leader of Christianity," Richard wrote to Saladin. "I have therefore sent a messenger who will be back in three months. If he authorizes this wedding, so much the better. If not, I will give you the hand of one of my nieces, for whom I shall not need papal consent."

Between the impossibility of remaining idle for three months, Joanna's opposition to el-Adel, and el-Adel's opposition to Eleanor of Brittany, Saladin did not favor this message with a reply. It was time to get back to the business of war. Richard made a final desperate effort to conclude the conflict through diplomacy. Through his newfound friend and prospective brother-in-law, he renewed his request for a personal meeting with Saladin. The Sultan's emirs were interested, but Saladin's reply was the same.

"It would be a disgrace for kings to fight one another after they had met," he wrote. "Let the issue between us be settled first. Only then would it be fitting to have an interview and talk over serious business. Only then can we lay the foundation for a sincere friendship between the two nations."

# 3

## LAISSEZ-ALLER!

As these surreal contacts went forward in October, the armies were not idle. The probing and skirmishing continued unabated on the plain of Ramla, as the foraging parties of the respective sides encountered one another. Saladin had received the distressing news that the farmers to the north around Acre were providing the Crusader army generously with grain and meat, dashing his hopes of starving the invading force in the hinterland. From deserters he also learned that Richard would soon leave Jaffa and march on Ramla.

With this intelligence Saladin continued to destroy fortresses ahead of the Crusader advance. He marveled at the splendor of the St. George Church in Lydda before he leveled it. Its sister church, the Cathedral of St. John at Ramla, along with the fortress, next fell victim to his ram and pickax. The inhabitants of the town were ordered to evacuate, their consolation the right to take with them the grain in the government stores. On October 4 the Sultan admired the well-fortified fortress at Latrun, also known as Toron of the Knights, before he ordered its five towers to be demolished. Early in the month of Ramadān he made a secret three-day trip to Jerusalem to survey its war stores and to order the strengthening of certain battlements. The Holy City was ready.

In late October the Crusader army finally left the delights of Jaffa. Proceeding past the important pilgrims' way station at Yazūr, it camped in the ruins of Lydda and Ramla. In that inhospitable place of strewn bricks and half-standing walls, it was mired down for twenty-two days, largely because of the weather. For several weeks violent rain and hail poured down on the soldiers. The wind tore out the tent pegs. Horses drowned; bread was ruined; coats of mail rusted on the knights' bodies. The earth turned to a sea of mud and made further movement impossible. But the deluge did not prevent the enemy from raining its arrows down on the encampment.

As he laid waste the land ahead of the invasion, Saladin's camp was rife with rumor and bad news and political setbacks. The Sultan was told, erroneously, that the King of France had died on his return to Europe. Whatever joy that may have occasioned was soon transformed into grief and tears with the report of Taki-el-Din's death in Syria.

Saladin had been close to this fierce commander. "I ask the pardon of God," Saladin said amid his tears, and then he quoted the Koran: "We are His, and to Him we return." His nephew's vibrant hatred of the Christians had made him a powerful presence in the field, and his loss now was a significant blow not only to Holy War but to the solidarity of his empire. The tragedy caused disruption and competing claims in his Mesopotamian provinces, and troops had to be diverted from the front to quell the violence. Then a dispatch arrived from the August and Prophetic Court in Baghdad in which the Caliph, al-Nasir li-dini'llah ("he who helps the religion of God") rebuked Saladin for political actions he had taken in the eastern part of the empire. Between the unrest in Mosul and the disapproval in Baghdad, the Sultan could expect little help from the East. The defense of the Holy City would have to rest with his Syrian, Egyptian, Turkish, and Kurdish contingents.

The Muslim advance guard remained ahead of the invaders in the hills, and the bedouins stayed on the attack against the enemy's line of communication to the sea, while Saladin moved his main force into Jerusalem. He did not expect the siege to begin until the dry weather of the spring, but he was uncertain about its defense and afraid that its stockpile of war supplies was insufficient. "If no help comes next spring, the affair will be hard," he wrote to a distant emir. Some Muslim troops were drifting away in this dismal season, but the Sultan did receive an infusion of fresh soldiers from Egypt at about this time under the command of the estimable Abu 'l-Haija' the Gross.

On December 12, with a break in the weather, the Crusaders were on the move again. From Ramla they moved to Toron of the Knights to camp amid its fallen towers. After a day there they moved to a recently vacated place called Beit Nuba, three miles to the northeast of Latrun. The liberators were now only twenty miles from Jerusalem. Again the rain and the snows halted them.

Ironically, in these miserable conditions, the morale of the Crusaders was soaring. They were camped at the foot of the Judean hills with their distinctive boulders and narrow valleys. The Christian soldiers took in the landscape of their dreams and prayers. Here at last were the rounded hills where their Savior had walked in his sandals and preached to the multitude. The Via Dolorosa of Jerusalem was now so close they could almost smell it. No one wanted to miss this final, glorious triumph. Even the casualties in Jaffa insisted on braving the perils of the bedouin-infested road so that they, too, could share the joy. Many were brought on stretchers to Beit Nuba, even though the bedouins had no compunction about descending on these convoys of the sick and wounded and defenseless.

They were coming again like the liberators of 1099. Their King, Richard, came as the new Guy de Bouillon, who eighty years before had made the alleys of Jerusalem run with the blood of Muslims and Jews, who had demurred to be king but who had reigned simply as "Advocate of the Holy Sepulcher." The grave of Guy de Bouillon had been inscribed thus:

Marvellous star, here lies Duke Godfrey
Egypt's terror, putter to flight of Arabs, scatterer of Persians;
Though elected king, king he would not be entitled
Nor crowned; but he was the "slave of Christ."
His was the care to restore to Zion her rights
As a Catholic to follow the sacred dogmas of right and equity;
Thus also with the saints could he deserve a diadem
The army's mirror, the people's strength, the clergy's anchor.

Their glory would be as great. They were about to redress the lament of Pope Gregory, who invoked the 79th Psalm: "O God, the heathen have come into Thine inheritance. Thy holy temple have they defiled. They have laid Jerusalem in heaps."

In the mud and snow the camp rejoiced. Soldiers tossed their weapons back and forth in playful games. "Despardieux!" Knights talked about the lists they would organize after the liberation, just as they had staged their tournaments after the capture of Acre. "Laissez-aller!" the cry of the charge rang through the tents in expectation. In their shelters they shined their armor and their lances, washed their surcoats, brushed their quilted vests, preened their banners, in readiness.

"Lord God, Thy grace has conducted us," they chanted. "Here we are at last on the True Path."

# CHAPTER TWENTY-FOUR

# SACRED AND
# DEMONIC
# FLAME

✠

**B**ETWEEN CHRISTMAS OF 1191 AND THE TWELFTH night of Epiphany, the fate of the Third Crusade hovered in the balance. In these critical days Richard the Lionheart wobbled wildly between bursting confidence and gnawing self-doubt. Amid the mud and the jubilation of Beit Nuba, he was to have his own epiphany. While his Templars rode out boldly into the countryside around the Holy City and returned with two hundred head of fat cattle—raw meat to energize the Christian host in its last superhuman vault over Jerusalem's walls—the king brooded.

Far away the actions of magi other than Saladin were influencing

Richard's state of mind and his future course. His mother, Eleanor, his rod and his staff in Europe, was in Normandy, at Bonville sur Toke, keeping a skelly eye on her late husband's mistress Alais in Rouen and holding together her far-flung Plantagenet domain like strands of wool. His younger brother, John, was at Howden in Yorkshire with Hugh, the excommunicated Bishop of Durham, seething with resentments against Richard, gaining in audacity as he gathered under his control more English castles and land, bursting with evil designs on his brother's kingdom.

And just before Christmas the linchpin of the conspiracy, King Philip Augustus of France, finally arrived back in Paris. To his doting subjects he presented himself as the hero of the Third Crusade. He paraded through the streets as the captor of Acre and the tiger of the Mediterranean. Prostrating himself sanctimoniously before the altar of St. Denis, he gave thanks for his safe return. And so he might. Only a quarter of the French soldiers who had departed with him from Vézelay in high spirits and piety would return to their homeland. Disease as well as war had taken a terrible toll. Philip of Flanders was only the most prominent of the victims. Reverently the King laid a swath of priceless Oriental silk on the altar as a token of his heroic service and then took himself off to Fontainebleau to hatch his plot.

He was obsessed with Richard. Perhaps he had always been obsessed with him, as if Richard were the story of Philip's life. Their relationship had run the gamut of emotion, but now Philip's emotions settled permanently into loathing. In early 1192, almost as if it were a New Year's resolution, he dropped all pretense of abiding by his promises to Richard and the Pope or of respecting the Truce of God. He wanted Flanders. He wanted the Vexin and Normandy and anything more he could snatch from the vast Plantagenet dominion while its lord was sorely taxed in the Holy Land.

"How faithfully he kept his oath the world knows well enough," an English scribe would write bitterly about the ease with which the French King closed the book on his lofty Crusade, shed his inhibitions, and returned to his scheming ways.

Early in 1192, Richard was receiving dispatches from his boorish, potbellied chancellor, Longchamp, informing the King of his brother's sedition in England, reporting that John was demanding oaths of fealty from the barons, warning Richard about the implications of Philip's return, and beseeching the King to give up his Holy War and return home on "wings of the wind" if he meant to keep his kingdom.

If Richard dismissed this missive from so untrustworthy and self-serving a source, other urgent dispatches from more credible quarters arrived, until the compendium of them seemed to speak with one voice. That his news was always two months old must have increased his anxiety. How dire a consequence the return of his erstwhile lover and ally would have on the scene, he could only imagine.

In fact, Philip was wasting no time. On January 20, 1192, he appeared at the walls of the strategic Norman castle at Gisors, the old meeting place of the French and English Kings, once festooned by the famous elm tree. There he confronted one William Fitz Hugh, the seneschal of Normandy, and demanded of that high officer the release of his sister, Alais, from her captivity in Rouen. This was more than a sentimental gesture. Philip had good reason for his request, for the much-used and -abused Alais was to be exploited once again for whatever residual value she possessed. Secretly, Philip's emissaries had been to England and had presented John with a devilish proposition: Come to France with a force, marry the lovely if somewhat shopworn Alais, and with her take possession of the borderlands that Richard had promised as Alais's dowry. That John was already married seemed to both Philip and John to be a trifle, easily remedied.

At the walls of Gisors, Philip produced an official-looking document. It was, he professed, a solemn treaty that had been struck with Richard in Sicily. In it the return of Alais and her valuable lands was promised. That Philip's document was a forgery was apparent on its face. To the common knowledge of all, Richard had made no promises or concessions about Alais in Sicily. In fact, quite the contrary was the case. At Messina he had ended the matter once and for all, dropping his father's mistress flat and paying Philip a modest gratuity to ease his pain. Still, William Fitz Hugh prolonged his discussions with Philip to get this clarified from a higher authority.

Enter Eleanor. With spry step and commanding voice the tireless seventy-year-old Queen Mother stepped forward and took charge. Her spies had already informed her of the unholy contact between Philip and John. The proceedings at Gisors were the easy part. Her youngest son was the thorny problem. To William Fitz Hugh she sent curt instructions: Inform his majesty, King Philip, that his treaty is a palpable fake, that the seneschal had received no instructions from King Richard about turning over persons or lands to France, that to do so would be in violation of the Truce of God. Soon enough Philip skulked back to Paris, seething and empty-handed. The

Queen, meanwhile, made haste to England to deal with her "light-minded" son John.

"With all her strength," wrote the English chronicler Richard of Devizes, "she wanted to make sure that faith would be kept between her youngest sons . . . at least, so that their mother might die more happily than had their father."

The Queen arrived at Portsmouth on the ides of February, February 11, shocked to discover that John was gathering a fleet and soldiers in Southampton. This was not her only shock. As she made her way to her dowered houses in Ely, the common people streamed out of their houses and besieged her on the muddy streets of their villages, barefoot, in tatters and in tears. They horrified her with stories of chaos and disruption. With an absentee King and a scheming pretender of a younger brother, with the high clergy in disarray, some bishops excommunicated and others acting like warlords, with soldiers romping through the countryside representing one faction or the other, even the dead were not being decently buried. England was falling apart.

Distraught and determined, Eleanor rode on to Windsor, then to Oxford, London, and Winchester. At each stop she prodded and bewitched and bullied the peers into denying John the support he needed for his ships and mercenaries. To John himself she sent an unequivocal message. To go to France against her word was to lose all his English lands and estates. Reluctantly, sullenly, temporarily, John relented.

With this goal accomplished, Eleanor turned her unflagging energies to the civil strife that was all around her. She strove with an iron constitution to reconcile the various factions in the church, from her hated stepson, Geoffrey, the powerful archbishop in York; to her son John's consort, the excommunicated Hugh of Durham; even to the despicable Longchamp, who lurked in France, longed to return to England, wished once again to wield his power as Richard's chancellor and as Bishop of Ely. By charm and threat and by the sheer force of her will she sought to make peace for the sake of order. But as Lent again approached, after the terrible season of constant motion and difficult diplomacy, some success and more disappointment, she was exhausted, and she sat down to write to Richard.

He must abandon his Crusade in the Holy Land. He must return to his realm if he wished to hold it. Above all others, this was a voice to which he was compelled to listen. But Eleanor's request did not reach him until the summer of 1192. By then he had come to his own conclusions. He had long since had his own epiphany.

2

## DOLT OR SAGE?

At the beginning of January, on the day of Christ's circumcision, Richard gathered his council to plot his next move. By contrast to the ecstasy and heady anticipation in the camp, the mood in council was somber. Saladin, the councils had learned, had moved out of Jerusalem through the back hills and was once again behind them at Tell Jezer, five miles south of Ramla. And so it seemed the game would forever be played: The Christians would move forward toward their cherished goal, only to find their nemesis snipping at their rear and hovering above them in the mountains.

In council Richard deferred to the native Franks to assess the situation. Their view was pessimistic. To besiege Jerusalem now, in these miserable conditions, was pointless. The rain, the mud, the hail, and the wind made military operations impossible. If the Crusade moved to the walls of the Holy City, Saladin's men would surely fall upon their men from the mountains. If by some divine miracle they were to take the city, who would hold it? To defend Jerusalem would call for a large, permanent garrison of the best knights, and yet who was prepared to stay? Once the Holy City was taken, the goal of the holy pilgrimage was achieved. The Europeans would scurry home as fast as the wind could take them. The native Franks had no chance to hold a conquered city without foreign aid.

And thus the Crusade found itself with a devilish dilemma. To take the city was to lose the army; not to take it was to undermine the entire purpose of the Crusade. The irony of the situation did not end there. The most fearsome, committed warriors, the Templar and the Hospitaler military monks, concurred in the native view. It made more military sense, they argued, to withdraw for a few months to Ascalon and rebuild that strategic city as an obstacle to Saladin's reinforcements from the south. Perhaps in the dry days of summer they could return for another assault on Jerusalem. Later the poet of the Crusade would render the sentiment of the military monks into verse:

> Unless the city were straightway
> Peopled with folk who there would stay.
> Since every pilgrim, dolt or sage;

*Having performed his pilgrimage*
*Would promptly to his land return*
*Back to home where he was born*
*And with scattering of the host,*
*The land would once again be lost.*

Who should now step forward to dispute this defeatist strategy—but the French! Having complained and malingered through the entire Crusade, having been embarrassed by the desertion of their King, the French now heaped contempt on the idea of retreat. The troops would never stand for it, they argued.

Of course, they were right. When the news of the withdrawal spread through the ranks, jubilation turned to shock and disbelief, then to despair and self-flagellation. Soldiers cursed the day they were born and the day they had committed themselves to this craven enterprise. Desertions were immediate and legion, especially among the French. Some seven hundred French knights departed for the pleasures of Jaffa and Acre and Tyre, spewing their recriminations against Richard and protesting that only they had the backbone to persevere.

From the hills Saladin's soldiers watched the retreat in amazement. It was as if they now were the beneficiaries of divine Providence, for, truth be known, behind Jerusalem's walls their defenses were weak and probably would have fallen precipitously to any serious siege. When it was clear what was happening, Saladin himself gave his army permission to disband and return to their homes, with orders to report again in May, fresh and ready for new adventures.

For the next two weeks it seemed to the heartsick Crusaders as if their Savior was punishing them for their cowardice. The rain and hail continued without letup, and the legions slogged their way through the hellish mud, discarding their equipment and leaving horses to die in the mire. At Ramla the remainder of the indignant French force, led by the Duke of Burgundy, ignored the orders of their most prominent leader, Henry of Champagne, and took the north fork to Jaffa as Richard turned south toward Ibelin.

Finally, on January 20, the main force arrived at its destination. Ascalon was a pile of rocks, and the soldiers had all they could do to climb over the rubble that was once the proud city's main gate. For eight days after their arrival the rains continued, and no galley could enter the harbor to reprovision the dispirited, bedraggled, and famished pilgrims.

Through February the weather conditions improved. Gradually, with his customary energy and leadership, Richard began to reinvigorate his army, if only by putting it to hard labor. For once class differences were set aside, as knights worked shoulder to shoulder with esquires and even women to rebuild the city. Towers began to rise again over the walls—one, constructed by a team of criminals, called the Bloody Tower, another by friendly bedouins, a third built by women and called the Tower of Maidens. With this palpable progress the cheer of the soldiers returned, to the point that Richard could think about reenlisting the help of the French. From Acre and Tyre had come reports of internal bickering. The old antagonisms had surfaced: The supporters of King Guy were fighting those of Conrad of Montferrat, the Pisans were fighting the Genoese, and the French had given in to the harlots and the tavern keepers. The Duke of Burgundy himself had been unhorsed by his detractors and thrown indecorously into the mud.

The King sent dispatches to the French, pleading with them to rejoin the army in Ascalon. "It is desirable that all the army should be together when we deliberate, for division will only weaken us and expose us to the attacks of the enemy." This was the first signal that new negotiations with Saladin were imminent. By accounts coming from Tyre and Acre, it would be hard to persuade the French to give up their urban pleasures. "They delighted in dancing women," wrote an admittedly biased English chronicler. "Their luxurious apparel bespoke their effeminacy, for the sleeves of their garments were fastened with gold chains, and they wantonly exposed their waists which were cinched with embroidered belts. Around their necks they wore collars glittering with jewels and on their heads garlands interwoven with flowers of every hue. They carried goblets, not falchions, in their hands. After spending whole nights in drinking and carousing, they went, heated with wine, to the houses of prostitutes."

After such a description as that, who would want them back? Still, the news of a negotiation assuaged the grumbling French temporarily, and many agreed to come to Ascalon—but only until Easter. If nothing had happened by then, they demanded freedom to leave and to take safe passage back to Europe. Having no choice, Richard agreed to this compromise.

The King had less success with Conrad of Montferrat. At a conference at Casale Imbert north of Acre, the insurgent rebuffed the King's effort to persuade him to rejoin the Crusade. To the English it seemed as if Montferrat was doing everything in his power to undermine Richard's authority. Word spread through the camp that the marquis was hiding from the King's wrath in his wife's chambers in Tyre.

Toward Easter, Ascalon began at last to take on the look of a functioning medieval city once again. For this Richard rejoiced. There were other reasons to celebrate. On a reconnaissance mission to the most southerly outpost, the fortress of Darum, which was the only fortress on the coastal plain that Saladin had not destroyed, Richard came upon a caravan of some twelve hundred Christian prisoners and liberated them without a fight when their guards fled at the sight of the King's fearsome banner. Perhaps because the deadline for the French departure had been set for Easter and perhaps because Richard hoped to retain his fickle allies in the pride of their accomplishments at Ascalon, the King made a sumptuous feast of the holiday, spreading magnificent fare before the soldiers and lavishing them with gifts and bonuses. "Where nobleness of heart harmonizes with deeds of renown," wrote the court poet,

> The stingy mind suits not the bounteous hand,
> But rather checks its givings; let each gift
> Be e'er attended with a generous heart.

But the banquets and bonuses had no effect on the resolve of the French to leave. Sadly, reluctantly, bitterly, Richard fulfilled his promise. He watched the French soldiers disappear down the road to Jaffa—and then promptly sent a swift message to his commanders in Acre not to admit the French into the city when they arrived.

Far away in Jerusalem, Saladin received the news of these latest developments happily. Perhaps this was the turning point. Once his spies informed him of the French desertion, the Sultan sent an exultant dispatch throughout his empire. Its tone of exaggerated optimism was forgivable under the circumstances: "The French have, from ill will, departed and left the land almost without a defender. The strength of the war and power of the Christian army are fallen. We trust that in short order we shall gain possession of Acre and Tyre."

On both sides it was a moment for dreams and fantasies. An English scribe would write that in his Easter exuberance King Richard had knighted the son of el Melek el-Adel; the purpose of such a bizarre ceremony was left unstated, unless it was to suggest a cordial preliminary to an agreement between the two sides. Even more fantastic was the English report of a miracle at the Holy Sepulcher. Legend held that every year on Easter Eve a beam of holy fire descended from heaven to light a lamp at Calvary within the holy church. On this Easter, so the scribe wanted his audience to believe, Saladin himself had become curious about the legend and had mingled among the Christian captives in the church, to witness the holy combustion. True to legend, the fire came as expected, to the hosannas and hallelujahs from the Christian faithful. But Saladin doubted—and ordered the fire to be extinguished. Once doused, it burst into flame a second time. It was snuffed out again, and miraculously lit itself a third time. The Christian captives turned to their Proverbs: "What use is it to fight against God's invisible Power?" they mumbled. "There is no counsel against God, nor is there any one who can resist His will."

So moved was Saladin, wrote his English enemy, that the Sultan prophesied the loss of Jerusalem to the enemy within a year—or his own death.

The Muslim chronicle of this time makes no mention of the Sacred Fire in the Sepulcher. Instead something more concrete marks the time. During Easter, Saladin received a message from Richard:

"I am anxious to have an interview with el Melek el-Adel to discuss a matter that would be equally advantageous for both sides. For I understand that the Sultan has entrusted the business of negotiations to my brother, el Melek el-Adel."

Perhaps this was the breakthrough. Perhaps it comprised merely more pointless words. "We have had a great many interviews without any good result to either side," Saladin replied to Richard. "It is useless for us to meet if the conference you now propose is to be like its predecessors . . . unless you show me that there is a likelihood of a speedy settlement of the question."

# 3

## The Lesser Evil

On the day after Easter, travelers from the semiannual passage from Europe to Syria began to arrive in the East. Among them was the Prior of Hereford, who brought with him the message from Richard's chancellor, Longchamp, about discord in England and the pretensions of his brother John to the English throne.

"Fair sire, I pray you with respect to come home and wreak vengeance on those who have wrought all this ill, else they will do still more evil. When they have seized the whole domain, you shall regain your land only with great strife."

Stricken and yet suddenly determined in his course, Richard gathered his barons and shared Longchamp's dire message with them. He must now leave the Crusade and return home. Three hundred knights and two thousand sergeants would remain to carry on the struggle at his expense. Who among them would stay and who would return to Europe with the King?

Much agitated, the barons left the royal chamber to deliberate. Who would rule and who would lead in Richard's absence? Was there any in their number bold enough in war and skilled enough in diplomacy to prosecute the Crusader cause? It was as if the clock had been turned back five years. The insidious choice once again was between an incompetent and a traitor. The erstwhile King of Jerusalem, Guy of Lusignan, was faithful but inept, while the Marquis of Montferrat was deceitful and was already treating with Saladin for his own personal advantage.

In time the knights returned to Richard's quarter. Their recommendation was unanimous. Unless his replacement was someone in whom they could all have trust and confidence, they intended—all of them—to return home with Richard. Under Guy there was no chance for success, the cause was hopeless, for he was not respected and would not be obeyed. Conrad was clearly the more forceful of the two. He might just rise to this higher calling. Not only did he have the skill and fortitude, he also had the French. Richard grumbled and prevaricated. "There is many a slip between the cup and the lip," quoth the proverb. Eventually the King yielded. Led by Henry of Champagne and graced by the local dignitaries, Balian of Ibelin and Reynaud of Sidon, a delegation set out for Tyre to bring back the new King of Jerusalem in glory.

In the meantime the loser in the political struggle, King Guy, came to Richard proposing a consolation prize. The year before, after paying Richard forty thousand gold pieces as a down payment, the Templars had taken charge of Cyprus. To be sure, the island had served the Crusade well as its breadbasket. But from their arrogance and their rigidity, not to mention the high taxes they had imposed upon the Cypriot population, Templar rule was beset by trouble and rebellion. After a second rebellion in April 1192, the Templars had given the island back to Richard, since it had proved itself to be more trouble than it was worth. Guy now offered to buy the island and put another sixty thousand gold pieces in Richard's hands. The request pleased Richard, for it solved two problems at once. Guy sailed off happily for Famagusta, and most of Palestine was glad to see him leave. But he would have the last laugh. For he began the Lusignan line of Cypriot royalty, which would last for nearly another three hundred years.

Meanwhile, at Tyre, after he heard of his election, the usually abrasive Conrad fell to his knees humbly and raised his arms to heaven. "O Lord God! who hast created me and infused life into my body, who art a just and merciful King. I pray Thee, O Lord, if Thou thinkest me deserving to govern Thy Kingdom, grant me my crown. If, however, Thou judgest otherwise, consent not to my promotion." And then he strode magnificently into the streets of his city to acknowledge the jubilation of his subjects. Once before he had saved his own city from Saladin. Now the whole kingdom was his to rescue.

How short was his joy! How short the jubilation of his subjects!

# CHAPTER TWENTY-FIVE

# The Dagger
# on the
# Pillow

EVERAL DAYS AFTER HENRY OF CHAMPAGNE HAD
left for Acre, where he was to be measured for his coronation
gown, Conrad was still in a sociable mood. Looking forward to an
evening in the company of the amiable Bishop of Beauvais, the
count grew impatient when his wife dallied too long at her bath, and he went
off to the archbishopric alone, in a connubial huff. To his disappointment he
found that the good bishop had already dined, and Beauvais was unable to persuade the count to take a meal nonetheless. No doubt annoyed at the delay his
wife's bath had caused, he set out to retrace his way home.

In the Muslim telling of this scene, the fate of this formidable enemy was
prefigured. "He was condemned to Hell," wrote a Muslim chronicler of this
journey through Tyre's close quarters. "The angel Mālik awaited his arrival,

and Tartarus was on the watch for his coming. The deepest circle of hellfire was burning, the blaze blazed and the flame flamed as it waited for him. The moment was at hand when the abyss would receive him and the fires of Hell would burn for him, and the Angels of Justice were even now building the foul place where they would torment him. Hell had already opened its seven gates, gaping to engorge him."

In the marketplace Conrad came into a narrow street, and halfway down it he recognized two familiar monks of his household, men who had been in his service for over six months and through stout labor had gained his trust. They sat on either side of the street. Upon his greeting them, one rose up, offering a letter to Conrad. As the marquis reached out for it, the man pulled a knife and ran it into the prince's side, as the other man leaped onto the rear of Conrad's horse and stabbed the count repeatedly in the other side, until Conrad of Montferrat fell gasping into the dust.

In the noise and commotion the two attackers ran. One was caught and immediately killed. The other fled and hid in the very church where the bleeding Conrad was brought, with still a flicker of life in him. Again the assailant pounced on him "like a mangy wolf," according to the Muslim source, and finished him off. Dragged from the church and interrogated, the murderer loudly protested at first that the King of England had sent them on their mission. To many this had the ring of truth, for it was well known that Conrad had not been Richard's choice to be King. But upon further interrogation a much more terrible explanation emerged.

The pair were members of the sect of the Assassins, the tribe of Ismaelites, whose very name induced both the Christians and Muslims of Palestine to quiver with fear and horror. The murderers had been sent by their imam, Sinan, known to the Christians as the "Old Man of the Mountain." This was Rashid al-Din Sinan, "Orthodox in Faith," an Iraqi who had come to Syria as the *dai* of the cult forty years before, establishing a community of about sixty thousand followers and a network of impregnable castles in the wild Ansarian mountains of northern Syria. The most prominent of these strongholds were Masyaf, a bastion on a butte overlooking a town of his followers on the edge of the Syrian desert, and al Kahf, his "Eagle's Nest," deep in the mountains on a peak over ten thousand feet, to which the Old Man retreated when he was pressed.

Sinan was brilliant, clairvoyant, ruthless, deceitful, pious, mystical, and ascetic, with eyes fierce as meteors, a physician's power of healing, and a

tyrant's power of awesome destruction. The stories of his supernatural gifts
and his evil were legion. So great were his powers of telepathy, it was said
that he could answer a letter without ever reading its contents.

Over the decades he had developed political murder into a fine art. It
proved to be an excellent tool for protecting his independence and prevent-
ing the consolidation of Syria under a single leader. Sinan had under his spell
a cadre of young novitiates, known as *fidai*, whose allegiance to him personally was absolute. Only through the wisdom of the *dai* himself lay the path
to Purification and Enlightenment and Paradise. As an expression of their devotion only to their messiah, these *fidai* were prepared for any suicide mission. Once, to prove the devotion of his followers to a Crusader leader, Sinan
had given a fleeting hand signal to two *fidai* high in a tower at Kahf, whereupon the two leaped to their death in the ravine below. Would the Frank like
to see the act of obedience repeated? He demurred, saying he was convinced.

Another story was told of the Old Man summoning his *fidai* to his chamber, where upon a gold plate rested the bloody head of a fellow Assassin that
had been brought back from a murder mission. Once the *fidai* were arranged
in their seats, Sinan addressed the head, asking if the martyr wished to return to earth. The head replied with a glowing report about the joys of Paradise. "God with His angels assist Your Majesty and cast your enemies into
Hell!" it said. "This world is nothing, and whoever deludes himself will repent when penitence is of no avail. I am of those who have turned away from
worldly goods and renounce them." After the *fidai* filed out, the Old Man un-
coupled the head from the gold plate and a young man crawled out from the
hole in the floor where he had given his performance—only for Sinan to lop
off his head for real and send him to his coveted Paradise for good.

The very name Assassins found its derivation in the word "hashish," for
part of the indoctrination of the *fidai* came in a ceremony where the young
men were given a potion laced with the cannabis, put to sleep, and then
transported into the perfect garden of the *dai*. When the youths awoke, they
felt that they had arrived in Paradise. And it was in such a ceremony that the
assassination orders were delivered. In the fog of hashish and in the joy of his
total devotion to the *dai*, the Assassin would extend his hand and receive a
dagger. "Go thou and slay Conrad of Montferrat," the *dai* might say, "and
when thou returnest, my angels shall bear thee into Paradise. And shouldst
thou die nonetheless, even so will I send my angels to carry thee back into
Paradise."

Sinan hailed from Basra in Iraq, but the religious roots of his faith were in Persia, in the Shi'ite branch of Islam. Even in the twelfth century the competition between Shi'ism and Sunnism was intense and passionate, and Sinan blamed Saladin for defeating and expunging the Shi'ite Fatamid Caliphate of Cairo and imposing Sunnism in its stead. Twice he had made an attempt on the life of Saladin. In the first attempt in 1174 the Assassins were intercepted only a few feet from the Sultan and slain. Saladin was furious. As he consolidated his gains in northern Syria, he moved his army against these mountain terrorists. The second attempt came in response to this invasion and nearly succeeded; then the murderer, posing as one of the Sultan's body-guards, brought his dagger slashing down on Saladin's skull. Though bleeding and terrified, the Sultan fended off the murderer until his guards could dispatch the intruder. Saladin survived only because he wore a mailed head-dress beneath his turban.

The close shave instilled forever in Saladin a paranoia about this virulent and uncontrollable cult. The paranoia deepened sometime later, when, instead of an actual third attempt on his life, the Assassins left their calling card of a dagger and hot cakes on the Sultan's pillow. How had the murder-ers slipped into the Sultan's most intimate space without being detected? From that time forward, Saladin always traveled in a wooden pavilion and took care never to talk to unknown persons in his camp. He left the Old Man well enough alone in his wild mountain enclave.

The territory of the Assassins lay in the mountains between the Orontes River and the Mediterranean west of Hama, and it was contiguous to the provinces ruled by the military monks. The great Hospitaler fortresses of Margat and Krak des Chevaliers, and the Templar strongholds of Castel Rouge and Castel Blanc (Safita) formed a protective ring to the south, safe-guarding the Christian province of Tripoli and the city of Tyre.

The Latin Christians were not Sinan's main enemy—he was most con-cerned with the Muslim viziers to the north in Aleppo and Mosul—and so over the years the Old Man made his accommodations with the foreign ele-ment. In some ways the Assassins and the military monks had much in com-mon, for they were all ascetic fanatics, and they seemed to understand one another full well. Assassination against the military orders was pointless in any event, since the Grand Master was chosen from the members of the order. Nevertheless, when the Latin Christians crossed the line and threatened the cult, the Assassins had no qualms about plying their deadly art. After a boundary dispute in 1154 they took the life of Raymond II of Tripoli. The Templars responded by butchering a number of Muslims in retaliation. Thereafter an accommodation was reached. For a time the Assassins paid the Templars a hefty tribute to be left alone.

Over the decades of Sinan's tenure in the mountains, his allegiance to the far-distant Persian imams dwindled, partly because the imams in Persia disapproved of Sinan's claim of divinity. Consequently his belief in the tenets of Shi'ism lessened. His followers were permitted to drink wine and eat pork. He even began to take an interest in Christianity, mastering the Bible thoroughly. It appeared that he was open to conversion to Christianity, if only the Templars would lift the burden of his annual tribute.

"The noble doctrine of Christ," wrote the Bishop of Tyre, "when compared with that which the miserable seducer, Muhammad, had transmitted to his deluded followers, caused Sinan to despise the beliefs which he had absorbed with his mother's milk and to abominate the unclean tenets of that deceiver." The Templars probably rejoiced at the interest Sinan was displaying in their faith.

In the meantime his own imams rejected him. "Their prophet is a devil in man's disguise called Sinan," wrote an Islamic traveler, Ibn Jubayr, in this period, "who deceives his followers with falsehoods and chimeras embellished for them to act upon. He bewitches them with these black arts, so that they take him as a god and worship him. They abase themselves before him, reaching such a state of obedience and subjection that should he order one of them to fall from the mountaintop he would do so, and with alacrity that he might be pleased. God in His power allows to stray those whom He wills, and guides whom He wishes. There is no Lord but He, and only He should be worshipped."

In straying from Shi'ism, in investing himself with divinity, and in toying with but not embracing Christianity, Sinan became a heretic to all sides. As such, the Old Man in the Mountain became that much more dangerous. The fierce reputation of this suicide cult and its fanatical leader had spread rapidly around the world. In a bizarre twist, it became the stuff of romantic poetry, with the element of drug-crazed violence carefully sanitized from the verses. To aspire to the Assassins' level of blind obedience was the height of romantic love. "You have me more fully in your power than the Old Man of the Mountain," wrote one poet. "Just as the Assassins serve their master unfailingly, so I serve love with unswerving loyalty," wrote another. "I am your Assassin who hopes to win paradise by doing your commands," wrote a third.

In 1191 the haughty Conrad had crossed one too many dangerous lines. Having determined to pass up King Richard's Crusade, the Count of Tyre was paying a high price for his own independence. He had turned his back on the English and harbored the French defectors from Richard's army. The count was hard-pressed for cash. From nowhere a surprise gift fell into his hands. A ship of the Assassins, brimming with valuable cargo, blew into the port of Tyre during a storm, and Conrad seized its payload, imprisoned its crew, and killed its captain. The Old Man of the Mountain asked reasonably for the return of his ship, its cargo and crew, and reparation for the death of his comrade. Conrad scoffed at these demands. It was not the Old Man's habit to make such requests more than once. Coldly and calmly, he gathered his faithful together and proclaimed his *fatwa*. Less than a year later, Conrad entered that narrow alley that led to the deepest circle of Muslim hellfire.

"In this year, on 13 rai' II, the Frankish Marquis, the ruler of Tyre and the greatest devil of all the Franks, Conrad of Montferrat—God damn him!—was killed," wrote the Muslim chronicler Ibn Al-Athir.

# CHAPTER TWENTY-SIX

# The Parable
# of the
# Weeds

✠

The ASSASSINATION OF CONRAD THREW THE SIT-
uation once again into confusion. It provided no advantage to
Saladin, for Conrad had been his wedge to cause division among
the Crusader ranks. Each time Conrad had sent an envoy to attempt a separate peace, Richard would hear of it from his spies and send his
own envoy with a better offer. So Saladin had lost his stalking horse and his
troublemaker within the Latin ranks. Only four days before the assassination,
Conrad's ambassador had been in Saladin's camp. So long as Tyre was independent from the Crusade, serving as an enclave for the disgruntled among
the Christians, Saladin's range of possibilities was great.

Nor, of course, did the demise of Conrad help Richard. For a start, it undid his plan for an imminent departure. His agreement to put Conrad on the throne had been his last political act of getting his house in order. The house was in disarray again, and the French suspected him of being behind the murder. In this chaos his departure had to be postponed. The king contemplated with dismay another round of political maneuvering.

Henry of Champagne stepped boldly forward. Though young, he was the logical choice now, for he was related by blood to both the French and the English dynasties. There was even a popular song about him: "By the assent of divine Grace the Count of Champagne alone reawakens the spark of hope. A faithful son of Jerusalem, like another Heraclius, he fights with faith and sword." The Muslims regarded him as reasonable, capable, and tolerant, and to the Franks he had proven himself to be a good fighter. He would even visit the Old Man of the Mountain in due course, only to watch two faithful *fidai* sail to their deaths as a demonstration of their total devotion to their messiah on earth.

To cement his ascension to the throne, Henry, at Richard's insistence, was to marry Conrad's widow, Isabella, even though she was pregnant with the late count's child. This proposal led to a sharp interchange between Henry and his uncle. If Isabella's child was male, Henry protested, then the boy stood to inherit the throne. "And then I will be stuck with the woman and never be able to return to Champagne."

"I shall give you more than you would ever get by going back to Champagne," Richard replied. "I promise that if God grants my return to England, I shall come back here to you with such a great armed force that I shall conquer the whole kingdom for you and many of the pagan lands as well. I expect to have such great power that on my return I shall conquer the empire of Constantinople. I shall give you the island of Cyprus as well, since King Guy had not paid me the whole price."

Hot air though this was, Henry had no choice but to accept it. Four days after Conrad was laid to rest in the Hospital of Tyre, Henry married his widow and took charge of his city. This unholy union occasioned disgust among the Muslims when they heard of it. "She is pregnant," wrote a Muslim chronicler, "but this does not prevent Henry's uniting himself with her, something even more disgusting than the coupling of the flesh. I asked one of their courtiers to whom paternity would be awarded and he said, 'It will be the Queen's child.' You see the licentiousness of these foul Unbelievers!"

In the weeks and months after the assassination, rumors continued to swirl around the question of who had been the real perpetrator. The Assassins of Ansari were regarded as merely the tools of the crime, in the hands of some greater authority. Both Richard and Saladin were whispered to be the real culprit, although the French were not whispering but shouting Richard's guilt from the towers. Eventually news of the assassination reached Europe and France. As usual with rumors, the story became embellished. By the time it reached the ears of King Philip, it had acquired greater menace. Not only had Richard used the Assassins to murder Conrad, he had the same fate in mind for Philip! Immediately Philip strengthened his personal guard and shrank away from any unknown person at Fontainebleau.

To describe the situation an English chronicler turned to the parable of the weeds in the Gospel of Matthew. In that parable the good man sows his good seeds, but when he sleeps, his enemy creeps in and spreads the seeds of weeds among the good seeds. "When the blade was sprung up and brought forth fruit, then appeared the weeds also," said the Word of the Lord. But the farmer lets them grow up together until harvest time, when his reapers gather the weeds in bundles and burn them, and then harvest the wheat separately.

The parable of the weeds was now turned against Philip. Philip had sown the seeds of noxious weeds in Richard's good and holy wheat field, and the weeds had begun to choke out the grain. But when the time came, the weeds would be first harvested with a scythe and then burned. Despite its enemies, the fruit of the Kingdom of Heaven would be saved.

## 2

# A Chaplain's Plea

By May the fair season for fighting had returned, and both sides waited to see how their adversary would utilize the dry and hot weather. Richard was pulled in opposite directions. With his warrior nature he was itching for more combat, but he was politically astute enough to hope that his latest diplomatic overture to Saladin would bear fruit. More messengers were arriving with conflicting news from Europe, some portraying a dire situation at home, others saying that the rebellions were under control, some arguing for Richard to come home immediately, others pleading with him to complete his pilgrimage. Between fighting and negotiating, he was one day preparing to abandon his Crusade and the next day preparing to stay. One day he dismissed the mischief of King Philip; the next day he was preoccupied with the proverb "He who has a bad man for his neighbor is sure to find something wrong in the morning."

Saladin's situation was more passive. He could play the waiting game, biding his time to see the implications of the assassination—Henry of Champagne's popularity among all sectors of the Crusader army was a minus—and awaiting further developments on the diplomatic front. While the short term was troubling, at bottom he was animated by the knowledge that he was in his own land, with his own people. Time was on his side, not Richard's.

On his way to Jerusalem in the early spring, just before Conrad's murder, el Melek el-Adel, Saladin's brother and diplomatic go-between, had had further contact with Richard. To the Sultan, Richard's message was conveyed optimistically. "We consent to the division of the country," Richard had written. "Each side shall keep what they now hold, and if one side has more than half, what is their just share? They shall give the other side a proper concession. The Holy City shall belong to us, but the coastal plan shall be reserved for you."

Saladin's emirs pronounced the essence of this offer to be quite satisfactory. When el Melek el-Adel returned to the Sultan's pavilion two weeks later with the news of further refinements and concessions by the Crusader side, they were even more pleased. Richard was now prepared to cede the citadel of Jerusalem to the Muslims as well as the Dome of the Rock itself, the Al Aqsa Mosque, while the rest of the Holy City was to be divided equally. In the area around Jerusalem the villages were to be apportioned equally to each side.

While these developments were encouraging, Saladin also received a dispatch from the south that deflated his optimism. The Crusaders, he was informed, had ventured out from Ascalon to the vicinity of Darum, the most southerly of the coastal fortresses, which Saladin had purposely not destroyed and still held. The fortress was his last remaining supply depot on the southern coastal plain, and potentially his fallback position if Jerusalem were taken. A Muslim camp had been attacked outside the city, several believers had been killed, and the raiders had carried off a thousand sheep. The communication annoyed Saladin, and he dispatched a company of crack troops to find and punish the marauders. The provocation showed that Richard was of no mind to give up the fight just yet.

If domestic revolts back home in Europe troubled Richard, Saladin had domestic problems of his own. His grandnephew, one el Melek el-Mansur, a young prince with big ambitions, was asserting his independence in northern Syria, demanding sway over several important cities, including Edessa, and over lands beyond the Euphrates. Saladin was livid at the impertinence of the youth, especially at so inopportune a time, and was inclined to teach the stripling a stern lesson. But his emirs brought the Sultan to his senses in a tense meeting.

"We are your servants and your slaves, Your Majesty," said one, "but young men, especially when they are afraid, will form alliances with one another. It is quite impossible for us to carry on two wars at once, one against Muslims and the other against infidels. If the Sultan wishes to fight the Muslims, he must let us make peace with the infidels. Then we will happily cross the Euphrates and fight under your leadership. If, on the other hand, you wish us to persevere in the jihad, pardon the young prince and grant him peace." The other emirs applauded this sensible advice, and Saladin relented. He deputized his brother to make an accommodation with his grandnephew and turned back to the more important matter at hand. He would deal with the naughty boy later.

At about this time the Sultan received an interesting visitor from Constantinople. He was the honorable envoy from the Emperor of Byzantium, and he came bearing gifts and interesting proposals. Most enticing was the offer to purchase the True Cross of Calvary for two hundred thousand gold pieces. This was an immense fortune and might be put to very great use in Saladin's war effort. Further, the envoy wished for Saladin to grant to the priests of the Greek Orthodox persuasion the dominion over the Holy Sepulcher. This, too, had its attractions. It would remove the holiest church in Christendom from the domination of Rome. And finally the envoy sought the help of Saladin in mounting an expedition against Cyprus, to wrest the valuable and strategic island from Crusader control and to return it to its rightful and historic relationship with Byzantium. All three overtures had much to recommend them, but Saladin rejected all three. As the Greek envoy turned to go home disappointed, Saladin better appreciated the collateral of the True Cross.

Until he could make up his mind to stay or to leave, Richard was incapable of standing still. It was mid-May, and time was a-wasting. The foray the month before to Darum had proved that city's importance, its bounty, and its vulnerability. To take this southern outpost now, even as negotiations with Saladin were active, would strengthen Richard's hand for a settlement.

Once again the French declined to join this latest adventure. The bulk of them were still feting Henry of Champagne in Acre. So Richard determined to attack Darum alone. As his siege engines were loaded aboard ship, the King moved his forces around his chess board. With the requirement to garrison Ascalon and the rest of his conquered territory, he could ill afford to take a large force so far away from the center of the action. And so he set off with only a battalion of his household troops, mainly men of Normandy and Poitou.

Because of its strategic location below Gaza, Darum was no ripe or easy catch. With seventeen towers, a high wall, a moat, and a gritty commander, 'Alem ed-Din Kaisar, it was a well constructed, well stocked, and well defended Muslim fortress. On May 17 the King arrived in front of this imposing bastion, dismounted his Cypriot horse, and put his own shoulder to that of his men as they carried the heavy beams and rods and struts of his massive siege engines on their backs the mile from the coast to the city's walls.

The Muslims could see that Richard commanded only a small force. At first they made bold in skirmishing the points. But the supreme warrior's reputation preceded him. The mere sight of his royal banner, with its three elongated lions against the heraldic red, projected an air of invincibility. Like a bloody shirt, the mere sight of it was enough to shatter the enemy's confidence.

His skill as a planner was immediately evident. Concentrating his siege engines and his compact force in front of the principal tower, the King gave the order for the boulders to fly against the battlements relentlessly, while his sappers went to work in undermining the foundations. The pounding went on for three days, until the main gate collapsed and burned. At that setback three Arab commanders appeared with a white flag, asking to surrender in exchange for their lives, wives, and possessions. Richard refused. Surrenders take place only before the blood is shed, he informed them, not at the point of total defeat. Within hours the main tower collapsed in rubble, and the banners of various Crusaders—Stephen of Longchamp and the Earl of Leicester, then the Pisans and the Genoese—were raised joyously on the walls. Before the defenders cowered into their homes to await the inevitable, they disabled their horses by cutting their hamstrings, so as to deprive the invaders of the animals.

The day after the fall of Darum, a French contingent including Henry of Champagne waltzed in just in time for the victory celebration. Since the departure of Philip, Richard had ceased to be competitive. History would record his triumph at Darum without the French now; his glory was secure. He was in a mood to be generous. It was the great feast of Pentecost, after all, seven Sundays after Easter, and no doubt there were locker room jokes about Henry's descending, well after the crisis, like the Holy Ghost on the Apostles. As three hundred Muslim prisoners filed by on their way to slavery, their hands tightly bound behind them, Richard presented his nephew with this new prize for his tenuous kingdom. And then the Kings and blood brothers rode north, past the Castle of the Figs, which a thousand Muslims had quickly vacated the day before, and past an evacuated castle called the Canebrake of the Starlings, toward a fateful decision.

As the procession moved north, through the plains of Ibelin and past Hebron, where Anne, the mother of the Virgin Mary, was born, the euphoria of Darum dissipated with the dust of their hoofprints. At the Canebrake of the Starlings, Richard had received another piece of bad news from England, and he seemed now to recede into silent doldrums. It was the general impression of his barons that their King was spending his last days in the Holy Land.

Independently, with their leader so remote and distracted, the knights held a council of state. Never had the Crusade been so united; there seemed to be goodwill everywhere. The French suddenly felt a solidarity with the English, the Normans with the men of Poitou, the Pisans with the Genoese. Their opinion was now unanimous. Regardless of what King Richard did, stay or leave, the pilgrimage must go on. They were determined to move on Jerusalem.

When the news of this baronial decision filtered out to the army, there was great joy. Fires were lit. There was singing and dancing as "they passed the lifelong night in wakeful glee." But the barons' decision and the army's spirits seemed to drive Richard into an even greater depression. A lame duck now, his dilemmas seemed irrelevant. And as if his army were being punished for his disloyalty, it was suddenly beset by a pestilence of fierce tiger beetles that swarmed over the camp in battalions and stung the men on their faces and arms until the soldiers looked like lepers.

On June 4 the column rejoined the main force at Ascalon. On the day after, Richard was wandering aimlessly in an orchard outside the city when he came upon a humble prior from Poitiers, who had been regarding the King from afar and down whose cheeks tears were streaming.

"Sir Chaplain, I pray you, tell me what is the cause of your weeping, especially if I am the cause of it?"

"I cannot speak before I know that Your Highness will not be angered with me for what I say."

When Richard gave the prior this assurance, he did speak: "My lord, I weep on account of the ill repute in which you stand with the army, because you intend to return home. But may God forbid that uncertain reports from overseas turn you away from recovering this desolated land. For we believe that it would redound to your eternal disgrace. Let not a hasty retreat undermine the glory of a most splendid enterprise. Nor let it be said that you returned home before your enterprise was finished. If you thus derogate your glory, how different will the end be than the beginning. Take heed, sire, lest your glory, so well earned at first, fade and tarnish in the end!"

The humble prior beseeched the King to ponder the qualities with which God had endowed him, quoting the Epistle of Paul to the Ephesians, "according to the riches of His Grace." He enumerated Richard's many triumphs: how as Count of Poitou he had subdued all his enemies; how he had obtained his kingdom through his victories over lesser lords and how he had become feared in all of Europe; how he had captured Messina and subdued the Greeks; . . . and the island of Cyprus and its Emperor; how because of his generalship Acre had fallen; how he had overcome his illness of arnaldia; how he had triumphed at Arsuf and at Darum and set the Muslims scattering and had liberated hundreds of Christians.

"Remember that when you came hither from the Western world, you were everywhere victorious and your enemies lay in chains at your feet." He compared Richard to the giant Antaeus, in Greek mythology, who grew stronger each time he touched the earth, and he compared the Muslim enemy to Hydra, who grew two more heads every time Richard cut one off. "And now the Sultan trembles at your name. The people of Egypt are astonished, and the pagan is struck with awe. Need I say more? All agree in declaring that you are the father, the champion, the defender of Christianity. If you desert them, it is the same as if you gave them up to be destroyed by the enemy. O King, succor this people, for their hope is entirely in you. You are their natural protector. May you, with the aid of Christ, still continue to prosper."

The following day Richard summoned his herald. He was to proclaim throughout the army that the King would not depart for home but would stay until the following Easter, when all of the Holy Land would be theirs.

They should prepare for the siege of Jerusalem.

When they heard his orders, his soldiers dropped to their knees in prayer:

"O God, we adore and thank thee that we shall soon see the city of Jerusalem, which the Infidels have held too long. O how blessed are our expectations, after so long a delay. How deserved have been our sufferings. The sight of Thy Holy City will repay us for all!"

# CHAPTER TWENTY-SEVEN

# SAMSON'S COUNTRY

N JUNE 7, 1192, THE CRUSADE WAS COMING TO its climax. Full of joy and expectation, the siege force set out from the land of the Philistines, on the ancient road to Jerusalem. A sense of purpose filled the air, and the generosity of the men toward one another was evident. In rebuilding Ascalon, class lines had come down, and they stayed down. Between knight and sergeant, esquire and knave, a joviality and intimacy prevailed, for as in Samson's riddle, "out of the strong comes sweetness." The chants of *"Sanctum Sepulcrum Adjuva* . . . Help, help for the Holy Sepulcher" had taken on concrete meaning. Song was again in their throats, especially one entitled *"Chanterai por*

*mon coraige,"* whose refrain was "Dear God, when they cry 'Forward!' assist the pilgrim, for whom I tremble. For the Arabs are treacherous." They had nearly completed their pilgrimage. Hallelujah! The spirit of Vézelay had returned to the Crusader force.

As they moved out of Ascalon and across a river of sweet water and into the land of Samson, the spectacle was magnificent. Looking for all the world like Samson himself, Richard led the way on his magnificent Cypriot stallion. The King was resplendent, confident, a giant among ordinary men, as if he, too, like Samson, could catch three hundred foxes or slay a lion barehanded or slaughter his enemies by the thousands, hip and thigh, with the jawbone of an ass. The King reveled in the harmony that at last his righteous cause enjoyed, and for a time the attractions of his homeland were laid aside. Behind him the column was a riot of color, a welter of hoofbeat, dust cloud, polished steel, and song. The banners of eminent European houses, of holy orders, of nations grand and small, fluttered in the wind and blistering heat. The tromp of a thousand horses was punctuated with the syncopated beat of drum and tambourine, the wail of bagpipes, shawn, and krummhorn.

In the first day's march the army accomplished nineteen miles. At a strategic crossroads called Blanchegarde or White Custody they camped where the easterly road met the north-south road leading from Beit Jibrin in the south to Emmaus in the north. Fifty years earlier the Christians had built a four-towered fortress on a hill to protect Ascalon against invasion. Now Richard's Crusaders came upon another ruin, for Saladin had dismantled the outpost a few years before, as he had its twin at Beit Jibrin, and left only rubble. Here in the Valley of Elah, where David slew Goliath, the Wadi al Sant provided them with abundant water. For two days they rested at this place, a respite marred by a bad omen: A knight and a sergeant were bitten by snakes and died.

While the Crusaders tarried at Blanchegarde, Saladin, in Jerusalem, learned of their movement from his spies. There could be no doubt that this activity signaled the final move on the Holy City. Saladin put out the call to his far-flung emirs to come for an urgent council of war. They had to be precise now about what was the source of this Samson's strength and what might make him weak as other men. They would have to discover this themselves, for they had no Delilah; the Delilahs had been assassinated or had returned home.

As the Sultan waited for his chiefs to convene, the Crusaders moved eleven miles north to Toron of the Knights and stayed on its hilltop only one night before moving even closer, to their old encampment at Beit Nuba. Once again they had returned to the Valley of Ajalon, where Joshua had asked the Lord to make the sun and moon stand still so that he could avenge himself on the Amorites. They had come again to the spot where they had been the preceding fall and from which they had evacuated only because of the winter rain and mud. No such adversity burdened them now. It was prime fighting season. Jerusalem was twelve miles away.

Saladin's alarm was acute. Frantically he handed out his assignments for the defense of the walls and ordered that raids on the Crusader supply lines to the sea be stepped up. Only the recent arrival of superior commanders gave him some comfort. His wise man, the scar-faced Kurd Mashtūb, was at his side at last, having been Richard's personal prisoner after the fall of Acre and having been ransomed for thirty thousand gold pieces. Bedr ed-Din Dolderin, the lord of Tell Basher, formerly a Crusader castle near the Euphrates called Turbessel, came with a large contingent of Turks, and Abu el-Heija the Gross had also arrived. The latter was a seasoned veteran of internal struggles in northern Syria and an able general, despite the fact that his grotesquely fat body had to be carted about in an enormous chair. Most important Saladin's son, el Melek el-Afdal, had been summoned from Aleppo, where he had been punishing the insolence of the Sultan's grand-nephew. His soldiers, some of whom were under the command of another of Saladin's sons, el Melek ez-Zaher, took up their positions on the western ridges.

In the Sultan's tent the emirs finally gathered for their council of war. All were aware that their jihad had reached its moment of destiny. Beha al-Din, Saladin's chief adviser, friend, and scribe, spoke first, setting the tone, summoning them to make a blood oath at the Dome of the Rock, the *as Sakhrah*.

"When the Prophet—Pray God for him!—was suffering great tribulation, his comrades swore to fight for him to the death. That is the example which we must now imitate. Let us meet together at the *Sakhrah* and swear to stand by one another to the death. Only through the sincerity of our purpose will we see the enemy driven back."

Rather than shouts of approval, perfunctory mumbles greeted this rallying cry, for there were undercurrents, and the Sultan sensed them. The emirs waited for their lord to speak. For a considerable time he was silent in reflection, his eyes lowered, his legs crossed and unmoving on his pillow, his hands clasped before him. Respecting his silence, tense in their worry and discord, no emir dared to break the leader's reverie. They were, wrote the scribe, "as still as if a bird was on their heads."

"Praise be to God and a blessing on His Messenger!" Saladin finally said as he lifted his head to the assemblage. "Today you are the army and the support of Islam. The blood of the Muslims, their treasures and their children are under your protection. Only you among Muslims can resist the enemy. If you give way—which may God forbid!—they will roll up this land, as the Koran teaches us, like the rolling up of a scroll. You will be answerable, for it is you who undertook its defense. You have received money from the public treasury. On you alone depends the safety of Muslims. I wish you well."

Again there was silence until the first among the emirs, Mashtūb, spoke up.

"My lord, we are your servants and slaves. You have been gracious to us, and made us great and mighty and rich. We have nothing but our necks, and they are in your hands. By God! not one among us will turn back from helping you till we die."

Again came the grumbles of assent, which seemed to satisfy Saladin. They moved to a somber evening meal and then withdrew to their commands.

Within a day the discord of the council surfaced. Abu el-Heija the Fat sent Saladin a secret communication: "Many of the memluks have come to me, complaining about the plan for the siege. They do not agree with us shutting ourselves up within the city. They say no advantage can result from such a course, and that if we shut ourselves up in the citadel, we shall surely meet the same fate as the garrison at Acre. In the meantime all the Muslim land will fall into the hands of the enemy. It would be better to risk a pitched battle, they say. Then if God grants us the victory, we shall be masters of all they now hold. If not, we would lose the Holy City, but the army would be saved. Islam can be protected without the Holy City!"

This assessment was worrisome enough, but the fat man's message carried a warning: "If you wish to remain in the Holy City, you must stay with us, or else leave some member of your family in command. For the Kurds will not obey the Turks, and the Turks will never obey the Kurds!"

This dissent and division sorely troubled the Sultan. To abandon Jerusalem was to abandon Allah, to defile the memory of His messenger's nocturnal journey to heaven, to throw away Islam's third-holiest place. The devout man in Saladin could not bear the thought of such a sacrilege. To the

military man in him an evacuation made sense. His emirs were right: drawing his entire force into the small, confined space of the city's walls was madness. They would be trapped, surrounded, starved, eventually crushed and
slaughtered. The Sultan's quandary lay between sentiment and practicality.

For several nights he fretted. His friend, Beha al-Din, stayed with him
through his nocturnal tribulation, until dawn broke and the haunting cry of
*muezzin* at the al Aqsa Mosque called them to prayer. *God is most Great! Come
to Prayer! Prayer is better than sleep!* The Arabic words wafted over the ancient
stones.

After they had washed, Beha al-Din asked for permission to speak his
mind, and it was granted. "Your Highness is taxed with anxiety, so much so
that you can hardly bear up. Worldly means are useless. You can only turn to
God Almighty. Today is Friday, the most blessed day of the week, the day
when prayer is most heard, and here we are in the most blessed of all places.
Let the Sultan perform ablution and then distribute alms in secret, then say
a prayer of two *rek'a* between the *azan* and the *ikama*, beseeching your Lord,
confessing your inability to carry out what you have undertaken. Perhaps
God will take compassion on you and grant your prayer."

Saladin did as he was advised. Between the announcement of divine service on that Friday and the second call to prayer, the two men knelt at the al
Aqsa Mosque and prayed together. From the corner of his eye Beha al-Din
watched while his lord and mentor performed his prostrations and his ritual
bowings and said two *rek'a*. His words were mumbled painfully. *He begets not,
and is not begotten. . . . Nor is there anyone like unto him. . . .* Tears rolled from
the Sultan's eyes, ran down his thin cheeks, and fell to the prayer carpet.

Hours later his decision became known. He would withdraw his main
army and leave only a token force in Jerusalem under the command of his
grandnephew, Mejed al-Din. In the spirit of martyrdom, as the captain of
Islam's ship, he was tempted to remain himself. But he was persuaded otherwise. In the interests of Islam he would leave. Jerusalem must be made
ready to be sacrificed for the greater good. Their song was like a funeral
hymn.

> Fill my goblet, O Cupbearer.
> I am overwhelmed with passion.
> The day I see you is the day of joy.
> You are as perfect as the full moon.

*You are more graceful than the willow branch.*
*The garden is fragrant with your scent*
*You outshine all the flowers.*

## 2

# FALSE LEADS AND RICH DIVERSIONS

Meanwhile, at Beit Nuba, Richard settled in to wait for the Count of Champagne. Henry had been dispatched to Acre and Tyre to collect the stragglers and loafers and to escort the transportation of the siege engines. The journey from Acre to the Crusaders' forward camp was sure to be dangerous, for there could be no doubt that the enemy infested the countryside all around them. Already he was receiving reports of ferocious raids along the supply route to Jaffa.

In one skirmish two hundred Turks pounded out of the hills on their fast horses, screaming the Muslim war cry "Help from God and a speedy victory!" and fell on the rear guard of a French convoy. Killing two guards, they unhorsed a rash Flemish Hospitaler whose ardor had carried him alone into the Turkish host, and who was saved only by commandeering the horse of a sergeant (who himself was killed). Even the charge of Hospitalers and Templars did not intimidate the Turks, as they stood their ground, giving blow for blow. Had it not been for the intercession of the Bishop of Salisbury, riding to the rescue, the French would surely have been routed.

"Brave fighting 'twas," wrote a scribe. "Ye had seen men deal many a fair stroke, and then wheel and turn, and many a sword blade flash, and many a combat fought with dash, many a stout and valiant deed, many an empty-saddled steed."

For his indiscipline and the endangerment of his comrades, the impetuous, overzealous knight Robert of Bruges was court-martialed in the field, for the lessons of the Battle of Cresson a few years before were still fresh, and the Crusader force could ill afford to lose a single knight more than was necessary. After a rebuke, his fellow military monks pardoned him, taking their generous forgiveness from the third chapter of the Book of Zephaniah, "In that day shalt thou not be ashamed for all thy doings, wherein thou hast transgressed against me. For then I will take away out of the midst of thee them that rejoice in thy pride, and thou shalt no more be haughty because of my holy mountain."

On the day after the army arrived at Beit Nuba, Richard got word of Turks lying in ambush a few miles to the west at the holy fountain of Emmaus. This was the place where after his death and resurrection Jesus had walked with two of his disciples, and they had not recognized him. The waters of Emmaus were sacred and said to cure all ailments. For pagans to infest the place was unconscionable, and so Richard mounted an expedition to chase them away.

Not long after dawn he caught the bushwhackers unawares and slew twenty of them. In their number was Saladin's herald; he was spared, for he was more valuable alive than dead. Buoyed by this sport, Richard and his men bounded off into the round hills looking for more trouble. They had no real sense of where they were as they drifted east toward a place called Nabi Samwil. On a narrow ridge they caught a few more unlucky Arabs. Richard knocked one from his horse, and then, as he withdrew his Excalibur from the chest of his victim, he raised his gaze and saw in the distance . . . Jerusalem!

The sight was a surprise and a shock. It tormented rather than gladdened him. Its proximity, a mere three miles away, was sheer torture, for it was so beautiful and so close, yet elusive and perhaps unattainable. His longing was almost unbearable. The city was like the holy flame and he the lowly moth, and his wings were singed by the heat. As an unworthy Crusader he shielded his eyes and shrank away from the glare, as if gazing upon Jerusalem without capturing it were a disgrace and a sin.

"Sweet Lord," he said, "I entreat Thee. Do not suffer me to see Thy Holy City, since I am unable to deliver it from the hands of Thine enemies."

Later, when Saladin's decision to evacuate the Holy City was known, the chroniclers would say wistfully that had Richard had his army with him at that moment, there at a place the Christians called Montjoie, he could have captured his prize in a day. There by the grace of St. George . . .

Ten days later another magnet drew him to disappointment. On St. Alban's Day, June 22, the abbot of the famous Cistercian abbey near Nabi Samwil wandered into Richard's camp. This holy man, with a long beard and a shock of white hair, was a terrible sight, for, since Saladin's capture of Jerusalem, he wore only rags and ate only bitter herbs and roots. It was said, however, that he possessed the gift of prophecy. Now he brought news that he knew the whereabouts of the Holy Cross. During Saladin's capture of

Jerusalem five years before, it had fallen to him to hide the remains of the Holy Rood, and he had sealed it up within the walls of a chapel. By the abbot's account, Saladin had pressed him hard about where the relic was, but he'd lied and said it had been lost in the capture of the city. In haste Richard set out for the hiding place with the abbot and a large contingent. There they found not the Cross itself but a small wooden crucifix. The abbot professed that the crucifix was made of the Cross, even if it was not the Cross itself.

And then the abbot turned to Richard solemnly and said that the King would not be successful in gaining control of the Holy Land. To show the truth of his prophecy, the abbot also predicted that he himself would die in seven days. Disheartened by this prophecy though he was, Richard had the relic brought back to the camp, where it was set up in the middle, and the soldiers came by to venerate and kiss it. Seven days later the abbot died.

As Richard was on this diversion with the Cistercian abbot, an Arab spy came to him with a more prodigious temptation. The King had a number of these Arabs in his service, for he paid them handsomely in silver when they came forward with hard intelligence—though whenever silver alone was their only motivation, the King had to be careful about the source. This one excitedly babbled about a huge caravan from Cairo, replete with thousands of horses and camels, burdened with Egyptian riches, making its way through the Judean desert to the south. At first Richard was skeptical of so tantalizing a report, and so he put a few trusted men in bedouin disguise and sent them out to confirm the report.

Once confirmed, the prize was too delicious to pass up. Temporary amnesia descended on Richard, as he seemed to forget why he was in the Holy Land. Jerusalem was within arm's reach, and his siege engines were about to arrive, and yet the King leaped onto his great steed, marshaled a force of seven hundred knights on horseback, a thousand foot soldiers, and a thousand Turcopoles, and galloped out on a hunting expedition thirty miles to the south in the blistering wasteland of the Judean desert. When it came to booty rather than heavenly grace, he did not lack for volunteers. Even the French agreed readily to go, so long as they were promised one-third of the lucre.

In a day the raiding force was at Blanchegarde, where they were spotted from the hills. The Muslims had their own spies, of course, and the Sultan was soon informed of the enemy movement. By a swift messenger he sent urgent word to the caravan then watering its huge number of horses and camels at the seven wells of Abraham and Isaac at Beersheba, at the southern limit of the Promised Land. The commanders were to avoid a clash with the advancing Crusaders at all costs. The best way to guard against that was to take the caravan by quick march into the high country under cover of darkness.

This imperial directive was ignored, probably because the obtuse caravan leaders were afraid of the delay of the mountaintop route and of the confusion that a night march might bring. Their scouts had not yet determined that Richard was within striking distance. They preferred to make a bolt for Jerusalem along the shortest route, and yet they tarried one critical overnight too long, waiting for dawn so they could pack up in good light. Thus the Crusaders were lucky in the incompetence of their quarry. For unexplained reasons the train was split into three, with one contingent diverting east on the hajj road around the south end of the Dead Sea toward el Kerak, and another taking the desert road past Hebron to Bethlehem.

On its second night out the raiding party was at Tell el Hesi when Richard was told of the third part of the caravan watering its animals at the foot of the Hebron hills fourteen miles to the south at a place known as Round Cistern. Several scouts in bedouin disguise were dispatched to make sure. (Muslim chronicles later reported that Richard himself doffed the bedouin cloak to have a look.)

Quickly but quietly under the full moon, the raiding party moved out. At dawn it fell upon its rich prize, just as the camels were being loaded up. The startled guards scattered in all directions, like hares before the hounds. As always Richard was in the midst of the melee. Of his behavior in battle, his troubadour would quote Horace: He was the "flower of valor and the crown of chivalry, and bore away the prize from all." He swung his lance so furiously that it eventually broke, and he resorted to his sword. "Those among the Egyptian soldiers who passed for brave men were glad to owe their lives to the swiftness of their horses," a Muslim chronicler later wrote contemptuously of this skedaddling.

If the carnage was terrible, the booty was beyond belief: three thousand camels and an equal number of horses; hundreds of mules loaded with spices, gold and silver, silk, purple and scarlet robes, weapons, tents, barley and grain, medicines and money—and military dispatches. Not since the caravan that Reginald de Châtillon had captured six years before, touching off the Third Crusade, had so rich a hoard been commandeered. As the mule and camel drivers had surrendered immediately, they were pressed into service to drive their animals north to Jerusalem.

On the evening of the same day, Saladin was told of the disaster. He was saddened, but he was also angry at the Egyptian commanders for disobeying his orders. A disaster had become a disgrace. The Sultan's problem now was to ensure that disgrace did not become total defeat. Already he had borrowed considerably from the Egyptian army for the defense of Jerusalem. The scattering of the Egyptian soldiers at the caravan weakened that defensive line even more and laid the way to Egypt completely open to the Crusaders. With the immense number of camels and sumpter horses now in his possession, an invasion across the Sinai to Cairo was possible for Richard. Once again, Al Anketār, as they called Richard, commanded the force of an Alexander the Great or a Caesar Augustus.

In his rage the Sultan now took a last desperate measure to deny Jerusalem to the enemy. He declared that every well was to be poisoned, every spring polluted, every cistern smashed in a two-mile cordon around the city. Water had been the key to his great victory at Hattin five years before. Let it be so again. If Richard's soldiers dared to advance through this poisoned zone, they would have to bring their water with them. Within a few days in the rocky tableland around the city, this policy was implemented with a thoroughness that brooked no exceptions.

Oblivious to Saladin's final measures, Richard rode north triumphantly with his spoils. At Ramla, Count Henry came in with his corps of malingerers, and they stood in awe at the sight of so many camels and horses. Richard, with the expansiveness of a King David, began to distribute the beasts liberally to the soldiers, not only his fighters but the newly arrived French. For it had been King David's law in the Negev desert that "the share of him who stays by his gear shall be the same as who goes down into battle." It was the law of Israel. And so King Richard might have used the words of King David: "Behold a present for you of the spoil of the enemies of the Lord!" A number of the camels were slaughtered for their meat and roasted. By all accounts the white flesh and exotic flavor was much to the soldiers' liking.

Within a few days of this banquet the self-congratulation of the Crusader force would sour dramatically.

# CHAPTER TWENTY-EIGHT

# The
# Dry Tree
# of Hebron

✠

O N JUNE 24 THE GREAT CRUSADER ARMY RE-
turned to its forward position at Beit Nuba. Immediately the
camp was abuzz about their next order. When would they
move? Who would have the privilege to be in the vanguard?
What section of the wall would they attack first? And whose flag would first
be planted on the parapets? Should they not avoid the citadel and take the
high ground first, on the north side of the city, around the Damascus Gate? It
was surely the most vulnerable. Would the nave of the Holy Sepulcher again
run with the blood of Muslims and Jews? Who would surpass the feats of the
heroes of the First Crusade? Who, after brave Richard, was their Godfrey of
Bouillon? Or Raymond of St. Giles? These murmurs of excitement reached
the ears of their leaders. The high command gathered to ponder its next move.

What happened to Richard the Lionheart upon his arrival back at Beit Nuba no historian has ever adequately explained. His command was united; the French were finally eager to attack; his siege engines were assembled and cocked; Jerusalem was nearly in sight; Saladin was evacuating the city; the Franks were confident and primed; even the camels seemed to bray their readiness.

Suddenly, inexplicably, disgracefully, the Lionheart became fainthearted. Glum-faced and disconsolate, he went before his barons with a dire assessment of their situation. Within a day, it seems, he had concluded that the quest for Jerusalem was hopeless. Perhaps the bleak prophecy of the holy abbot had unnerved him.

"You shall never see me guide men other than I rightly ought," he began. "Who blames me for it I care not. Wherever our army goes, Saladin knows our plan, the course we plan to follow, the number of our force. We are far distant from the coast. If he should move around our flank and take his army into the Ramla plain and block the passage of our provisions, it would be disastrous to our besiegers. They would pay and pay dearly. Moreover, the perimeter of Jerusalem is long, and its walls are thick and strong. It would take a great number of our soldiers to breach these walls. Who then would protect our supply lines? No one. These supply trains would be destroyed one and all, if there were no one to relieve them."

To knight or lowly squire, to any person who had shared the pain and the triumph and the sacrifice of the past two and a half years with Richard, it seemed a bit late to be touting the skill of the opposition or harping upon the daunting defenses of Jerusalem. Were they not on the brink of success? Had these two years been spent for nothing? Had the deaths of so many been pointless? Doubts and fears? Why now? After all their sacrifice? The assemblage listened in stunned silence at this total collapse of will and courage. Perhaps Richard did not care, for his speech got worse. Beyond the timidity, it would take on an element of self-pity

"If I should lead the host to besiege Jerusalem the way you advise and the endeavor should come to defeat, all my life long I should be blamed, even shamed and reviled. I am aware, of course, that there are people here and in France who would love to see me make such a mistake, so that they might broadcast it far and wide and bring infamy to my spotless name. But with such a doubtful result, I deem it wrong to rush rashly forward. We are ignorant of the narrow roads and defiles between here and Jerusalem. If we knew more, we might safely proceed, but we do not. We could wait and seek the advice of natives. And we should wait until we have heard from the Knights of the Temple and of the Hospital."

The once fearless, noble, proud man called Lionhearted, who so often in the past had expressed such contempt for the weak and the indecisive, blustered on with his indecision.

"Yes, we must wait and seek the advice of those who know the ways of this land. We must ask them whether it be better to lay siege here, or to try to capture Egypt or Beirut or Damascus. Once we have consulted them, we would not be so divided as we are now. If you insist upon proceeding to Jerusalem, I will not desert you. I will be your comrade, but not your commander. I will follow, not lead you."

It was a strange moment for him to resign his command. Authority was shifted to a committee of twenty. Five Templars, five Hospitalers, five natives of Syria, and five French nobles withdrew to confer on strategy without Richard's participation. They returned with the recommendation of pulling back from Jerusalem and proceeding immediately to invade Egypt.

It was as if the high command was flapping around like a fish on the floor. The situation was fast moving from indecision to farce. In the supreme irony it was the French, so vacillating and tardy through the entire effort, who now howled the loudest at the decision to forsake Jerusalem. Egypt was not the reason they had come to Palestine. They were pilgrims! They had taken the cross and pledged to deliver their Lord's tomb from the hands of the heathen! What did Cairo have to do with that?

"We left our own country only for the sake of the Holy City," said one bravely, "and we will not return until we have taken it!"

"All the springs in the neighborhood of the city have been polluted," Richard retorted. "There is not a drop of water to be had. Where shall we find water?"

Had not the heroes of the First Crusade faced the same sort of pollution? And had they not brought water from the river Jordan?

"We will drink the brook of Teku'a," the French baron replied, referring to the Tekoah of Amos and Absalom in the Old Testament, an underground stream about ten miles south of Jerusalem.

"How can we water there?" Richard asked.

"We will divide the army into two sections," the Frenchman said. "One will ride out to the watering place, while the other remains close up to the city to carry on the siege. We will go to water once each day."

"As soon as one division of the army has gone to the watering place with their beasts, the garrison will sally out from the city and attack the troops that remain, and destroy all Christendom!"

In the face of the French contempt, Richard was losing respect and losing control. Instead of acting like Godfrey of Bouillon, he was sounding like Judas Iscariot, or worse, like Philip Augustus. His words began to sound like whining. Perhaps money would assuage them. "If the French will agree to our plan for the invasion of Egypt," Richard said, "I will give them my fleet, now at Acre, fully equipped. It can carry their provisions, and the army can march along the coast in safety. At my expense I will contribute seven hundred knights and two thousand foot soldiers to the cause. If anyone doubts my commitment, I promise to march with my own soldiers only."

When word of the withdrawal reached the soldiers, they were dumbfounded. Cursing the day they had joined this ill-fated enterprise, they rolled in the dust in self-flagellation, and then they turned their ire on their King. Their despair was far greater than it had been the previous fall when Beit Nuba was evacuated the first time around. At least then the rain and the mud made an assault impossible. But now! Quarrels broke out between the various factions.

The French heaped scorn on Richard personally. Overtly they began to separate themselves from the rest of the army. Hugh, the Duke of Burgundy, went so far as to compose a wicked jingle about Richard, which made fun of him and questioned not only his leadership but his manhood. Soon enough, soldiers took up the song with cackling, until in due course it reached Richard's ears. He was not amused. In revenge he composed his own catty little song about the Duke of Burgundy. As the chronicle of the Crusade reports, he had no lack of good material.

The Third Crusade had entered its time for recriminations.

To a troubadour it did not matter who was to blame. He could think only of the ancient oak tree at Hebron. It was known as Abraham's Tree, for it was as old as the world, and nearly dead. Christians in the Holy Land believed that the tree had withered on the day that Christ was crucified. In the intervening centuries just enough life was in the trunk that the Crusading Christians professed fervently that Abraham's Tree would spring to life once again when a Christian prince captured the Holy Land.

On July 6, almost exactly five years after the disaster at the Battle of Hattin, the Crusader force began its second retreat from Beit Nuba.

As the withdrawal got under way, the poet could feel the last sap of life drain away from the Dry Tree of Hebron.

# CHAPTER TWENTY-NINE

# The Ram Backs for Butting

�֍

I

N HIS SPEECH TO HIS BARONS, CONCEDING THE DE-
feat of his Crusade, Richard had complained that Saladin seemed
to know every move the Crusaders made, even before they made it.
It was true that the Sultan had a mole high in the ranks of his opposition. Within a day of the Crusaders' decision to withdraw from Beit
Nuba, Saladin knew not only what had been decided but how it was decided
and who had argued for what position. In a dispatch reporting on the strife
between the King and the French, the actual dialogue between the parties
was repeated verbatim.

As word of the retreat raced through the Muslim ranks, and as the forward elements watched the sad procession of knights move down the road to Ramla, there was great rejoicing. Saladin himself rode out to have a look. Yet he could not give way completely to his emotions. For he feared the invasion of Egypt almost as much as a siege of Jerusalem.

Soon he called for the ambassador who represented Henry of Champagne. When the envoy appeared in the Sultan's presence, he was exceedingly brash for one whose side was skulking out of the vicinity. The envoy carried with him a message from Henry: "The King of England has given me all the land on the coast, and it is now in my hands. Now give me back my other lands, and I will make peace with you and be as one of your children."

At this impertinence Saladin flew into a rage and ordered the ambassador out of his sight. But the envoy would not relent. "The count is anxious to know how much of the county now in your hands you will give him?" he stammered. Saladin rebuked him further for this rudeness. It was not for the victor to give away the spoils. A day later, however, after he had calmed down, Saladin again called for the ambassador.

"All negotiations between us must be restricted to Tyre and Acre. We must proceed on the basis of conditions accepted by the marquis, Conrad of Montferrat, before he was killed. We will make peace with Count Henry as Lord of Acre, since that city has been granted to him. As to the rest of the land, we shall make our arrangements only with the King of England."

Several days later, when the Crusaders were already on their way from Ramla to Jaffa, Saladin's own ambassador, Hāji Yusuf Sāhib el-Meshtūb, arrived from Richard's court. During the retreat the King had summoned the envoy from Nablus to carry a new peace initiative to Saladin. Two of Richard's lieutenants accompanied el-Meshtūb, ostensibly to be sure that the message was delivered accurately. The royal message was this:

"Tell your lord that he and I can go on no longer, and the best thing for us to do is to put an end to the shedding of blood. But do not think I say this because I am weak. It is for our common good. Act as mediator between the Sultan and me, and do not be deceived by the maneuver of withdrawing my camp. The ram backs for butting."

Saladin must have enjoyed this brave flourish, for he knew well from his spies that with the discord in the Crusader ranks, Richard's ram was growing weaker by the day and would not be butting anytime soon. Three days later Richard was in Acre, and he sent yet another embassy to Saladin.

"I am anxious to deserve your friendship and goodwill. I have no desire to be Pharaoh to rule over this land, and I do not suppose you wish to be so either. It is not right for you to allow all the Muslims to perish, nor for me to suffer all our Franks to be killed. Now, there is Count Henry, my sister's son, whom I have put in possession of all these districts. I commend him and all his troops to you. If you invite him to accompany you on an expedition to the East, he will be willing.

"On many occasions monks who have been turned out have petitioned you for churches, and you have never shown yourself niggardly. Now I beg you to give me the church of the Holy Sepulcher. I promise to renounce all that was unpleasing to you in my former negotiations with el Melek el-Adel, and to relinquish all idea of it. Will you not, then, give me a barren spot, and the ruin of its shrine?"

This modest plea for the modest church in Jerusalem's center seemed to soften Saladin. Unlike their diplomatic interchange the previous November, when Richard had arrogantly demanded all lands as far as the Jordan River, now Saladin held the advantage. He was negotiating from strength, and he was in a position to be generous. Moreover, it was time to heed the spirit of the Koran. It counseled the faithful to smile upon sincere efforts at peace by an enemy. "If the enemy inclines toward peace," it is written in the Koran 8:61, "do thou also incline toward peace and trust in Allah. For He is the One that heareth and knoweth all things."

On July 11, Saladin replied to Richard, "Count Henry shall be as a son to me, and the Basilica of the Resurrection shall be given you. The rest we will divide. You shall have the shore and the plain. We will hold the mountain fortresses already in our hands. Ascalon must be destroyed, but we will let you retain its dependencies."

Judging from Richard's response to this message, they seemed to be getting somewhere. For the King's reply arrived along with the gift to Saladin of two prize, well-fed falcons. He was grateful for the terms Saladin had offered, Richard wrote, but wanted the right to station twenty stouthearted Hospitalers in Jerusalem's Citadel. On July 13, Saladin reacted bluntly:

"You shall have no rights in the Holy City, except those of pilgrims. Ascalon must be dismantled, but you may have the territory around it for the expenses of the fortifications. Darum must also be destroyed, but you will have the coast and its fortresses from Jaffa to Tyre."

They had hit a snag, and its name was Ascalon. For the fortress to remain in Christian hands was, to Saladin, an impossibility. It would disrupt the co-

ordination between the two halves of his empire. The last eighty years of
Arab history, including the most recent twenty years with Saladin as supreme
leader, could be explained as the constant thrust to unify Egypt and Syria.
Saladin had personally accomplished that unification; it was his crowning
achievement. Only through it had the Crusader kingdom shrunk and become
endangered. Ascalon was the hinge at the elbow, and in Crusader hands it
could unhinge the precious, hard-won Arab unity.

In Richard's view the rebuilding of Ascalon after the first retreat from
Beit Nuba had saved the morale of his dispirited men. For six months his soldiers had poured their strength and sweat into its reconstruction, and once
again its towers rose proudly above the sea. Indeed, for it and Darum to be
in Christian hands, as the forward positions pointing toward Egypt, ensured
the balance of power between the two sides and gave the King of Jerusalem
a reasonable chance for survival.

On July 16, Richard replied vaguely, as if he were not getting the point.
"If the Christians are to be contented with one single church in the Holy
City, surely three fortresses are not too much for them to ask. Let them re-
tain what they have from Darum to Antioch."

Again Saladin's reply was curt. "Let the people of Antioch negotiate for
themselves. They are not included in our negotiations. The towns you ask for
cannot be given up, but you may have Lydda as compensation for your efforts
and expenses at Ascalon." (Lydda, southeast of Ramla, had once possessed the
fine Cathedral of St. George, which Saladin had destroyed. Let Richard rebuild a cathedral instead of a strategic bastion.)

On July 20, Richard replied with his own curtness. "We cannot displace
one stone of Ascalon."

With that insult Saladin prepared to renew the war.

## 2

## JAFFA

The momentum of the conflict had now shifted to the Muslim side. Saladin's strength, his purpose, and his military intelligence gave him an
immense and unexpected advantage. The Crusaders were retreating in disarray and discord, with the French and Richard going in different directions.

The ram had lost its butt and its horns. His spies reported that only the sick and the exhausted had stopped over in Jaffa, while the main body of Richard's army had followed the King to Acre. Most important, a bulletin came from Acre signaling that Richard, giving way to his impetuosity, had taken a shipful of marines even farther north for an expedition against Beirut. That put the King more than four days distant from any new emergency in the south.

The way was open for Saladin to go on the offensive. By late July all his main divisions and his major commanders had arrived from distant corners of the empire, ostensibly for the defense of Jerusalem. Indeed, the army's ranks swelled with fresh, eager recruits, who had signed up with the news of the Crusader withdrawal from the Holy City, as if the Muslim side was moving in for the kill. Saladin's force was now more than full strength.

On July 26 his divisions appeared before the walls of Jaffa. Saladin thought the city would be easy to snatch, for it was defended by a token force of merely five thousand, supposedly exhausted and sick men. With the left commanded by his brother, el Melek el-Adel and the right by his son el Melek ez-Zaher, the offensive enveloped the town, and the Sultan expected to take it in a day.

To his astonishment the defenders put up an exceedingly stiff resistance. The siege engines, two catapults and four mangonels, were brought forward, while porters were sent to the hills for boulders to arm them. After three days the outer wall had been breached through the combined effort of miners and artillerymen. But when a section of the wall tumbled down, the Crusaders lit a huge bonfire behind it, creating a curtain of fire, and this made it impossible for the Muslims to pierce the perimeter.

The baron who commanded the defense was one Alberi of Rheims. Initially the baron did not comport himself in the highest tradition of chivalry. In fact, when the wall fell, Alberi made a bolt for safety in a small boat, rightly fearing for his life. But his comrades blocked his way, and the erstwhile leader was brought back in chains as a deserter to the cause. Once back and under watch in a tower, peering down on the Muslims picking away at the defenses, the French baron declared theatrically, "Here then we shall devote our lives to God's service," a remark later noted by a chronicler with the wry comment that "it was the only thing that remained for him to do."

Time was now the critical factor. As usual, when Richard abandoned his ill-considered move north on Beirut and was hastening south to the rescue, Saladin knew it immediately. The Sultan urged on his Kurds at the parapets eloquently. They must capture the city before Melech Ric arrived! But they were manifestly tired and incapable any longer of heroic effort.

Meanwhile, the defenders played for a delay. Command had been assumed by the newly elected Patriarch, the previous bishop of Bethlehem. The priest proved himself to be "a man whom no fear of death could vanquish, nor any danger could terrify." Moreover, he was clever. He sent ambassadors through the lines to Saladin humbly offering to surrender the city if only a prisoner exchange could take place, if only they could pay for their lives with the old ransom formula from Jerusalem four years before: ten gold bezants for every man, five for every woman, three for every child. If only . . . if only . . .

Saladin rejected this conditional offer out of hand and later regretted it. For the very sight of ambassadors moving back and forth with the prospect of an imminent truce or surrender not only wasted precious time and diverted him from the siege, but it further weakened the resolve of the Muslim soldiers. Their siege became even more anemic than before.

Still, five days after the siege began, the eastern gate facing Jerusalem was a ruin. Hand-to-hand combat was taking place at several openings in the wall. Steadily the defenders were being pushed back toward the citadel, on a hill in the town's center. Again the Patriarch asked for terms, sweetening his previous offer by suggesting he would give up important hostages as security as part of the peace package. This time Saladin eagerly accepted. The hostages filed out, led by the woeful Alberi of Rheims.

The defenders withdrew inside the citadel, hoping to hold out until Richard turned up, but preparing themselves for martyrdom. Meanwhile the Muslim soldiers entered the city and gave themselves over to an orgy of looting. Saladin could do nothing to restrain them, for his soldiers were frustrated at the long delay since the Muslim side had taken a Christian town. But he stationed his best Kurds at the city's gates, and as his soldiers came out heavy laden, the Kurds stripped them of their booty.

At dawn on the sixth day of the siege, a day celebrated in the Christian calendar as St. Peter in Chains, a fleet of thirty-five galleys appeared on the horizon. Richard perched on the prow of his royal ship, *Trenchemere*, which was painted red and flew a red sail and an enormous standard of the King, his three lions against a heraldic background. The vessels were manned by the bravest Hospitalers and Templars, as well as Pisans and Genoese, "who did great deeds when they were needed."

The King was two days late, however, for adverse winds had held his fleet at Haifa. Stuck and frustrated at the lack of a favorable wind, the King had raised his head skyward and shouted, "Mercy, O Lord! Why do You hold me and retard me when I go upon Your quest?" If this was the Lord's unfathomable plan, he was making things difficult. As Richard's fleet had set out from Acre, another contingent of Hospitalers and Templars had started out overland. But a combined band of Saladin's soldiers and Assassins had blocked them between Caesarea and Arsuf and pinned them down.

On that Saturday morning the ransom of the Christians was already under way. Nearly fifty knights had already paid their ten bezants and had been freed. But when the sound of the trumpets reached the tower of the citadel and its defenders rushed to the walls to see the King's red sail in the distance, they cried out with the words of Isaiah that "they shall cry unto the Lord because of the oppressors, and He shall send them a Savior, and a great one, and He shall deliver them." The surrendering abruptly stopped, the door was bolted again, the remaining defenders strapped on their armor and withdrew into the tower of the citadel.

As the same trumpet sounds reached Saladin's pavilion, he was already in early-morning discussions with the Christian Patriarch on the last details of the surrender. The Patriarch was hustled out, and Saladin took charge of the military situation. Understanding thirty-five ships as a modest force, he ordered the beach in front of the city to be filled with a horde of Muslim soldiers. Their mission was to prevent the Crusaders from landing.

Viewed from the Christian galleys, the rabble on the beach presented a formidable obstacle. The defenders were crammed together like straw without room to move; archers waded into the water and let fly a fusillade that darkened the sky; behind them cavalry tried to restrain their eager horses. The defenders raised a menacing racket, shouting their war cries and chants of *"Tahlil"* and *"Takbir"* about the greatness of their one God and clicking their tongues in an unnerving, ethereal manner. Richard could not be sure whether the citadel was still in Christian hands, for everywhere on the walls the Muslim banners fluttered. If it was not, there was no point or urgency about a frontal assault. In his own council there was sharp disagreement about what to do next.

Amid this indecision, suddenly, from an enormous height in the tower, a distant figure dropped to the beach, as if he had commended his soul to the Messiah. He scrambled into the water and swam furiously for the royal ship. When he was pulled on board, the messenger turned out to be a priest.

"Most noble King, the remnant of our people await your arrival," he blurted out.

"Good friend, how say you? Are some still alive?"

"As says the Psalm, for thy sake are we killed all day long. We are counted as sheep for the slaughter . . . unless divine grace shall bring you to their rescue."

"Some still live?"

"Aye, but hemmed in and at the last extremity in front of yonder tower."

"Please God, then, by whose guidance we have come," cried the King, "we will die with our brave brothers in arms, and a curse light on him who hesitates." And with that the galleys moved toward the swarming beach.

The King was the first to leap into the water. He had stripped off his leg and waist armor, and at first the sea came up to his midriff as he waded forward, crossbow in one hand and sword in the other. His men followed him eagerly, feeling, like Saul's men at Gibeah, that their hearts were touched by God. So daunting was the sight of this huge man, this superb athlete moving against the press of humanity that almost by instinct the Muslim fray fell back in awe and fear. The reaping began. It was not long before their beachhead was established. Planks and barrels were brought on shore to form a barricade; behind it the archers fell smartly into their ranks.

Richard found his way to a spiral staircase that led from the beach into the Templars' house, and he was soon in Jaffa's streets with a band of bloodthirsty military monks. As soon as they could manage it, they raised the King's standard on the wall, so that it could be seen by the hard-pressed tower in the distance.

When he heard about the swiftness of the Crusader advance, about their beachhead, about his soldiers' panic as they quailed before the enemy, about the King already in Jaffa's streets and making his way to relieve the tower as the tower's defenders had sallied forward to meet up with their King, Saladin was incredulous at the incompetence and cowardice of his troops.

"How can this be?" he gasped. "By what superior disposition have they been able to accomplish this? In infantry and cavalry our army is far superior!" Richard had begun the morning with three horses. Now the Crusader force had about twelve horses, and the entire Muslim force was fleeing on foot and on horseback.

His emirs shrank from their Sultan in shame.

"My lord, it is not as you think," sputtered one of his advisers. "Still, I think that their wonderful King could easily be surprised, for he lies almost alone in his tent, and fully worn out with fatigue." And so they were reduced to that: Their only hope was to remove the King himself. Saladin turned away in disgust.

# 3

# TWO ARABIAN HORSES

In the three days after his recapture of Jaffa, Richard camped outside of the city, on the hill from which Saladin had tried to defend it, where he focused on rebuilding the damaged walls of the city. But it was true, he was exhausted from the exertions of battle and draped himself on his divan in the hope of some rest.

During this hiatus he and Saladin exchanged a number of communications. With their representatives riding furiously between the two headquarters, the contacts became so intense and frequent that it was almost as if the two great leaders were having a face-to-face discussion. In the first contact, during the preliminary courtesies with Saladin's ambassador, Richard taunted his great adversary.

"Your Sultan is mighty. There is none greater or mightier than him in this land of Islam," Richard said jovially. "Great and good God! I should have thought he could not take Jaffa in two months, and yet he made himself master of it in five days! Why then did he make off at my first appearance? By God! I was not even ready to fight. I was still wearing my sea boots. Why did you retreat?"

There was, of course, no answer to this humiliating question. The King seemed to be enjoying himself, and he pushed forward cheerfully.

"Greet the Sultan for me and tell him that I beseech him, in God's name, to grant me the peace I ask. This state of things must be put to a stop. My own country beyond the seas is being ruined. There is no advantage to either you or me in suffering the present condition of things to continue."

Increasingly their exchanges took on the tone of banter rather than of real negotiations.

"You began by asking for peace on certain terms," Saladin wrote. "At the time the question of Jaffa and Ascalon formed the main point at issue. Jaffa is now in ruins. You can have the country from Tyre to Caesarea."

"Among the Franks," Richard replied, "it is customary for a man to whom a city has been granted to become the ally and servant of the giver. If, therefore, you give me these two cities, Jaffa and Ascalon, the troops I leave there will be always at your service. If you have any need of me, I will hasten to come to you and be at your service, and you know that I can serve you."

At the facetiousness of this dispatch Saladin's reply seemed equally flippant. "Since you place such trust in me, I propose that we share the two cities. Jaffa and what is beyond it shall be yours whilst Ascalon and what is beyond it shall be mine."

Richard thanked him for the rights to Jaffa but still insisted on the same assurances for Ascalon. If peace were concluded in the next six days, Richard promised to leave promptly for Europe.

It was now time for Saladin to taunt Richard. But his taunt had more the tone of a father challenging his son. "It is absolutely impossible for us to give up Ascalon," the Sultan replied. "In any case the King will be obliged to spend the winter here. He knows full well that if he departs, all the country he has conquered will fall into our hands without fail. That will most certainly happen, please God, even if he remains.

"If he can manage to spend the winter here, far from his people, and two months' journey from his native land, while he is still in the vigor of his youth and at an age that is usually devoted to pleasure, how much easier is it for me to remain here not only during the winter, but during the summer also? I am in the heart of my own country, surrounded by my household and by my children, and able to get all I want. Moreover, I am an old man now. I have no longer any desire for the pleasures of the world. I have had my fill of them and have renounced them forever.

"The soldiers who serve me in the winter are succeeded by others in the summer. And above all I believe that I am furthering God's cause in acting as I do. I will not cease therefrom until God grants victory to whom He will."

While he talked, Saladin was actually on the move. Southeast of Jaffa he ordered yet another Crusader outpost called Beit Dejan to be destroyed before moving his army to Ramla to consider his next move. From scouts he learned of another relief force on its way from Acre to "succor" Richard's small force at Jaffa. Saladin determined to prevent this reinforcement at all costs.

"It is better to attack now than to wait for the enemy's armies to join up and then go into the mountains like a beaten force," Saladin said. "Now we shall go like pursuers."

The emirs' plan to launch a surprise attack on Richard in the hope of capturing him seemed more sensible by the hour. Leaving his heavy baggage at Ramla, the Sultan marched through the night. In the morning he came upon a mere twelve tents, including the royal tent, with their occupants slumbering peaceably on the plain outside Jaffa.

Quietly the Muslim forces stole forward until near dawn they were close to Richard's tent. Then, in a bit of Alphonse-and-Gaston slapstick that was later ascribed to God's grace, two Muslim commanders fell into a disagreement about who was to attempt the seizure of the King.

"You go on foot to take the King and his followers while we will remain on horseback to prevent their escaping into the castle," said one grandly.

"Nay, it is your place to go in on foot," replied the other, "because our rank is higher than yours. We are content with the service which is our duty. This service on foot belongs to you rather than us."

Neither one, of course, was too eager to knock on the tent door and rouse from his peaceful sleep the greatest warrior and Arab slayer on earth. Their conversation became loud enough that it was heard in the Crusader camp, and the alarm was sounded.

Richard raced from his tent, strapping on his armor and barking orders. In an incredible display of discipline and close-order drill, his soldiers fell into a defensive line, as seven Muslim squadrons, comprising several thousand horsemen, swooped out of the darkness and fell upon the formation. In his front line Richard's foot soldiers knelt shoulder to shoulder, thigh to thigh, behind their shields and with their spears pointing outward. Behind them his crossbowmen crouched in pairs, one loader and one shooter, who discharged his bolts as fast as his mate could hand him a reloaded weapon. Behind them some eighty knights stood at the ready for a charge. They had only a dozen battle horses and a single mule. At first Richard raced along the back line exhorting his soldiers. The outcries later ascribed to him were probably better formed than they had been at the time.

"Bear up against the frowns of fortune! . . . Adversity sheds light upon the virtues of mankind! . . . Brave men conquer nobly or die gloriously! . . . Before we die, let us avenge our own deaths! . . . This will be the end of labors, men, the termination of life and of our battles! . . . Let us receive our martyrdom with a willing mind!" Or words to that effect.

Though they were outnumbered more than four to one, the Crusaders' fusillade took a terrible toll on the attackers and their horses. As Saladin watched from a knoll in the distance, his soldiers were never able to close on the tight company of Crusaders. When the initial wave was blunted, Richard burst through his line and charged into the center of the enemy, followed by ten other knights. "The King was a very giant in the battle, and was everywhere in the field—now here, now there, wherever the attacks of the Turks raged the hottest," reported the chronicler, until unbelievably he was unhorsed!

"Sire, see him there! On foot!" one of Saladin's sergeants shouted to his lord excitedly. Saladin had seen it all.

"How can this be?" he said calmly. "That a King should be on foot with his men! It cannot be!" And then turning to his brother, el Melek el-Adel, he said, "Go. Take these two Arabian horses and lead them to him. Tell him that I send them to him, and that a man so great as he is should not be in parts such as these, on foot, with his men."

It was the crowning act of chivalry in the entire Third Crusade. The present was "for the brave deeds he had done and all the prowess he had won," el-Adel said when he reached Richard in the melee. He requested only that the King remember the gift later if he should be so lucky as to return from this battle alive.

The battle continued and spread into the town itself. Before long, so many arrows had stuck in Richard's armor and quilted cuirass that he looked like porcupine. At one point he was completely surrounded by the enemy, one against a multitude, and yet he emerged from a pile of dead unscathed. It was as if he were possessed, as in the words of Deuteronomy, "I will make mine arrows drunk with blood, and my sword shall devour flesh; and that with the blood of the slain and of the captives, from the beginning of revenges upon the enemy." At another point an emir, on a richly caparisoned horse and frustrated at Richard's flair and genius and almost supernatural skill in battle, charged the King, only to have not only his head but half his shoulder and right arm sliced off with it. The Muslim fighters recoiled at this ghoulish sight. As the day wore on, they gave Richard a wide berth, for the King had become a one-man killing machine. He was the Lionheart, and as the Proverb said, "A lion which is strongest among beasts, turneth not away from any." By nightfall the battle slackened. The Muslim side had reportedly lost more than seven hundred men and fifteen hundred horses, while the Crusader side had lost but two dead and a number of wounded.

"And on that day," wrote Saladin's scribe, Beha al-Din, with both disdain and admiration, "the King of England, a lance in his hand, rode down the whole length of our army, and none of our men did come forth to challenge him."

This was the last battle of the Third Crusade.

And it is remembered as much for Saladin's generosity and respect for his great adversary as for any bravery or prowess displayed by Richard himself in combat.

CHAPTER THIRTY

# Here Is My Hand

AFTER THE BATTLE OF JAFFA, RICHARD COLlapsed from fatigue and from the stench of the battlefield. For days his body shook with intermittent fever and chills. His doctors diagnosed his condition as semitertian and warned him that few recovered from the disease. He was not alone. The air had become so fetid with the smell of death and the danger of ptomaine poisoning that soldiers on both sides dropped by the score and died.

As the rumor spread through the camp that he was about to "migrate from this world," the King appreciated the danger of his illness to his entire effort. Too often only his presence had saved the day. "If Saladin knew that Richard was dead," wrote the English chronicler Richard of Devizes, "he would instantly pelt the French with cow dung, and intoxicate the best of the English drunkards with a dose which should make them tremble." Now, not only could the King not remove himself if there were another attack, but once again the French, snug and dissipated in Acre, had refused to come south to Jaffa in succor.

Saladin learned quickly of Richard's condition. He had sent his chamberlain, Abu Bekr, across the lines on some pretext. Not wanting the envoy to see the state of the town and its weak defense, Richard came out of the city walls to greet the Sultan's gatekeeper, looking like death itself. Inevitably the conversation turned to peace.

"How long am I to go on making advances to the Sultan that he will not accept?" Richard said. "I was anxious above all things to be able to return to my own country. Now the winter is here, and the rain has begun. I have, therefore, decided to stay, so that question no longer remains to be decided between us."

Abu Bekr carried this hollow threat to Saladin, along with a full report on Richard's decrepit state. The Sultan immediately called his emirs together.

"The King of England is very ill, and it is certain that the French will embark very shortly and return to their country," Saladin said. "Now that they have exhausted all their resources, the enemy is weighed down by the mighty hand of God. We ought then to march against Jaffa and take that city by surprise, for we have a good chance of a favorable outcome. Alternatively, we could march by night and fall upon Ascalon. Then if our courage does not fail us, we will carry our purpose through. We have become accustomed to fighting the jihad. In it we have achieved our aim."

Customary reverence greeted this new call to arms. At last, haltingly, an emir spoke up. "It is as you say. You must act as you think, and the right decision is the one that you make. Only what you settle stays firm, and what you establish remains stable. Divine grace assists you in all you bind and loose, all that you give and take away. You alone have looked to yourself, as one accustomed to happiness, to the desire to serve God, to the acquisition of eternal virtue, to the taking of measures necessary to success, to disdain for idleness and dislike for keeping oneself aloof. In yourself you find force and tenacity, and your indestructible faith marks you out as the one to achieve the aims we strive for."

This was an extraordinary preamble to a disagreement, but it was the Oriental way. Saladin was the Defender of the Faith. The agony of his duty was awesome, almost divine, and his emirs honored the difficulty of his position. "It is my job, with God's help, to take the most determined and resolute course," Saladin had told them. "It is difficult to break off what is customary. We have no other occupation than that of making war, for we are not among those who are beguiled by games or led astray by dissipation. If we give up this work, what shall we do? If we destroy our hope of defeating them, what shall we hope for?"

Once the emir had expressed his respect, he moved to his disagreement with measured words. "But look to at the state of the country!" he said. "It is ruined and trampled underfoot. Look at your subjects. They are beaten down and confused. Look at your armies. They are exhausted and sick . . . at your horses: they are neglected and ruined. There is little forage. Food is short; supply bases are far away; the necessities of life are dear. All supplies have to come from Egypt, confronting the murderous perils of the desert. Again this concentration of troops may well decide to disperse, and your lengthy explanation of the situation will in that case have little effect, with provisions cut off, roads blocked, the rich reduced to hunger, the poor to destitution, straw more precious than gold, barley unobtainable at any price.

"And if they fail to get their truce, they will devote all their energies to strengthening and consolidating their position. They will face death with high courage in the course of achieving their aims. For love of their faith will they refuse to submit to humiliation. The best thing for you to remember is the verse revealed by God: 'And if they incline to peace, you, too, should incline to it.'"

To quote the Koran to Saladin was close to the last resort. However eloquently his emirs might couch their respect and obedience for their lord, they, too, had exhausted their resources. They had no more to give. Their lord might report that Richard was sick, but he was like no other man. "Since the beginning of the world we have never heard of such a knight, so brave and so experienced in arms," said one emir. "In every deed at arms he is without rival, first to advance, last to retreat. We did our best to seize him, but in vain, for no one can escape his sword. His attack is dreadful. To engage with him is fatal. His deeds are not human."

To the astonishment of his counselors Saladin responded with an admission of fear. Richard did not scare him. "I am afraid of making peace," he said, turning to his scribe, Beha al-Din, "and I do not know what may happen to me. The enemy will increase his forces, and then he will come out of the lands we are leaving in his possession, and recapture those we have taken from him. You will see that each one of them will make a fortress on some hilltop. I cannot draw back, because the Muslims will be destroyed if we make peace."

In succeeding days, however, Richard's actions were very human indeed. He made no effort to conceal his indisposition from Saladin. Instead he sent requests to the Sultan for ice and fruit, especially peaches and pears and snow, as shaved ice was known, for which he had great hunger. For sound military reasons, as well as his natural courtesy, Saladin obliged. From his fruit man he learned that the Crusaders were concentrating on the repair of the citadel's fortifications and neglecting the battered city walls and that Count Henry of Champagne had had no success in persuading the French to pitch in. The town seemed to have about three hundred healthy knights still. To confirm the report a Muslim force was dispatched to Jaffa to lure the defenders out to be counted. Indeed, about three hundred rode bravely out, trying to hold on to their dignity. For most of them rode out on mules! Chivalrous knights on mules? It had come to that.

Not long after, Abu Bekr had another audience with the King in which Richard renewed his call for Saladin's brother to enter into serious negotiations. From past contacts he trusted and respected el Melek el-Adel as liberal and reasonable. "Beg my brother, el Melek el-Adel, to consider what means can be used to induce the Sultan to make peace. Ask him to request that the city of Ascalon may be given to me. I will take my departure, leaving here only a very small force. The Sultan will take the remainder of the territory out of the hands of the Franks. My only object is to retain the position I hold amongst the Franks. If the Sultan will not forego his pretensions to Ascalon, then let el-Adel procure for me an indemnity for the sums I have laid out in repairing the fortifications."

On the surface this seemed like Richard's same old position. Still, the words of the Koran rang in Saladin's head: If they incline to peace you should incline to it as well.

And so, too, did the words of the emirs in council: "If you make peace, then the farmers and inhabitants will return to their lands. Harvests and fruits will abound during the time of truce. The armies can renew their equipment and rest. When war returns again, we, too, shall prepare for war and shall renew the means of striking a blow with point and blade. This does not mean abandoning the service of God. It is simply a means of increasing our usefulness and our strength and success. The Franks will not keep faith long or abide by sworn treaties.

"Therefore, sire, make a truce with them all, which will enable them to break up and disperse, enduring the blows they have suffered and leaving no one in Palestine capable of resisting and standing up to us."

This prodding broke through the inertia that gripped Saladin. Now he perceived a crack in Richard's previous inflexibility on Ascalon. To his brother, the Sultan forwarded Richard's statement along with this urgent message: "If they will give up Ascalon, conclude the treaty of peace, for our troops are worn out by the length of the campaign and have spent all their resources."

When el-Adel came into the royal quarters, a very different Richard presented himself. The King's condition was worsening, to the point that Richard himself was now worried that he would not be able to recover. Moreover, he had no illusions about his soldiers. They had lost their will to fight. No longer could they be moved by a common cause; only money moved them. As a good commander he knew that money alone was a poor motivator.

From his bed the monarch had no bravado. There was no posturing. He spoke philosophically from the heart, as one whose fate was sealed, either in death or in his remaining life. "The time is close when the sea becomes unavailable, and the crests of the waves swell up on high," he said. "If you agree to a truce and enable me to, I shall fulfill my desire to go. But if you fight and oppose me, I shall pitch my tents and fix my dwelling here. Both sides are exhausted. I have renounced Jerusalem and will now renounce Ascalon. I am not misled by this mass of enemy troops assembling from everywhere, for I know they will disperse when winter comes. If we persist in our miserable conflict, we shall destroy ourselves. So fulfill my desire and win my friendship. Accept my respect. Make a pact with me and let me go."

When they moved to the details, Richard gave up his demand for Ascalon and his demand to be reimbursed for the cost of rebuilding the city. At last they had come to a point where an agreement was possible.

In Ramla, Saladin's scribes reduced the terms of the settlement to paper. Ascalon was to be destroyed with a combined force of Christian and Muslim engineers. It was not to be rebuilt for three years. After three years whoever could seize the city could fortify it. Jaffa and its environs were to stay in Crusader hands, with the exception of the strongholds to the east: Ramla, Lydda,

Yebna, and Mejdel Yaba. The coastal cites of Caesarea, Arsuf, Haifa, Acre, and Tyre were also to remain in Crusader hands, along with their dependencies, except the strongholds of Nazareth and La Safouri on the road to the Sea of Galilee. Free movement and free commerce were assured for both Franks and Arabs in the other's territory. Christian pilgrims were to be permitted to visit the Holy Sepulcher in Jerusalem without hindrance or fee.

Saladin conveyed these terms to Richard with a cryptic covering message: "These are the boundaries fixed to your territory. If you accept peace on these terms, well and good. I will give you my hand upon our promises. Let the King send a man to the Sultan empowered to swear in his name. Let this be done the day after tomorrow. Otherwise, we shall believe you are only stalling to gain time, and we shall break off negotiations."

When the Sultan's envoys entered the King's presence, Richard was dizzy with fever. Solemnly the ambassadors read the treaty's language. Where was the provision for a reimbursement of his expenses at Ascalon? the King asked doggedly, until his advisers calmly reminded him that days before he had given up that demand. "If I did, I will not break my word," he said weakly, falling back on his bed. "Tell the Sultan that it is well. I accept the treaty. I trust myself to his generosity, and know that, if he does anything further in my favor, it is to his kindness I shall owe him the next favor."

The treaty was handed to him, but he turned away.

"I am not strong enough to read it," he whispered. "But I solemnly declare that I will make peace." And then he turned back and reached out feebly to them.

"Here is my hand," he said.

# CHAPTER THIRTY-ONE

# A Slender String

I N Acre, through September of 1192, the sur-
vivors of the Third Crusade gathered together their weapons and
their souvenirs, packed up their mangonels and other heavy baggage,
and prepared to leave the Promised Land. There is no accurate figure
of how many men were still alive after their long ordeal. The emphasis was more
on how many had died. It was estimated that merely one in twelve who came
originally stood at the end on the stone pier in those emotional days at Acre,
waiting to board their galleys for home, looking out on the Tower of Flies and
back on the walls they had stormed fifteen months earlier. The chief Christian
chronicler of the Third Crusade put the dead at the siege of Acre alone at one

hundred thousand and the total dead at three hundred thousand. These figures are absurdly high, but the death toll was beyond imagination and beyond accurate accounting. Disease and famine had taken more men than combat.

Had they all died in vain? Not if it was martyrdom that sent them directly to heaven. At this sad juncture the purpose of the entire grand enterprise seemed to have been entirely about martyrdom.

"Each, in his own way, endured a kind of martyrdom," the chronicler wrote, of both the living and the dead, as he surveyed the ragtag survivors. "Every one of those, with simple and devout hearts, had exposed himself for the love of God to this distant pilgrimage. Who can doubt the salvation of the souls of such noble and excellent men? These surely may be supposed to have gone to heaven."

Nor were the dangers over. Fresh opportunity for martyrdom lay ahead on the perilous journey home. As the galleys spread their sails in Acre, the unpredictable winds of fall took them in sundry directions. Many were blown off course and would not reach their destination for many months. Some were shipwrecked. And many of the pilgrims were still to succumb to the lingering effects of the battlefield's putrescent stench.

King Richard was carried tenderly first to Haifa and then to Acre, where his Queen, Berengaria, and his sister, Joanna, the former Queen of Sicily, and his loving minstrel, Blondel de Nesle, nursed him slowly back to health. In the waning weeks of summer he suffered as much from his sense of unworthiness as a pilgrim as from the poisonous vapors of the killing fields. Doggedly he hung on to the fantasy that he was merely going home temporarily for the three-year span of truce, to save his realm and his crown. After that he would return again in this higher calling with another great army to fulfill the goal of his pilgrimage and to reclaim Christ's tomb.

Even in his feverish exhaustion he was able to muster the energy to announce his intention to return, through ambassadors, to Saladin. Saladin must have smiled at this bold Parthian shot. With the largesse of a victor the Sultan replied, Allah as his witness, that if he must lose his dominions, he would just as soon lose them to so magnificent a King as Richard. For, Saladin proclaimed, Richard was a man of honor, of magnanimity, and of general excellence. The feeling was mutual.

In reporting this last exchange between Richard and Saladin, even Richard's own doting chronicler remarked upon the elusive nature of fate. Many uncertainties lay ahead. Of any future plans for more crusading armies and further epic quests, Richard had forgotten the poet's lines:

*Reflect how every human being*
*Hangs suspended on a slender string.*

The Queens and troubadours left on September 29, but Richard, still burdened with unfinished business, tarried for another eleven days. One solemn act of chivalry remained to be handled, the matter of William des Préaux. He was the brave and selfless Norman knight who had saved Richard from capture a year before in those woods near Lydda when the royal party had been surprised and, seeing the disaster unfolding, had shouted out that he, not that other large man, was the famous Melech Ric. Now for the steep price of ten of the most important Muslim prisoners, who were willing to purchase their freedom for a huge pot of gold, William alone was exchanged, without a further penny expended, and Richard's final account in Palestine was settled.

As he boarded his royal galley, there was general lamentation. "O Jerusalem, thou art indeed helpless, now that thou art bereft of such a champion," they wailed on the quay as the King pushed off. "If by chance the truce is broken, who will protect thee from thy assailants in King Richard's absence?" Only Saladin's word of honor would protect them, that was the honest answer, and in his word they could have confidence.

When Richard was far out to sea, watching the shore grow dim on the horizon, he was heard to say, "O Holy Land, to God do I entrust thee. May He, of His mercy, only grant me such space of life that, by His goodwill, I may bring thee succor. For it is my hope and intention to aid thee at some future time." And then the slender string that bound him to Palestine snapped, and he turned his eyes westward.

2

# ODYSSEUS

From the moment Richard Coeur de Lion turned his eyes away from the Holy Land and westward toward home, his story ceased to be an epic of history and became a personal romance. His diligent chroniclers had left him to concentrate on their own struggle to return home safely, and the novelists took over. In the odyssey of his return journey the legend of Richard the Lionheart was born. He was the new Odysseus, only his sirens and lotus eaters and one-eyed monsters would take the form of revenge-seeking dukes, pining minstrels, a traitorous brother, silly squires, and simpering maidens. His adventures would include disguises as a Templar and a cook, mountain-top castles, dark dungeons, bloodhounds, feats of incredible strength and daring, and ultimately, a huge pot of money.

No longer was Richard's story the same as that of his Crusade. He was finally, utterly on his own. The denouement of his heroic tale was elaborated upon over the centuries, with a heavy dose of imagination and invention, and finally it presented itself to us in modern times as the stuff of bedtime stories. And thus we must navigate with the few scraps of hard evidence we have and enjoy the incredible stories for what they are.

For six weeks, as the hot sirocco winds off the Libyan desert clashed over water with the cold fronts of the north, the King was blown around the Etruscan Sea like a feather. He made a brief stop at Cyprus to place his blessing personally on the rule of Guy of Lusignan, but after that he lost his way. At one point his galley hovered near the Barbary Coast, at another a mere three days out of Marseille.

The foul winds were, in a sense, the least of his worries. The hero had become the hunted. His band of twenty men had some sense of the risk they ran no matter where they might land in Europe. Everywhere they looked on their maps, there were traps. Across the Continent a confederation of enemies past and present was arrayed against them: in France, Germany, Italy, Greece, and Byzantium. They had turned away from Marseille when they learned from passing ships that the Count of Toulouse, the grandson of the legendary hero of the First Crusade, Raymond of St. Giles, and an old enemy from the pre-Crusade days of internecine struggle, had laid traps for him in southern France. Elsewhere in central Europe they could count on King Philip Augustus to lay snares wherever he could, not only in France but elsewhere. Diplomacy was Philip's forte, and he was cunning and bent on revenge.

No doubt the King of France was slandering Richard to whoever would listen. In fact, Richard could not fathom the full extent of the libel. Throughout Europe his old companion was defaming him with wild charges that had the combined passion of the spurned lover and the shamed warrior: that from the moment Philip had arrived in Judea, Richard had tried to betray him to Saladin; that as soon as Richard gained access to Tyre, he murdered Conrad of Montferrat; that he had poisoned the Duke of Burgundy;

and that he had sent Oriental assassins to slit the throats of various sitting monarchs of Europe who had opposed him.

Through Germany and Italy many listened eagerly. From the intelligence of other arriving Crusaders these enemies were on the alert for the imminent appearance of Richard. In the Piedmont the relatives of Conrad of Montferrat were still seething over Conrad's apparent murder, and in all Italy the enemies of King Tancred of Sicily, the usurper with whom Richard had allied himself, were legion. In Germany the Tancred connection was also the problem, since the new Emperor of the Holy Roman Empire, Henry VI, had backed the wrong candidate and was smarting from his mistake. In fact, the Emperor had commissioned every town in his realm to apprehend the King of England if they could catch him and then extradite him to the Emperor. In Byzantium the potentates were still livid over Richard's humiliation of Isaac Comnenus in Cyprus. And along the Danube lay his worst enemy of all, the Duke of Austria, who had had his treasured banner dragged through the dust after the fall of Acre and had held Richard personally responsible for the desecration.

In short, there was no safe way back to England. Even there, trouble awaited him. His brother John was seizing castles, demanding fealty, and laying hopeful wagers that Richard would never reach the English shore. In all the world, it seemed, only his mother, Eleanor, in Rouen, hoped for the safe return of her beloved third nestling.

On his homeward journey a hearty band of his closest confederates accompanied Richard. There was Baldwin, the advocate of Bethune, who had been his liege man as far back as the struggles in Anjou. There was the King's clerk, Philip, his chaplain, Anselm, and his young valet. The rest were tough military monks from the Order of the Temple.

Six weeks after they left Acre, the band landed in Corfu. They seemed to have settled on a dangerous route through the Adriatic and then overland through Germany to get to England. Their goal may well have been Saxony, where Richard's brother-in-law, the venerable and cunning Henry of Saxony (known as "The Lion") was in open rebellion against the rule of the new German Emperor. In the past, Richard had provided aid and succor to the old Duke of Saxony, and he could be sure that the favor would be returned. But Saxony's capital, Wittenberg, was far to the north, beyond the hostile regions of Austria and Bavaria. Theoretically they could have passed through the Straits of Africa and sailed all the way home, but in November the perils of

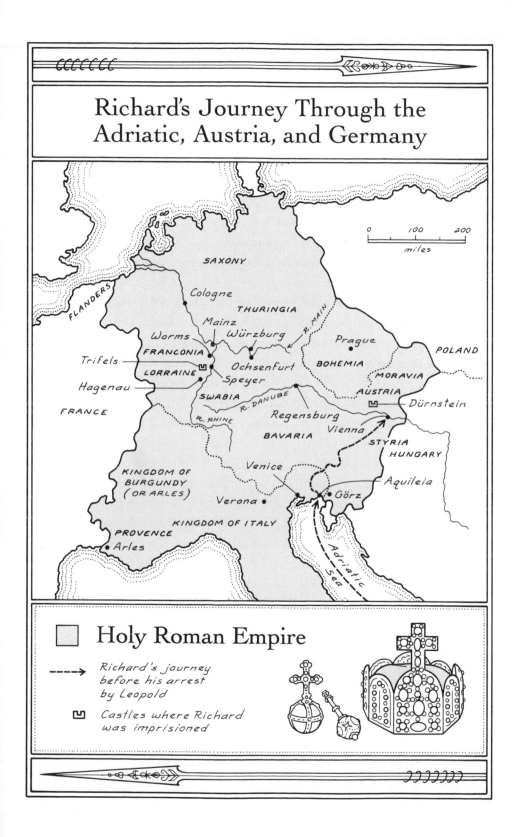

# Richard's Journey Through the Adriatic, Austria, and Germany

SAXONY

FLANDERS

Cologne

THURINGIA

Mainz

R. MAIN

Worms

Würzburg

FRANCONIA

Prague

POLAND

Trifels

Ochsenfurt

BOHEMIA

LORRAINE

Speyer

MORAVIA

Hagenau

SWABIA

R. DANUBE

AUSTRIA

FRANCE

Dürnstein

R. RHINE

Regensburg

Vienna

BAVARIA

STYRIA

HUNGARY

Venice

KINGDOM OF
BURGUNDY
(OR ARLES)

Aquileia

Verona

Görz

KINGDOM OF ITALY

PROVENCE

Adriatic Sea

Arles

0    100    200
miles

## Holy Roman Empire

- - - - > Richard's journey
before his arrest
by Leopold

Castles where Richard
was imprisioned

the sea were even greater than the perils of land. At least on land mere mortals opposed him, whereas the supernatural power of the sea was beyond his control.

In due course he landed on Corfu, an island off the western coast of Greece. In those times it was a nest of pirates—indeed, the entire Adriatic Sea was infested by them—and this redounded to the benefit of the King on the run. The law rather than outlaws was his problem. Richard promptly forsook his royal galley and retained the services of two pirate ships to take him farther north along the Dalmatian Coast. (Later Richard's alliance with pirates was portrayed as the result of an initial fight that so gained the admiration of the pirates for Richard's skill and bravery in battle that they signed up to help.)

The royal party was next spotted at Ragusa, otherwise known as Dubrovnik. Some reports had him shipwrecked on the tiny island of Lacroma, across from Dubrovnik's medieval castle, and so grateful was he to have survived that he supposedly built a monastic church for the Benedictine monks who inhabited the island. Whether the shipwreck was there or farther north at the headwaters of the Adriatic—or both or neither—does not matter. In any event, he turned up next at a place called Aquileia, north of Trieste.

Shipwrecked or not, the King reconsidered his situation and found it desperate. Due north was the dominion of Leopold, the Duke of Austria, who harbored the most passionate of private grudges against him. To the west lay the dominion of Venice, whose merchants would sell anything under the sky to the highest bidder, and beyond that the Piedmont of Conrad of Montferrat.

Here at the headwaters of the Adriatic the wily lord was one Count Meinhard, the ruler of Görz, who was the nephew of Conrad of Montferrat and therefore on especially high alert for any suspicious wayfarer of royal bearing who might happen along. Thinking that the Truce of God might still hold some sway, Richard tried to pass his party off as returning Crusaders led by Baldwin of Bethune and one wealthy merchant named Hugh. "Hugh" sent along an expensive gold ring, festooned with a ruby, to placate the count, but this lavish gift had the opposite effect of making the count suspicious. Hugh was none other than the treacherous Richard, he whispered to his minions, but then set a plan that was too clever by half.

To gain a little time to muster his raiding party, he said to Richard's messengers, "I have sworn to seize all palmers, and to receive no gifts from them. But by virtue of the honor done to me by your lord, I will return the gift and give him leave to depart." Richard smelled the deception instantly and fled on horseback in the dead of night, disguised as a Templar.

Now that his enemies knew that he was in the vicinity, his dangers increased. In Friuli, Richard's band found itself in the fief of Count Meinhard's brother, Frederick of Pettau. This petty lord was no less eager to capture the royal prize. To aid in the endeavor he designated a Norman in his employ, one Roger of Argenton, to search every inn in the land where returning pilgrims were staying and listen for the French tongue. If he should capture the King, Roger was promised half the houses of his town.

When Roger came upon Richard in Templar dress, he persisted in his questioning until Richard revealed his identity. At that, instead of clapping the King in chains, Roger was overcome with emotion and fell to his knees in homage. The Norman spilled out the full extent of the danger Richard was then in, and instead of irons, he provided the King with a fast horse for his getaway. At the alarm Richard's band of twenty fugitives scattered in different directions. Returning to Frederick, Roger professed, somewhat unsuccessfully, that no King was to be found, but only a group of Templars under a knight called Baldwin. In a rage Frederick had every pilgrim in his fief arrested, and no doubt the faithful Roger went to prison with them. By this time Richard was moving north through the Alps into Carinthia. His band was now down to three.

Could he have known where he was headed? According to lore, he traveled for three days through the mountains without food; perhaps his hunger addled his brain and deprived him of his bearings. He was riding directly and almost magnetically to Vienna and the lair of Duke Leopold. By the time he was in the outskirts of the town, he surely appreciated his jeopardy and hid in a small inn. His young valet was dispatched to the market for provisions, but the silly boy spent a bit too lavishly and strutted about boastfully speaking of his master as a man of consequence. Inevitably this aroused curiosity. Upon his return visit the squire marched grandly between the vegetable vendors with the King's own embroidered gloves tucked into his belt. He was seized and tortured.

When the magistrates broke noisily into Richard's inn, the King grabbed a soiled cloak and raced to the kitchen, where he tried to look like kitchen staff, turning chickens on a spit and donning a woeful peasant's expression.

But noble Kings do not easily or swiftly transform themselves into kitchen help. When the magistrate came upon the ridiculous scene, he acted as if he were ashamed for the King.

"Sire, get up," he said scornfully. "You have tarried here too long already."

Within hours Richard was brought before Leopold. Once Leopold vividly recapped his humiliation at Acre at the hands of English soldiers, the prisoner handed over his sword to his captor. Soon after, the King was escorted west along the Danube to the towering castle of Dürnstein and imprisoned.

The imprisonment of Richard was, of course, a gross violation of both the law of nations in Europe at the time and the law of the church and the Truce of God. No Crusader could be taken advantage of while he was "on God's service," and Richard had reminded his captors of this fact when they took him roughly into custody. But he was now a prize of considerable value, both politically and monetarily. The Holy Roman Emperor, Henry VI, promptly ordered his vassal, Leopold, to hand King Richard over to him. At a conference in Würzburg they haggled over the price of the arrangement and finally made a contract on February 14, 1193, settling on sixty thousand pounds of silver as a finder's fee for the enterprising duke.

Henry's visceral grudge against Richard had to do with the loss of Sicily, formerly a province of the Holy Roman Empire, to the usurper Tancred. And the German Emperor was also related to the late Conrad of Montferrat. But Henry VI had an additional motive. His quarrel with Rome was the same old eternal struggle between the authority of church and state. A prominent bishop had been assassinated in Liège, and the papacy held Henry VI responsible. Much of Henry's empire was siding with Rome, and the wily old veteran of these struggles, Henry the Lion, was leading the rebellion from his capital in Wittenberg. Richard, therefore, was held as the ultimate hostage and pawn in that struggle as well. From Henry's viewpoint Richard had fallen into his hands almost by divine grace to aid in his battle with Rome.

Promptly the German Emperor conveyed the joyful news to Philip Augustus in France. Citing the "treason and treachery and accumulated mischief" of which Richard had been guilty in the Holy Land, and inasmuch as Richard "had always done his utmost for your annoyance and disturbance," he was glad to convey the tidings of the King's capture. He did not, however, reveal the location of Richard's prison.

The messenger bearing this happy news was welcomed by Philip Augustus "above gold and topaz." Philip laughed especially at the manner of

Richard's capture: For his old mate to have been apprehended in the disguise of a "kitchen-knave," tending roasted chickens, was simply too endearing.

Slowly the news of Richard's capture made its way around the courts of Europe. Prince John in England might have paid actual "gold and topaz" for this splendid, unexpected news when Henry's message was forwarded to him by Philip Augustus. He immediately crossed the channel to Normandy, declared himself to be his brother's heir, demanded the allegiance of the Norman barons, and plotted with Philip Augustus. He had more success with Philip than with the Norman barons, however, for they reaffirmed their allegiance to Richard.

But Rome was not amused. For the imprisonment of the royal pilgrim and the Judas silver he derived from his unseemly deal with Henry VI, Duke Leopold of Austria was eventually excommunicated. Celestine III threatened Henry VI with the same fate if he did not promptly release Richard. To the Pope, Philip Augustus was as treacherous as any of them, for the Pope had been singularly unimpressed with the French King's intentions in their meeting in Rome eighteen months before, when Philip had hectored the Pope about lifting the ban on attacking Richard's lands. Should the French King lay a finger on a single inch of Richard's land now during this disgraceful imprisonment, Philip, too, would be placed under anathema.

Several months passed by without any change. Richard's supporters wondered what ailed the Vatican. A political poem heaped scorn on the cowardice of the Holy See: *"Ha! quid Roma, quid nobiles, quid ue!"* the poem went. "What of Rome and of the nobles, what gives! Why does noble Rome delay so long in drawing the sword of Heaven." This sentiment was echoed even more fiercely by a group of Norman bishops who felt that action was a moral imperative. They invoked the story of Simon Peter drawing his sword in the Garden of Gethsemane and cutting off the ear of the high priest's servant, who had come to arrest Jesus. To Celestine III they wrote, "This unjust captivity is detested by all laws, both new and old, is lamented by the people, deplored by the provinces, and makes our Church cry out.

"Let go your hand, most merciful father, and draw the sword of Peter."

But Celestine III stayed the heavenly sword of Peter in its earthly sheath, for he was unprepared to draw it and slice off the ear of his very own Holy Roman Emperor.

# CHAPTER THIRTY-TWO

# The Last Conquest

✠

hen Saladin was assured that Richard's
ship had finally left the shores of Palestine, he marked the
moment by declaring his intention to make a pilgrimage of
thanks to Mecca. For the Sultan the pilgrimage would
complete his observance of the last of the five columns of faith (after prayer
and fasting at Ramadān, tithing for charity, and belief in the unity of God)
upon which Islam is built. Just as the road was now open for Christian pilgrims to visit the Holy Sepulcher in Jerusalem, so the hajj road from Syria to
the Arabian holy sites was now safe from Crusader bandits. Just to be sure
Saladin dispatched his son el Melek el-Afdal to the old Crow's Nest of the in-

famous Reginald de Châtillon, the bastion of el Kerak, to inspect the preparedness of its garrison.

Before the Sultan could go to Arabia, however, he needed to survey the new kingdom that had been created. With a very light guard he rode past the maritime cities that had been ceded to the enemy. Ascalon preoccupied him most of all. He had dispatched a hundred miners to destroy the walls. They were to be joined by an equal number of Christian engineers, and the demolition was to go forward as a joint operation. Richard had left his men with a cryptic order: "When you have demolished it, you will have leave to depart."

After this brief swing around the southernmost strongholds, Saladin repaired to Jerusalem, to his dim cell off the Via Dolorosa, and to quieter affairs of state. Apart from its basic core, his army had disbanded, and so there was some routine administration to attend to, as well as some diplomacy. The military work ahead was mainly for the engineers, to repair the structural damage to his cities and their fortifications. During this respite in Jerusalem he ordered the construction of a hospital and a college in the city. The pace of the Sultan's life slackened for a time as he receded into the pleasures of his family and into the adulation of his people.

During this time his son, el Melek ez-Zaher, prepared to leave the Holy City to resume his duties as lord of Aleppo. He was Saladin's third son and the apple of the Sultan's eye, who went by the nickname *"al-Mushammer"* because when his father had divided his states among his elder brothers, el Melek ez-Zaher had blurted out, "I also am ready" *(mushammer)*. In his own mind Saladin had already settled on his nineteen-year-old son as his eventual successor. After praying at the Dome of the Rock, el Melek ez-Zaher asked permission to see his father for a final farewell. When they were alone, the Sultan displayed a father's concern for his son's well-being, for the success of his new endeavor, for the boy's development as a leader.

"I commend you to God Almighty. He is the source of all good," the Sultan said. "Do the will of God, for that is the way of peace. Beware of bloodshed. Trust not in that, for spilt blood never sleeps. Seek to gain the hearts of thy subjects, and watch over all their interests, for thou art only appointed by God and by me to look after their good. Endeavor to gain the hearts of thy emirs, thy ministers, and thy nobles. I have become great as I am because I have won the hearts of my people by gentleness and kindness. Never nourish ill feeling against any man, for death spares none. Be prudent in thy dealings with other men, for God will not pardon unless they forgive you. But as to that which is between God and thyself, He will pardon the penitent, for He is gracious."

In the meantime the first delegation of Christian pilgrims arrived in the outskirts of the city. They had had a harrowing journey across the plain of Ramla, for they were unarmed, and their sole protection was the safe-conduct pass that had been issued to them at Acre. This first contingent was led by Andrew of Chauvigny, a distinguished military monk from Cluny who had been a guarantor of the treaty with Tancred of Sicily and a stalwart at the siege of Acre. But their advance party had fallen asleep in a wood and had failed to warn the Muslim commanders ahead of their approach. When they came into the midst of some two thousand glowering Islamic soldiers outside the city wall, there was a tense moment. Saladin was informed of their presence by a few firebrands who thought this was an excellent chance to avenge the deaths of their sons and brothers. But Saladin calmed them.

"It would be a deep stain upon our honor, if the treaty which has been made between you and the King of England should, by our interference, be broken. Forever afterward, the faith of the Arabs would be called into question."

The terrified pilgrims were given permission to proceed to the city walls. But a Christian observer well stated the measure of their high anxiety as the pilgrims passed through the Muslim ranks and spent their last night at the foot of Mount Joy: "They grinned and frowned on us as we passed, and it was manifest by their looks what enmity they harbored in their hearts, for the face is the index of the mind. Our men at that moment were so confounded that they wished themselves back again at Tyre, or even Acre, which they had just left. Thus we passed the night, near a certain mountain, in a state of great alarm."

In fact, Richard had tried to curtail the flow of pilgrims after his departure by requiring an official visa to visit Jerusalem, to be issued in Acre and shown to the Muslim authorities. This was an unabashed attempt to prevent the French from visiting, since they had deserted him at the Battle of Jaffa and elsewhere. And in this trivial and unworthy effort he had tried to enlist Saladin's cooperation.

But Saladin disregarded Richard's wishes. Any pilgrim who got the chance to complete his pilgrimage with a visit to the Holy City would speedily leave the country, Saladin believed, and so he was quite happy for every last foreign invader to pay respects and then be gone. The Sultan told his men, after this first delegation, that no official papers from Christian authorities were required. All along the road to Jerusalem he posted soldiers, not to make the Christian pilgrims feel anxiety, but on the contrary, to make them feel secure.

In the Holy City itself Saladin went out of his way to entertain the Christian pilgrims. He encouraged them to kiss the True Cross of their Lord, which had been carried into battle at Hattin and lost, to visit Mount Zion and Golgotha and the Garden of Gethsemane. It had not been Muslims who had crucified their Savior, after all, and Jesus was one of Islam's prophets. Then he invited them to his banquet table, where he engaged them in informal conversation and entertained them lavishly. He even sent a message to Acre detailing his generosity.

"There are men here who have come from afair to visit the holy places," he wrote. "Our law forbids us to hinder them."

The third delegation to visit the Holy City was led by the Bishop of Salisbury, Hubert Walter, one of the grand and wise men of the age, who would upon his return to England become the Archbishop of Canterbury and the justiciar of the realm. He had also been a valiant soldier who had come to Palestine before Richard and had been throughout the ordeal one of the King's most trusted advisers. Saladin received this dignitary expansively and invited him to stay in the Sultan's palace. But the biship demurred.

"We are pilgrims," he said with humility. Living lavishly was not appropriate.

Nevertheless, when the bishop viewed the True Cross, Saladin escorted him and afterwards entertained the distinguished prelate at a banquet. In due course Saladin inquired curiously about what manner of man this Richard really was.

"I will only say what justice demands," replied the bishop, "that he has no equal among all the knights in the world, either for valor or for generosity. He is in every respect distinguished for every excellent quality. In short, in my humble opinion, if anyone, debating your majesty's sins, were to bring your virtues into comparison with those of King Richard, and were to take you both together, there would not be two other men in the world who could compete with you."

Saladin listened to this elaborate praise with an air of indulgence. "I have long been aware that your King is a man of the greatest honor and bravery," he said solicitously, "but he is imprudent, not to say foolishly so, in thrusting himself so frequently into danger. He shows too great a recklessness of his own life. For my part, however large the territories are where I am King, I would rather have abundance of wealth, with wisdom and moderation, than display immoderate valor and rashness."

As their evening wore down, the good feeling between the men deepened. Finally Saladin invited the bishop to ask for anything he liked, and it would be given to him.

At so important an invitation, Hubert Walter asked permission to ponder the offer overnight. On the following morning, back in audience with the Sultan, the bishop complained that the manner of worship presided over by Syrian Christians at the Holy Sepulcher was corrupt. His request was that two Latin priests with two properly consecrated deacons be permitted in residence at this most holy of Christian shrines, and that an equal number be posted at Bethlehem and Nazareth as well.

"*Erat quidem petitio magna, Deo ut creditur gratissima. . . .* This petition is one of great importance," said the bishop, "and, we believe, pleasing to God."

Saladin granted the request without hesitation.

2

# BARLEY WATER AND TEARS

As winter approached, Saladin was eager to move on to Damascus, his favorite city and the place where his family resided in force. Through Nablus he rode on to the great fortress high above the southern rim of the Sea of Galilee, which the Crusaders had built and called Belvoir but which he knew as Kaukab. Until it was conquered, the Muslims had regarded Kaukab as "an inviolable woman, a maid who could not be asked for in marriage." Indeed, they had feminized all the major Crusader castles as if they were objects of desire and conquest to be romanced or raped. They were women either to be married or violated by force or beseeched to submit, but submit they must. From his conquest of Belvoir the Sultan looked down with satisfaction on the historic route he had traversed on his way to the glorious Battle of Hattin, and across the valley to the castle of Qal'at 'Ajūn, which he had built in 1184 to counterbalance Belvoir. After inspecting the garrison at Kaukab, he proceeded to Beirut and finally arrived in Damascus in mid-November 1192.

There his subjects greeted him jubilantly and heaped honors on him. Throngs accompanied his movements through the streets. Poets sang their verses about their great protector.

"He spread the wings of Justice over all," wrote one, "and rained down gifts on his people from the clouds of his munificence and kindness."

It could be no mystery why this city was his favorite. The oldest inhabited city in the world, it was also the most beautiful city in Syria. In effect it was a huge oasis, refreshed by the water of the Barada River, upon the vast, dry plain of Ghutah. Its mud-brick houses were so ancient that they were said to exist before the time of Noah. Its libraries and palaces were many. Its Great Mosque, with its magnificent mosaics, was unrivaled in all Islam, and its citadel was the Sultan's favorite in all of his empire. Its gardens "encircle it like a halo round the moon," wrote the Arab traveler Ibn Jubayr, "and contain it as if it were the calyx of a flower." This was the paradise of the Orient. Indeed, as the common saying went, "If paradise is on the earth, then Damascus without a doubt is in it. If it be in heaven, Damascus is its counterpoint on earth."

In this paradise a family reunion awaited Saladin. His brother, el Melek el-Adel, had returned from his inspection of el Kerak and tarried before he proceeded to his new dominions beyond the Euphrates. Saladin's son el Melek ez-Zaher came down from Aleppo, and the two other sons gathered with their families. Banquets were laid on, and there were hunting expeditions to the region of Ghabāgheb twenty miles south of the city, where the large-eyed gazelles were plentiful. With his sons and wives and mistresses and grandchildren all about him, there were also interludes of song and poetry, for Saladin was beginning to feel his age. Among his favorite verses was a couplet about the custom of old men dying their hair black:

"It is not for the uncomeliness of gray hair that they are dyed; for certainly, hair, when it loses its color, is still more uncomely. But they do so because, when youth is dead, its dwelling place is blackened to show how greatly the loss is regretted."

When he would recite this verse, he would accentuate the phrase "youth is dead" and pull his mistress close to him. "Yes, by Allah," he would say, looking deeply into her eyes, "youth is dead."

Amid this familial bliss the Sultan seemed to unwind. He inquired of his vizier about the number of fasting days he had missed in recent years due to the press of war. For he now wished to fulfill his obligation. When a delegation of Crusaders came to call on him, it was much to his amusement that their shaven faces, short, cropped hair, and funny costumes frightened the children, who hid behind curtains until the foreigners had left. At least it had not been the dreaded Melech Ric who had come calling. For throughout Palestine, mothers had invoked the name of the terrible English King as a way to frighten and motivate their children: "If you don't clean up your room, Melech Ric will come to get you!"

Through the winter months, when the rain was heavy and the roads were awash in mud, the Sultan seemed to sink into a torpid languor. For weeks he canceled banquets and showed little interest in food other than rice boiled in milk and other light refreshment. He curtailed his visitors. The talk of a pilgrimage to Mecca ceased. At these first signs of illness his scribe and adviser, Beha al-Din, was summoned from Jerusalem. But the road was so muddy that it took him nineteen days to make the journey. When the scribe was rushed into the Sultan's presence, he found his lord to be weak, thin, emaciated, and suffering from indigestion.

As best he could, Beha al-Din tried to buoy his master's spirits. They went out on the road to greet pilgrims returning from hajj, but out in the country, amid the throngs of well-wishers, Beha al-Din noticed that the Sultan was not wearing his wadded tunic, the *kazāghand*. This oversight was badly out of character, for all his public life Saladin had been obsessive about his personal safety, especially with the danger from Assassins, and had never exposed himself to unnecessary danger. When his companion pointed out the omission, Saladin replied as if he were in a dream, calling for the master of the wardrobe, who could not be found.

"The Sultan is asking for something he never used to be without, and he cannot get it!" Beha al-Din said to himself apprehensively, and he considered this to be a bad omen. They beat a hasty retreat along a deserted back road.

"I was heavy at heart, for I feared very much for his health," wrote Beha al-Din later.

In late February, Saladin's lassitude turned to sickness, and he took himself to bed in the summer house of the Damascus citadel. To his advisers, even in his distress, he remained convivial, but he was unable to eat and had difficulty in drinking. Once his valet brought him lukewarm water, and he sent it away because it was too hot. Another glass was brought, and he found it too cold.

"Oh, God, is there no one in the land who can make the water the right temperature!" he complained.

His scribe turned away in tears. "What a great soul the Muslims will love!" he said. "Any other man in his place would have thrown the cup at the head of the man who brought it."

For several days Saladin's chief physician deserted him, as if to convey the message that nothing could be done. News of this bad omen spread rapidly through the city, and measures were taken to prevent public chaos. Merchants, afraid of looting, emptied their stalls in the *souq* nearby. As his father failed, his firstborn son, el Melek el-Afdal, assumed the royal chair at the banquet hall and began to lobby among the emirs for their allegiance to him, much to the distress of some who thought the son's act disrespectful and presumptuous. The governors of Damascus and of Sahyun (the great fortress east of Latakia) readily agreed. Others followed, including three emirs of the Kurds. El Mashtūb, the Scarred One, consented on the condition that he receive a generous donation of land. One emir imposed the condition that he never be made to raise a sword against one of el-Afdal's brothers.

As Saladin was bled and struggled to sip his barley water, the emirs filed before Saladin's son to swear their oath of fealty. The oath contained the warning called the "triple divorce" clause: "If I break my oath, I swear that my wives are divorced, my slaves are set free, and I must go barefoot on a pilgrimage to Mecca."

On the tenth day of the Sultan's illness he was given an enema, which gave him some relief, and he was able to drink more barley water. Soon after, perspiration appeared on his legs, an excellent sign, and hours after that the physicians reported in astonishment that the sweating was so profuse that his mattress was soaked through. Could this be a miracle? But on the twelfth day he took a turn for the worse, and his mind began to wander. The sheik attending him read continually to him from the Koran, especially Surah 59, Verse 22: "Allah is He. There is no other God who knows all things both open and secret."

"It is true," mumbled the patient.

And then, according to legend, he called for his standard bearer, the man who had carried the banner of the Sultan in many of his great battles. "You, who have borne my banner in the wars, carry now the banner of my death. And let it be a vile rag which you shall bear through all Damascus upon a lance and proclaim, 'Lo at his death the King of the East could take nothing with him save this cloth only.'"

On March 4, 1193, Saladin died. "May God have mercy on him and sanctify his soul!" wrote one scribe, "for he was the ornament and the admiration of the world."

As was the custom, the body was washed and wrapped in a shroud. His personal clothes—including his short, yellow vest, his *kabā,* with its distinctive black cuffs—were tied carefully in a packet. The funeral arrangements were awkward, for upon his death the Emperor was found to have no property—no estates or houses or lands or gardens and virtually no gold or silver in his safe, save forty-six Nasirian dirhams, less than one pound sterling. Accordingly his followers had to borrow money to purchase the necessities, even down to the halfpenny needed to buy the straw to mix with the clay to make the sun-dried mud bricks that would line his tomb. His bier was covered with striped cloth, and before the hour of the *'asr* prayer the body was laid to rest in the garden near the summer house of the palace where he had endured his final illness.

"The castle, the city, the whole world were plunged into grief, the intensity of which God alone could fathom." So wrote his devoted scribe Beha al-Din.

The streets of Damascus were packed with swaying mobs of mourners. During the first twenty-four hours after his passing only emirs and men of the turban (as doctors of law were known) were admitted into the citadel. The sons, meanwhile, went into the streets to console the people, for in their collective grief, as the Koran says, "their hearts have come even to their throats." On the second day el Melek el-Afdal gave a public reception to receive the condolences of the people. At first poets were barred from writing elegies to their lord, for it was the humility of Saladin, above all his other noble qualities, that had so impressed his colleagues. In Cairo he had founded three colleges and a hospital; in Jerusalem, a college and a hospital; in Damascus, two colleges. None of these institutions bore his name, and so it would be said, "For this favor, that of escaping vainglory, he was indebted to the grace of God." How different he was from Richard!

To the grief-stricken Beha al-Din, who had dedicated his life to chronicling the exploits of this great man, the days after Saladin's demise had an intensely surreal quality. "So passed those years and men," he wrote, "and seem, both years and men, to be a dream."

Eventually, of course, the testimonials rolled out in a torrent. "Though he possessed so extensive a kingdom and such vast dominions, he was extremely kind and condescending," went one. "Being affable to all men, tender-hearted, full of patience and indulgence. He befriended the learned and the virtuous, admitted them into his society and treated them with beneficence. Toward talents of all kinds he was favorably inclined and, being a great admirer of good poetry, he would repeat pieces of verse before the company at his assemblies . . ." At last the poets were given free rein to attempt *kasīdas* in his honor. This was the exceedingly difficult form of verse whose exacting constraints in rhyme scheme had tyrannized and paralyzed Arabian poets for centuries. Of all the attempts, this one was the most successful:

> I *see victory attached to your yellow standard; proceed therefore and conquer the world, for you are worthy of its possession.*

He had not conquered the world. But at his death his empire stretched from Libya to the Tigris River, from the Indian Ocean to the Caspian Sea.

Three years after his death, Saladin's body was removed from the citadel and placed in a mausoleum to the north of the great mosque of Damascus. The mausoleum took the shape of a domed chapel, with a grated window that looked toward his college. This *kubba* received his casket in December 1195. Engraved in the marble were these words,

> Almighty God! *Let his soul be acceptable to thee and open to him the gates of Paradise, that being the last conquest for which he hoped.*

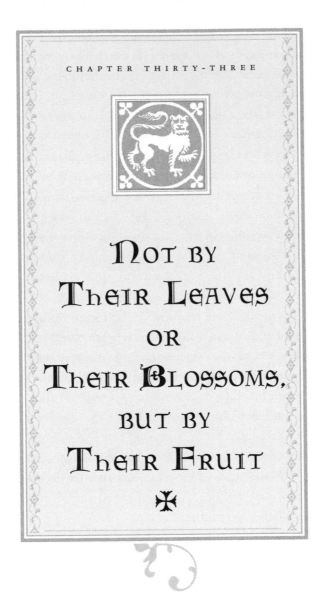

# CHAPTER THIRTY-THREE

# Not by Their Leaves or Their Blossoms, but by Their Fruit

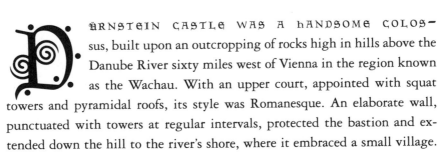

ÄRNSTEIN CASTLE WAS A HANDSOME COLOS-sus, built upon an outcropping of rocks high in hills above the Danube River sixty miles west of Vienna in the region known as the Wachau. With an upper court, appointed with squat towers and pyramidal roofs, its style was Romanesque. An elaborate wall, punctuated with towers at regular intervals, protected the bastion and extended down the hill to the river's shore, where it embraced a small village.

Leopold had chosen it as Richard's prison as much for the loyalty of its lord, one Hadmar II, as for its remoteness. Hadmar held the title of *küeringer* or brave fighter, and indeed, in the Austria of that time, the barons needed to be brave. Leopold's domain was the first line of defense for the Holy Roman Empire against the wild, Oriental horsemen of Hungary to the east.

In this forbidding place Richard was kept under strict watch. In his commodious rooms, guards surrounded him with swords drawn, but beyond that indignity, he was accorded royal treatment. He was able to have visitors and minstrels for his entertainment, and he was supplied with good food and plenty of the crisp, white wine for which the Wachau region was famous even then. Though his supporters later charged that he was being mistreated, he was never manacled or tortured. According to legend, the King developed a playful relationship with his guards, never losing his sense of humor and amusing himself with them by various games of strength.

Later, in preparing the fable of Richard's imprisonment for children's bedtime stories, romantic writers did not find jokes and wrestling matches quite dramatic enough, and so spectacular episodes were grafted onto the bare facts of his imprisonment. The Duke of Austria, Leopold, became the evil villain of the piece while his minions and guards became the foils. One tall tale spoke of a duel of "pluck-buffet" (or "hot cockles," as it was called in England) between Richard and the son of the evil Duke. This was a barbaric game of chicken, dating back to Greek times, but which had a sad association with Christ's mockery by the Roman soldiers after his arrest, when they blindfolded him and "buffeted" him and cried out, "Prophecy unto us, Christ. Who is he that smote thee?"

Here, the "game" had a peculiarly German twist: one man was to stand still, blindfolded, while the other coldcocked him with a blow to the head, thereby putting his pluck on display. If this first victim remained on his feet from his buffet, he was then to have his turn. Like Richard, the Duke's son was huge and strong, and by rights of being the warden, he got the first punch. Richard took the vicious blow and staggered more from it than his dignity required. His "weakness," he felt, came from malnourishment, and therefore he requested permission to delay delivering his return blow until the following day, so that he could have a good meal. His young opponent, honorable and stupid lad that he was, agreed immediately.

After a huge meal of meat and wine, Richard spent the night waxing his fist, and, by morning, the wax had the temper of steel. When the King's turn came, his fist shattered the jaw of the Duke's son, and the boy died soon thereafter. This did not result in Richard receiving more privileges in jail.

Even better and taller was the story of the Duke's beautiful daughter—all bedtime stories require this stock character—who immediately swooned in love over the gorgeous King, and confounded the rules of the dungeon, by slipping Richard various treats and sweetmeats, then by disguising him as a squire and slipping him into her chamber at night. (This particular tale overlooks Richard's proclivities.) Inevitably, so the story goes, the tryst was discovered, and the prisoner was dragged before the court. The wicked Duke, of course, pressed for immediate execution, but his chief judge had a better idea, more acceptable to the courts of Europe. So this was Richard Coeur de Lion! Why not starve the huge lion in the Duke's menagerie and then turn him loose in the prisoner's cell? Then they would see who really had a lion's heart.

The Duke's tremulous daughter was so horrified at this diabolical plan that she raced to her King's cell with the offer to aid him in an escape. The noble Richard refused, of course, asking only that the daughter provide him with forty of her favorite, perfumed silk scarves. On the appointed day, the door of his cell swung open, and the King stood ready, with his arm sheathed tight in his lady's scarves. When the lion charged, Richard stepped nimbly aside at the last moment and gave the beast a tremendous uppercut to the body as it went flying by. The king of beasts turned and roared its hurt and indignity. Seeing its jaws wide open, Richard leaped forward, thrust his sheathed arm far down its throat, and tore out the lion's heart! According to legend, he paused piously to give thanks to God, then strode to the banquet table of the wicked Duke, where he lifted the lion's heart, squeezed all the blood from it like a dishrag, dipped it in salt, and ate it!

If this is the best of the legends about Richard's captivity, it is not the most famous. That distinction goes to the story of how the location of Richard's prison was finally discovered. According to the folktale, the grieving Queen Berengaria eventually made it back to England and closeted herself in the royal keep in Oxfordshire, hoping desperately for miraculous news. She was accompanied there by Richard's minstrel who, as the stories sweetly say, occupied a very special place in the affections of the King. Richard and Blondel had idled many hours together since childhood, hunting and cavorting together, while Blondel sang songs of love and loyalty to the King, and the King in turn lavished favors on his poet. They had thought a great deal about their love, and about love in general, and had even composed a number of amorous songs together. Their favorite was called, *Cuer Disirrous Apaie* ("The Longing Heart").

As several months passed with no word of the King, Berengaria grew more and more distraught, until finally Blondel could comfort her no longer. She should weep no more, he declared finally, for now was "not the time to cry but to act." He confided in her a plan to find the imprisoned King somewhere in the vast German empire, but his scheme was to be their secret alone.

"Where force of arms and the subtlety of diplomats fail, art will triumph!" he proclaimed, and set off heroically for the Continent.

Over a period of weeks he passed by one castle after another, strumming his lute and singing the song of their dual composition:

> The longing heart is appeased through sweetness and succor,
> and I am dying of true love's kisses.
> If another kiss is not soon mine, I will sure die.

And when he tired of that, he would sing one of his many well-known chansons.

> I am on fire with a love
> which compels me to sing.
> I act like a man taken by surprise
> who cannot resist.
> And yet I have gained something
> to boast of:
> that long ago I learned
> to love loyally.

Eventually, he came to the Danube and passed by each castle melodiously.

> A secret kiss is love's wound;
> Agonizing but not visible.
> Alas, why be so boastful about this illness
> when healing can come only
> If again you violate my mouth.

Until finally, he came to the imposing ramparts of Dürnstein. Beneath its towered walls, he launched full-throated into their sweet air:

*No woman can make herself the mistress of my spirit and sensibility*
*If I choose to bestow my favors on others.*
*I should rather live all alone, hated and shunned,*
*Than to divide my life's force and affections.*

When suddenly from a slit window high in the tower, came back the second verse in the booming, powerful basso of the King:

*To see you, my gallant charmer, is to love you.*
*But your heart, alas, does not know how to throb.*
*That is why I shall bear the burden of my aching pain,*
*Since all my rivals must bear it the same as I.*

When the royal captive had finished the verse, he let out a whoop that had been the rallying cry of the hunt when the boon companions had romped through the forest of Aquitaine together. Blondel was, say the chroniclers, "marvelous glad" when he heard his friend and King bellow forth.

What happened after this duet was at last consummated, is told differently in various versions over the ages. In one version Blondel is invited into the Dürnstein castle and kept for weeks as entertainment for the guards, until he talks his way out. In another version the guards become suspicious at this hearty singing and boisterous whooping of hunting calls and strike out after the troubadour with bloodhounds. Either way, it has come down to us that through Blondel's ministrations the site of Richard's captivity was discovered. It was the minstrel who brought word of the prison's location back to England.

## 2

## IN SPLENDID CONFINEMENT

By the spring of 1193, Richard's circumstance had become well known in the royal courts of Europe. An Emperor held a king hostage: That was big news, and cause for Continental crisis. Diplomatic efforts became intense, with Pope Celestine III in Rome serving as the magnet for a number of initiatives—and the butt of much criticism for his inaction.

Richard himself was permitted to write letters home, for that seemed to serve the Emperor's purpose. On March 26, Richard wrote to the prior of Canterbury, the richest see in England, describing his imprisonment as tolerable, yet announcing the breathtaking news that the Emperor was demanding one hundred thousand marks of silver for his freedom. This was an immense fortune, truly worthy of the phrase "a king's ransom." It was the equivalent of half the treasury of the realm. Richard begged the church to lend him what money it could and to help in raising the rest. If the ransom was worthy of a king, Henry's extortion was beyond imperial—and imperious. It was an effort to do nothing less than bankrupt England and render it harmless in Europe, while at the same time shifting the wealth and power of the Continent to Germany.

During this limbo period, as England tried to digest the enormity of the crisis, Eleanor of Aquitaine generated the most important communications. She was in London trying to keep John's offenses against the family in check. In three letters to the Pope, Eleanor presented herself both grandly as the Queen of the English (ignoring the insignificant Berengaria), as the Duchess of Normandy and the Countess of Anjou—and humbly as a wretched and grieving mother, whose son was the victim of a dastardly conspiracy against God and England. The King "is in straits, beset on all sides," she wrote to Celestine III. "Behold his condition and the ruin of his kingdom, the malice of the times, and the cruelty of the tyrant who out of the furnace of his avarice is ever forging weapons against the King whom he [Henry VI] seized when on a holy pilgrimage under the protection of the God in heaven and the tutelage of the Roman Church." Her phrase, "out of the furnace of his avarice," and a later reference to the "maw of insatiable greed" indicate that she knew of Leopold's sale of Richard to Henry VI. She implies that Henry bought Richard merely to flip the deal into the more lucrative sale of the royal prisoner back to his people.

With passion and sarcasm, with anger and veiled threat, Eleanor pled her case. She complained that the Pope had not sent a single papal legate to Henry in protest, nay, not a single subdeacon or acolyte. Like the bishops of Normandy, she wondered why the sword of Peter had not been brandished before the insolent and disobedient Emperor and his lapdog, the King of

France, for (quoting Ephesians) the sword of the Spirit is the word of God. "The kings and princes of the earth have conspired against my son, the anointed of the Lord," she wrote. "One keeps him in chains while another ravages his lands. One holds him by the heels while the other flays him. And while this goes on, the sword of Saint Peter reposes in its scabbard." And she excoriated the empty words of his cardinals. "Alas, I know today that the promises of your cardinals are nothing but vain words. Trees are not known by their leaves, nor even by their blossoms, but by their fruits. In this wise we have known your cardinals."

Menacingly, she charged that the Vatican's inaction raised again the horrible specter of schism within the community of Catholic nations. "The fateful moment is at hand when the tunic of Christ shall be rent again, when the bonds of Saint Peter shall be broken, the catholic unity dissolved." It was as if the schism this time was a reversal of the circumstances twenty years before with Thomas à Becket. Then the Prince of the Church was held hostage by the King; now the King was held hostage by the inaction of the Church. The consequences of dissolution, she suggested, were the same.

Before Easter, several English bishops, including the notorious William of Ely and his close adviser, Hubert Walter, the Bishop of Salisbury, were dispatched to Europe to find Richard and evaluate his situation. They tracked him down in Swabia, for after his sale as a virtual slave by Leopold of Austria to Emperor Henry, he had been moved from Dürnstein to a dismal castle on the Swabian border called Trifels. This was a notorious dungeon, hundreds of years old, of which it was said that before entering its dark passages one should honor his parents, for it might be his last act before he died.

The bishops found Richard in gay spirits, in no way bent or broken by his confinement, with all his pluck and dash still on display. He peppered his countrymen with questions about England and the state of the realm in general. Eagerly, he listened to their tales about the shenanigans of his brother John. When he was told of their mixed success, Richard quipped wryly, "My brother John is not the man to subjugate the country, if there is a single person able to make the slightest resistance to his attempts."

Under guard, the group was moved from Trifels to Ochsenfurt, and eventually to Speyer, on the left bank of the Rhine. The episcopal see of Bavaria, Speyer was known for its magnificent sandstone basilica, where the Emperor was to hold his Easter court. Ironically, Speyer had been one of the six towns on the Rhine where nearly a hundred years earlier Christian mobs had massacred Jews before the Crusaders went off to the "glory" of the First Crusade.

It had been in Speyer that St. Bernard of Clairvaux had passionately preached the Second Crusade nearly fifty years earlier, promising divine protection for all who went to the Holy Land and heavenly salvation to any who died. So Henry was now adding to the curse of this place in Crusader annals. Still Richard seemed oblivious. He was on the move and liberated from dark and dank dungeons, and his spirits were rising. The diplomatic wheels were turning in his behalf, and he would soon have the chance to confront his accuser. On the road he was good company.

"It was the admiration of all," wrote the chronicler Roger of Hoveden, "how boldly, how courteously, how becomingly he behaved."

At last, on Palm Sunday, he was brought before Henry VI. While the Emperor's main motivation in this outrage was political and monetary, he harbored genuine ill-feeling toward Richard, anger which had been stoked by the deliberate misinformation that Philip Augustus had eagerly supplied. Now, while his captive stood glowering before him, the Emperor spilled out his complaints. Due to Richard's treachery, his empire had lost its dominion of Sicily and a considerable sum of soldiers and money with it. With malice Richard had mistreated his relation, the Emperor of Cyprus, Isaac Comnenus, and even held him still, reportedly in silver chains, somewhere in Palestine. Richard had wickedly assassinated his heir, Conrad of Montferrat, and had dispatched Oriental Assassins to murder Philip Augustus of France. And lastly, with disrespect and contempt, he had allowed the sacred banner of Austria to be ground into the dust at Acre.

The hand of Philip was all too apparent in these fulminations, but Richard adopted a tolerant cordiality in his defense. The Emperor was merely misinformed. Before the assemblage of skeptical German barons, he took the charges on, count by count, speaking "clearly and convincingly," according to an observer. He could do nothing about Sicily and Cyprus, for he had done what any great leader of a Holy Crusade would have done to use those islands as a staging area for his Crusade. He could deny outright any interest or complicity in assassinations of any sort, past or present, and promised to provide further evidence of his innocence on this point. And he had had no part in the indignity his troops visited on the Austrian flag. Indeed, the episode had appalled and embarrassed him, though not nearly as much as the drowning of Henry's compatriot, Frederick Barbarossa. Had that great German

Emperor not drowned in Turkey, the Third Crusade would surely have had a successful result.

After this virtuoso performance, the imprisonment of Richard I moved into a surreal twilight zone. By all accounts, Henry's personal animus toward Richard disappeared altogether. He accepted the King's representations completely, and they became fast friends! Richard was invited into Henry's court as an equal; there the rulers shared in ceremonials, banquets, and entertainments of poetry, song, and music. When the Emperor's court moved from Speyer to the Imperial palace at Hagenau in Alsace, where the imperial crown, globe, and scepter, as well as the sword of Charlemagne were kept, Richard went along.

Within a few weeks he wrote a letter to Eleanor (whom he addressed as the Queen of England) that veritably gushed about his honorable treatment by the Emperor and his entire court. It was as if the court censor stood at his shoulder when he wrote this valentine to his extortionist. For they had formed a "mutual and indissoluble bond of friendship," so much so that Richard had decided to "prolong" his stay with his new friend.

Had Richard gone soft?

In the second part of his letter to Eleanor, Henry's extortion was presented as if it were a gift rather than a crime. The King would remain with Henry until they had concluded their "business" together: to wit, "until we have paid him seventy thousand marks of silver." Eleanor and the justiciars were to set a good example to others by raising the kidnapper's demand and putting the arm on the churches to contribute the bulk of their gold and silver. As if to confer dignity upon the abomination, the King's words were conveyed to the Queen "under the golden seal of our lord and emperor."

In June 1193, the arrangement took the form of a contract between Richard and Henry. Much of its language pertained to the manner in which the Judas silver was to be submitted and weighed by imperial bankers before the king would be free to depart. As security some sixty-seven hostages, worth an additional fifty thousand pounds, were to be presented. For his leading role in the conspiracy, Leopold, the Duke of Austria, was to be rewarded with Eleanor, Richard's niece and the Princess of Brittany, who would be betrothed to Leopold's son.

In the short run, his kidnapping of King Richard had benefited the Duke of Austria handsomely. True, he had been personally excommunicated, and the Pope had put his entire fief under interdict (meaning that no mass could be celebrated in the land). But with the lucre he received from Henry and Richard, he was able to widen the boundaries of Vienna, fortify the city of Enns, and found two new towns.

Eventually, however, his sins caught up with him. In 1195 various pestilences descended on his land of Austria: drought, poor crops, and disease. The Danube flooded, and it was said ten thousand people were drowned. The Duke himself was kicked in the leg by his horse. His leg swelled up horribly and turned black, and his physicians could do nothing for it. Amputation was necessary, but no one was willing to perform the act on the accursed man. So, according to the chronicle, Leopold took an ax and cut it off himself. Soon after this, his body was aflame with fever. Only then did he tell his bishops that he wished to repent.

"At length, he acknowledged the wicked crime which he had committed out of malice against the King and his followers," wrote the chronicler. "On persuasion of the bishops who came to him, he gave up the hostages, and the remainder of the money due for the ransom of the King, and gave his word that he would also return what he had received, and promised henceforward to be obedient to the judgment of the church."

But there would be no henceforward. Even though his bishops, seeing his pain, lifted his excommunication, he died in agony. Since no one would touch it, his body was left to rot and was consumed by worms.

# 3

## "UNRANSOM'D, BEARING A TYRANT'S CHAIN . . ."

To fulfill so daunting an obligation as raising Richard's ransom would take considerable time—if it even could be fulfilled under the chaotic conditions that prevailed in England. Indeed, when the Bishop of Ely returned to England to raise the money, the initial reaction of the church was chilly. In the expanses of England that the King's brother controlled, John siphoned off a substantial portion of the ransom for his own use. Unaware of such difficulties, Richard moved around the German empire in his splendid confinement. On July 5 the court was in Worms, where the Emperor gathered the princes of Germany to sanction his extortion. As the days went by, it became clear that Henry VI was stalling—to wring more and more concessions from the English.

Meanwhile, Richard generated a slew of letters to various corners of Europe, often complaining to various barons about their lack of support. He reminded an old companion, the Count of Auvergne, for example, of their many trials together, of how Richard had supported and enriched his vassal, and of how in previous times, the count had given him "such faith as a chicken might have in a rooster." But once his lord was captive, the count had deserted and robbed him.

"Who keeps their faith in Richard, the law will protect to the end," he wrote menacingly. "But whoever keeps his own faith will receive the worst of it."

He was given to depression and self-pity. In one of those bouts he wrote his famous ode to false friends, *Ja Nus Hons Pris,* that has come down through the ages as his enduring achievement in poesy. His song speaks with the doleful voice of the captive:

> Yet to the sad 'tis comfort to complain
> *Friends I have many, and promises abound;*
> *Shame will be theirs; if, for winters twain,*
> *Unransom'd, I still bear a tyrant's chain.*
> *Full well they know, my lords and nobles all,*
> *In England, Normandy, Gascony, and Poitou*
> *Ne'er did I slight my poorest vassal's call;*
> *All whom money could buy from chains withdrew.*
> *Not in reproach I speak, nor idly vain,*
> *But I alone, unpitied, bear the chain.*
> *They know this well who now are rich and strong*
> *Lusty bachelors of Anjou and Touraine*
> *That far from them, in hostile bonds I strain.*
> *They loved me much, but have not loved me long.*
> *Their plains will see no more fair lists arrayed,*
> *While I lie here betrayed.*

Unfair and outrageous though his situation surely was, it might have been worse. In his spring doldrums he received a communiqué from Enrico Dandolo, the venerable Doge of Venice, patriarch of an illustrious Venetian family, founder of the Venetian colonial empire, and pivotal figure in the next Crusade, who would go on to capture in Constantinople the four horses which adorn the facade of St. Mark's Basilica:

"To his most serene lord Richard, by the grace of God, king of England, duke of Normandy and Aquitaine, and earl of Anjou, Enrico Dandolo, by the same grace, Duke of Venice, Dalmatia, and Croatia, health, and sincere and dutiful affection. Know ye that it has been intimated to us from a source that can be relied on, that Saladin, that enemy of the Christian religion, is dead."

The news was four months old.

What might have been the fate of his epic Crusade, Richard might well have thought, if his great adversary had died seven months earlier.

# 4

## The Devil Is Loosed

In the fall of 1193, an air of the bizarre and the surreal hovered over the efforts to free Richard from his Teutonic captivity. Reeking of false cordiality, the extortion proceeded as if this were a common transaction of international banking between honorable merchants.

The treasure chest for the King's ransom was slowly filling with the gold and jewels of England, Aquitaine, Anjou, and Normandy. To raise the ransom, each knight had been taxed twenty shillings, each lay person one-quarter of his income, and every church was to give up its chalices and any other valuable object it might possess.

As the money was delivered to the authorities, Richard masqueraded as monarch in absentia. With the permission and the censorship of his captor, he wrote his orders and proclamations to his realm from afar. Among them were occasional political instructions about various affairs of state, including his efforts to secure the appointment of his old friend and adviser, Hubert Walter, the Bishop of Salisbury, (and recent visitor to the captive King himself and to Saladin in Jerusalem) as his Archbishop of Canterbury. This appointment would expedite the squeezing of the church's remaining wealth for the ransom. The bishop's elevation, therefore, was in the interest both of Henry and of Richard.

Deepening the surreal atmosphere was the conspiracy of Henry VI's allies,

Philip Augustus and Richard's brother, Earl John, in slicing away Richard's domains in his absence. While Richard wrote his sad songs and stern directives, Philip Augustus invaded Normandy, subdued the Vexin, and seized the critical towns of Gisors, Dieppe, and Evreux.

He then presented himself at the gates of Rouen and exclaimed to its defenders, "John, the Earl of Mortaigne, has done homage to me for England, and has given up to me Normandy and all other lands on this side of the sea. I have come to take possession of this city, the capital of Normandy. Allow me to enter peaceably, and I will prove a kind and just master to you!"

Behind the walls the chortling had to be suppressed. "See, the gates are open," came back the loud answer from Richard's loyal companions. "Enter if you like. No one opposes you." Whatever else he was, Philip was no fool. He declined to enter and withdrew his forces, vowing to return with a "rod of iron."

If the news of these various robberies made Richard salivate for the battlefield, he must have cackled at the report of Philip Augustus's second betrothal around the same time. For the greater glory of France rather than in the name of love, the French King had married Ingelburg, the sister of Canute, the King of Denmark, in the hope that the Vikings would not again invade England. She must have been a stolid Viking wench, for Philip Augustus fled the bridal chamber in terror on their wedding night, never to return. He immediately divorced the saucy Dane.

Meanwhile, another bizarre bit of old business was cleared up in the fall of 1193. In his protestations of innocence to Henry VI concerning the various charges leveled against him, Richard had promised to provide further exculpatory evidence. And so he had sent messengers to, of all people, the chief of the Assassins, Rashid al-Din Sinan, requesting that the Old Man of the Mountain write to his first captor, Leopold of Austria, about the facts of Conrad of Montferrat's murder. In September the reply of the fanatic Grand Master of assassination arrived.

"The Old Man of the Mountain to Leopold, Duke of Austria, greeting. Whereas several kings and princes beyond the sea have accused our lord Richard, King of the English, of the murder of the marquis, I swear by the God who reigns eternally, and by the law which we observe, that no blame attaches to him in regard to the death of that noble." The messiah of the hashish cult went on to describe the theft of his ship by Conrad and his assassination order as a result. And then, oozing with sanctimony, as if to affirm that honor existed among murderers, he concluded his letter with the line, "Be assured that we do not kill any man in this way for the sake of reward or for money, but only when he has first inflicted an injury on us." What a relief!

Going the extra mile, Sinan wrote a second letter to all the princes and all the people in the Christian religion:

"We have also learned that it is said of the same King Richard that he has engaged us, as if we were more corruptible than others, to send some of our people to lay ambush for the King of France. This is false. God is our witness that he never proposed anything of the kind to us. Our honesty would not permit us to allow such an evil to be attempted against one who has not merited it."

Since the issue was not guilt or innocence but money, these letters did not carry much weight with Henry VI.

For his part Earl John was having only mixed success in displacing his older brother from the throne. When Bishop Hubert Walter returned to England from his visit with the imprisoned King in Germany, John's frequent argument that his brother was dead was weakened. Although his effort to enlist the King of Scotland in his claim to the throne failed, he had more success with the English-hating Welsh, who supplied his ranks with soldiers and eagerly waged war against various English castles coveted by John. Over the months of 1192–93 the important castles of Windsor and Wallingford in the south of England changed hands several times, but John lost them finally as the year 1194 dawned. Besides his lands in Cornwall and Devon in the west, his stronghold was reduced to two castles in Nottinghamshire. This would be important later to the legend of Richard and Robin Hood.

Richard's adversaries made a pair. Needful yet distrustful of one another, they made a pact to cover the grim eventuality of Richard's imminent release. One tired aspect of their agreement was that Philip, yet again, shopped his sister Alais as John's wife. Of such cement great empires were not likely to be built. Still, months before the event, both displayed their utter fear and high anxiety about Richard's liberation. In mid-1193, Philip wrote to John that unless they did something dramatic quickly, the terms of Richard's release were close to being fulfilled.

"Take care of yourself," wrote Philip, "for the devil is loosed."

During the Christmas season of 1193, after the release date was set for

February, the coconspirators made a last-ditch attempt to keep the devil in his place. They offered to match the ransom terms with an equal amount of cash: Philip would pay one hundred thousand pounds, John the additional fifty thousand if only Henry would turn the captive over to them, or at least keep Richard prisoner for another year. Most of all, the royal conspirators needed at least another nine months of captivity to shore up their defenses against the hurricane they knew was coming.

No doubt with mischief in his heart, Henry VI waved the offers from Philip and John in front of Richard on February 2, 1194, merely to extract a final measure of emotional pain. The ransom money was raised, and had been handed over to the Emperor's exchequer in London. Their contract was fulfilled. Honor the terms, Richard insisted. For a day Henry pondered his delightful dilemma, as he also pondered the invasion of Sicily that he would soon launch and finance with the ransom money.

On February 4, in Metz, in the presence of his mother, Eleanor, his chancellor, William of Ely, and his archbishop of Canterbury, Hubert Walter, Richard was released. On the day of his release, ever the romantic, the King dispatched a messenger, one Salt of Bruil, to Palestine, with a letter to Henry of Champagne, informing his nephew, the Crusader King of Jerusalem, of his release and stating cheerfully that once he wreaked vengeance on his enemies and secured his kingdom, he would come again to the Holy Land to conquer the pagans. A few days later the happy group arrived in Cologne. There, in the great cathedral, a mass was said for the King. Its text was taken from Acts 12:11:

"Now I know for sure that the Lord hath sent His angel, and hath delivered me out of the hand of Herod."

Soon enough the news of the release reached the Plantagenet realm, and the people and the poets rejoiced. The King's arrival to resume his rule and settle his scores was eagerly awaited. The most famous troubadour, Bertran de Born, was ecstatic, for this was the grist of epic verse. The lion was coming home. Beware of this noble animal, for he is not cruel to a conquered creature, but "proud against pride." He would catch the oath breakers, like wolves in a noose.

"Now comes the charming season when our ships will reach the shore and the King will come gallant and worthy," the troubadour wrote. "King Richard has never been so great before!"

On March 12, at Sandwich, Richard set foot at last on English soil. To

Canterbury he went first to pay homage to the shrine of Thomas à Becket and then proceeded to London, where the town turned out a royal welcome.

In anticipation of Richard's homecoming, his cohorts had stepped up their campaign against John's league of traitors in the land. Days before Richard arrived, a messenger of the Earl had been waylaid, bearing instructions from John to his strongest castles to prepare for war between the brothers. These scurrilous instructions horrified the bishops of the land, who met and excommunicated John forthwith for "disturbing the peace of the kingdom."

Then the good bishops had strapped on their armor and fanned out across England to lay siege to John's remaining bastions. The Archbishop of Canterbury commanded the campaign in the south, and soon, John's castles at Marlborough and St. Michael's Mount were in his hands, as was Lancaster in the north. The bishop of Durham went to the heart of John's resistance in Nottinghamshire where two castles, Tickhill and Nottingham itself, were still putting up a stout defense. Tickhill surrendered first but only after its skeptical leaders were taken into the presence of Richard to prove his reincarnation as King of England.

That left the castle of Nottingham itself. Richard had hastened to its vicinity on the Day of Annunciation, but instead of being treated like the Angel Gabriel, he was greeted with a scene of chaos. The castle's defenders refused to believe that Richard had actually returned and turned aside any suggestion of the fact proven to them. In exasperation, the King called for his stone siege engines and erected a gallows outside the walls to hang some of John's cohorts. After a few days of this, the nasty business ended with the predictable scene of the traitors on their knees before the King pleading for their lives. At a council of the King's advisers at which Eleanor of Aquitaine was present, Earl John was ordered to stand trial for insurrection within forty days or forfeit all his royal holdings.

And thus the ground for legend was laid. Under the cruel and evil rule of the wicked Earl John, traitorous Nottinghamshire had spawned a band of outlaws, loyal to Richard, in nearby Sherwood Forest. Their leader was known as Robin Hood, a knight of noble lineage whose creed it was to rob from John's rich and give to the poor, and thus he became a popular hero to the common people. His nemesis was the wicked Sheriff of Nottingham, who was forever trying to catch the bandit with such ruses as offering a golden arrow to the winner of an archery contest. Robin's purpose was to flout John's tyrannical laws and to keep the dense woods of the forest safe from the turncoats until King Richard returned from captivity.

Robin had one hundred archers, among them Will Scarlet and Friar Tuck. All were clad in Lincoln green and their skill with the longbow was unparalleled. It was said that Robin and his gigantic mate, Little John, could shoot an arrow the full length of a mile or 1,760 yards. And of course there was the romantic angle, with the lovely maid Marian, "A bonny fine maid of a noble degree, With a hey down, down, adown, down. . . . For favor and face, and beauty most rare, Queen Helen she did excel. For Marian then was prais'd of all men, That did in the country dwell. . . ." And then the story is then told in poetry.

> King Richard hearing of the pranks
> Of Robin Hood and his men,
> He much admir'd, and more desir'd
> To see both him and them.
> Then with a dozen of his lords,
> To Nottingham he rode:
> When he came there, he made good cheer
> And took up his abode.

According to the chronicle of Roger of Hoveden, Richard did, in fact, visit Sherwood Forest on the day after Nottingham Castle surrendered, and the woods, full of deer and lusty loyalists, "pleased him greatly." Whether the King met there a dashing bandit and a beautiful Saxon maiden, threw off his friar's cowl to reveal his kingly garb, or said to the bandits, "Rise Ye Men of Sherwood!," or restored the bandit to his castle and lands, and blessed the union of Robin Hood and Maid Marian . . . Well, of course, he did!

At Easter time the dignitaries of the land gathered at Winchester for the second coronation of Richard I of England. Donning his heavy royal robes, wearing a crown of gold, carrying in his right hand the royal scepter topped with a cross and in his left, a wand of gold topped with the figure of a dove, he was conducted beneath a canopy of silk to the altar. There, Queen Eleanor and her ladies were arrayed in splendor and looked on proudly.

Within a week of this ceremony, the King left England for Normandy and a long campaign to reclaim his patronage from Philip Augustus. On May 28, with a few more castles reclaimed, he was in the town of Lisieux, in the company of the archdeacon there, when he noticed the discomfort of his host.

"What is the matter?" Richard said, and then he understood. "I know you have seen my brother John. Do not deny it. Tell him to come to me without fear. He is my brother and should not be afraid. I will not hold his folly against him."

The archdeacon bounded happily to John's nearby hiding place.

"Come out, you are in luck," he called to the earl. "The king is gentle and merciful, kinder to you than you would have been to him."

Fearfully, John slunk into his brother's presence and threw himself at his feet.

"Think no more of it, John," Richard said cheerily, begging his brother to rise and have supper with him. "You are only a child who has had evil counselors."

Forty days had passed since the council of Nottingham had summoned John to trial. Since he had not appeared before the English magistrates, he had forfeited all his lands. He was again landless in England, at the mercy and sufferance of his indulgent brother.

For the time being, the Earl of Mortaigne would have to content himself with a hearty meal of salmon. For pink fish and crumbs were all he could expect from now on from the king's table.

# Epilogue

✠

For the next five years after his glorious return from captivity, Richard the Lionheart preoccupied himself, one way and another, with his endless quarrel with Philip Augustus of France. They were two spitting cats, backs arched, hackles raised, teeth bared, tails waving menacingly. Neither would ever have justice or satisfaction or the retribution he required. Neither could let his guard down. To Philip, Richard was an interloper in France. To Richard, Philip had stolen his inheritance. But behind it all the matter was personal. They fought and made peace and fought again, just as lovers fight and make up and fight again.

Through 1194, Richard reclaimed his castles at Vermeuil, Loches, and Montmirail, as Philip maneuvered and threatened and schemed and inevitably lost whenever the Kings actually came into direct combat. In July, Richard staged a night attack on Philip's wagon train and captured not only horses and money but the royal seal and the rolls of Philip's treasury, so that the Gallic clerks had to create again the royal payrolls from scratch.

At one point, in ridiculous frustration, Philip proposed a gallant and absurd resolution for the disputes between them. Let there be a tournament of royal teams in which the five best knights of Capetian France and of Plantagenet England would fight to the death, "so that," wrote Philip, "the issue should make manifest to the people of both realms what was the mind of the Eternal King as to the rights of the two earthly sovereigns." Ever a fancier of tournaments, the proposal pleased Richard, and he agreed immediately, "provided that each of the Kings should be one of the five combatants on his own side, and that they should fight each other on equal terms, armed and equipped alike." Philip Augustus against Richard the Lionheart in single combat? To the death? Philip decided to drop his proposal.

Through these years important players left the stage. Henry of Champagne died in Jerusalem, and after conquering Sicily, Henry VI died in Germany. In France, Alais, the whore of Europe, finally got married. For the English King, England was an afterthought. To be sure, Richard did return to make legal once again the glorious and bloody spectacle of the jousting tournament. This was more a matter of fundraising than of chivalry, for the exchequer profited from the ticket sales. Once again colorful tents and pavilions dotted the landscape. Crowds filled the galleries again to watch their champions compete for laurels or coronets of flowers or the love of ladies. They fought, these veterans of the Crusade, with blunted swords and headless spears, but they still killed or maimed one another in imitation of war. The crowds loved it.

Through 1196–97, Richard and Philip maintained an uncertain truce. Richard filled the time by building his greatest castle, called Gaillard, a wonder of the age, on the towering rock of Andely above the Seine River. This massive fortress was to be the protection for his lands in Normandy, and Philip could only watch its construction and curse. When Richard threw three French prisoners off its walls to their deaths, Philip shook his fist and exclaimed that he would have Normandy and Aquitaine, regardless of what Richard might build or what atrocities he might commit. And Richard responded by saying he could defend his redoubt even if its walls were made of butter rather than stone.

After a period of quiet threat, their war broke out again in 1198 more violently than ever, and the poets cheered. "War pleases me," wrote the troubadour Bertran de Born. "For I see courts and gifts and pleasure and song all enhanced by war. War makes a peasant courtly." Across Normandy the armies squared off again, and this time the Pope interceded. Crusade was again on the mind of Rome. This brotherly combat must cease. After posturing and threatening and preening, Richard finally acquiesced, and a treaty of five years was concluded between France and England.

Once his accounts were finally settled with Philip Augustus, Richard might have been expected to settle into a quiet complacency, to enjoy at last the governance of his realm in relative peace. But he was a war lover. Combat was all he knew and all he cherished. Internal annoyances rather than foreign affairs captured his attention. In the south of the Plantagenet realm, impertinent barons scoffed at his rule, and where there were impertinent barons, Richard was soon to show up. In Limoges the viscount of a castle called Chalus was withholding a portion of a treasure of gold and silver that had come into his possession. And so Richard was promptly in front of his walls with his army and siege engines.

It was a nasty little spat, beneath the dignity of a great King, and unworthy of the risk it entailed. But Richard was inured to risk. After so many great battles where the odds were against his survival, he flaunted the sense of his own invincibility. If only Saladin's words had rung in his ears: "But he is imprudent, not to say foolishly so, in thrusting himself so frequently into danger. He shows too great a recklessness of his own life. For my part, however large the territories are where I am King, I would rather have abundance of wealth, with wisdom and moderation, than display immoderate valor and rashness."

The knights defending this petty castle had already offered to surrender if their lives could be spared and if they could retain their weapons. But Richard was in a sour mood: he would take no compromise, he would storm their walls and hang them all when he had overwhelmed them.

Paying no attention to the danger, he was strutting around the walls, within plain sight of the defenders and without his armor, when a young crossbowman, one Peter Basil, let a bolt fly. It struck Richard and lodged deeply in his arm. In a rage Richard ordered a full-scale assault, as he struggled to mount his horse and then rode to his quarters, where he was attended by a physician. Not a physician, wrote the chronicler Roger of Hoveden, but a butcher who mangled the job and the arm and extracted first only the wood, leaving the metal tip still lodged. With more butchering, the tip of the bolt was finally removed, but quickly the arm started to blacken with gangrene.

By the time Richard realized the severity of the situation, his men had taken Chalus. Richard ordered its defenders all to be hanged, save only Peter Basil. For him a special fate would be reserved. The King ordered his assassin to be brought before him. The young bowman was dragged forward, and he showed himself quickly to be neither repentant nor afraid of Richard.

"What harm have I done to you that you have killed me?" Richard demanded.

"With your own hand you killed my father and my two brothers, and you intended to kill me," the youth replied. "Therefore, take any revenge on me that you want, for I will endure the greatest torments you can devise, so long as you have met with your end. For you have inflicted many and great evils on the world."

Such bravado must have struck some deep chord in Richard. The King's men waited eagerly for their lord to define the manner of a ghoulish death that the youth might expect. The youth demanded honorable death by the sword. The King's men thought something slower and more painful would be appropriate.

"I forgive you my death," Richard said finally. He ordered the marksman released and that one hundred shillings English be given to him.

"Live on," Richard said. "By my bounty behold the light of day. Let the vanquished learn by my example."

He turned his mind to the order of his affairs. At last he proclaimed Earl John officially to be his successor. To his younger brother he willed all his castles and lands and three-quarters of his treasure, the other quarter going to his servants and to the poor. And then he divided up his body. His heart was to go to Rouen, a present to its wonderful citizens who had always shown him unquestioned loyalty. His body itself was to be buried at the feet of Henry II, in Font-Evrault, as a last act of penance for the destruction he had visited on his father. And his entrails were to remain here, in Poitou, to stink up the region that had perpetually and treacherously resisted his rule. But that was not his only deathbed whimsy. His soul also wanted dividing, and his principal vices needed shedding. To the Cistercians he left his avarice. To the mendicant friars he left his love of luxury. And to his favorites, the Templars, he left his pride.

On April 6, 1199, he died.

Before the unlucky shot of that youth no obstacles had slowed him, "no rage of the sea, no abyss of the deep, no mountain height, no roughness of path nor winding of the road, no fury of the winds, no thunder or dreadful visitation, no murky air." So wrote a poet. The lion had been slain by an ant.

The balladeer was also at work.

*Ah! Lord God you who are the true pardon,*
*true God, true man, true life, be merciful!*
*Pardon him, for he is in want,*
*and do not, Lord, look at his faults.*
*Instead, remember how he went to serve you.*

# Acknowledgments

✠

In all of America there is no more medieval place than the Smithsonian Castle in Washington, and it was there, in the spring of 1997, that I got the idea for this book. At the time, as a fellow at the Woodrow Wilson Center for International Scholars, I was exploring, under the patronage of the director, the late Charles Blitzer, the idea of a sequel to my millennium book, *The Last Apocalypse*, which would be published the following year. My notion for the spinoff was a collection of ten essays called *The Man of the Millennium*, in which I would write about the significant figures of each of the past ten centuries and, at the end, declare a winner in a bald-faced attempt to upstage *Time* magazine. (*Time* eventually would choose Albert Einstein as its man of the millennium; my choice would have been Galileo.)

There, high in the main tower, with my panoramic view of the Mall, the Capitol, and the Washington Monument, I began my march through the ages. But I never got beyond the twelfth century. The struggle in the Third Crusade between Saladin and Richard the Lionheart captured my imagination immediately, and it has never let go.

In the three years it has taken to research and write this book, my locus shifted east from the Smithsonian Castle to the Library of Congress, where I became a scholar-in-residence in 1998, thanks largely to the good offices of Dr. Carol Armbruster of the European Division. In retrospect, it is hard for me to imagine how I could have managed this project without the prodigious help of so many people at the world's greatest library. Most important was the Office of Scholarly Programs, housed in secret spaces off the magnificent dome of the Library. Its directors, Prosser Gifford and Lester Vogel, provided me with a kind of contemplative heaven to do my work in peace, without interruption or telephone. But they were unfailingly helpful whenever I was in need.

Behind them stood the remarkable resources and staff of the library, and I made the most of both. I remember well my first day of orientation, when the courteous and always affable Bruce Martin told me, with a hint of apology, that I could have only a hundred books at a time in my commodious carrel. In the two years that followed, I recall with particular fondness some of the more exotic challenges I gave to that stellar corps of reference librarians. Thomas Mann tracked down the nature of the disease called arnaldia mentioned in the chronicles, from which both Richard and Philip Augustus suffered in Acre. (It was a form of trench mouth.) And later, when I showed him a reference in the chronicles to a species of stinging fly called cincenelles which had swarmed over the Crusaders in a place called Canebrake of the Starlings, Mann discovered it to be a nasty, airborne tiger beetle. David Kelly, the master of all games at the library, sleuthed out the kind of barbaric personal combat called "pluck-buffet," which Richard supposedly "played" with his captors in Austria. (The game consisted of one knight coldcocking another just for the fun of it.) I put Phoebe Peacock, the library's classics expert, on the trail of an obscure Aristotle quote applied to a castle in Germany, and Carol Armbruster translated the songs of Blondel from medieval French for me. George Selim and Mary Jane Deeb of the Middle Eastern Division helped countless times when I was at sea with Arab sources. Across town, at the Mullin Library at Catholic University of America, Bruce Miller, a specialist in Vatican history and literature, helped me on various obscure quests with this book, as he has helped me with previous work.

I also pressed my advantage with family scholars. After the appropriate grumbles, my brother, Tom, a notorious Francophile and a former spinmeister at the U.S. State Department, translated certain arcane poems and songs from the French, giving them a decidedly carnal spin. His wife, Vicki Kiechel, with her wonderful mind and Oxford education, helped out with Olde and Middle English.

I made two research trips to the Middle East. The first, in the spring of 1999, early in the writing, took me to Jerusalem, northern Israel, Syria, and Cyprus, where I visited a number of Crusader castles, drank in the landscape over which these great battles were fought, and visited with medieval scholars. In Syria, Dr. Sadik al Azm, a former fellow at the Wilson Center, introduced me to a number of knowledgeable authorities and guided my expeditions in his country. His article on "Jihad and History" gave me a far broader understanding of the Muslim concept of Holy War. In Damascus, I spent two long and fascinating evenings with the preeminent medieval scholar in Syria, Dr. Suheil Zakar. Dr. Zakar has spent his whole life studying the Crusades, or as he prefers to call it, the struggle for Arab unity in the face of European invasion. His patience at my persistent questions and his wisdom have been an important influence on the approach of the book. Ironically, Zakar has never been able to visit the battle sites in Israel, like Hattin, to which he has devoted so much attention.

In Israel, I was blessed with prior friendships from the Wilson Center and the Library of Congress: David Passow, Gabriel Sheffer, and Amnon Sella helped with personal concerns and professional contacts as they plied me with good food and great conversation. On that first trip, Dr. Benjamin Kedar, the most knowledgeable of authorities, gave me wise counsel about how to organize my time in Israel and would direct me toward Sednayia in Syria, which he longed to visit himself but could not. In Acre, Dr. Eliezer Shatran of the Israeli Antiquities Department briefed me on his excavations of Crusader facilities there. Through the good offices of Dr. Israel Roll, I got a special tour of the medieval town of Arsuf, now under excavation. And in Galilee, Rabbi Yitzchak Snitkoff from the nearby Kibbutz Lavi has made himself an expert on the Battle of Hattin, and we walked the battlefield together one foggy morning in March 1999.

On my second trip to the Middle East, in April 2000, I concentrated on Saladin and the Arab perspective. In East Jerusalem, I had long and useful conversations with Dr. Bernard Sabella, Dr. Nazmi Al-Ju'beh, and Dr. Mustafa Abu Sway. On a subsequent occasion Dr. Abu Sway braved the Easter crowds to show me the tiny, dark cell in the mosque, contiguous to the Holy Sepulcher, where Saladin directed his efforts in A.D. 1192. And for my foray to the great castle of el Kerak, beyond the Dead Sea in Jordan, where the agent provocateur of the Third Crusade, Reginald of Châtillon, did his dirty work, Mahmoud Abu-Sham, the cultural attaché of the Jordanian Embassy in Washington, smoothed the way.

On my return trip home I laid over for a long weekend in Austria in order to make a visit to the castle of Richard's captivity, Dürnstein. Dr. Werner Maleczek, a medievalist at Vienna University, had already pointed me to the important primary sources about Richard's interlude by the Danube. And at the lovely village of Dürnstein itself (where I stayed at the Hotel Richard Löwenherz) the local expert, Gerhard Fischer, gave me an excellent tour of the castle ruins.

On the literary side, I must thank Father James Devereaux, Jesuit, Shakespeare scholar, Renaissance man, bird-watcher extraordinaire, and former colleague of mine in the English Department at the University of North Carolina, for reading the manuscript and, as always, making many trenchant suggestions for revision. Finally, I'm deeply grateful to my superb editor at Doubleday, Amy Scheibe, who labored heroically on my manuscript under the most difficult personal circumstances, and who has had a profound effect on the final shape of this book.

# Selected Bibliography

✠

CONTEMPORARY ACCOUNTS

Ambroise. *The Crusade of Richard Lion-Heart*, Merton Jerome Hubert, trans. New York: Columbia University Press, 1941.

Archer, T. A. *The Crusade of Richard I.* New York & London: Putnam's, 1889.

Ibn-el-Athir el-Bahir: History of the Atabergs of el-Mosil. *Recueil des historiens des Croisades: historiens orientaux,* tome ii., 2, Paris, 1876.

Beha ed Din. *The Life of Saladin.* London: Committee of the Palestine Exploration Fund, 1897.

Benedict of Peterborough. *The Chronicle of the Reigns of Henry II and Richard I,* Rolls Series, no. 49. London: Longmans, Green, Reader, and Dyer, 1867.

Benjamin of Tudela. *The Itinerary of Benjamin of Tudela.* New York: Joseph Simon, 1983.

Bertran de Born. *The Poems of the Troubadour, Bertran de Born.* Berkeley: University of California Press, 1986.

Blondel de Nesle. *Les Oeuvres de Blondel de Nesle.* Reims: P. Dubois, 1862.

Brundage, James A. *The Crusades: A Documentary Survey.* Milwaukee: Marquette University Press, 1962.

Capellanus, Andreas. *The Art of Courtly Love*, John Jay Parry, trans. New York: Columbia University Press, 1941.

Edbury, Peter. *The Conquest of Jerusalem and the Third Crusade: Sources in Translation.* Brookfield, Vt.: Scolar Press, 1996.

Ernoul. *Chronique d'Ernoul et Bernard le Trésorier,* Mas Latrie, ed. Paris: Mme. Vij. Renouard, 1871.

Fetellus. *Description of Jerusalem and the Holy Land.* London: Committee of the Palestine Exploration Fund, 1897.

Fichtenau, Heinrich. *Urkundenbuch zur Geschichte der Babenberger in Osterreich.* Vienna: A. Holzenhausens Nachfolger, 1950.

Gabrieli, Francesco. *Arab Historians of the Crusades.* Berkeley: University of California Press, 1969.

Gervase of Canterbury. *The Historical Works of Gervase of Canterbury.* William Stubbs, ed. London: Longman & Co., 1870.

Gerald of Wales. *Opera,* J. S. Brewer, ed. London: Longman & Company, 1861.

al-Harizi, Judah. *The Tahkemoni,* vol II. Jerusalem: Raphael Haim Cohen's Ltd., 1973.

Ibn Jubayr. *The Travels of Ibn Jubayr.* R. J. C. Broadhurst, trans. London: Jonathan Cape, 1952.

Imad ad din al-Isfahani, *Conquête de la Syrie et de la Palestine par Saladin,* H. Masce, trans. Paris: Libraire orientalistic, 1972.

Stubbs, William, ed. *Itinerarium Peregrinorum et Gesta Regis Ricardi,* Rolls Series, vol. 38. London: Longmans, Green, Reader, and Dyer, 1864.

John of Würzburg. *Description of the Holy Land.* London: Committee of the Palestine Exploration Fund, 1897.

al Kātib al Isfahānī, 'Imād al-Dīn Muhammad ibn Muhammad. (1125–1201) al Fath al-Qussī fi al-fath al-Qudsī. ed. Landberg, vol. I, Leiden, 1885.

Ibn-Khallikan Wefaydt el-A'ydn. *Biographical Dictionary,* 4 vols., MacGuckin de Slane, trans. Beirut: Libraire du Luban, 1970.

Matthew of Paris. *Historia Anglorum.* London: Longman, Green, Reader and Dyer, 1866.

Migne, J. P., ed. *Patrologiae Latina,* vol. 206. Paris: J. P. Migne, 1855.

Neophytus. *Neophytus de Calamitatibus Cypri,* in *Rerum Britannicarum Medii Aevi Scriptores,* Rolls Series, vol 38. London: Longman, Green, Reader, and Dyer, 1864.

Odo de Deuil. *De Prefectione Ludovici VII in Orientum,* Virginia Berry, trans. New York: Columbia University Press, 1948.

Palestine Pilgrims' Text Society, vols. 5–13. London, 1896.

Ralph de Diceto. *Historical works.* London: Longman & Co. 1876.

Ralph of Coggeshall, *De expungnatione Terrae Sanctae libellus.* Rolls Series, vol. 66. London: Jos. Stevenson, 1875.

Richard of Devizes. *Chronicle concerning the deeds of King Richard the First, King of England.* London: H. G. Bohn, 1848.

Rigord. *Oeuvres de Rigord et de Guillaume le Breton, historiens de Philippe-Auguste,* 2 vols. Paris: Libraire Renouard, 1882–1885.

Roger of Hovedon. *Annals,* 2 vols., Henry Riley, ed. London: H. G. Bohn, 1853.

Roger of Wendover. *Flowers of History.* London: H. G. Bohn, 1849.

Stone, Edward Noble. *Three Old French Chronicles of the Crusades.* Seattle: University of Washington Press, 1939.

Upton-Ward, J. M., trans. *The Rule of the Templars: The French Text of the Rule of the Order of the Knights Templar.* Rochester, N.Y.: Boydell Press, 1992.

Usamah Ibn-Munqidh. *Kitab al-I'tibar* [An Arab-Syrian Gentleman and Warrior in the Period of the Crusades]. New York: Columbia University Press, 1929.

de Vinsauf, Geoffrey. *Itinerary of Richard I and Others, to the Holy Land.* London: H. G. Bohn, 1848.

*Itinerarium Peregrinorum et Gesta Regis Ricardi.* London: H. G. Bohn, 1848.

William of Newburgh, *Historia rerum anglicarum, in Chronicles of the reign of Stephen, Henry II, and Richard I,* vol. 1, Richard Howlett, ed. Rolls Series, vol. 82. London: Longman & Co., 1884.

William of Tyre. *A History of Deeds Done Beyond the Sea,* 2 vols., Emily Atwater Babcock and A. C. Krey, trans. New York: Columbia University Press, 1943.

## SECONDARY WORKS

Appleby, John T. *John, King of England.* New York: Knopf, 1959.

Armstrong, Karen. *Holy War.* London: Macmillan, 1988.

Arnold, Benjamin. *German Knighthood 1050–1300.* Oxford: Clarendon Press, 1985.

Ashdown, Charles. *British and Foreign Arms and Armour.* London: T. C. & E. C. Jack, 1909.

————. *Armour and Weapons in the Middle Ages.* London: George G. Harrap Co., 1925.

Ayton, A. J. *Knights and Warhorses.* Rochester, N.Y.: Boydell Press, 1994.

Bahat, Dan. *The Illustrated Atlas of Jerusalem.* Jerusalem: Israel Map and Publishing Co., 1990.

Baldwin, John W. *The Government of Philip Augustus,* Berkeley: University of California Press, 1986.

Baldwin, Marshall W. *Raymond III of Tripoli and the Fall of Jerusalem (1140–1187).* Princeton: Princeton University Press, 1936.

Barber, Richard W. *The Knight & Chivalry.* London: Harlow, Longman, 1970.

Bedier, Joseph. *Les Chansons de Croisade.* New York: B. Franklin, 1971.

Benvenisti, Meron. *The Crusaders in the Holy Land.* New York: Macmillan, 1970.

Blair, Claude. *European & American Arms, circa 1100 to circa 1850.* London: B. T. Batsford, 1962.

Bradbury, Jim. *The Medieval Siege.* Rochester, N.Y.: Boydell Press, 1992.

Bradford, Ernle. *The Shield and the Sword: The Knights of St. John.* London: Hodder and Stoughton, 1973.

Broughton, Bradford. *The Legends of King Richard I, Coeur de Lion.* The Hague: Mouton & Co., 1966.

Brundage, James A. *Richard Lion Heart.* New York: Scribner's, 1974.

———. *Medieval Canon Law and the Crusader.* Madison: University of Wisconsin Press, 1969.

Bumke, Joachim. *The Concept of Knighthood in the Middle Ages.* New York: AMS Press, 1982.

Burns, Ross. *Monuments of Syria, an Historical Guide.* London: I. B. Tauris & Co., 1992.

Cartellieri, Alexander. *Philipp II. August, König von Frankreich.* Leipzig: Dyksche Buchhandlung, 1899–1900.

Castiglione, Baldassare. *The Book of the Courtier*, George Bull, trans. Harmondsworth: Penguin, 1967.

Chrétien de Troyes. *Arthurian Romances*, D.D.R. Owen, trans. London: Dent, 1987.

Conder, C. R. *The Latin Kingdom of Jerusalem.* London: Palestine Exploration Fund, 1897.

Contamine, Philippe. *War in the Middle Ages.* New York: B. Blackwell, 1985.

Crouch, David. *William Marshal: Court, Career and Chivalry in the Angevin Empire.* London: Longman, 1990.

Demmin, A. *An Illustrated History of Arms and Armour.* London: G. Bell & Sons, 1911.

Edbury, Peter W. *Crusade and Settlement.* Cardiff: University College Cardiff Press, 1985.

———. *Kingdom of Cyprus and the Crusaders, 1191–1374.* Brookfield, Vt.: Ashgate, 1999.

Ffoulkes, Charles, *Armour and Weapons*. Oxford: Clarendon Press, 1909.

Folda, Jaroslav. *The Art of the Crusaders in the Holy Land, 1098–1187*. Cambridge: Cambridge University Press, 1995.

―――. *Crusader Manuscript Illumination at St.-Jean d'Acre, 1275–1291*. Princeton: Princeton University Press, 1976.

Franzius, Enno. *The History of the Order of Assassins*. New York: Funk and Wagnalls, 1969.

Gibb, Hamilton. *The Life of Saladin*. Oxford: Clarendon Press, 1973.

Gillingham, John. *The Life and Times of Richard I*. London: Weidenfeld and Nicolson, 1973.

Grousset, René. *Histoire des Croisades*, vol III. Paris: Perrin, 1936.

―――. *The Epic of the Crusades*. New York: Orion Press, 1970.

Hill, Raymond Thompson, ed. *Anthology of the Provençal Troubadours*. New Haven: Yale University Press, 1941.

Hitti, Philip K. *History of the Arabs*. London: Macmillan, 1937.

Holt, P. M. *The Age of the Crusades*. London: Longman, 1986.

Hutton, W. H. *Philip Augustus*. Port Washington, N.Y.: Kennikat Press, 1970.

Hyland, Ann. *The Medieval Warhorse from Byzantium to the Crusades*. Gloucestershire: Alan Sutton, 1994.

Jackson, W. H., ed. *Knighthood in Medieval Literature*. Woodbridge, England: D. S. Brewer, 1981.

James, G. P. R. *The History of Chivalry*. London: Henry Colburn and Richard Bentley, 1830.

Jeffery, George. *Historic Monuments of Cyprus*. London: Zeno, 1983.

Johnson, Paul. *A History of the Jews*. London: Weidenfeld and Nicolson, 1987.

Kedar, B. Z., ed. *The Horns of Hattin*. Jerusalem: Israel Exploration Society, 1987.

Keen, Maurice. *Chivalry*. New Haven: Yale University Press, 1984.

Kelly, Amy. *Eleanor of Aquitaine and the Four Kings*. Cambridge, Mass.: Harvard University Press, 1950.

King, E. J. *The Knights Hospitallers in the Holy Land*. London: Methuen & Co., 1931.

―――. *The Rule, Statutes and Customs of the Knights of Malta*. New York: AMS Press, 1980.

Laking, Sir G. F. *Catalogue of the Armor and Arms in the Armoury of the Knights of St. John of Jerusalem*. London: Bradbury Agnew & Co., 1903.

*Lancelot of the Lake*, Corin Corley, trans. Oxford: Oxford University Press, 1989.

Lane-Poole, Stanley. *Saladin and the Fall of the Kingdom of Jerusalem*. Beirut: Kyayats, 1964.

Le Strange, Guy. *Palestine Under the Muslims.* London: Committee of the Palestine Exploration Fund, 1890.

Lipman, V. D. *The Jews of Medieval Norwich.* London: Jewish Historical Society of England, 1967.

Llull, Raimon. *The Book of the Order of Chivalry,* Robert Adams, trans. Huntsville, Tex.: Sam Houston State University Press, 1991.

Lyons, Malcolm and Jackson, D. E. P. *Saladin: The Politics of Holy War.* Cambridge: Cambridge University Press, 1982.

Maalouf, Amin. *The Crusades Through Arab Eyes.* New York: Schocken Books, 1985.

Makhouly, N. and C. N. Johns. *Guide to Acre.* Jerusalem: Government of Palestine, 1946.

Mann, Horace K. *The Lives of the Popes in the Middle Ages,* vol. 10. St. Louis: B. Herder, 1914.

Meade, Marion. *Eleanor of Aquitaine: A Biography.* London: Frederickmuller, 1978.

Meller, Walter Clifford. *A Knight's Life in the Days of Chivalry.* New York: AMS Press, 1981.

Müller-Wiener, Wolfgang. *Castles of the Crusaders*. New York: McGraw-Hill, 1966.

Murphy-O'Connor, Jerome. *The Holy Land.* Oxford: Oxford University Press, 1980.

Newby, P. H. *Saladin in His Time.* London: Faber and Faber, 1983.

Nicholson, Helen. *Templars, Hospitallers and Teutonic Knights. Images of the Military Orders, 1128–1291*. Leicester: Leicester University Press, 1993.

Norgate, Kate. *Richard the Lionheart.* London: Macmillan, 1924.

————. *John Lackland.* London: Macmillan, 1902.

Oman, C. W. C. *History of the Art of War in the Middle Ages,* vol. 2. New York: B. Franklin, 1959.

Owst, G. R. *Literature and Pulpit in Medieval England.* New York: Barnes and Noble, 1961.

Paterson, Linda M. *The World of the Troubadours: Medieval Occitan Society 1100–1300.* Cambridge: Cambridge University Press, 1993.

Perlesvaus. *The High Book of the Grail,* Nigel Bryant, trans. Ipswich, England: Brewer, 1978.

Prawer, Joshua. *The World of the Crusaders.* New York: Quadrangle Books, 1972.

————. *The History of the Jews in the Latin Kingdom of Jerusalem.* Oxford: Clarendon Press, 1988.

Regan, Geoffrey. *Saladin and the Fall of Jerusalem.* London: Croom Helm, 1987.

Riley-Smith, Jonathan. *The Atlas of the Crusades.* London: Times Books, 1991.

————. *The Knights of St. John in Jerusalem c. 1050–1310.* London: Macmillan, 1967.

————. *The Oxford Illustrated History of the Crusades.* Oxford: Oxford University Press, 1995.

Rogers, R. *Latin Siege Warfare in the Twelfth Century.* Oxford: Clarendon Press, 1992.

Roth, Cecil. *The Jews of Medieval Oxford.* Oxford: Clarendon Press, 1951.

Runciman, Steven, Sir. *History of the Crusades*, vol. 3. Cambridge: Cambridge University Press, 1951.

Scott, Sir Walter. "An Essay on Chivalry." *Encyclopaedia Britannica*, 5th ed. London, 1816.

Setton, K. M., ed. *A History of the Crusades, II.* Madison: University of Wisconsin Press, 1969.

Seward, Desmond. *The Monks of War: The Military Religious Orders.* London: Methuen, 1972.

Smail, R. C. "Crusaders' Castles in the 12th Century." *Cambridge Historical Journal*, vol. 10, 1951.

————. *Crusaders Warfare (1097–1193).* Cambridge: Cambridge University Press, 1956.

Smythe, Barbara. *Trobador Poets.* London: Chatto & Windus, 1911.

Stubbs, William. *Historical Introductions to the Rolls Series.* New York: AMS Press, 1971.

Tuchman, Barbara. *Bible and Sword.* New York: New York University Press, 1956.

Walpole, Horace. *A Catalogue of the Royal and Noble Authors of England, Scotland, and Ireland.* New York: AMS Press, 1971.

Warren, W. L. *King John.* London: Eyre & Spottiswoode, 1961.

Warton, Thomas. *The History of English Poetry.* London: T. Tegg, 1824.

Wilkinson, Henry. *Engines of War.* Richmond, Va.: Richmond Publishing Co., 1973.

Wilkinson, J.; J. Hill; and W. F., Ryan, eds. *Jerusalem Pilgrimage 1099–1185.* London: Hakluyt Society, 1988.

# Index